Counselling Psychology

A newly emerging discipline, with its foundations in academic psychology, counselling psychology has the unique potential to develop and sustain a powerful model for the integration of research and practice in counselling. Practitioners are sometimes reluctant to introduce research into their place of work, seeing it as a distraction from the counselling process. This book shows how a blend of theory, research and supervised practice can be employed in ways which will benefit both counsellors and their clients. It also encourages students to take up and extend research that is already under way.

The nineteen contributors to *Counselling Psychology* are all actively engaged in ethically aware and culturally sensitive research and, through supervision, promote its integration into the therapeutic encounter. They argue that comparative study of theory serves to highlight common ground between different theoretical orientations, and helps practitioners avoid dogmatic adherence to a single approach. By addressing the professional dimensions of counselling psychology, their aim is to bridge the divide between academic study and counselling practice, whatever the setting, and to ensure the future research base of this rapidly expanding discipline.

Counselling Psychology is not designed to be read from start to finish, but will provide a secure grounding for trainees, and a valuable sourcebook for experienced practitioners.

Professor Petrūska Clarkson is a consultant counselling and clinical psychologist, an accredited psychotherapist, supervisor and organisational consultant with some 120 publications in these fields. She is Chair of the BPS Counselling Psychology Diploma Examinations Board, and she teaches internationally and in the UK (University of Surrey, Roehampton Institute, University College London, and at PHYSIS, London).

Counselling Psychology

Integrating theory, research and supervised practice

Edited by Petrūska Clarkson

Routledge
Taylor & Francis Group

LONDON AND NEW YORK

First published 1998
by Routledge
27 Church Road, Hove, East Sussex, BN3 2FA

Simultaneously published in the USA and Canada
by Routledge
270 Madison Ave, New York NY 10016

Transferred to Digital Printing 2008

Routledge is an imprint of the Taylor & Francis Group, an informa business

© 1998 Petrūska Clarkson

Typeset in Times by Keystroke. Jacaranda Lodge, Wolverhampton

British Library Cataloguing in Publication Data
A catalogue record for this book is available from the British Library.

Library of Congress Cataloging in Publication Data
Counselling psychology : integrating theory, research, and
  supervised practice / edited by Petrūska Clarkson.
      p.   cm.
   Includes bibliographical references and index.
   1. Counselling–Great Britain. 2. Psychotherapy–Great Britain.
   I. Clarkson, Petrūska, 1947– .
BF637.C6C676   1998
158'.3–dc21   97–9536
                                                     CIP

ISBN 978-0-415-14523-7

Publisher's Note
The publisher has gone to great lengths to ensure the quality of this reprint
but points out that some imperfections in the original may be apparent.

070055408

Contents

List of figures and tables   ix
List of contributors   xi
Preface   xv
Acknowledgements   xviii

1 Counselling psychology: the next decade   1

Part I Counselling psychology practice as integrating research and theory

2 Organisational counselling psychology: using myths and narratives as
   research and intervention in psychological consultancy to
   organisations   19
   Petrūska Clarkson and Marie Angelo

3 How counselling psychologists can employ a role enactment
   methodology to examine possible causal relationships amongst
   internal events   37
   Frank W. Bond and Windy Dryden

4 Qualitative research in counselling psychology: using the counselling
   interview as a research instrument   56
   Adrian Coyle

5 Researching the 'therapeutic relationship' in psychoanalysis,
   counselling psychology and psychotherapy: a qualitative inquiry   74
   Petrūska Clarkson

6 Cross-cultural issues in counselling psychology practice: a
   qualitative study of one multicultural training organisation   95
   Petrūska Clarkson and Yuko Nippoda

7 Psychological counselling in primary health care: a review   119
   Linda Papadopoulos and Robert Bor

8 Therapeutic factors in group psychotherapy 134
  Jorge Ribeiro

9 Transformational research 157
  John Rowan

Part II Counselling psychology research and practice: some professional dimensions

10 Investigating the learning experiences of counsellors in training: a research question

  Introduction 179
  Helen Cowie, Annemarie Salm et al.

  Section 1 Balancing the qualitative and the quantative in counselling psychology research 182
  Martin Glachan

  Section 2 The research question: significant learning experience in counselling training – a longitudinal study 189
  Annemarie Salm

  Section 3 Illuminative case studies: a solution 194
  Helen Cowie and Annemarie Salm

  Section 4 Content analysis of qualitative data 199
  Regina Pauli and Diane Bray

  Section 5 Grounded theory: a potential methodology 204
  Jean O'Callaghan

  Section 6 Discourse analysis: a possible solution 212
  Paul Dickerson

  Section 7 Commentary 220
  Annemarie Salm

  Section 8 Eros and Hermes: the twin pillars of the 'New Paradigm' of qualitative research in psychology 222
  Jamie Moran

11 Chartered counselling psychology qualification by the independent route and the role of the training co-ordinator: a little research 231
  Petrüska Clarkson

12 Learning through Inquiry (the Dierotao programme at PHYSIS) 242
  Petrüska Clarkson

13 Phenomenological research on supervision: supervisors reflect on
'Being a supervisor' 273
Petrüska Clarkson and Orit Aviram

14 Writing as research in counselling psychology and related disciplines 300
Petrüska Clarkson

15 The psychology of 'fame': implications for practice 308
Petrüska Clarkson

Name index 325
Subject index 332

Figures and tables

FIGURES

1.1 Venn diagram of the relationship between counselling, psychology and psychotherapy   6
5.1 Diagrammatic summary of entire research process to date   82
6.1 Pie diagram to show categories of replies according to percentage   106
6.2 Graph to show positive and negative statements according to percentage   107
9.1 The cycle model   163
9.2 Representation of basic empirical research   164
9.3 Representation of existential research   165
9.4 Representation of action research, intervention research and personal research   166
9.5 Representation of participatory research, collaborative research, experiential research and endogenous research   166
9.6 Representation of John Heron ASC research   167
9.7 Representation of transformational research   168
9.8 Types of knowledge   171
10.1 Correspondence analysis plot showing importance of different course elements at different times   203
13.1 Phenomenological research on supervision   281

TABLES

5.1 Summary of method with reference to Lincoln and Guba (1985)   87–88
5.2 Summary of other postmodern features of this inquiry   89
6.1 Self-descriptions of trainee counsellors (obtained from replies to question 1)   106
6.2 Subdivision of positive and negative responses   107
8.1 Final order of the weekly results from the four groups   139
8.2 Overall rank of the final mean for each group   141

8.3 Rating of the efficacy and helpfulness of the psychosocial
    psychotherapeutic factors in the opinion of the group in its last
    session   142
8.4 Presence and efficacy in Groups I, II, IV   144
8.5 Correlation between therapeutic factors in the four groups   145
8.6 Final sum of the factors order in the four groups   151
9.1 A comparison of four positions in personal development   159
10.1 Frequency with which course components are mentioned at three
     points of time during counselling training   202
11.1 Four fictional case examples (provided by Pat Didsbury)   233
11.2 Record of results of study   234–35
12.1 The two kinds of education   245
13.1 Demonstration of a report protocol   278
13.2 Thirty-seven groups of statements describing 'Being a supervisor'   279
13.3 Six dimensions of 'Being a supervisor'   280

Contributors

Petrŭska Clarkson MA, PhD, Fellow of the British Association for Counselling, Fellow of the British Psychological Society, is a professor and consultant chartered counselling and clinical psychologist with twenty-five year's successful experience as an accredited psychotherapist, supervisor and organisational consultant. She is an international visiting lecturer/supervisor, the author/editor of twelve books and over a hundred professional papers, the principal/co-founder of several major organisations in the field, and Chair of the BPS Counselling Psychology Diploma Examinations Board. She combines supervision, practice and research, particularly in the fields of supervision, ethics and organisations. She teaches internationally and in the UK (University of Surrey, Roehampton Institute, University College London, and at PHYSIS, London).

Marie Angelo MA, PhD is Senior Lecturer in Psychology at Richmond College, London, where she writes and researches on Archetypal Psychology and is developing a Practitioner Masters Degree in Archetype and Culture. She trained in dance therapy, occupational psychology and psychoanalytic studies, and studies counselling psychology with Petrŭska Clarkson at PHYSIS. She is a 'founding friend' of the London Convivium for Archetypal Studies, and has over twenty years' experience of supervised active imagination work with the cosmology of the Sapphire Tree.

Orit Aviram PhD (Psychology) is a lecturer and researcher in psychology at institutes in Israel. She has conducted research at Lund University, Sweden and Metanoia Psychotherapy Institute, London. Her broad research experience includes work in the fields of pain, brain hemispheres, sleep, dreaming and sleep disorders. In recent years, her work has expanded to include clinical practice and phenomenological research of psychotherapeutic issues.

Frank W. Bond PhD is Research Fellow at the Department of Psychiatry and Behavioural Sciences, University College London Medical School. His research interests include examining the validity of various cognitive-behavioural psychotherapy theories and investigating the effectiveness of psychological job stress interventions.

Robert Bor DPhil, CPsychol, AFBPsS, is Professor of Psychology at City University, London, and a Chartered Clinical and Counselling Psychologist. He received his family therapy training at the Tavistock Clinic, London, and is a member of the Tavistock Society of Psychotherapists and a UKCP registered Family Therapist. His main research and practice interests are psychotherapy in health care settings and counselling families affected by medical problems. He is also a Churchill Fellow.

Diane Bray BSc, PhD is Senior Lecturer in Psychology and Counselling at Roehampton Institute, London. Her interests are risk-taking behaviour, women's issues, individual differences, crimes, mood and cognition, and teaching and learning strategies.

Helen Cowie is Professor of Psychology at Roehampton Institute, London, a Fellow of the British Psychological Society and a chartered counselling psychologist. Her research interests include children's social and emotional development, with a special focus on peer support initiatives and strategies to counteract school bullying. She has published widely in these areas.

Adrian Coyle PhD is a lecturer in psychotherapeutic and counselling psychology in the Department of Psychology at the University of Surrey. His writing and research have focused on lesbian and gay psychology, psychosocial aspects of HIV/AIDS and qualitative research methods.

Paul Dickerson BA is Senior Lecturer in the School of Psychology and Counselling at Roehampton Institute, London, and a member of the BPS. He is interested in the use of discourse analysis to explore various psychological issues, particularly political talk on television.

Windy Dryden is Professor of Counselling at Goldsmiths College, University of London. He has authored or edited over a hundred books including *Facilitating Client Change in Rational Emotive Behaviour Therapy* (Whurr, 1995) and *Daring to be Myself: A Case of Rational-Emotive Therapy*, written with Joseph Yankura (Open University Press, 1992). In addition, he edits twelve book series in the area of counselling and psychotherapy including the *Brief Therapy and Counselling* series (Wiley) and *Developing Counselling* (Sage Publications). His major interests are in rational emotive behaviour therapy, eclecticism and integration in psychotherapy and, increasingly, writing short, accessible self-help books for the general public.

Martin Glachan PhD, AFBPsS, CPsychol, is Principal Lecturer at Roehampton Institute, London. His major research interests are in the area of family relationships and how adults' early life experiences influence their own parenting behaviours. Most recently he has investigated how parents' network of close relationships relate to the quality of experiences they have with their young children.

Jamie Moran BA, PhD has trained in child psychotherapy and has also practised with adults for sixteen years working from a broadly existential base. He is currently Senior Lecturer in Psychology and Counselling at Roehampton Institute, London, and his research interests include counselling process in situated action mode, issues in the New Paradigm and spiritual psychology.

Yuko Nippoda MA is a UKCP registered psychotherapist. She has seen clients at Nafsiyat Intercultural Therapy Centre and University College London, and also in primary care and organisational contexts through Personal Performance Consultants, UK as a bilingual counsellor. She also engages in organisation development consultancy focusing on cross-cultural issues (particularly between Britain and Japan), and in collaborative research at the Independent Centre for Qualitative Research at PHYSIS, London. Her current interest is in the difference in group dynamics between collectivistic societies and individualistic societies.

Jean O'Callaghan BEd, MA (PsyEd), DCG (NUI) is Senior Lecturer at Roehampton Institute, London, and her interests include narrative in counselling, children's and adults' developing sense of self, counselling in the workplace, identity development in career transitions, and interpersonal process recall.

Linda Papadopoulos BA, MSc, Post MSc Diploma in Counselling Psychology is a counselling psychologist working in primary care. She received her undergraduate degree in psychology from York University in Toronto, and went on to obtain an MSc in Health Psychology from Surrey University and a post MSc diploma in counselling psychology from City University, where she is currently undertaking doctoral research into the use of counselling with disfigured patients. She also works as a visiting lecturer at City University.

Regina Pauli BSc, PhD is Lecturer in Psychology at Roehampton Institute, London. Her research interests are in the areas of individual difference in cognitive skill acquisition, learning to interpret medical images and research methods.

Jorge Ponciano Ribeiro MA, PhD is Professor of Clinical Psychology at Brasilia University, has been a psychotherapist for over twenty years, and has been trained in group analysis and in Gestalt therapy. He is author of two very important books on Gestalt theory: *The Group Process: a Gestalt Approach*, and *Gestalt Therapy: Retracing the Path*, both in Portuguese. He is founder and President of the Gestalt Institute of Brasilia.

John Rowan is the author of a number of books, including *The Transpersonal in Psychotherapy and Counselling* (Routledge, 1993), and *Healing the Male Psyche: Therapy as Initiation* (Routledge, 1996). He is a past Chair of the Humanistic and Integrative Section of the UKCP. He is a Fellow of the British Psychological Society and a member of the Counselling Psychology Division. He teaches, supervises and leads groups at the Minster Centre in London.

Preface

I think of the discipline of counselling psychology as the professional application of the integration of psychological research and supervised practice in the amelioration of distress and the improvement of quality of life for individuals, groups, families and organisations within the relevant historical and cultural contexts. I believe that the primary vehicle for this endeavour is through relationship – with the people, between the specialities and between this discipline and others.

As Chair of the British Psychological Society Counselling Psychology Diploma Examination Board and as an active professional practitioner, teacher, supervisor and consultant in this and cognate disciplines, I know how much this has been a counsel of perfection rather than an accurate statement about our everyday work. In the planning and preparation for this book, I found that there were many contributors who were in principle interested in contributing to this volume within such terms of reference. However, there were but relatively few authors who eventually delivered.

Shortly before going to press I discovered that, in the preface to his book on the practical implications of research for counselling and psychotherapy, Dryden (1996) wrote about his own experience that virtually all contributors to that book (which he had edited with a similar intent to that which I bring to this present book, in the much wider fields of counselling and psychotherapy) 'had difficulty' with addressing the basic task of integrating research and practice.

The BPS Division of Counselling Psychology is little more than three years old and there are only some fifty chartered counselling psychologists in Britain at the moment. So, Dryden's and my experience is perhaps not unexpected. However, we should delight at the richness and variety of material which people who have published on this theme in this country – and also in this book – have felt generous and brave enough to make available at this stage.

However, I also agree with Dryden (1996: xi) that 'If the research–practice divide is to be traversed, then research, skills training and supervised clinical practice need to be far more closely integrated on training courses than they are at present'. We have a long way to go. And there are few maps and even less travellers who have returned knowledgeable and victorious from trying publicly to harvest their work in this field. (Writing is indeed speaking publicly, as Bakhtin said (Hirschkop and Shepherd, 1989).)

Counselling psychology on the other hand is perhaps the mental health discipline which, because of its very youth and recent emergence in this country, its philosophy of openness and inquiry, and its lack of dogmatic adherence to singular approaches, methods or ideologies, could be most hospitable to the development and celebration of less traditional and perhaps more innovative and experimental forms of integrating research and practice.

According to Barker, Pistrang and Elliott (1994) some of the reasons which clinical and counselling psychologists give to explain why they do not do research are the following: the irrelevance of research to ongoing work with patients or clients ('journals are filled with rigorous but irrelevant studies' (p. 26)); the emphasis on generalities and lawfulness rather than individual uniqueness; the positivist paradigm which still has hegemony in the academy is seen to be reductive and simplistic, patriarchal, Eurocentric, dualistic, Newtonian, etc. Research is also feared to be intrusive and disturbing to the therapeutic relationship. making disproportionate demands on professional time compared to clinical work. and it is not encouraged, supported, valued or rewarded by managers or colleagues. Furthermore technical expertise is felt to be lacking with 'journal editors and other gatekeepers setting prohibitively high standards that discourage those beginning research' (p. 27). There are also (as there should be) ethical concerns affecting the integration of practice and research – particularly when the research paradigm or process 'dehumanises' the 'subjects'. (Of course one could raise the question of whether unresearched clinical practice or lack of accountability for one's work is ever ethical.) Many clinical and counselling psychologists also specifically mentioned feeling threatened by anxiety about being scrutinised and the possibility of coming up with findings which do not support one's convictions or beliefs. 'Sometimes these feelings of threat may find their expression in the form of some of the other reasons listed' (p. 28).

Yet. unless we understand the process and demands, the potential as well as the impossibilities of research. we can hardly be effective – even at evaluating the previous research of our colleagues, upon which *the body of psychological knowledge* which is the underpinning of all our professional work is based. Furthermore. if we all refrained from undertaking this task of integrating our practice with research, for any combination of these (or other) reasons, students and colleagues perhaps would also be reluctant to engage in this work. Worse, they would be deprived of the joys, excitement and satisfaction that comes so richly from the effort of carving out new land where before there was only a choice between jungle and weeds on the hand, and, on the other, the artificially cultivated gardens of factory farms. I am interested in work in progress as much as in finished products – and I rarely believe in the latter. Sometimes there is more to learn from seeing a craftsman or craftswoman at work than just buying (financially or metaphorically through introjection) the outcome of their labours. Some of these papers show ideas in embryo, some at halfway stations, and others circling back already along the feedback loops of increasing confidence and understanding.

Therefore I took the bit between the teeth and forged ahead anyway presenting here what we could find now, not as perfect pieces of completed research, confident that they have been crafted as the next step in the advancement of science in the modernist idiom of the Enlightenment Project, but as moments of punctuation and communication along the road of discovery and mistake, map-making and shopping for instruments, model-building as well as experimenting with unusual and even sometimes controversial forms and themes.

This book is not necessarily meant to be read from beginning to end. It is probably more useful as a source to be consulted for argument, inspiration, education or amplification as the need or curiosity dictates. It is divided into two parts. Part I acts as orientation and introduction where the field is defined and outlined *vis-à-vis* adjunct disciplines, and contains a rich harvest of chapters focusing on integrating research and theory as counselling psychology practice, bringing together practitioner–scientists from a wide variety of orientations and settings who apply their very different kinds of energies to this endeavour. Part II continues in this vein, but with the emphasis on application to professional dimensions of counselling psychology research integrated with supervised practice.

May our colleagial conversations continue as our relationship thrives with increased communication in the bookshops as well as in the conference halls, in the academy as well as in the consulting rooms. All of the work in this book can be developed further 'had we but world enough and time'. We also look forward to seeing such improvements on our own work, and that of other colleagues yet to join us in print, as we endeavour to advance the frontiers of competence in our shared professional discipline.

REFERENCES

Barker. C., Pistrang, N. and Elliott, R. (1994) *Research Methods in Clinical and Counselling Psychology*, Chichester: John Wiley.

Dryden. W. (ed.) (1996) *Research in Counselling and Psychotherapy: Practical Applications*, London: Sage.

Hirschkop, K. and Shepherd. D. (eds) (1989) *Bakhtin and Cultural Theory*, Manchester: Manchester University Press.

Acknowledgements

Chapter 1 by Petrūska Clarkson is a revised version of a paper first published as 'Counselling psychology in Britain – the next decade' in *Counselling Psychology Quarterly* 8, 3: 197–204. 1995 (© Journals Oxford Ltd, reprinted with permission of the Editor).

Chapter 4, 'Qualitative Research in Counselling Psychology: Using the Counselling Interview as a Research Instrument', by Adrian Coyle, is an extended and elaborated version of a paper, co-authored with Clare Wright, which appeared in 1996 in the *Journal of Health Psychology* 1: 431–40.

Chapter 5, 'Researching the "Therapeutic Relationship" in Psychoanalysis, Counselling Psychology and Psychotherapy – A Qualitative Inquiry' by Petrūska Clarkson was first published in *Counselling Psychology Quarterly* 9, 2: 143–62, 1996 (© Journals Oxford Ltd, reprinted with permission of the Editor).

Chapter 7, 'Psychological Counselling in Primary Health Care: A Review', by Linda Papadopoulos and Robert Bor was first published in *Counselling Psychology Quarterly* 8, 4: 291–303, 1995 (© Journals Oxford Ltd, reprinted with permission of the Editor).

Chapter 10 was originally published in 1996 in *Counselling Psychology Review* 11, 1: 4–42.

Chapter 13, 'Phenomenological Research on Supervision: Supervisors Reflect on Being a Supervisor' by Petrūska Clarkson & Orit Aviram was first published in *Counselling Psychology Quarterly* 8, 1: 63–80, 1995 (© Journals Oxford Ltd, reprinted with permission of the Editor).

Chapter 14, 'Writing as Research in Counselling Psychology and Related Disciplines' by Petrūska Clarkson was first published in P. Clarkson (1995) *The Therapeutic Relationship*. pp. 266–75. Reprinted with permission of Whurr Publishers Ltd.

Excerpts from Federico Garcia Lorca (1980) *Deep Song and other prose* (edited and translated by Christopher Maurer) reprinted with permission of Marion Boyars Publishers Ltd.

Excerpt from Rainer Maria Rilke (1993) *Letters to a Young Poet* (translated by M. D. Herter Norton) reprinted with permission of W. W. Norton & Company Ltd.

Chapter 1

Counselling psychology
The next decade[1]

Petrūska Clarkson

INTRODUCTION

In this chapter a brief but necessary review of the boundary and definitional concerns which most affect the discipline of counselling psychology (Part I) is followed by an overview of what our future could look like (Part II).

PART I: COUNSELLING PSYCHOLOGY – WHAT IS IT?

The issues, concepts and disputes of disciplinary demarcations between the designations psychologist, counsellor and psychotherapist have been exhaustively discussed elsewhere and will no doubt continue in many voices. Three factors may change this preoccupation: (a) the legal protection of the term psychologist as currently being mooted by the British Psychological Society (BPS); (b) the possibility of a more generic training for all psychologists; and (c) the outcome of initiatives to establish a special designation of psychotherapist psychologist (or similar).

For our purposes here, acknowledging that there are vast areas of similarity, we will separate the descriptions of clinical and counselling psychologists as follows.

Psychologists and applied psychologists

Psychologists are professionals with at least one degree in psychology. Many move on to further postgraduate studies in applied psychology, one of which, these days, is counselling psychology.

The dictionary definition of psychology as 'the science of the nature, functions and phenomena of the human soul or mind' (Onions, 1968: 1700) is

1 This chapter is a revised version of a paper published as 'Counselling psychology in Britain – the next decade' in *Counselling Psychology Quarterly* 8 (3): 197–204, 1995, and of a paper given at the Division of Counselling Psychology 2nd Annual Conference in Birmingham on 12 May 1995. I am most grateful to Dr Michael Carroll for his input on the earlier article and to Dr Zoubida Guernina for presenting the latter on my behalf at the Conference.

somewhat restrictive in its view. Psychology is not only the 'science of the mind' but also the science of human behaviour in all its aspects. Psychology interprets the person (Carroll and Pickard, 1993) and results in a number of theories of personality and research methods for understanding the person. Its questions are person-related: Why do people behave the way they do? What motivates the individual? How do people grow and begin to think and use language? Can we isolate stages of life as individuals progress towards old age? From its academic base. psychology is divided into a number of subsections, such as development psychology, cognitive psychology, personality theory, biological basis of behaviour. abnormal psychology, psychological assessment. From this academic basis, psychologists move to apply their subject to the world.

Clinical psychologist

The key tasks of clinical psychologists are: Assessment, Treatment, Training/teaching and Research (both patient and service related) as well as Management (BPS, 1988b: 4).

The range of treatment techniques has grown considerably during the last twenty years, from the previously limited range of essentially educational or psychodynamic techniques. . . . Examples are the treatment of elimination disorders in children, phobic conditions in adults and the remediation of cognitive difficulties following different types of brain injury. Some of these treatments now offer positive alternatives to drug treatments (such as anxiety-management procedures), and supplement medical treatments in people with long-term-disabling conditions (BPS, 1988a: 5).

Behavioural methods (such as desensitisation), methods based on social learning principles (such as social skills training) and cognitive methods, used especially for altered mood states, are now widely used. In addition, a wider range of psychotherapeutic approaches has been developed, based on theories that are not essentially psychodynamic (such as personal construct theory). It has become apparent that there are a number of non-specific factors which are relevant to many apparently different techniques. A number of these approaches are used by counsellors and other non-psychologists to help people with less serious conditions (BPS, 1988a: 5).

The boundaries between clinical psychology as a discipline and other academic and health-care disciplines, are not fixed (BPS, 1988a: 1).

Counselling psychologist

This has become an avenue to chartered psychologist status and an independent Division of the BPS. At the time of writing it is a Special Group of the BPS, as Carroll (1992: 74) makes clear:

Counselling psychology moved from being a 'Section' in 1982 to becoming a 'Special Group' in 1988 with increasing aspirations to becoming a Division within BPS. Its membership . . . is still probably the fastest-growing section of the BPS. . . . Becoming a Division within the BPS would bring with it major implications for training, training courses, career structure and pay levels, status, and supervision. A proposed new Diploma in Counselling has been outlined as the next step on the journey to Division status.

One important, if not the most important, difference between counsellors and counselling psychologists is the conscious use of *academic psychology alongside practical counselling skills*. Counselling psychologists have a basic degree in psychology, and then further training in counselling psychology (MSc). Counselling psychology is here conceptualised as the overlapping area between counselling and psychotherapy in the Venn diagram (see Figure 1.1, p. 6) representing the three primary arenas of counselling, psychology and psychotherapy.

Counselling psychology is considered not identical with counselling (even when it is carried out by psychology graduates). In counselling psychology, there is an emphasis on the systemic application of distinctively psychological understanding, *based on empirical research of the client and the counselling process*, to the practice of psychological counselling. The relevant psychological knowledge is partly concerned with the presenting problems of clients, and partly with the procedures and processes involved in counselling. It would be remembered that counselling psychology involves work in an organisational context, as well as with individual clients, and synthesises elements of better-developed areas of professional work such as clinical and occupational psychology. Life-span developmental psychologies and the social psychology of interpersonal processes are among the areas that supply the academic foundations of counselling psychology. Of central scientific relevance, of course, are empirical investigations of the processes and outcomes of counselling and of related methods of psychotherapy.

The psychological understanding of counselling derives not only *from formal psychological inquiry but also from the interpersonal relationships between practitioners and their clients*. The essence of such relationships is one of personal exploration and clarification in which psychological knowledge is utilised and shared in ways which enable clients to deal more effectively with their inter- and intra-personal concerns. The capacity to establish and maintain such relationships ultimately rests upon the personal qualities and maturity of the individual counselling psychologist. Personal qualities, such as non-defensiveness and a capacity to experience and communicate emphatic resonance, constitute essential resources which the counselling psychologist draws upon. Whilst these characteristics may be enhanced by skills training they derive primarily from a foundation of personal experience and integrative maturity (BPS, 1989: 1).

Having made some distinctions between counselling and clinical psychologists, we now address common descriptions of two other professions which interlink and overlap in terms of many variables.

Counsellor

The British Association for Counselling, founded in 1977, defines counselling as follows:

Counselling is the skilled and principled use of relationship to facilitate self-knowledge, emotional acceptance and growth, and the optimal development of personal resources. The overall aim is to provide an opportunity to work towards living more satisfyingly and resourcefully. Counselling relationships will vary according to need but may be concerned with developmental issues, addressing and resolving specific problems, making decisions, coping with crisis, developing personal insights and knowledge, working through feelings of inner conflict or improving relationships with others.

The counsellor's role is to facilitate the client's work in ways that respect the client's values, personal resources and capacity for self determination (BAC, 1989: 1).

Psychotherapist

'Legislators and courts of law have found it almost impossible to define "psychotherapy" in such a way as to include, by universal agreement among therapists, that which *is* psychotherapy and to exclude that which is *not* psychotherapy' (Watkins, 1965: 1142). The professional body for psychotherapists is the United Kingdom Council for Psychotherapy (UKCP).

Here follow some definitions of psychotherapy:

Psychotherapy is defined as a form of treatment for mental illness and behavioural disturbances in which a trained person establishes a professional contact with the patient and through definite therapeutic communication, both verbal and non-verbal, attempts to alleviate the emotional disturbance, reverse or change maladaptive patterns of behaviour, and encourage personality growth and development. Psychotherapy is distinguished from such other forms of psychiatric treatment as the use of drugs, surgery, electric shock treatment and insulin coma treatment. (Freedman, Kaplan and Shadock, 1985: 2601).

Psychotherapy is the treatment by psychological means of problems of an emotional nature in which a trained person deliberately establishes a professional relationship with a patient with the object of 1) removing, modifying or retarding existing symptoms, 2) mediating disturbed patterns of behaviour, 3) promoting positive personal growth and development (Wolman, 1965: 118).

In discussions at the United Kingdom Standing Conference for Psychotherapy (as the UKCP used to be known), the following definition of psychotherapy had been used: 'the systematic use of a *relationship* between therapist and patient – as opposed to pharmacological or social methods – to produce changes in cognition, feelings and behaviour' (Holmes and Lindley, 1989: 3).

In the UKCP, the Psychotherapy Training Organisations are currently divided into the following sections:

1 Analytic Psychotherapy Section;
2 Humanistic and Integrative Psychotherapy Section (HIPS);
3 Family, Marital, and Sexual Section;
4 Experiential Constructivist Therapy;
5 Behavioural Psychotherapy Section;
6 Hypnotherapy Section;
7 Psychoanalytically-based Psychotherapy with Children Section;
8 Analytical Psychology.

It should be clear that membership of all of these divisions (with the exception of 3) is made on the grounds of avowed and practised adherence to one or more theoretical orientations.

Figure 1.1 shows each of the three areas – counselling, psychology and psychotherapy – as distinct in itself, but relating to each of the other two areas, and indicates the interrelationship between all three. The overlap between counselling and psychotherapy represents the work of counselling professionals with advanced practice qualifications or the psychotherapist using counselling skills. The overlap between psychotherapy and psychology represents psychotherapists with a psychology qualification or psychologists trained as psychotherapists. The overlap between counselling and psychology represents counselling psychologists (i.e. psychology graduates with counselling qualifications, but no special training in psychotherapy). Finally, 'X' marks the area which involves the work of psychology graduates who have training and experience in both counselling and psychotherapy. This may be the appropriate area for the profession of counselling psychology.

Research (Norcross, 1986) shows that theoretical differences between 'schools or approaches' are far less important in terms of successful outcome of counselling or psychotherapy than the quality of the *relationship* between counsellor and client and certain client characteristics, including motivation for change and the willingness to take responsibility for their part in the process. The literature and an extensive twenty-year-long qualitative research project is reviewed, discussed and amplified, for example, in Clarkson (1991, 1995a) and Chapter 5 of this volume.

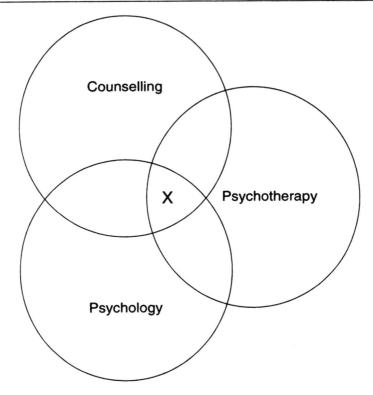

Figure 1.1 Venn diagram of the relationship between counselling, psychology and psychotherapy

Source P. Clarkson and M. Pokorny (eds) *Handbook of Psychotherapy*, London: Routledge, 1994.

PART II: COUNSELLING PSYCHOLOGY – THE FUTURE

In this part of the chapter. originally written in response to a specific assignment, I will survey some of the major trends developing in counselling psychology, which may shape the future of the profession into the next decade. For purposes of consideration rather than an attempt at spurious demarcation, the major themes of the discussion will be organised under the four headings of Professionalism, Theory. Practice and Research. I will use a device of polarisation to highlight the major issues as I see them now. It is not meant to be comprehensive or defini-tive. but a spur towards exploration, debate and development.

Professionalism

Counselling psychology has comparatively recently emerged as a separate pro-fession in Britain, largely in response to pervasive and large-scale changes in the socio-economic, political and cultural forces affecting the helping professions.

Some of these are the aftermath of the Thatcher years (such as what has been experienced as the dismantling of the National Health Service), the restructuring of care and medicine in terms of market forces and the popularization (through books, radio and TV) of self-development and counselling both as a resource as well as a career opportunity for many people of the middle classes in these uncertain times. (It has been one of the few professions relatively untouched by the recession and counselling schools have flourished while city firms and industry have languished and suffered.)

Quantity and quality

Emerging thus as a profession for and from our times, counselling psychology can both suffer and benefit from the upsurgence of recognition, demand and popularity. On the one hand, given the large numbers of professionals seeking registration as chartered counselling psychologists, the profession can capitalise on these boom times by recognising more courses, more psychologists, more professional opportunities. representation and influence in all probably and possibly relevant forums. On the other hand the energies and capacities of those concerned with professionalisation can be concentrated very specifically towards goals of quality and more discriminating selection procedures, more stringent examinations and qualifying criteria on par or better than the most demanding of neighbouring professions (for example, psychotherapy), thus focusing the profession more in the direction of quality and forgoing some of the populist arguments based on numbers (such as numbers of applicants for recognition). At a certain point in our history this was politically necessary in achieving our professional goals – for example, in dealing with the British Psychological Society. Hopefully, there will come a time in the next decade when a balance will be achieved. Quantity can provide the healthy base for the development and crystallising of quality. The criteria and consequences will have to be worked out over time in strategic response to changing conditions of the world in which our profession needs to make its way.

Uniformity and diversity

In the early development of professions, there is often a willingness to include (even if reluctantly) diversity. difference and a tolerance for idiosyncrasy. This was certainly the atmosphere of the early meetings of what has now become the United Kingdom Council for Psychotherapy. As soon as the criteria have been more or less agreed, the standards for inclusion start changing and people become more and more resistant to including those who do not quite fit in at the same time as the demands become more stringent and more difficult to meet. I have seen this and heard about it from colleagues in almost every professional organisation which currently exists. It is a well-known phenomenon in the psychology of organisations generally.

Classically and predictably, students and new organisations seeking to join then complain that 'they keep moving the goalposts'. Of course it is right and natural that developing professions are developing. Continuous review and revision of standards and improvements related to changing conditions and circumstances are what marks out the thriving from the dying in personal as well as professional life. However, what usually happens next is that this drive for acceptability to the status quo, commonly agreed standards and consensually developed criteria becomes a repository of conformity, uniformity and 'people who are like us'. The unusual, the challenging, questioning of the basic assumptions underlying the hard-won professional status (or similar) is often experienced as threatening, untrustworthy and therefore to be excluded or marginalised.

Somewhere I came across a book on organisational behaviour, which I have not been able to trace since. It tells of the metaphorical barbarians who break new ground, machete their way through the jungle and struggle with their ox-wagons over the mountains; the bureaucrats on the other hand end up balancing the books and decreeing how wide the paths should be and how much those who don't do it correctly should be fined. In this way the creativity and counter-dependent energies often end in schismatic breaks (Jung from Freud, the BCPC from the UKCP, the Social Democrats from the Labour Party, etc.) rather than in fruitful fertilisation, enhanced diversity and delight in increased choices in the organisation itself and an enrichment of its creative and discriminating capacities.

Elitism and access

The third theme which can be noticed around the issues of professionalism for counselling psychology in the next decade is that between the ideal of open access in dialogue, engagement or contest with the desire for exclusivity, professional/academic excellence and a sociologically normal 'closing of the ranks' when resources (of, for example, finance, status or support) are threatened. Although Accreditation of Prior Experiential Learning (APEL) has been instituted in this country, in order to give equal opportunities to people who have non-academic learning and experience, this worthy goal still seems to be more honoured in the breach than in the observance. Graduate basis for registration is still necessary, as far as I understand it, in order to begin to engage in recognition processes to become a chartered psychologist or chartered counselling psychologist. This necessitates a particular culture-bound accomplishment which research has amply shown to mitigate against women, non-whites and the disabled (to mention only some examples).

Therefore people with less conscientious academic training, people with unconventional kinds of wisdom or unusual experiential backgrounds, people who come from cultures which have valued less rational, left-hemispheric, patriarchal forms of education are automatically disadvantaged. Yet if precisely these people are (however subtly) discouraged or disallowed from entering and starring in our profession, it appears inevitable that we will continue to serve effectively only certain sections of the population in a certain language, who have access to certain privileges in certain very narrowly prescribed contexts – and even so in ways which can disable by the very prejudicial gulfs in which they are rooted.

Theory

Conservatism and revolution

I hope that the next decade will see a good and solid tournament joined between conservative and revolutionary forces within counselling psychology theory. Classicism, fundamentalism even, has a certain purity of form even if it does act as some Procrustean bed upon which to slice or stretch all human phenomena. The ideas and ideals which have guided some hundred years in psychoanalysis, cognitive-behavioural therapy and humanistic/existential psychotherapy have each their own integrity, soundness and coherence within their respective ideological, epistemological and aesthetic universes of discourse. The problem with such pure forms is when they acquire some hegemony of power, criteria-setting or reality definition. An instance of this is in a recent code of ethics formulated for Gestalt therapists in which the only psycho-technical terms are transference and countertransference: there is no representation of autonomy, responsibility or actualisation in the guidelines – the very radical theoretical and philosophical foundations of the originators of Gestalt therapy who formulated their work in such terms in rebellion against what they perceived as psychoanalytic reductionisms such as transference.

It is likely that as the forces of conformity, cohesion and scraping off of the barnacles of idiosyncrasy and individuality grow apace, counterforces will come into play. These could be and perhaps will be of the sudden discontinuous nature of revolutions in knowledge which Kuhn (1962) wrote about. Chaos and complexity theory have hardly touched psychology yet. In such event, much of what we take for granted now in psychology, counselling and psychotherapy will be redundant and the unlearning of our assumptions will be at least as, if not more, important than the learning of new knowledge, skills, attitudes and habits.

Integration and deconstruction

Given the fact that outcome research studies show little if any differential effectiveness related to theory, the debates, competitions and differentiations between different approaches seem less and less realistic, interesting or relevant to the needs of clients. The identification of more than 450 different approaches (Corsini, 1984); the lack of sound evidence of differential effectiveness (Norcross and Goldfried, 1992); the studies which point to a common factor such as the relationship (Norcross and Goldfried, 1992); or that senior people from different approaches resemble each other more than beginners and experienced practitioners in the same approach (Fiedler, 1950) – all these point in the direction of integration rather than exclusive or dogmatic adherence to any one approach. Indeed integration is the way in which the majority of American counselling psychologists now identify themselves and it is one of the fastest growing avowed orientations in the world. Few 'pure forms' remain and those are rapidly becoming inaccessible or unaffordable to anyone who may challenge the basic assumptions or simply want relief from their immediate pain or distress or even learning for dealing with similar problems in the future.

At the same time as many approaches are recognising their similarities, commonalities and integrating capacities (although these may be exercised within only one system (e.g. the colonisation of empathy by Kohut in Self-Psychology), there are also termites gnawing at the very roots of the psychological edifice of our *fin de siècle*. Is there such an entity as an individual? Does childhood have anything to do with adult pathology? Is it possible to practise psychotherapy without abusing power? How can we justify individual psychotherapy in a world riven with injustice, inequality and uninvolvement in the important social justice issues of our time? Powerfully intelligent voices from the postmodern Zeitgeist are questioning and problematising most of what we have accomplished or even taken for granted so far.

Individual and field perspectives

Psychology has drawn its inspiration and its models largely from science – particularly physical science. We can see this originating in the Wundt laboratories as well as in Freud's hydrostatic conceptualisations of psychic energy. However, physical sciences, particularly physics, currently hardly resemble the ideal which modernist positivistic empirical psychology is still striving after. Theories of psychological investigation or intervention based on notions of measurement or observation by objective observers or researchers (for example, most of the papers in the *Journal of Clinical Psychology*) are drawing on a model of scientific investigation which has been substantially discarded or radically revised in the light of new knowledge and new perspectives.

The observer not only is part of the field, but influences and affects the field perhaps to the extent that he or she is unaware of such influence. It has been said that 'there are only relationships' – there can be no possibility of measurement which excludes the values, expectations or effects of the experimenter. Perhaps there should be no theory which considers the individual separate from the field – the child from the family system, the woman from our advertising culture, a young man from the collective pressures of our economy, an employee's problem drinking from the organisation's relationship with environmental ethics. Counselling psychology is uniquely placed and can without too much historical baggage be the approach to evaluate and implement theories which are used as tools. as metaphors, as Wittgensteinian ladders rather than as laws set in tablets of stone. unresponsive to changing conditions, unaware of the interrelatedness of all our explanatory theoretical nets.

Practice

NVQ and creativity

One of the biggest challenges counselling psychology will have to grapple with in the next decade is the counterpoint between component analysis of competencies and the potential stifling of creativity and spontaneity. I have been active in and applaud our professional concerns with explicit measurable standards, learning objectives and specific skills, accountability, audit, NVQs, contracting, health insurance categorisation and so on. Yet the more uncertain our economic conditions. the more questioned our basic assumptions, the more our meta-narratives buckle under the combined onslaught of inner and outer challenges, the more we seek the security of structures, and the more we tend to develop an obsessive-compulsive preoccupation with the details, compartments, measurabilities, respectabilities, predictabilities, regulations, laws and ultimate control over all relevant aspects of practice.

How to be seated, how to make a contract, how to do an assessment, how to deal with one's countertransference, how many hours of what kind of super-vision. what standards in training, what kind of records to comply with the Data Protection Act, what kind of topics or movements are allowed in order to ensure no censure from either customer or colleague – these are the themes of so many professional meetings and indeed is the very stuff of professionalisation itself. Elsewhere (Clarkson, 1995b) I have expounded on how these valid, important and admirable accomplishments can lead to the emergence of a kind of 'defen-sive practice' which stifles the kind of creativity, discovery and novelty with fear. conformity and compliance. Counselling psychology will need to find ways, idioms and spaces for the jagged edges, the mistakes and the disordered random-ness of the creative process if it is not to suffocate itself in a misguided quest for an empty respectability.

Ahistoricity and cultural contextuality

Psychotherapy and psychological counselling have in recent years come under increasing attack for their irrelevance to the real world of the people who come to us for help. Counselling psychology will have to address the fact that it draws its origins from approaches, models and roots that essentially began a century ago and therefore in some very important ways need to be modified in terms of the changed cultural context in which we now live. I think the practice will have to change substantially in the direction of greater accountability, short-term interventions, flexibility from theoretical models and rapid responsiveness to situations. For example. ferry accidents, natural disasters, and rapid economic changes.

Individual and systems

Much as the practice of counselling psychology has focused on the individual and the bulk of the literature concerns interventions with individuals, the urgency and epidemiology of psychological distress will necessitate increased skills in the practice of systemic interventions, whether these be through families, groups or organisational interventions. It has become obvious, for instance, from people working in HIV counselling that the demand on counsellors, whether volunteer or qualified, rapidly exceeded the one-to-one practice paradigm.

This has enormous implications for training, requiring knowledge and facility in conceptualising as well as working effectively in the great variety of settings. In particular, if we take into account that most people spend more of their life in work settings (or the expectation of organisational settings), the fluctuations in education, jobs and the corporate mushrooming of our time, a thorough understanding of the organisational context and intervention skills of an organisational consultancy nature will be essential to every practitioner. We can no longer work as if an individual is not part of a system. In this way it is possible that the ambitions to be purely and exclusively clinical will conflict with consumer demand for counselling approaches which are also preventive, educational and equip people specifically, not only in working with their own familiar psychological heritage but also with the collective pressures, demands and opportunities.

Research

Positivism and postmodernism

The traditional, positivistic research tradition of psychology has grown such strong and healthy roots and such far-reaching branches that psychologists sometimes seem to believe 'that oranges are the only fruit'. The effects of the postmodernist turn in our cultural worldview will certainly reverberate for the next decade. At least during this time we can develop a postmodernist attitude to research which does not privilege any one particular form but welcomes and supports a psychology of practice which can develop a pragmatic body of knowledge, for example, by collecting the knowledge from clinical experiences of experienced and expert practitioners to find the patterns, models or interventions which have been found to work in the clinical setting (Polkinghorne, 1992).

New paradigms and old paradigms

One of the most encouraging contributions of counselling psychology already has been its welcoming of models of research and investigation which are non-traditional, non-parametric and even qualitative. On the examination board we have specifically allowed for the necessity of counselling psychologists in their training to become knowledgeable and familiar with qualitative and pheno-menological research methods. In this sense counselling psychology has a major contribution to make to the neighbouring disciplines of clinical psychology and psychotherapy, hopefully infecting them in a positive sense with new vision, a fresh approach and the willingness to make serendipitous discoveries rather than to continue indefinitely and unquestioningly with the old style positivistic, experimental models of research. Of course this does not mean relinquishing the enormous benefits of our classical traditions. It does mean a growing mutual respect and understanding.

Following and leading

The research component of most academic psychology programmes is the one that is often least attractive to students and most burdensome to the teachers. Counselling psychology as a newly emerging discipline in Britain has a unique opportunity to develop, encourage and sustain a model of blending practice and research in an ongoing, interesting and satisfying way. Process as well as out-come will be investigated perhaps even considered equally important (Elton Wilson and Barkham, 1994). New research questions and new kinds of research questions can follow the interests of clinicians rather than the funding priorities of the laboratory. The divide between the academy and the consulting room could potentially become a meeting place as their inhabitants learn to speak and work and supervise in the same language.

RECOMMENDATIONS

In particular I am suggesting that the practice of the clinic should not be separated from rigorous and constant research borne from and bearing theory. For example, a qualitative research project such as a disciplined and methodologically informed case study is not something to be done once for a dissertation or paper – I believe it needs to be conducted with every client, every session, for as long as a clinician/supervisor thinks and works in the profession.

It would therefore also be necessary for all professional supervisors to be skilled in acting as co-researchers in every case or situation brought to dis-ciplined reflection – also subjecting their own clinical and supervisory work to investigation. This may need to be done – not once or twice in a life time, but all the time. Although there will probably always be important differences in experience, interests and expertise, conjoining the work of *doing and reflection* in this way might even begin to signal the end of the difference between research and clinical supervision in training. This could potentially be to the benefit of all concerned – not least the clients. Learning with the client in such a way introduces a praxis of the recovery of knowledge which is surely at the very heart of the therapeutic endeavour itself.

In conclusion, for the purposes of this discussion, I have separated four areas of counselling psychology practice and supervision – professionalism, theory, practice and research. I would wish for the next decade that, for all practical purposes, they become inextricably interwoven.

REFERENCES AND FURTHER READING

Bandler, R. and Grinder, J. (1975) *The Structure of Magic: A Book about Language and Therapy*, vol. 1, California: Science and Behavior Books.

Brady, K. and Considine, M. (1988) *The London Guide to Mind, Body and Spirit*, London: Brainwave.

BAC (British Association for Counselling) (September 1984) Code of ethics and practice for counsellors, (Form no. 20), Rugby: BAC.

BAC (British Association for Counselling) (October 1989) Invitation to membership, (Form no. 1), Rugby: BAC.

British Psycho-Analytical Society (September 1990) In *UKCP Member Organisations' General Information and Training Courses*, London, UKCP.

BPS (British Psychological Society), Division of Clinical Psychology (1988a) *MPAG Project on Clinical Psychology Services, Manpower and Training Issues: Key Tasks of Clinical Psychology Services*, Leicester: BPS.

BPS (British Psychological Society), Division of Clinical Psychology (1988b) *The Representation of Clinical Psychologists: Interim Briefing Paper*, Leicester: BPS.

BPS (British Psychological Society), Membership and Qualifications Board (20 November 1989) *Report of the Working Party on the Diploma in Counselling Psychology*, Leicester: BPS.

BPS (British Psychological Society) (March 1991) *Code of Conduct, Ethical Principles and Guidelines*, Leicester: BPS.

Carroll, M. (1991) Counsellor training or counsellor education? A response, *Counselling* 2 (3): 104–105.

Carroll, M. (1992) *The Generic Tasks of Supervision*, private publication.

Carroll, M. and Pickard, E. (1993) Psychology and Counselling. In B. Thorne and W. Dryden (eds), *Counselling: Interdisciplinary Perspectives* (pp. 107–27), Milton Keynes: Open University Press.

Clarkson, P. (1991) A multiplicity of psychotherapeutic relationships. *British Journal of Psychotherapy* 7 (2): 14–163.

Clarkson, P. (1995a) *The Therapeutic Relationship*, London: Whurr.

Clarkson, P. (1995b) 'Vengeance of the Victim.' In *The Therapeutic Relationship* (pp. 53–61), London: Whurr.

Corsini, R. (ed.) (1984) *Current Psychotherapies*, Itasca, IL: R.E. Peacock.

Duffy, M. (1990) Counselling psychology USA: patterns of continuity and change, *Counselling Psychology Review* 5 (3): 9–18.

Dryden, W. (ed.) (1984) *Individual Therapy in Britain*, London: Harper & Row.

Elton Wilson, J. and Barkham, M. (1994) A practitioner-scientist approach to psychotherapy process and outcome research. In P. Clarkson and M. Pokorny (eds), *The Handbook of Psychotherapy* (pp. 49–72), London: Routledge.

Fieldler, F.E. (1950) A comparison of therapeutic relationships in psychoanalytic non-directive and Adlerian therapy, *Journal of Consulting Psychology* 14: 436–445.

Freedham, A.M., Kaplan, H.I. and Shadock, B.J. (1985) *Comprehensive Textbook of Psychiatry*, vol. 2, Baltimore: Williams & Wilkins.

Gelso. C.J. and Carter, J.A. (1985) The relationship in counselling and psychotherapy: components, consequences, and theoretical antecedents, *The Counselling Psychologist* 13 (2): 155–243.

Holmes. J. and Lindley. R. (1989) *The Values of Psychotherapy*, Oxford: Oxford University Press.

Karasu. T.B. (1986) The psychotherapies: benefits and limitations, *American Journal of Psychotherapy* 40 (3): 324–343.

Kohut. H. (1959) Introspection, empathy, and psychoanalysis: an examination of the relationship between modes of observation and theory. In P.H. Ornstein (ed.), *The Search for Self* (pp. 205–232). New York: International Universities Press.

Kuhn. T.S. (1962) *The Structure of Scientific Revolutions*, Chicago: University of Chicago Press.

Laplanche. J. and Pontalis, J.B. (1988) *The Language of Psychoanalysis*, London: Karnac Books.

Loughly. J. (1985) Personal communication at BPS Counselling Psychology Conference.

Norcross. J. (ed.) (1986) *Handbook of Eclectic Psychotherapy*, New York: Brunner/ Mazel.

Norcross. J.C. and Goldfried. M.R. (1992) *Handbook of Psychotherapy Integration*, New York: Basic Books.

Onions. C.T. (1968) *The Shorter Oxford English Dictionary*, Oxford: Clarendon/Oxford University Press.

Polkinghorne, D.E. (1992) Postmodern epistemology of practice. In S. Kvale (ed.), *Psychology and Postmodernism* (pp. 146–165), London: Sage.

Rogers. C. (1961) *On Becoming a Person: A Therapist's View of Psychotherapy*, London: Constable.

Watkins. J.G. (1965) Psychotherapeutic methods, in B.B. Wolman (ed.), *Handbook of Clinical Psychology* (pp. 1143–1167), New York: McGraw Hill.

Wolman. B.B. (ed.) (1965) *Handbook of Clinical Psychology*, New York: McGraw Hill.

Part I

Counselling psychology practice as integrating research and theory

Chapter 2

Organisational counselling psychology

Using myths and narratives as research and intervention in psychological consultancy to organisations[1]

Petrūska Clarkson and Marie Angelo

Myth and story go beyond mere explanation and give us access to our inner wisdom. They help us escape from the confines of linear, rational thinking. This is absolutely vital if we are to embrace the chaos and complexity of post-modern life and not stick our heads in the sands of reductionism. Contrary to literary convention, stories (at least myths, legends and fairy stories – which are essentially non-literary) do not have a linear form with beginning, middle and end. Such stories are fragments of the never-ending story. They are currents and eddies in the great sea of stories. They exist independently of any person – a fact recognised in some cultures when the storyteller thanks the story and bids it farewell until the next time it is told. Nor must we typecast ourselves in one role in one story. Our psyches contain all the characters and all the plots of all the stories – even those dark murderous aspects of the shadow which we hesitate to own – and so too do our organisations.

(Mead, 1997: 22)

INTRODUCTION

We have been researching ways in which the counselling psychologist can 'befriend' research and practice with organisations, through developing a perspective on myth and narrative. To work with 'the organisation as client', rather than with the individuals within an organisation, is to work at a new level of complexity, which myth and narrative are arguably well placed to provide. As this is essentially a new domain, and a new theoretical framework for counselling psychologists, we have chosen to bring the two together, focused through the reflective processes of qualitative research.

This chapter represents selections from a larger project on organisational coun-selling psychology, in which we have investigated the theoretical foundations in

---

1 A full account of the research to which this chapter refers may be obtained from the authors c/o The Independent Centre for Qualitative Research, PHYSIS, 12 North Common Road. London W5 2QB.

depth. and use insights from the research to propose practical applications (Clarkson and Angelo, in preparation). Ten co-researchers contributed, each a practising organisational consultant who uses myth and narrative in his or her work. These consultants were interviewed about their reasons for using myth and narrative, the particular advantages and disadvantages this brings to their work, and any further developments they could envisage. Each has an individual story to tell. which contributes to the 'grand narrative' of the research, but the final storytellers are ourselves, using the interview transcripts to create our own narrative about applications of their work for organisational counselling psychology. For the purposes of this chapter, therefore, the selections have been made in order to focus on 'the heart of the matter': the qualitative research process itself.

This reflective stance encouraged us to look closely at the role of the researcher, for the perspective of myth and narrative emphasises the importance of the storyteller as well as the story. As a result, we have examined the assumptions we bring from our specialist fields of practice – counselling psychology, organisational consultancy and archetypal and cultural psychology and psychotherapy. Each of these specialist fields is extensive in its own right, but our work is at that singular and essentially unexamined place where the disciplines intersect in embodied work; a fragment, but one which is a fractal of the whole. From the discipline of our academic trainings, we were prompted to begin with an extensive literature review of each field, and amassed an extensive critique concerning the developing role of counselling psychology in the workplace, the practice of qualitative research and the power of myth and narrative as a perspective.

We were particularly interested in the correspondences between the reflective processes of qualitative analysis and the reflective processes of counselling psychology itself. Throughout, we have appreciated Eckhartsberg's insight that to be human is 'to be entangled in stories' (1981: 90), and have followed Polkinghorne's lead (1988) that it is a narrative approach which will best serve the multiplicity and complexity of the organisational system. In the mythic language of archetypal psychology, we have sought to apply 'a hermetic eye' not only to the material, but, and this is of key importance to the qualitative researcher, to *the way we look at the material*.

THE RESEARCHERS AS STORYTELLERS

As researchers, we brought to the data our experience and training in the disciplines of counselling psychology and psychotherapy, organisational and management consultancy and research and academic psychology. Our interest in qualitative research spans our entire professional careers, although we both have experience in quantitative research (for example, Clarkson's Masters and Doctoral degrees were obtained on the basis of quantitative research considered to be of *cum laude* level. and Angelo has worked in both quantitative and qualitative research consultancy, and teaches the full range of methodologies).

The impetus for our research came from our mutual interest in the overlap between the application of psychology to organisations, a commitment to living and practising a personal and professional life where inquiry, especially inquiry into quality, is privileged and a recognition of the power of archetypes and myths as 'deepest patterns' shaping human experience in positive or negative ways.

We feel that it is from the archetypal and cultural psychology perspective that the key to an integrative method can be found which will bring the various disciplines together. The philosopher Robert Avens (1980) speaks not only for archetypalists but also for practitioners struggling to bring 'dry' theory to bear on 'wet' practice, when he comments that

> Academic psychology, in its eagerness to be as scientific as physics, has devoted all its energies not to understand but to explain the soul (psyche) from the view-point of natural sciences. In this way the soul has been exorcised from the only field which is traditionally dedicated to its study: it has been explained away, reductivised. (Avens, 1980: 32).

Archetypal and cultural psychology places the insights of story and narrative against the widest and most comprehensive of backgrounds. It is a discipline in which the study of story and narrative as social construction is grounded in mythic structures which at once extend and enliven the processes and procedures of one's work. In our examination of the research data, therefore, it is the insights of archetypal and cultural psychology which inform the method of examination.

Looked at archetypally, the place where the contributing disciplines meet to form the new practice of organisational counselling psychology is an archetypal ground. An interface such as this is a borderline, and thereby is inhabited by the mercurial, changeable. flexible god of borders, wit and lively intelligence – Hermes, messenger of the gods (and his many incarnations in other cultures). The successful organisational counselling psychologist will not emerge by holding on to old patterns of research, sedimented attitudes, single-theory perspectives and single levels of explanation. There is a need for the simultaneity and multiplicity which characterises an integrating and questioning perspective in counselling psychology. When this perspective opens out to find its imaginal grounding in multi-cultural myth, we find that *all along*, an integrative perspective is an archetypal approach, a polytheism (cf. Angelo 1997). As Charles Handy (1985) writes in *Gods of Management*, 'Differences, then, are necessary and good for organisational health. Monotheism, the pursuit of a single god, must be wrong for most organisations' (p. 39).

It is also wrong for the organisational counselling psychologist, and it is the archetypal perspective which enlarges and enlivens the field of discourse. This 'meta-integrative' approach provides an imaginal space sufficiently complex to contain, and to do justice to, and to tolerate, the multiple, emergent, intractable, ambiguous operations of organisations. It enables these operations to be perceived with lively imagination as living, dynamic co-created entities, rather than through mechanistic frameworks which fail to convey any dynamic. It makes it possible to envisage, differentiate and manage the workings of power, influence, politics, money, gender, culture and ambition, forces which retain an emphasis in organisational work in a way which is not so evident in counselling psychology itself. It is a mode in which the practitioner is a specialist storyteller, messenger of the gods, enlivened by their complex multiplicity.

TELLING THE STORIES: THE PRELIMINARY METHODS OF ANALYSIS

With the archetype Hermes informing the examination of the data, how do we proceed?

To establish a place from which to begin the 'work of Hermes', we started the analysis through immersion in the tape and transcript data, enjoying the rich flow of comment and example, talking together over a five hour session and jotting down initial observations. This was done with the intent of brainstorming a preliminary gestalt, with no consciously applied structure or form. From this 'naive role play', six initial categories emerged as themes in the data, which are given below, each with the key material which was spontaneously recalled as evidence. The responses that illustrate the categories below are drawn from our interviews with co-researchers.

1 *The overwhelming power and importance of narrative and story in organisations*

'Stories carry the energy and is where the work needs to be done', for, 'An awful lot of what goes on in organisations is story-telling', and, 'stories create the culture, and they keep it going and flowing in a whole range of ways, and they are like the sub-cultures as well, that are maintained, through myth and story, through various sections, particular grades of staff, operating at different levels ... '.

2 *The way story is a different, sometimes difficult, mode*

'When ideas are abstract they are ungrounded – and it's a closing off of possibilities. Images are concrete, specific – it's particularly where the power lies'. Hence, 'whenever people start telling stories they then shift to that mode'. However, 'we don't know enough about this kind of discourse – it speaks to a different part of us we haven't studied', and, 'there's a bit of me that finds it ridiculous'.

3 *The extra value which narrative can add to consultancy work (sometimes surprising, even for a consultant already working in the field)*

'To tell a narrative is to become aware of situating yourself – it is very hard to escape from narrative – when people tell stories they become caught in them in some way, they can't deny the responsibility in some way – so. . . . It's tapping into people's realisation that they do create worlds; they bring forth worlds together in which they act – and that realisation is incredibly powerful'. Hence, 'the use of stories is how you tap the blood flow in an organisation – it's how you tap an aliveness . . . the other story is a dead one – because it is a story – the analytical and mechanical one – and it is a non-living story – anti-organismic – and therefore I think it's very noticeable that as soon as you tell a story that is based on life you see that people actually become aware of being alive and being a living part of what it is they are weaving'.

4 *The potential dangers of leaving the stories unexamined*

'If these powerful stories aren't noticed and addressed, people are influenced without their knowledge'; 'You get cast as a character, such as being seen as something feminine and witch-like, and everything I did was cast in terms of the stories people knew about witches. . . . I was catapulted into big stories . . . I didn't know anymore what was my sense of myself and all these reflections I was being offered. . . . I felt caught up – who was to say whose story is what? This is how people have breakdowns. . . . It took a long, long time for the whole cycle to work its way through. We have extremely little power to do anything about it – it taught me the power of the collective. Identities are co-created in those kind of intense working environments – powerfully co-created selves end up working together – that's the real lesson of this – it happens elsewhere in organisations in no less intense but equally influential ways'. 'I know there is danger that I am going to be in it – when I am very stressed I'm in it without even knowing it. . . . it is amazingly powerful – it sort of draws you in spite of your stronger awareness – and you can't help not be, in a strange way.'

5 *The potential dangers of using the stories in consultancy*

'I think I used to be reluctant about using them [images] because of my own fear . . . I used to be very fearful of straightaway starting with pictures – I used to take care of them for a bit – in the rescuer mode – and then encourage them'; 'you could be seen as entirely off the wall – an image like Jonah and the whale is culturally specific – and people could say "it's crazy, there's no point". Some people really want to drum you out for that . . . people are so threatened by it'; 'I can also be threatened by the weirdness and strangeness – when you see it's the matriarchy/patriarchy thing – you are reconstituting a very ancient battle – and I'm careful about how I use mythology and to whom'.

6 *People use fragments of stories (clichés, metaphors) to carry the whole, and only rarely are full stories articulated – even for the consultant concerned*

'It's about shifting goalposts . . . sorry about that, I can't be original'; 'everyone has their nickname in the story – the two [chief protagonists] are called "Monsieur Oui" and "Madame Non" '; 'it's the ogre perspective – the organisation as ogre'; 'I do sometimes connect things up – with the *Anansi* stories – which are very Caribbean in their origin . . . and Anansi is sometimes somewhere that I go for help when I'm trying to understand what's going on in the black community of an organisation. . . . That's a bit like *Brer Nancy* stories as well – *Brer Nancy and the Briar Patch*. . . . When it comes to being in a team meeting or in a group situation when somebody stands up and identifies something as discriminatory or whatever . . . it's quite often met by silence, nobody supporting them, and I guess that's all part of that fear of falling into the Briar Patch . . . getting stuck with all the prickles – and I guess some of the work I do with people is trying to give them ways of doing just that – helping them out of the Briar Patch without getting stuck themselves – so how can we assist each other in ways that are safe – I shall go home and read up on *Brer Nancy* stories to see what wisdom might lie in them!'.

RETELLING THE STORIES – THE QUALITATIVE 'WORK OF HERMES'

These categories contain interesting and exciting material, but they are of limited value. They are fragments of narrative which lack the coherence of a structure/pattern, and hence they have neither the elevation of a conceptual overview, nor the deepening of its imaginal equivalent, which is mythical grounding. They are not yet a story, for they are not going anywhere. They do not connect and lead the imagination into further insights: they do not teach. In the language of archetypal and cultural psychology, the fragments are messages from the gods which have not yet been carried and informed by the work of Hermes, the master storyteller.

The archetypalist Ginette Paris, writing in *Pagan Grace* (1990: 84), describes Hermes as 'par excellence, a God of mythic thought . . . [for] as Messenger of the Gods, he brings the fundamental message of all Gods – which is myth'. We are now beginning to recognise that he is, too, a god of qualitative rather than quantitative research (cf. Moran, 1996). Paris gives us a wonderful picture of some of the qualities of Hermes, and when we read them we need only replace the names of Hermes and Apollo with 'qualitative researcher' and 'quantitative researcher', to see 'who is behind' our work; for as she explains:

The Hermes myth places communication at the intersection of all levels of language, at the point where complexity threatens to become confusion. He is comfortable somewhere between the explicit and the implicit and never tires of inventing nuances of voice, tone or gesture to place his message in the right context. Whereas Apollonian communication carries a single meaning – to be straight and clear like an arrow – communication under the sign of Hermes borrows from twisted pathways, shortcuts and parallel routes; it makes many round trips and ends up sometimes in meaningful dead-ends. The paths of

Hermes are multiple . . . he knows a trick or two about the complexities of human exchange [pp. 63–64]. . . . Apollo leads us on the linear roads (or highways perhaps) of science, while Hermes is the guide into the complex network of symbolic relationships (Paris, 1990: 105).

As guide to the analysis of the data, Hermes prompts the qualitative researcher to ask four questions about the material.

1 *Where is the story being told?*

This is the question which identifies the domain of discourse, the level of analysis, the archetypal ground. It examines the conceptual/structural enhancement which is brought to the story via its location in a particular cosmos or body of psychological knowledge and professional training.

2 *Who is telling the story?*

This is the primary method of archetypal psychology, the phenomenological turning from the story to the teller who is constructing the story. It asks, not just 'what is going on?', but 'who is speaking?', to reveal the various ways in which a conscious attentiveness to the contribution of each of the professional frameworks can add to and deepen the analysis.

3 *How well is the story being told?*

This is the question which focuses further on the discipline of systematic research inquiry. It points out that good qualitative research is a craft akin to that of the good storyteller.

4 *How can the story change?*

This is the question which looks closely at the narratives of the co-researchers and focuses on their insights. In telling the stories of consultancy, it teaches the way of doing such work, not only through conceptual frameworks, but through imaginative empowering.

We shall find and tell this narrative of organizational counselling psychology by being attentive to each question in turn:

1 Where is the story being told?

A particularly powerful enhancement is brought to the story via its location in a specific cosmos or body of psychological knowledge and professional training; one which is both clarifying conceptually/structurally and imaginatively animating. Exemplar papers of this approach are found in the volume *On the Sublime in Psychoanalysis, Jungian Analysis and Archetypal Psychotherapy*, with Angelo (in press) on 'Placing the sublime: cosmology in the consulting room' and Clarkson (in press) on 'The archetopoi of supervision', in which different supervision activities are located in different archetypal spaces; 'the hunting grounds', 'the academy', 'the home', 'the market', 'the temple'.

Hermes is a god of intelligence who is informed by extensive knowledge. This is particularly the case in an earlier incarnation of the god as the Egyptian Thoth. As Angelo (1997) has pointed out in the paper 'When the gods were intelligent and education was enchanting' the 'plasticity' of the Thoth archetype enables it to function as the intelligence at the heart of each god. Hence, depending on whether or not Thoth is at the heart of the research, each mythic grid can be applied with or without intelligence. It is an indication that the Hermes work with data must itself be extensively informed. A counselling psychologist, trained in the canon of academic psychology, and with a specialist training, is well located amongst theory, which, if used with an hermetic eye, can also point beyond itself, to help the development of the skills of organisational counselling psychology.

Three particular hermetic skills of theory use can be identified, namely: Repertoire, having a range of theories upon which to draw; Responsiveness, having a theory-rich approach rather than one which is theory-constrained; and Recognition, the ability to notice gaps in one's theories and to look for new ideas. Below, we have outlined some examples of each skill area.

Repertoire

The knowledge of academic psychology will have given the graduate basis for registration (GBR) necessary in order to train as a counselling psychologist. This is a basis shared with other professional psychologists, such as the occupational and clinical. This in itself gives a number of particular narratives or ways of seeing and construing the data which are not available to the non-specialist, for the understanding of social constructionism (cf. Gergen and Kaye, 1992) informs us that each of the contributing disciplines is itself a narrative; a story-telling about what kind of problems there are and how they can be described, explained, and retold, in ways that change how we perceive and experience the world. In addition, the counselling psychologist brings an extended knowledge base of counselling theory and practice. These specifically psychological constructs and theories provide previously researched themes and explanatory frameworks for the data.

Even if a psychologist does not choose to use theories explicitly, these are narratives which have informed and shaped his or her identity as a psychologist, and they remain in the background, operating in the structures of assumptions. They form part of the repertoire of the researcher, which can be triggered by recognition or associations to a single statement, operating as an entire 'unit of imagination' (Hughes, 1977) lighting up all the associated story circuits and resonating with the 'grand narratives' or major perspectives of the field. Hence when a co-researcher reports that 'an awful lot of what goes on in organisation is storytelling – particularly in accounting for how they've dealt with a project or an issue – it's a kind of hindsight story that they tell', the resonance for the psychologist can run right throughout gestalt pattern-making, to embrace Bartlett's 'effort after meaning' in the classic *Remembering* of 1933, and onward to the entire field of active information-processing theory.

Responsiveness

The counselling psychologist, having been trained to apply a range of counselling perspectives. will be unlikely to make the type three error (the probability of solving the wrong problem) which results from a narrow focus on only one level of explanation and only one kind of solution; as the classic illustration puts it, 'the customers complaining because the lift took too long to arrive did not necessarily have to be solved by the massive expense of building a new lift – a more imaginative flexible consultant advised on the placing of a mirror by the lift – and the complaints ceased'.

This does not mean that no coherent use can be made of a single theory, but it points out that there is no single theory which will address the interactive dynamic of organisational life with all its levels and systems. Having access to a range of perspectives makes it possible to disidentify from any one of them, either to use them selectively, or to reach towards an integrating perspective (cf. Clarkson, 1995). Rather than approaching the interviews with the intention of making an analysis exclusively in terms of learning theory or attribution, or of psychodynamics. the meta-integrative approach can recognise how the narrative relationships are operating; to establish the working relationship as a basis. and look for which aspects of reparative, transferential, interpersonal or transpersonal relationships are operating.

Recognition

A 'grand narrative' provides a pattern, and it becomes possible to use it rather like a table of elements; gaps can be noted, predicted and new elements looked for. If the researcher starts to become aware of other narratives, these may identify places where a gap is being superficially filled through a gestalt drawn from the surrounding area. Such a 'blind spot' can be seen in the lack of literature on power in counselling psychology and its GBR canon. Co-researchers described the power of narrative to affect people, and were concerned about the difficulties in their own work in using this mode because of problems and pressures of status, yet there is very little language of organisational power either in academic psychology or in counselling psychology training. How can we speak of something for which we have no differentiated vocabulary? There are typologies (such as French and Raven's categories of position power, reward power, coercive power, expert power and charismatic power), but this is descriptive labelling and does not convey an interactive dynamic.

Organisational consultancy goes much further in acknowledging the central importance of power, and has developed a more detailed vocabulary of the relations between power, influence and authority. The pragmatics of leadership and conflict management are built into the trainings for Master of Business Administration (MBA) and consultancy, often forming the basis of taught courses, management studies and role play exercises (as, for example, in Open University Business School courses and residential workshops). It is the archetypal discipline, however, which offers the most sophisticated study of power, and speaks not only of *kinds of power* but of *the intelligent use of power* in organisations. This approach, presented in archetypalist Hillman's (1995) text of that name, gives a subtle differentiation of ideas of power which goes far beyond the simplistic and into the hermetic. As Hillman points out:

> A simple idea of power, any idea that defines it simply, lulls us into quiescent passivity, and so actually saps power. The mind needs richer foods and it likes to move subtly, like a snake or a fox, otherwise it will get blindsided by the narrowness of focus, thereby blocking access to power and the enjoyment of it. If we don't first disturb the mind's familiar concepts of power, we can hardly be smart when using it. If, for instance, I define power simply as 'control', I will never be able to let go of control without fear of losing power. Trapped by this concept into paranoid vigilance, competitive exertions and demonstrative leadership, I will never discover the subtle power of influence, authority, generosity or patient resistance (Hillman, 1995: 9–10).

An archetypally informed organisational counselling psychology will need to have extended its domain (that archetypal ground of the interface) so that its training, practice and research explore further into these issues.

2 Who is telling the story?

This question identifies the primary method of archetypal psychology, which is also a key to qualitative research. It is the phenomenological stance of turning from the story to the teller who is constructing the story, to ask not just 'what is going on?', but 'who is speaking?' The success of this phenomenological bracketing lies in the researcher's willingness to leave the forward rush of analysis in order to prepare the eye (the 'I') to be a high-quality instrument of perception. This is a form of stepping back, returning to oneself as an integral part of the research; to bracket assumptions, biases and expectation before looking much more closely at the detail itself; and to hold back from prioritising and interpreting.

To prepare the researchers, this hermetic discipline involves identifying and setting aside the limiting assumptions of each of the narrative frameworks. Who is speaking when the organisational consultant, the counselling psychologist or the academic research psychologist speaks? Inspired by Miller Mair's telling personification of clinical psychology (1989: 5–12), as part of the research exercise. we asked for spontaneous stereotypes of the three disciplines. Hermes is a mischief-maker and Trickster as well as witty and intelligent, and many of the images must remain confidential! However, they lead on to some useful insights about limitations in the initial categories.

For example, the eye of 'the organisational consultant' (stereotype: 'a whizz kid with confidence') may tend to move too swiftly into categories which lend themselves to actionable recommendations. In consultancy, results have usually to be represented to senior management, who will tend to have little interest in the techniques, but place every pressure of time, economy and clarity. A set of final recommendations may be the only part of the report that is really studied by the budget-wielding decision-makers. The pragmatics of this do not lend themselves to lengthy and delicate analysis, but often depend on an 'educated intuition' which might work directly from the initial categories. Interviews on myths and narrative might be undertaken in order to anticipate employee and client reactions, and to make decisions about which techniques to use in a particular intervention. The emphasis would certainly be on possible dangers and difficulties.

Reflecting back on the forming of the initial categories, it is noticeable that the consultant's eye picked out the problem areas of shock, upset, alienation, embarrassment. These were contrasted with the positive values of humour, energy. insight, selecting material to illustrate each side as one might present the case to the management. As a result, value and danger have been polarised, rather than differentiated, and the resulting categories do not unpack just when and where and in what circumstances the methods might be useful and in what terms. They are not the work of Hermes.

By contrast, the eye of 'the academic research psychologist' (stereotype: 'lords it over people who can't count') may be reluctant to engage with 'messy' issues which have personal valence. On reflection it seems that this 'eye' kept the initial categories 'clean' of the emotive issues of gender and culture, even though they were raised on numerous occasions by co-researchers. Some very powerful material appears in the quotations, involving witch-hunts, scape-goating. discrimination. yet no category was specifically raised to contain them. Gender and culture are such powerful forces that it is almost always important to reflect on the way attitudes to these may affect the emergence of categories. Why did they not appear here? As researchers we seem to have colluded, uncon-sciously. to omit the difficult and contentious, yet we both work in multicultural environments and have tangled with the gender problem in many discussions, critiques and experiences. It is not that these issues were ignored from our discussions, but they were set in the context of personal experience, which the academic eye will tend to exclude from its Apollonic research considerations unless informed by the hermetic intelligence.

And what of the eye of 'the counselling psychologist' (stereotype: 'nice, tired-looking person')? On reflection, this 'eye' appears to have focused on the helplessness of the individual in the context of the organisational environment, rather than a response to the organisation as a whole. Yet in consultancy it is the organisation which is the client, and this tendency to focus on the individual in an environment rather than the dynamic between individual and environment (cf. Brown and Lent, 1992) may mean neglect of material framed at an organisational level of explanation. In the initial categories, for example, nothing is said about the overall practice of consultancy, about negotiating a contract, making an organisational analysis, presenting the reports, despite the fact that these were described by the co-researchers. The focus is the more familiarly therapeutic one of paying attention to the individual and group responses of employees. The material which refers to being trapped and 'sucked in' has a particular emotional valence which prioritises it.

To be awake to such narrative frameworks is the Hermes work of preparing the eye of the researcher. It is a cyclical business too, for at each point in a narrative it is of value to know 'who is speaking' now.

3 How well is the story being told?

This is the question which focuses further on the discipline of systematic research inquiry. It points out that qualitative research is a craft akin to that of the good story-teller.

In order to select a method for the lengthy procedures of textual and structural analysis, it is usual simply to reflect on the research procedures which were part of professional training, and to consult a relevant text. However, one of the great attributes of the Hermes work is its side-stepping movement out of sedimented or stuck attitudes and the ability, suddenly, to see and name things differently. It is the phenomenological art of 'making the familiar strange', so that what was taken for granted and was transparent is suddenly perceived afresh. To bring the thoroughness and discipline of an established research tradition to qualitative interview data is not a separate set of skills. The counselling psychologist is already in possession of the essential research skills for qualitative inquiry, but they have been called therapeutic skills rather than research skills. What is more, not only are these good research skills, but they are superior research skills for organisational consultancy work.

Strong parallels between counselling psychology practice and good qualitative research have been pointed out elsewhere (Clarkson, 1996; Cowie, Salm et al. in Chapter 10 of this book), including an emphasis on skills such as a superior training and experience of interviewing, and attentiveness to the words. nuances, hints and unspoken themes of the therapeutic encounter, both in terms of process and content. A good practitioner will keep and reflect on good quality case notes, turning them over in the mind, examining, considering and returning to small points again and again. Details of cases will regularly be taken into supervision where the processes and events of sessions are subjected to minute scrutiny. Time is taken in the telling of a story, and no client will be rushed or the story they are telling trivialised. At once, we are in the realm of Hermes, master storyteller.

Then, since the storytelling has already begun, there is no sudden 'breaking off of relationship' in order to apply some formal, deadening method of 'research'. What has been created is a first draft, and Hermes, god of communication, makes use of the language of reflection and organisation to do the work of taking the first tellings of the story through their second, third, fourth draft stages. Writers have always known this, but the scientific mode has tended to present formal process as an alien structure, rather than as the shaping, crafting and participating further in the work which brings out the story. The phenomenological reduction is not to cut the transcripts down to a list of concepts, but to *reveal* the stories hidden in the spontaneous, repetitive and partly formed discourses of action, just as a sculpture is hidden in the stone. It is a work in service to the story, not to an austere god of abstraction.

4 How can the story change?

This is the question which looks closely at the narratives of the co-researchers and focuses on their insights. In looking with an hermetic eye at the stories of consultancy it teaches ways of doing such work, not only through conceptual frameworks, but through imaginative empowering which enlivens technique and generates new insights into organisational life.

Stories help make the transition from a person-centred style of counselling to an organisational-centred style, and then to find a place which inhabits the dynamic of interaction. Stories take place in contexts and with others; they are collective, community affairs. They can be looked at as telling the story of one individual and his/her many sub-personalities, and simultaneously as telling the story of one organisation and its sub-cultures. Story places the individual back into the collective:

> Our problems are inside our lives, yes; but our lives are lived inside fields of power, under the influence of others, in accord with authority, subject to tyrannies. Moreover our lives are lived inside the fields of power that are our cities with their offices and cars, systems of work and mountains of trash. . . . Dysfunctional ideas in the world of the present, rather than the wounds of the inner child of the past, claim our psychological care today (Hillman, 1995: 15).

Deriving 'story categories' for organisational analysis may seem a useful way to start some consultancy work, but not one of our co-researchers described such a technique. They spoke of getting the 'feel' of the organisation, but there was no classification system of 'seven types of story', 'four types of organisational culture', etc. Martin, Feldman, Hatch and Sitkin (1983) discuss the notion that organisations, cultures and, in particular, stories often seem to carry a claim to uniqueness, that an institution is unlike any other. They argue that a culture's claim to uniqueness is, paradoxically, expressed through cultural manifestations, such as stories, that are not in fact unique. They carry on to identify seven forms of narrative occurring in organisations, which Polkinghorne (1988) succinctly outlines, such as a story about rule-breaking in which a high-status manager breaks a rule which a low-ranking employee must then enforce; or a story concerning the amount of humanity and respect the boss displays in relationships with lower-status employees (Martin *et al.*, 1983: 122).

We have come to think that this kind of typology may indeed also paradoxically limit the potential of the consultant's intervention, particularly since it may be used to circumscribe the imaginative scope and narrative depth of the relationship to the story, in its uniqueness, idiosyncrasy and unrepeatable individuality for that moment and those people. A more hermetic eye brought to the work does not emphasise which 'story label' fits, but displays an attentiveness to detail which draws out the cliché and metaphor as a fractal of a fuller, grounded narrative. For example, a simple comment from a client that 'the research lab is like a car driving round a bend in the wrong manner', becomes a full story in the hands of a sympathetic and attentive consultant, who explained it in the context of metaphor opening up into a story:

> People use a lot of metaphor – a lot of straight similes – a lot – e.g. a fax in which this client suddenly goes off into a long paragraph in which he thinks of the laboratory being like a car. He then tells me a story about how a car gets driven round a bend and talks about what's happening in the research laboratory in that way – and once he's using the story you can tell how illuminating it is for him, how it's carried him away. He went into some detail about the particular way in which a car is driven around a bend in terms of the stresses that have to be in balance and the camber of the road – and when it isn't in control . . . the forces that are supposed to be in balance don't hold against the camber and it's no longer possible to steer it and the more you try the more impossible it is to steer – and then people make the wrong instinctive decision about what to do and this makes it worse – and therefore it ends up crashing over the edge of the precipice . . . the whole laboratory is the car, not him . . . he's saying, I'm a part of this and we ought to be working out what we are doing wrong.

What can be added to this subtle attentiveness by the work of the counselling psychologist? An hermetic mode which becomes available to the consultant via the discipline of counselling psychology is Clarkson's integrative model of seven levels of epistemological discourse (Clarkson, 1975, 1992). This model provides a differentiated 'place' for locating and ordering detailed observation without labelling it into story-categories of content which run the risk of becoming diagnostic labels. To do so would be to try and *use* the gods as grids or structural metaphors in service to our desires for system and order, rather than entering into *relationship* with them, and rendering them service, through the hermetic art of receiving their messages.

The seven-level model has recently been archetypally referenced (Angelo, in press) to display a mythic grounding in the image of the Tree of Life (which derives from old, magical Kabbalistic sources). This 'Tree' has the property of a cosmology, displaying the levels of existence simultaneously, from the physical and emotional to the social, cultural, intellectual and spiritual. Like all archetypal images it opens into complexity and ambiguity, but can also be presented in a simple manner, such as the listing below. Each level can be addressed conceptually, as in the listing, but also opens out mythically bringing with it the resonances of the gods. It represents the macrocosm of 'the greater whole' such as the organisation itself, or any larger system, and simultaneously the microcosm, or 'smaller whole', of the individual. Differentiating the levels and their interactions can provide a way of teaching and ordering the consultant's eye, leaving the stories free to come and go, and be expressed in a multitude of ways.

The seven levels are as follows:

1 Physiological (Sensing): roots, earth imagery, the physical environment and context;
2 Emotional (Responding): power-house of emotional energy, behavioural responses, outbursts, acting out;
3 Nominative (Naming): the names and nicknames given to individuals, the characteristic phrases people repeat;
4 Normative (Connecting): the way rivalries and sub-groups perceive each other, which may be disconnected or refer to different parts of stories and sub-stories. In-groups and out-groups, conflict management and mismanagement;
5 Rational (Using): the way the names and groupings are used to form entire scenarios, episodes, chapters and events;
6 Theoretical (Making): the overview, the whole picture, the complete story to date. This is also the only level at which it is possible to rewrite a story. Adjustments at levels below this inevitably distort back to the original form and repeat the scenario;
7 Transpersonal (Opening): intimations, hunches, synchronicities, that which is feared and hoped for, the doorway into the future and the question, 'where is the story going?'

If each cliché, nickname and chance metaphor in a narrative is in fact a fractal of a story, mythically related, then it is in the full use of the seven levels that the consultant is empowered to hear the story with more depth and accurate empathy. To see into the past and future also, for each narrative stretches across time and will tend to have a momentum that is pressing forward into level 7. It is at this transpersonal level that the work of the consultant is most fulfilling, in the rare moments when this multiple-layered complexity is realised by the organisation itself. Then,

> people begin to react with awe, which is an unusual kind of feeling for people in organisations on the whole – they react with awe, and they come nearest to realising that their mundane world, even in an organisation, may have some link with the sacred. I'm very aware that it's that aspect of the nature of life,

of what it is to be living, which somehow seems to penetrate – it's my main criterion of whether I think I'm doing a good job – and I touch it now and again – it's what I aspire for.

As Reason and Hawkins (1988: 99) point out, 'we need to do a lot more thinking about authentic and alienating uses of storytelling'. The archetypalist Miller, too, warns that 'The danger . . . lies . . . in how one views a story or how a story is used. Narrative form is no better than abstraction if it is used ideologically, that is, for ego security (1981: 17). The hermetic mode of qualitative research, with its question 'Who is telling the story?', finds that all too often, no matter what story is being told, it is the hero who is telling it, and it is heroic consciousness which is finding expression, like the co-researcher who described feeling 'sucked into a world in which there were only goodies and baddies – a macho place – and I clicked into the game where there would now be a power struggle with victors and resentment. There seems to be no alternative'. Hillman (1995), more than any other researcher, has been alert to this problem, emphasising again, in *Kinds of Power*, that the 'forward and upward' movement of classic heroism makes introspection the most difficult of all tasks for heroic consciousness.

> Looking inward to its own drive, the myth that propels it towards its cruel end: Hercules gone mad; Jesus crucified; Oedipus blind; Agamemnon murdered by his wife; Moses dead, away from the Promised Land. Can giant corporations like GM, IBM and K-Mart, and powerful nations like the United States that rose to pre-eminence by means of dedication to the heroics of expansion and improvement awaken to the tragic consequences of the model that once served so well? Can heroism shift its own paradigm? (Hillman, 1995: 31–2).

It cannot be pretended that to learn such ways of working is easy. As one co-researcher observed:

> I think it takes a while – I think you need time to work with this, for many people it's the shock of a paradigm shift. . . . I think working at this level really is a huge shift . . . it is a very profound challenge to the story of the person in control – it's a bit like – a slow sort of therapeutic exercise to taste what the world is like if I try telling this story rather than the other story – and it takes a little bit of time. It is not to be used as a fancy little tool – not a quick fix and not in a kind of entertaining way. . . . I've seen lots of people using it in ways that are supposed to be releasing creativity and imagination and are done through quick little exercises of drawing something or 'tell the fairy story that's most like your department's recent history', or 'what's the character you're playing?' – and all of these things could be powerful interventions but I think when they are used as a kind of short exercise and everybody has a quick ten minutes input I just think that it's really trivialising rather than getting people to appreciate the power of what is in a narrative.

It is the ability of the organisational counselling psychologist to contain these ambiguities, differentiate the 'universes of discourse' and embody this switch from the heroic to the hermetic which gives him or her authority in the role of change-agent, and opens up the scope of the entire mythic cosmos of organisational life. Intrinsic to the professional training of a counselling psychologist is the requirement for personal counselling of the nature and duration which matches subsequent practice. We might perhaps extend this idea to add the need for 'a therapy of ideas' which would initiate us into the archetypal perspective necessary to work at this new professional interface. The co-researcher who spoke of overcoming a fear of this material recognised that our imaginations are untrained for this complex, multiple and enlivening style of work. Yet, through self-tuition this consultant has developed a style of work in which clients are asked to draw and make collage, facilitated with such sensitive skill that it seems the most natural thing in the world 'even for the men in grey suits'.

As researchers, we look forward to the time when we can return to this theme and interview another generation of organisational counselling psychologists trained in the archetypal mode. They will fully inhabit the place where the disciplines intersect and have learned to cultivate the eye of Hermes and do the work of Hermes. Under the guidance of the master story-teller they will craft a further understanding of myth and narrative as research and intervention in consultancy to organisations.

I was with a group of managers from a high tech company talking about a failure of an initiative which had cost a lot of money. They began sharing their views about how it had come about – and it was endlessly recessive and they couldn't track it down. At the end there was a definite pregnant pause in the room while they came to the conclusion that there wasn't a simplistic answer, there really wasn't. That is the power of coming to an awareness of stories. I think certain kinds of inhuman behaviour become less possible; it becomes very clear that to blame x, get rid of y, demote z are unbelievably foolish responses to the situation. Story is the only way in which it is possible to ask people to take the difficult, complex, broader view of what we all do together that prevents the kind of one-sided action that leads to a lot of the ways that people damage each other.

REFERENCES

Angelo. M. (1997) 'When the gods were intelligent, and education was enchanting', in *Self and Society* 24. 6: 12–17.

Angelo. M. (in press) 'Placing the sublime: cosmology in the consulting room', in P. Clarkson (ed.) *On the Sublime in Psychoanalysis, Jungian analysis and Archetypal Psychotherapy*. London: Whurr.

Avens. R. (1980) *Imagination is Reality*. Irving, TX: Spring.

Bartlett. F.C. (1932) *Remembering: A Study in Experimental and Social Psychology*. Cambridge: Cambridge University Press.

Brown. S.D. and Lent, R.W. (eds) (1992) *Handbook of Counseling Psychology* (2nd edn), New York: John Wiley.

Clarkson. P. (1975) 'Seven-level model', invitational paper delivered at the University of Pretoria, November.

Clarkson. P. (1992) 'The seven-level model', in P. Clarkson and P. Lapworth, 'Systemic Integrative Psychotherapy', in W. Dryden (ed.) *Integrative and Eclectic Therapy: A Handbook*, Buckingham: Open University Press.

Clarkson. P. (1995) *The Therapeutic Relationship: In Psychoanalysis, Counselling Psychology and Psychotherapy*, London: Whurr.

Clarkson. P. (1996) 'Qualitative research as praxis in the supervision of counselling psychologists (a fractal example in post-modern vein)', delivered on 28 April at the British Psychological Society conference *New Horizons: Counselling Psychology in Different Contexts*, 26–28 April 1996, York.

Clarkson. P. (in press) 'The Archetopoi of Supervision – Parallel Process in Place' in P. Clarkson (ed.) *On the Sublime in Psychoanalysis, Jungian analysis and Archetypal Psychotherapy*, London: Whurr.

Clarkson. P. and Angelo. M. (in preparation) 'Researching Organisational Counselling Psychology'.

Eckhartsberg, R.V. (1981) 'Maps of the mind', in R.S. Valle and R. von Eckhartsberg (eds) *The Metaphors of Consciousness*, New York: Plenum.

French. J.R.P. and Raven. B.M. (1959) 'The bases of social power' in D. Cartwright (ed.) *Studies in Social Power*, Ann Arbor: University of Michigan Press.

Gergen. K.J. and Kaye. J. (1992) 'Beyond narrative in the negotiation of therapeutic meaning', in S. McNamee and K.J. Gergen (eds) *Therapy as Social Construction* (pp. 166–185), London: Sage.

Handy. C. (1985) *Gods of Management*, London: Pan Books.

Hillman. J. (1995) *Kinds of Power: A Guide to its Intelligent Use*, New York: Doubleday.

Hughes. T. (1977) 'Myth and education', in P. Abbs (ed.) (1989) *The Symbolic Order: a Contemporary Reader on the Arts Debate* (pp. 161–173), London: The Falmer Press.

Mair. M. (1989) *Between Psychology and Psychotherapy: a poetics of experience*, London: Routledge.

Martin. J., Feldman, M.S.. Hatch, M.J. and Sitkin, S.B. (1983) 'The uniqueness paradox in organizational stories', *Administrative Science Quarterly*, 28: 438–453.

Mead. G. (1997) 'A winter's tale or myth, story and organisations', in *Self and Society* 24. 6: 19–22.

Moran. J. (1996) 'Eros and Hermes: the twin pillars of the 'New Paradigm' of qualitative research in psychology', in this volume.

Paris. G. (1990) *Pagan Grace: Dionysos, Hermes, and Goddess Memory in Daily Life*, Dallas. TX: Spring.

Polkinghorne, D. (1988) *Narrative Knowing and the Human Sciences*, Albany, NY: State University of New York Press.

Reason. P. and Hawkins, P. (1988) 'Storytelling as inquiry', in P. Reason (ed.) *Human Inquiry in Action: Developments in New Paradigm Research* (pp. 79–101), London: Sage.

Chapter 3

How counselling psychologists can employ a role enactment methodology to examine possible causal relationships amongst internal events

Frank W. Bond and Windy Dryden

INTRODUCTION

This chapter is written for counselling psychologists who wish to conduct experiments that examine if and how an internal event, such as a belief, affects other internal events, such as emotions and inferences. As will be discussed, investigations of this sort are, indeed, lacking; and this fact may concern counselling psychologists who employ techniques that are based upon assumptions that one internal event affects other internal events (for example, the assumption that beliefs affect inferences and emotions). For those counselling psychologists who are concerned about this situation, our chapter explains how they can employ an experimental methodology to examine internal event-internal event causal hypotheses (i.e. hypotheses that posit that one internal event affects other internal events).

To this end, the chapter first maintains that internal event-internal event causal hypotheses remain untested, because of the current impossibility of manipulating internal events directly. It then suggests that a role enactment experiment may be able to circumvent this 'direct manipulation' problem and examine adequately these causal hypotheses. Role enactment experiments are then defined, and a major problem with employing them is mentioned. The chapter then presents role enactment procedures that attempt to maximise the reliability and external validity of this methodological paradigm; and, following this presentation, research is considered that indicates that role enactment experiments can produce results that are as reliable and externally valid as those obtained from non-role enactment experiments. Then, as an example of how to construct a role enactment experiment so that it is as reliable and externally valid as possible, a role enactment experiment by us (Bond and Dryden, 1997) is considered. This role enactment experiment examined how one internal event, beliefs, affects another internal event, the functionality of inferences. Finally, the chapter discusses (1) why counselling psychologists should examine if and how an internal event affects other internal events; and (2) the three conditions under which a role playing methodology should be employed.

INTERNAL EVENTS AFFECT OTHER INTERNAL EVENTS: THE DIFFICULTY OF TESTING THIS HYPOTHESIS

The number of possible internal event-internal event causal relationships that can be hypothesised is very great. For example, it can be posited that beliefs affect emotions, emotions affect beliefs, inferences affect emotions, and beliefs affect inferences. For simplicity's sake, the example, beliefs affect inferences, will be employed in this chapter, from henceforth, to represent all possible internal event-internal event causal relationships. Thus, even though this chapter will now discuss how to examine if and how beliefs affect inferences, it can be assumed that this discussion can be applied to all of the possible internal event-internal event causal relationships.

Unfortunately, it is very difficult for researchers to establish if and how beliefs affect psychological events such as inferences, because researchers cannot directly manipulate people's beliefs; that is, people's brains cannot be altered in some way so that a specific belief is isolated and its naturally occurring functions examined. Instead, researchers (and, of course, counselling psychologists) can only attempt to change people's beliefs indirectly by means of talking to them and having them 'test-out' the efficacy of alternative beliefs; thus, it is only through these indirect ways that researchers can hope to establish a relationship between beliefs and inferences. However, by examining beliefs and inferences in this indirect way, only a relationship of a correlational nature can be established between these two variables (a relationship such as the one established between internal variables in the experiments by Miranda and Persons (1988), Miranda, Persons and Buyers (1990), and Miranda (1992)). Unfortunately, only being able to establish a correlational relationship between beliefs and inferences is not very helpful when testing hypotheses that maintain that beliefs in some way *cause* inferences. (For a full discussion on theoretical and practical issues concerning the examination of internal event-internal event causal hypotheses, please refer to a special issue of the *Journal of Behaviour Therapy and Experimental Psychology*, 1995, 26(3).)

EMPLOYING ROLE ENACTMENT EXPERIMENTS TO EXAMINE IF AND HOW BELIEFS AFFECT OTHER INTERNAL EVENTS

As noted, the main problem in testing if and how beliefs affect inferences is that researchers cannot yet manipulate people's beliefs directly. There appears to be. however, an experimental methodology that can circumvent this problem of direct manipulation of people's beliefs; this is known as role enactment. Specifically, in role enactment experiments, internal events, such as beliefs, can be manipulated by having subjects first hold a belief and then employ that belief (and only that belief) to produce other internal events, such as inferences. It is important to note that with a role enactment methodology, beliefs are not being directly manipulated by the experimenter. Of course, an experimenter can manipulate the belief that subjects are asked to hold, but it is ultimately the subjects who are required to manipulate their beliefs, in that it is they who hold the belief that is given to them by the experimenter. Thus, in a role enactment experiment, researchers can give subjects a belief, but it is the subjects who need to hold it, and then imagine how that belief (and, hopefully, only that belief) would affect events such as inferences. The pitfalls of this methodology are, of course, very apparent (and are discussed below). Nevertheless, currently it is the only one available that can even attempt to examine experimentally if and how beliefs affect inferences.

It appears, then, that counselling psychologists can employ role enactment experiments to examine experimentally if and how beliefs affect inferences. The rest of this chapter discusses how counselling psychologists can best employ a role enactment methodology to investigate this type of causal hypothesis. However, before a valid and reliable role enactment methodology can be described, it would be helpful to define and discuss role enactment experiments.

DEFINING A ROLE ENACTMENT EXPERIMENT

A hypothetical research question is used to define and show the difference between role enactment experiments and their more popular and accepted methodological alternative, involved participation experiments. This hypothetical research question asks: Do people's ratings of self-worth differ, depending on whether they consider themselves intelligent or unintelligent? Each of the above two experimental methodologies can be used to answer this question.

Using an involved participation experiment, a researcher, for example, administers an intelligence test to subjects, and after grading it, he or she tells the subjects that they are either: (1) unintelligent, or (2) intelligent. Subjects then answer some questions about their self-worth.

In this example, these subjects really took a false intelligence test, and the experimenter only pretended to grade it. In fact, the experimenter randomly determined which subjects would be labelled intelligent or unintelligent before they even entered the laboratory. Why would researchers choose an involved participation methodology, when they must lie about the subjects' intelligence? Many experimental psychologists hypothesise that subjects should *truly believe* that the independent variable is being manipulated, if subjects are to produce externally valid and reliable results (Skinner, 1987; Cooper, 1976; Freedman, 1969; Aronson and Carlsmith. 1968). Thus, in this hypothetical experiment, subjects should truly believe that they are either intelligent or unintelligent. For, only then can they rate their self-worth accurately.

A role enactment experiment can also be used to answer the hypothetical research question: How does knowledge about IQ affect people's ratings of self-worth? In a role enactment experiment, a researcher, for example, asks subjects to imagine that they have just taken an intelligence test, which told them that they were either: (1) intelligent, or (2) unintelligent; and whilst imagining this scenario, the researcher asks these subjects to rate their self-worth. In this methodology, subjects do not *actually believe* that they are intelligent or unintelligent, as they do in involved participation designs; instead, they are asked to *imagine* that they are either one or the other. Put another way, subjects in this hypothetical experiment play a role in which they rate their self-worth, *as if* they really consider themselves intelligent or unintelligent.

WHY ROLE ENACTMENT DESIGNS MAY BE INHERENTLY INVALID AND UNRELIABLE

Some researchers hypothesise that role enactment experiments pose more threats to external validity than do involved participation experiments. As a result, these researchers consider the former more invalid and unreliable than the latter, in answering psychological questions (Aronson and Carlsmith, 1968; Cooper, 1976; Miller, 1972; Freedman, 1969); and these critical researchers offer one primary reason for this assertion.

People make inaccurate predictions about their behaviour

Many critics of role enactment experiments (e.g. Aronson and Carlsmith, 1968; Freedman, 1969; Miller, 1972; Mixon, 1979; Cooper, 1976; Greenwood, 1983) note that subjects who imagine themselves in a particular role may not be able to predict how they would react, were they actually in the imagined scenario. Cooper (1976) notes that, in a given situation, there is a multitude of stimuli to which subjects can attend. When imagining that situation, subjects may attend and react to one set of stimuli; however, if they were actually in the imagined situation, they might attend and react to another set of stimuli.

For example, as Orne (1962), Freedman (1969), Miller (1972), and Cooper (1976) note, subjects wish to appear and believe that they are psychologically healthy, in an experiment. Subjects may attend and respond to this 'appear healthy' belief (or stimuli) in a role enactment situation but may attend to another belief (or stimuli) were they really in the situation that they were imagining. Thus, in the above hypothetical experiment, subjects imagining that they are unintelligent may indicate that they are still worthy people. This would show the experimenter, and themselves, that they are psychologically healthy; however, if these subjects really believed that they were unintelligent, their desire to appear psychologically healthy may be deactivated and overridden by very worthless and hopeless beliefs; and these beliefs would probably result in very low ratings of self-worth. Thus, subjects who imagine that they are in a particular situation may not be able to predict how they would really behave, were they actually in the situation that they were imagining; and this inability to predict accurately how they would behave may make data from role enactment experiments unreliable and invalid.

This major criticism of role enactment methodologies may lead researchers to suggest that an involved participation design should always be employed in experimental research; however, as noted at the beginning of this chapter, involved participation experiments cannot address certain hypotheses that role enactment experiments can (e.g. the hypothesis that beliefs affect inferences). Thus, despite the major criticism of role enactment methodologies, it appears that they are better able to test certain hypotheses than are involved participation experiments. Given this apparent situation, it is fortunate that there is research indicating that role enactment experiments can produce externally valid and reliable results, and this research is discussed presently.

ROLE ENACTMENT METHODOLOGIES CAN PRODUCE EXTERNALLY VALID AND RELIABLE DATA

Despite the role enactment criticism discussed above, Geller (1978) and Mixon (1979) employed two different role enactment procedures in experiments that replicated an involved participation experiment. Specifically, they found that both role enactment and involved participation methodologies produced comparable data, when the design of the role enactment experiments met certain criteria. This indicates that role enactment methodologies can produce data that are as externally valid and reliable as those which are produced by an involved participation methodology. The criteria used in these two role enactment experiments are outlined by Geller (1978) and are presented below. After this presentation, there will follow a very brief discussion of Geller's (1978) and Mixon's (1979) experiments.

Categorising role enactment methodologies and which type may be the most externally valid and reliable

Geller (1978) categorises role enactment designs on two dimensions. The first concerns the *type of role* subjects are required to perform in the experimental scenario, and there are two types: (1) role taking and (2) role playing. In role taking methodologies, subjects imagine what another person would do in a given situation and then respond to the imagery, as if they were that other person. In role playing methodologies, subjects imagine themselves in a given situation and then respond to the imagery as themselves. Geller labels the second dimension, on which they classify role enactment methodologies, as *type of enactment*, and there are two types: (1) active role enactment, and (2) non-active, or passive, role enactment. In active role enactment, subjects physically participate in an enactment of an event; and in non-active role enactment, subjects enact an event, but only in their imaginations. As can be seen, Geller (1978) suggests that there can be four types of role enactment methodologies, and these four stem from interacting the two role enactment dimensions, type of role and type of enactment. Thus, through this interaction, the four types of role enactment methodologies are: an active role taking methodology, a non-active role taking methodology, an active role playing methodology, and a non-active role playing methodology.

Amongst the four types of role enactment methodologies, Geller (1978) hypothesises that an *active* role *playing* one produces the most reliable and externally valid data. In an experiment that employs an active role playing methodology: (1) subjects are physically participating in the scenario; (2) the dependent variables are behavioural and, perhaps, verbal; and (3) subjects are playing (as opposed to taking) a particular role. By way of contrast, in an experiment that employs a non-active role taking methodology: (1) subjects are imaginally participating in the scenario; (2) the dependent measures require *only* verbal responses (and the authors of this chapter would also add written responses); and (3) subjects are taking (as opposed to playing) a particular role (Geller, 1978).

Why an active role playing methodology might produce the most externally valid and reliable results: experimental realism and emotional involvement

As noted, Geller (1978: 220) maintains that, amongst the four role enactment methodologies, an active role playing one produces the most externally valid and reliable results. He arrives at this conclusion because he posits that an active role playing methodology generates in subjects the greatest amount of 'experimental realism' (Geller, 1978: 220), or intense cognitive and behavioural focus on the experimental tasks. Aronson (1992: 411) indicates that when researchers achieve a high degree of experimental realism, the 'experiment has an impact on the subjects, forces them to take the matter seriously, and involves them in the procedures'. Geller (1978) and Aronson (1992) note that achieving experimental realism should be the goal of researchers who use role enactment methodologies.

It is interesting to note that this goal of achieving 'experimental realism' in role enactment designs mirrors the goal of achieving a high degree of subject involvement, which Orne (1962), Aronson and Carlsmith (1968), and Cooper (1976) consider crucial for producing externally valid and reliable experimental results. They also hypothesise that only involved participation designs can achieve this high degree of subject involvement. Geller is attempting, however, to achieve this high level of subject involvement, in role enactment experiments, by attaining experimental realism; and this, they hypothesise, can be accomplished by employing active role playing procedures.

Geller hypothesises that by producing a high degree of experimental realism, an active role playing methodology increases the amount of emotional involvement in an experiment. This means that subjects move from an 'as if' participation in the experiment, to one of complete engagement; so that subjects are responding 'reflexively' to the manipulated variable, without having to think first: ' "What if" I were *really* in this situation?' (Geller, 1978). Miller (1972) and Geller (1978) hypothesise that this high level of emotional involvement increases the reliability and external validity of the role enactment methodology.

Beyond an active role playing methodology: other criteria for producing externally valid and reliable results in a role enactment experiment

In addition to using an active role playing methodology, role enactment experiments are more likely to produce externally valid and reliable results if researchers: (1) honestly convey to subjects the 'experimenter intent' (that is, the goal of the experiment) (Geller, 1978; Forward *et al.*, 1976); and (2) establish a subject–experimenter collaboration for a joint investigation (Geller, 1978; Forward *et al.*, 1976; Kelman, 1967). To accomplish these two aims, researchers need to ensure first that the experimenter intent is 'honestly' conveyed because it is likely that subjects will only feel emotionally involved in the study if they believe the experimenter's stated intent (Geller, 1978; Forward *et al.*, 1976). Complete honesty about experimental aims is not always possible, however, when obtaining certain measures; therefore, deception might be necessary when telling subjects the study's 'true' intent (Rosenthal and Rosnow, 1969). In this case, researchers should create a convincing and subject relevant cover story that produces a high amount of interest and emotional involvement in subjects; because, if subjects can identify with and are interested in the experimenter's intent, then they may be more likely to accept it as true and become emotionally involved in the procedures.

A convincing and subject relevant cover story can also help to maximise the subjects' sense of collaboration with the researcher. For subjects are probably more likely to assist an experimenter if he or she is investigating a topic that is relevant to them. For example, a clinical experimenter can tell subjects: 'By helping me in this research project, you will aid in the development of effective therapeutic techniques that will eventually help people who feel insecure (lonely, anxious, restless, or whatever is important to subjects)'. Thus, by using a convincing cover story that is relevant to the lives of subjects, researchers may be able to: (1) convince them of the experimenter's stated intent; and (2) involve them in a collaborative quest for knowledge. By accomplishing these two aims, researchers might be able to increase the external validity and reliability of a role playing experiment.

In summary, it is hypothesised that researchers would do well to use a role playing design and ensure that subjects are: (a) convinced about the honesty of the experimenter's intent; and (b) engaged with the experimenter in a collaborative search for knowledge. With these criteria fulfilled, researchers might increase the experimental realism and emotional involvement of a role enactment experiment; which, in turn, might also increase the external validity and reliability of its results (Geller, 1978).

Readers may note that one of Geller's (1978) recommendations for conducting an effective role enactment design was not included at the beginning of the previous paragraph. Specifically, it was not suggested that an *active* role playing methodology be used instead of a *non-active*, or imaginal, role playing methodology. The reason why this recommendation by Geller was not contained in the previous paragraph is due, in part, to an experiment by Mixon (1979), which is now discussed.

Role enactment experiments that replicated data from an involved participation experiment

In two experiments, Geller (1978) and Mixon (1979) demonstrated that role playing methodologies can produce data that replicate results from an involved participation experiment; thus indicating, perhaps, that role playing experiments can be as externally valid and reliable as involved participation experiments. In Geller's experiment, he showed that data from an active role playing design were similar to data obtained from an involved participation design. Contrary to what Geller's (1978) role enactment criteria might predict, Mixon (1979) showed that an active role playing design was not necessary to produce results comparable to those from an involved participation design; instead, he demonstrated that a scripted, non-active (or imaginary) role playing design could produce the same data as an involved participation design. In a scripted, non-active role playing design, subjects are not simply asked to imagine a scenario; rather, they are guided through a non-active scenario, using a script that highlights specific details of the imaginary situation (Miller, 1986)

To demonstrate the external validity and reliability of role enactment designs, Geller (1978) and Mixon (1979) conducted role playing versions of Milgram's (1963) first obedience experiment. Milgram's experiment was an involved participation experiment, in which subjects thought that they were shocking a person to death, although they really were not. In this obedience experiment, Milgram demonstrated that 65 per cent of subjects obeyed an experimenter's request to administer *deadly* shocks to another person. Geller replicated Milgram's experiment, using an active role playing methodology. Geller's experimental situation contained the same materials as did Milgram's, including an experimenter, a person who received the shocks (called the learner), and the same shock generator that Milgram used. Unlike Milgram's subjects, however, Geller's realised that they were not really shocking another person; instead, they knew that they were just involved in a role playing exercise. Nevertheless, Geller's results did not differ significantly from Milgram's in that the percentage of subjects who 'shocked' the learner to death was similar in both experiments (Miller, 1986). Specifically, in Milgram's experiment, 65 per cent of the subjects shocked the other person to death, and in Geller's experiment, 51 per cent of the subjects shocked the other person to death. These results indicated that subjects in Geller's active role playing procedure could imagine themselves in the shock scenario, to the extent that they responded in the same way as did Milgram's subjects.

This comparison between Geller (1978) and Milgram's (1963) results may contradict the hypothesis, by many researchers (e.g. Aronson and Carlsmith, 1968; Freedman, 1969; Miller, 1972; Mixon, 1979; Cooper, 1976; Greenwood, 1983), that role enactment subjects cannot accurately predict how they would behave if they were actually in the imagined situation. It should be noted, of course, that informally comparing the results of two independent experiments (with two different subject samples) cannot adequately address this hypothesis.

Geller's (1978) results, using an active role playing methodology, were replicated by Mixon (1979), who used a scripted, non-active role playing methodology. In Mixon's experiment, subjects were asked to imagine the same scenario that Milgram (1963) used in his experiment. Subjects were asked, therefore, to imagine the presence of an experimenter and a person who would receive shocks. Mixon guided subjects through a script that contained the experimenter's orders, and he then had subjects indicate, on a paper diagram of the shock generator, their responses to those orders. As noted, Mixon's results demonstrated that using a scripted, non-active role playing procedure produced data that did not significantly differ from results obtained by Milgram (Mixon, 1979). Specifically, in Milgram's experiment, 65 per cent of subjects 'shocked' the other person to death, and in Mixon's experiment, 50 per cent of subjects 'shocked' the other person to death. Thus, Geller (1978) and Mixon (1979) demonstrated that active and non-active (but scripted), role playing methodologies can produce data that are as externally valid and reliable as those which are produced by involved participation experiments.

MAXIMISING THE EXTERNAL VALIDITY AND RELIABILITY OF A ROLE PLAYING METHODOLOGY: AN EXAMPLE

The role playing methodology used in an experiment by us (Bond and Dryden, 1997) is described, in order to present an example of how counselling psychologists can maximise the external validity and reliability of role enactment experiments. As will be shown, we employed a scripted, non-active (imaginal) role playing methodology utilising the relevant guidelines that were described above. Briefly, our experiment examined the effects of different types of rational and irrational beliefs on the functionality of inferences (FI). Specifically, one of the hypotheses of our experiment was that subjects who hold a rational belief will form inferences that are significantly more functional than those that are formed by subjects who hold an irrational belief. In order to test this, as well as other hypotheses, subjects were required to hold a belief that the experimenter gave to them. Whilst they held this belief, they were asked also to imagine themselves in a scenario that was given to them by the experimenter; and, then, holding their assigned belief in this imagined situation, they were required to answer questions about how they would react in that scenario. The experimenter stressed to subjects that they were to answer the questions as if they *really held* the belief that he gave them.

For example, in our experiment, a group of subjects were asked to imagine that they held the following belief: 'I must absolutely control my anxiety; not having such control would be unbearable'. These subjects were then asked to imagine themselves holding this belief in the following scenario: You are sitting in the Union bar and notice a person whom you find attractive. You decide to talk to that person so you get up to do so. As you're walking over, you notice yourself getting fairly anxious. Subjects were instructed to answer questions about how they would react in this situation, and they were to answer them as if they were actually in the scenario whilst holding their belief. An example of questions that subjects answered are: (1) To what extent will other people in the bar think that you are pathetic?; (2) To what extent will other people in the bar think that you are unattractive?; and (3) To what extent will other people in the bar think that you have low self-esteem, and no pride in yourself?

It was necessary to construct carefully two important components of our role playing methodology, in order for it to achieve maximal experimental realism and emotional involvement; these two components were: (1) how the imagined beliefs and scenarios were presented to the subjects; and (2) the cover story that was used to convey the experimenter's intent. In addition, subjects were excluded from participating in our experiment if they did not meet certain criteria (which will be outlined below, pp. 47–8). This methodology attempted to increase the probability that our experiment produced the most externally valid and reliable results possible.

Presenting the beliefs and scenarios to subjects

Firstly, the beliefs and scenarios that subjects were asked to imagine in our experiment were scripted and read to them; in addition, subjects received written copies of these scripts so that they could consult them, when they formed inferences of the imagined situation. Thus, subjects were told precisely what scenarios to imagine, and they were reminded of these scenarios throughout the entire experiment. Also, by scripting the scenarios, our experiment attempted to ensure that subjects, within each condition, imagined the same situations and beliefs. In addition, by providing subjects with written copies of the scenarios, they could rehearse and refer to them, so as not to forget certain elements. In summary, then, by scripting the beliefs and scenarios we made it easier for subjects to imagine themselves in the scenario correctly; and this, consequently, left them with more 'attentional resources' (Borkovec, 1994) to adopt their imaginary role and achieve a high level of experimental realism and emotional involvement; which, in turn, may have increased the likelihood that subjects produced externally valid and reliable results.

Constructing a cover story

Our experiment employed a cover story that also attempted to increase the external validity and reliability of its results, and it was designed to accomplish this goal in two ways. Firstly, this cover story emphasised the pro-social and therapeutic applications of the experiment, which was helping people who experience stress; and it ignored the theoretical implications, which, perhaps, would have inspired less subject involvement than did the therapeutic implications. Emphasising that subjects were helping to produce therapeutic strategies to help people with stress (which may have included themselves) provided them with an opportunity to appear socially desirable, which is an impression that many subjects desire to manage (Cooper, 1976; Miller, 1972).

In order to increase the external validity and reliability of our experiment, the pro-social cover story that we constructed served, secondly, to disarm subjects from thinking that their 'personality', or other such private territories, was being examined. For example, subjects in our experiment were told that they were assisting the experimenter in a 'preliminary study', where the goal was to obtain new and unknown information that would help people who experience stress. The intention of this cover story was to relax subjects by emphasising that the experimenter was not 'testing' whether they produced right or wrong answers that would then reveal some telling psychological profile. By relaxing subjects it was hoped that they would have more attentional resources to concentrate on the experimental tasks, become emotionally involved in the experiment and, therefore, produce externally valid and reliable results.

The following was used for part of the cover story in our experiment, and it contained the elements just described:

Now, some people are interested in knowing what I plan to discover in this preliminary study; but the truth is, I just don't know. Since this is the first time that stress has been investigated in this particular way, your guess is almost as good as mine. This may provide you with some relief in knowing that I am not expecting you to respond in any particular way; and there are certainly no right or wrong answers. Rather, with your help, I am trying to decrease, eventually, the amount of stress that people experience. If you have ever felt stress, you know how uncomfortable this emotion is, and how important it is to decrease all of its negative effects. So really, you have kindly volunteered to work with me in finding a way to help people with stress. Do you have any questions about anything that I have just said?

Subject exclusion criteria

To increase, further, the external validity and reliability of the data in our experiment, non-psychology students were used. Psychology students are very aware of deception in psychology experiments, and it is harder to employ cover stories that they find believable. Thus, it may have been more difficult for these students to have attained a high level of experimental realism and emotional involvement in our experiment; because, as noted, if subjects are too suspicious about the experimenter's intent, then they may not get emotionally involved in the experiment; therefore the data that they produce may be externally invalid and unreliable (Geller, 1978; Forward et al., 1976).

Subjects were also excluded from our experiment if they were unable to hold their belief and imagine themselves in the 'bar' scenario to a satisfactory extent. In the experimental procedures, subjects were asked twice: 'To what extent can you imagine yourself in this situation, whilst holding your belief?' If subjects rated their ability to do this as less than a 'seven', on a nine-point Likert-type scale. then they were excluded from the experiment. Subjects were first asked this question by the experimenter before they completed a rating form (which was the dependent variable); and subjects responded verbally to the experimenter. The last item on the rating form also asked this question, and subjects answered by ticking the appropriate space, on a nine-point rating scale. These two manipulation checks were designed to increase the external validity and reliability of these experimental results in three ways.

Firstly, these manipulation checks allowed two opportunities for excluding people who could not imagine their role well enough to manipulate the independent variable. Secondly. using a manipulation check before subjects completed the rating form may have encouraged them to imagine their belief and scenario, as well as possible, whilst completing the form. Thirdly, during the first, verbal, manipulation check, subjects may not have wanted to displease the experimenter (Orne. 1962) by verbally indicating that they could not imagine their role adequately. Thus, the second, written, manipulation check may have allowed subjects to indicate this in a less direct, less threatening, and more anonymous way; and if subjects were not presented with a less threatening opportunity to indicate their inability to imagine their role adequately, their data would be analysed, and its external validity and reliability would be highly suspect.

In summary, there were three ways that our experiments attempted to obtain externally valid and reliable data, and they were by: (1) scripting and writing down for subjects their beliefs and scenarios; (2) having a carefully constructed cover story – one which relaxes, disarms, and fully engages subjects; and (3) excluding psychology students, and subjects who could not adequately imagine their role. By accomplishing these aims, it was hoped that subjects would be able to focus their attention. fully, on participating with the experimenter in a joint quest for socially desirable knowledge.

WHY A NON-ACTIVE, RATHER THAN AN ACTIVE, ROLE PLAYING METHODOLOGY WAS EMPLOYED IN OUR EXPERIMENT

As noted above, amongst the four possible role enactment methodologies, Geller (1978) hypothesises that an active role playing one produces the most reliable and externally valid data. Nevertheless, the experiment by Mixon (1979) (described above), and five other non-active role playing experiments (Dryden, Ferguson and Clark, 1989; Dryden, Ferguson and McTeague, 1989; Dryden, Ferguson and Hylton, 1989; Smith and Lazarus, 1993; and Stopa and Clark, 1993), indicate that a non-active (imaginal) role playing methodology is powerful enough to manipulate independent variables and yield results that are as externally valid as those that are produced by an involved participation methodology. Based upon this empirical support, we felt confident about employing a non-active role playing procedure in our experiment.

One of the reasons for wanting to use a non-active, rather than an active, role playing methodology, in the first place, concerned the improbability of obtaining the resources necessary to stage an active role playing situation. Specifically, subjects were asked to imagine that they see an attractive person at the college bar, and they then start walking over to speak with that person. To act out this scenario would have required enough people to have represented accurately a bar environment, and a room large enough to contain them. Moreover, these people would have needed to participate in over 240 runs of the experiments, which would have been a request that would probably not have been fulfilled. Thus, the practical requirements of running these experiments, using an active role playing methodology, would have been unobtainable.

Furthermore, using an active role playing methodology might have compromised the ability of subjects to imagine themselves, vividly, in the role playing scenario. For example, if the experimenter, or another person, had role played the 'attractive person', this target person may have been the wrong sex, or he or she may not have been attractive to some of the subjects. In any event, either of these two situations might have resulted in certain subjects not being able to imagine themselves, vividly, in the role play, thus compromising the external validity and reliability of the results.

Using a non-active role playing methodology hopefully allowed subjects to imagine, as vividly as possible, an attractive person that they would have really wanted to meet. With a stimulus target that subjects really wanted to meet, their ability to imagine themselves in the role playing scenario, and to generate inferences about it, was, most likely, fairly good. Thus, a role playing methodology that was non-active was employed in our experiment because: (1) research has shown that it can produce results that are similar to data produced by an involved participation experiment; (2) it would have been difficult to have obtained the resources necessary to have staged an active role play situation; and (3) it probably best allowed subjects to imagine, vividly, a person that they really found attractive.

Although we thought it was necessary to employ a non-active role playing design in order to examine our experimental question, other empirical questions might be answered very well by using an active role playing design. Clearly, the decision regarding whether to employ an active or a non-active design needs to be made by each researcher, based upon the experimental question that is under consideration. As with any methodological decision, however, whether to use an active or a non-active design should be consistent with the goal of maximising emotional involvement and experimental realism; because, with this goal realised, a researcher can help ensure that the external validity and reliability of results are at acceptable levels.

In summarising thus far, it is recommended that counselling psychologists, who wish to employ effectively a role enactment methodology, ensure that: (1) they employ a role playing design (as opposed to a role taking design); and assure that subjects are: (2) convinced about the honesty of the experimenter's intent, and (3) engaging with the experimenter in a collaborative search for knowledge. How these latter two recommendations are enacted depends upon the individual experiment and researcher(s). As one example of how to enact all three of the above recommendations, a role playing experiment that we conducted was just presented. It is thought that by fulfilling the above three criteria, researchers stand to increase greatly the experimental realism and emotional involvement of a role enactment experiment, which, in turn, may also increase the external validity and reliability of its results (Geller, 1978).

WHY COUNSELLING PSYCHOLOGISTS SHOULD EXAMINE IF AND HOW AN INTERNAL EVENT CAN AFFECT ANOTHER INTERNAL EVENT

This chapter has shown how counselling psychologists can employ role playing experiments to investigate if and how an internal event affects other internal events. Since an involved participation methodology cannot be used in such an investigation, it is certainly unfortunate that role playing experiments have not been employed previously to examine this internal event-internal event causal hypothesis. For both experimental and counselling psychologists have much to gain from knowing if and how internal events, such as beliefs, affect other internal events, such as inferences and emotions. Exactly why counselling psychologists, who sit face-to-face with clients, should be interested in investigating potential internal event-internal event causal relations has not been clearly outlined in this chapter; and this needs to be done, because, if practitioners are to conduct role playing experiments to investigate these putative, causal hypotheses, they need to know how it will benefit their counselling.

The present authors believe that when it is known if and how an internal event affects other internal events, then counselling psychologists can become even more effective counsellors. To be specific, the present authors maintain that an accurate psychological theory of emotion has the potential to yield the most effective psychotherapy; and that untested (and perhaps incorrect) psychological theories may yield (at best) psychotherapies that are not as effective as they could be, or (at worst) psychotherapies that are harmful to clients. Of course, a psychotherapy can be demonstrably effective, even though the theory upon which it is predicated is untested (or even false); however, even a beneficial therapy should be made as effective as possible, and for that to occur, the therapy needs to stem from a psychological theory that has been confirmed empirically; because an accurate psychological theory of emotion can point to interventions that are more likely to be highly effective than can a theory that is incorrect.

Thus, role playing experiments offer counselling psychologists one way to establish a highly effective approach to counselling. Specifically, these experiments can examine hypotheses that cannot be tested by using involved participation methodologies (for example, the hypothesis that internal events can affect other internal events); and findings from these role playing experiments can then be employed to establish, eventually, highly effective psychotherapeutic interventions that counselling psychologists can employ with their clients.

WHEN ROLE PLAYING METHODOLOGIES SHOULD BE EMPLOYED

In this chapter, we have argued that role playing experiments should be used when determining if and how an internal event affects other internal events. In this section, it is argued that there are, in fact, three conditions in which role playing experiments should be employed, and they are discussed below. In suggesting that the use of role playing experiments be limited to three conditions, it is not being maintained that these types of experiments are inherently unreliable and invalid. (On the contrary, as discussed above, two experiments (i.e. Geller. 1978 and Mixon, 1979) have been conducted that demonstrated this is not the case.) Rather, it is thought that the controversial status of role playing experiments may mean that their findings are not as readily accepted by the psychological community as are results from involved participation experiments. (As noted above, many researchers question the validity and reliability of role playing designs (e.g. Aronson and Carlsmith, 1968; Freedman, 1969; Miller, 1972. 1986; Mixon, 1979; Cooper, 1976; Greenwood, 1983).) For practical concerns, therefore, researchers may find it advantageous to employ involved participation experiments where possible.

Nevertheless, despite any negative views of role playing experiments, it is thought that they offer an experimental methodology that can be effectively and ethically employed under three conditions: (1) when involved participation experiments cannot address certain hypotheses (e.g. internal event-internal event causal hypotheses); (2) when it is not feasible to conduct involved participation experiments; and (3) when it is unethical to employ involved participation experiments. The first condition in which it is suggested that a role playing methodology be used has been the focus of this chapter, because, unlike the second two, the first condition has not been identified, much less discussed, by any previous author.

In particular, with regard to this first condition, our chapter has provided an example of when an involved participation experiment cannot address certain hypotheses. This example was provided in the form of an experiment by us that investigated whether or not different types of rational and irrational beliefs differentially affect the functionality of inferences (FI). It was noted above that we employed a role playing experiment because an involved participation one could not examine relationships between internal events. Our experiment also provides a good example of when it is unfeasible and unethical to employ an involved participation methodology in experiments.

When it is not feasible to employ an involved participation methodology: our experiment

Quite apart from the fact that an involved participation methodology could not have addressed our experimental hypothesis, it would have been unfeasible for us to have conducted our experiment by employing such a methodology. Specifically, as noted above, subjects in our experiment were asked to imagine that they see an attractive person at the college bar, and they then start walking over to speak with that person. To have truly enacted this scenario, as would be required in an involved participation experiment, each subject would have had to have been placed in the college bar, have identified a person whom they thought was attractive, and then have walked over to talk with him or her.

The problems of conducting an experiment that employed these involved participation procedures would have been overwhelming for us. To begin with, the amount of time it would have taken us to conduct the required 240 runs of the experiment would have been prohibitive. In addition, the probability would most likely have been fairly low that many subjects would have consented to endure these anxiety-provoking procedures; therefore, the amount of time it would have required to have actually found 240 willing subjects would have been very great indeed. Furthermore, in order to increase the probability that subjects could have found a person at the bar whom they thought was attractive, experimental sessions would have had to have been conducted in the evening, when the college bar would have been most full; however, it is likely that very few subjects would or could have participated in a highly anxiety-provoking experiment during the evening. As can be seen, it would have been highly unfeasible, if not impossible, to have conducted our experiment using an involved participation methodology. Fortunately, under impracticable conditions such as these, a role playing methodology can and should be employed as an efficacious alternative.

When it is unethical to employ an involved participation methodology: our experiment

Even if it were feasible to conduct our experiment by employing an involved participation methodology (e.g. if we had a great deal of money to hire many experimenters), it is unlikely that using this methodology would be ethical. To elaborate, we consider it extremely unethical for subjects to have any opinions of themselves adversely affected by participating in an experiment; and we consider it fairly possible that people's opinions of themselves could be negatively affected after being subjects in an involved participation experiment that employed our 'bar scenario'.

For the 'bar scenario' required subjects to approach and talk with an attractive stranger in a bar, and it is likely that many people find such a task difficult if not 'impossible' to do. Thus, *actually* being in this (probably novel and potentially punishing) situation may lead to a great deal of emotional distress in some subjects; and this degree of emotional distress may alarm some subjects. In fact, some subjects may be so surprised and alarmed by how they react to this bar situation that they begin to think differently about themselves. For example, some subjects may begin to wonder if they are emotionally able to tolerate stressful interpersonal events and then conclude that they are 'weak' and 'vulnerable' people. Thus, these subjects may leave the experiment with a new opinion of themselves that is represented by the dysfunctional belief: I am vulnerable; and if subjects do leave the experiment with this new and negative opinion of themselves. then, according to these authors, this involved participation experiment is unethical.

In order to avoid denigrating subjects' opinions of themselves, it is recommended that experimental procedures such as the above 'bar scenario' be enacted using a role playing methodology (as we did) instead of an involved participation methodology. Of course, even a role playing experiment could denigrate subjects' views of themselves (and thus be unethical); but it is thought that these types of experiments provide a greater protection against damage to a subject's self-opinion than does an involved participation experiment. Clearly, careful contemplation and the advice of others, such as a human subjects committee, should guide any decisions that may affect the physical and psychological integrity of all experimental participants. (The topic of employing role playing experiments when it is unethical to use involved participation experiments has been discussed fully by Miller (1986), amongst others, and readers who wish for more information on this topic are encouraged to refer to this detailed source.)

In summary, it was maintained, in this section, that role playing experiments can be effectively and ethically employed under three conditions: (1) when involved participation experiments cannot address certain hypotheses (e.g. internal event-internal event causal hypotheses); (2) when it is not feasible to conduct involved participation experiments; and (3) when it is unethical to employ involved participation experiments.

SUMMARY

In this chapter, we have maintained that role enactment experiments, unlike involved participation experiments, can be employed by counselling psychologists to determine if and how an internal event affects other internal events.

Specifically, in this chapter, criteria were discussed that attempt to maximise the external validity and reliability of results that are obtained from role enactment methodologies. In addition, an experiment was presented that showed that role playing procedures can produce data that are comparable to results obtained from an involved participation experiment; and this *may* indicate that subjects are able to predict accurately their behaviour, when imagining a scenario under certain role playing conditions. It appears, then, that if role playing experiments follow certain procedures, they may be able to test effectively hypotheses that cannot be examined by employing involved participation experiments. Finally, this chapter discussed (1) why counselling psychologists should examine if and how an internal event affects other internal events; and (2) the three conditions under which a role playing methodology should be employed.

REFERENCES

Aronson, E. (1992). *The Social Animal*. San Francisco: W.H. Freeman.

Aronson, E. and Carlsmith, J.M. (1968). Experimentation in social psychology. In G. Lindzey and E. Aronson (eds), *The Handbook of Social Psychology*. Reading, MA.: Addison-Wesley.

Bond, F.W. and Dryden, W. (1997). Testing an REBT Theory: the effects of rational beliefs, irrational beliefs, and their control or certainty contents on the functionality of inferences: I. In a social context. *Journal of Rational Emotive and Cognitive-Behavior Therapy*, 15(2), 157–88.

Borkovec, T.D. (1994). The nature, functions, and origins of worry. In G. Davey and F. Tallis (eds), *Worrying: Perspectives on Theory, Assessment and Treatment*. Chichester: Wiley.

Cooper, J. (1976). Deception and role playing: on telling the good guys from the bad guys. *American Psychologist*, 31, 605–610.

Dryden, W., Ferguson, J. and Clark, T. (1989). Beliefs and inferences: a test of a rational-emotive hypothesis: 1. Performing in an academic seminar. *Journal of Rational-Emotive and Cognitive-Behavior Therapy*, 7(3), 119–129.

Dryden, W., Ferguson, J. and Hylton, B. (1989). Beliefs and inferences: a test of a rational-emotive hypothesis: 3. On expectations about enjoying a party. *British Journal of Guidance and Counselling*, 17(1), 68–75.

Dryden, W., Ferguson, J. and McTeague, S. (1989). Beliefs and inferences: a test of a rational-emotive hypothesis: 2. On the prospect of seeing a spider. *Psychological Reports*, 64, 115–123.

Forward, J., Canter, R. and Kirsch, N. (1976). Role-enactment and deception methodologies: alternative paradigms? *American Psychologist*, 31(8), 595–604.

Freedman, J.L. (1969). Role playing: psychology by consensus. *Journal of Personality and Social Psychology*, 13, 107–114.

Geller, D.M. (1978). Involvement in role-playing simulations: a demonstration with studies on obedience. *Journal of Personality and Social Psychology*, 36, 219–235.

Greenwood, J.D. (1983). Role-playing as an experimental strategy in social psychology. *European Journal of Social Psychology*, 13(3), 235–254.

Kelman, H.C. (1967). Human use of human subjects: the problem of deception in social psychological experiments. *Psychological Bulletin*, 67, 1–11.

Milgram, S. (1963). Behavioral study of obedience. *Journal of Abnormal and Social Psychology*, 67, 371–378.

Miller. A.G. (1972). Role playing: an alternative to deception? A review of the evidence. *American Psychologist*, 27, 623–636.

Miller. A.G. (1986). *The Obedience Experiments: A Case Study of Controversy in Social Science*. New York: Praeger.

Miranda. J. (1992). Dysfunctional thinking is activated by stressful life events. *Cognitive therapy and research*, 16(4), 473–483.

Miranda. J. and Persons, J.B. (1988). Dysfunctional attitudes are mood-state dependent. *Journal of Abnormal Psychology*, 97, 76–79.

Miranda. J., Persons, J.B. and Buyers, C. (1990). Endorsement of dysfunctional beliefs depends on current mood state. *Journal of Abnormal Psychology*, 99(3), 237–241.

Mixon. D. (1979). Understanding shocking and puzzling conduct. In G.P. Ginsburg (ed.), *Emerging Strategies in Social Psychological Research*. New York: Wiley.

Orne. M.T. (1962) On the social psychology of the psychological experiment: with particular reference to demand characteristics and their implications, *American Psychologist* 17: 776–83.

Rosenthal. R. and Rosnow. R.L. (eds), (1969). *Artifact in Behavioral Research*. New York: Academic Press.

Skinner. B.F. (1987). *Upon Further Reflection*. Englewood Cliffs, NJ: Prentice-Hall.

Smith. C.A. and Lazarus, R.S. (1993). Appraisal components, core relational themes, and the emotions. *Cognition and Emotion*, 7(3/4), 233–269.

Stopa. L. and Clark, D.M. (1993). Cognitive processes in social phobia. *Behaviour Research and Therapy*, 31(3), 255–267.

Chapter 4

Qualitative research in counselling psychology
Using the counselling interview as a research instrument[1]

Adrian Coyle

QUALITATIVE RESEARCH AND COUNSELLING PSYCHOLOGY

Qualitative research and the practice of counselling psychology are closely related. The characteristics of qualitative research have been described as a focus on viewing experiences from the perspectives of those under study in an unprescriptive way; a concern with detailed, contextualised description and understanding of events and experiences; a focus on process; and an openness and flexibility, allowing unexpected experiences to be addressed (Bryman, 1988). These overlap considerably with the characteristics of counselling interactions.

Skilled practitioners of counselling psychology often employ specific forms of qualitative inquiry in their work, although they may not be aware of the link between their practice and qualitative research methods. For example, when trying to construct a more complete understanding of what is happening in a therapeutic situation, the counselling psychologist may focus upon not only the meaning of what a client says but also the functions that the client's talk is performing, for example, blaming, absolving or legitimating. Similarly, the practitioner may be sensitised to the ways in which their language use can shape the therapeutic space. They may therefore attend closely to the potential ramifications of their own language use in order to avoid creating a suboptimal therapeutic environment. Such concerns with the social functions of language are shared by discourse analysis, which is a domain of social psychology (Potter and Wetherell, 1987; Coyle, 1995). Many discourse analysts would differ from counselling psychologists in their insistence that social and psychological realities are constructed through language use rather than simply being reflected in language. This means that discourse analysts would generally not assume the existence of an intrapsychic world which can be accessed through language. However, some counselling psychologists and psychotherapists have successfully

1 This chapter is an extended and elaborated version of a paper, co-authored with Clare Wright, which appeared in the *Journal of Health Psychology* in 1996 (Vol. 1, pp. 431–40).

incorporated ideas about the constructed nature of intrapsychic 'realities' into their practice and operate within social constructionist frameworks (McNamee and Gergen, 1992).

To take another example of the link between counselling psychology practice and qualitative research, sometimes a counselling psychologist encounters difficulty in fitting a client's experiences within the therapeutic frameworks available to them. If they know little about the substantive issue that the client raises, they may need to engage in *ad hoc* theorising about the nature and meaning of the client's experiences in order to arrive at a therapeutically useful formulation of the client's problems. This involves working in partnership with the client to construct a theory that satisfactorily accounts for the client's experiences and suggests further fruitful lines of inquiry and/or activity. Such theorising arises from and is grounded in the client's understanding of their experiences. This process of abstracting theory from qualitative data is central to the qualitative research method of grounded theory (Glaser and Strauss, 1967; Henwood and Pidgeon, 1992; Pidgeon, 1996; Pidgeon and Henwood, 1996), although in a research context the process of data analysis is more formal and systematic than in a therapeutic setting.

The overlap between qualitative research and counselling psychology/psychotherapy has also been noted by some qualitative researchers. For example, in describing their method of analysing interview data, Brown and Gilligan (1993: 15) state that 'Like . . . a psychotherapist, we attend to recurring words and images, central metaphors, emotional resonances, contradictions or inconsistencies in style, revisions and absences in the story, as well as shifts in the sound of the voice and in narrative position'. This chapter explores how this overlap can be formalised in order to perform research and therapeutic functions simultaneously within counselling psychology.

THE COUNSELLING INTERVIEW IN RESEARCH

Research relevant to counselling psychology often addresses sensitive issues which clients may bring to the therapeutic situation. A research topic has been deemed sensitive if it 'potentially poses for those involved a substantial threat, the emergence of which renders problematic for the researcher and/or the researched the collection, holding and/or dissemination of research data' (Lee and Renzetti, 1993: 5). The qualitative research method of in-depth interviewing is often employed in the study of such topics because the one-to-one interaction involved allows the skilled interviewer to be sensitive to any distress the interview may cause to the interviewee. Such distress may arise if the interview process re-stimulates painful memories and feelings. If this happens, interviewers must be equipped to deal with interviewees' distress. It verges on the unethical for a researcher to address sensitive issues with respondents, re-stimulate painful experiences, record them and then simply depart from the interview situation (Finch, 1984). The interviewee may wish to explore further some of the painful experiences that have been aroused. It is unreasonable to expect research interviewers to undertake prolonged, formal, therapeutic interventions with interviewees outside the research context. However, having re-stimulated distressing memories, the interviewer should at least be able to suggest resources that the interviewee might use to work through them (Breakwell, 1995). This may require the interviewer to be familiar with local counselling and psychotherapeutic resources and self-help groups that are concerned with the issue(s) that caused distress to the interviewee.

How, though, can the interviewer respond to an interviewee's distress in a beneficial way during the interview without losing sight of the research focus? Lee (1993: 106) has suggested that, when faced with a distressed respondent, an interviewer should be able to 'undertake the difficult task of enduring and sharing the pain of the respondent'. However, he does not specify exactly what this process might involve. Locating an in-depth research interview within a counselling framework can be an effective strategy for enabling interviewers to respond to interviewees' distress in a way that can help them come to terms with their distressing experiences (presuming that the interviewer is sufficiently skilled in basic counselling practice), while at the same time advancing the research aims of the interview. The fundamental counselling attributes and skills focused upon in this chapter are those suggested by Rogers (1951), although others have described a range of additional counselling skills which could be fruitfully employed within a research context (for example, see Nelson-Jones, 1993). Rogers (1951) advocated the development of the attributes of empathy, genuineness and unconditional positive regard for the person and saw these as being conveyed chiefly through the use of counselling skills such as attentive listening, paraphrasing the content of the material offered, reflecting feelings, summarising and using open questions.

From a therapeutic viewpoint, paraphrasing content and reflecting feelings may help the interviewee to clarify their experiences and to become aware of the feelings underlying their words. To the extent that counselling techniques encourage the interviewee to disclose and elaborate their experiences and feelings, they may facilitate cathartic expression. If interviewees express emotional distress, interviewers should respond with acceptance and empathy. They can do this by remaining with the person in their distress rather than seeking to minimise it or inhibit its expression, for example, by moving quickly to a less sensitive question on the interview schedule. The interviewer could then use counselling skills to encourage the person to elaborate the thoughts and feelings associated with their distress. The process of relating traumatic events to an attentive, accepting listener may help to divest those events of their power to threaten. This process may also help the interviewee to construct an account or narrative of their experiences, which can render these experiences more understandable and more psychologically tolerable (Harvey, Weber and Orbuch, 1990). The cultivation of counselling attributes and the careful use of basic counselling skills can also help foster a sense of connectedness between the interviewer and the interviewee. It is this sense of interpersonal connectedness – 'the presence of a meaningful shared relationship with another person' (Herth, 1990: 1254) – which is often valued and found beneficial by those who are or have been in emotionally distressing circumstances. The supportive and therapeutic aspect of the interview continues after the interviewer has worked through the interview schedule. It is the interviewer's responsibility to try to ensure that respondents are not left distressed by their involvement in the research. At the end of each interview, therefore, the interviewer should allow for a debriefing period in which interviewees can express how they feel and can explore further any particularly problematic issues that were raised during the interview. In this context, the interviewer continues to use counselling skills, with the aim of ensuring that the person is in a state of relative equanimity after the interview.

The deployment of counselling attributes and skills also helps fulfil the interview's research function. The importance of establishing good rapport in research interviewing is often stressed as it is believed to promote open and honest reporting by the interviewee (Massarik, 1981). Such rapport is said to involve the interviewer being 'nonargumentative, supportive, sympathetically understanding, or facilitating' (Brenner, 1985: 158). The fostering and conveying of such qualities requires a high level of interpersonal skill. However, books and articles on interviewing tend not to specify exactly what skills are required if interviewers are to develop good rapport or how these skills should be deployed. The recommendation that research interviewing might sometimes be usefully located within a counselling framework goes some way towards rectifying this frequent oversight. The use of counselling skills can also help the interviewer to obtain detailed information and a clear understanding of the interviewee's experiences and feelings and to check that they have understood what has been said. Understanding is thereby maximised, thus helping the interviewer to develop 'intimate familiarity' with the person's experiences and feelings, which has been identified as a principal aim of research interviewing (Brenner, 1985).

SO WHAT'S NEW ABOUT USING THE COUNSELLING INTERVIEW IN RESEARCH?

How does the counselling interview used for research purposes differ from other forms of in-depth research interview? In the standard in-depth interview, the *prime* concern is with collecting valid research data rather than providing the interviewee with a psychologically beneficial experience (Breakwell, 1995). Indeed, it has been contended that in research interviews, the interviewee is often viewed as little more than a seam of data to be mined (Oakley, 1981; Stanley and Wise, 1993). Feminist interviewing, however, stresses the importance of sensitive and meaningful engagement between the interviewer and the interviewee in an attempt to avoid the 'objectification' of respondents (Roberts, 1992). Within the feminist framework, the personal involvement of the researcher is seen as enhancing and legitimating both the research process and the research outcome

(Stanley and Wise, 1993). While doubt has been cast on the possibility of creating a truly equal relationship between researchers and respondents (Coyle, 1996), the principles of feminist interviewing suggest that it is possible to ensure that both researchers and respondents can derive benefit from the interview process. When used in a research context, the counselling interview shares the aims of feminist interviewing but specifies exactly how the interviewer can create conditions in which the interviewee can derive therapeutic benefit (in the broadest sense) from their interview experience. This foregrounding and systematising of both the therapeutic and research aspects is what distinguishes the research counselling interview from other forms of in-depth research interview.

CRITICISMS OF USING THE COUNSELLING INTERVIEW IN RESEARCH

Some people have reservations about research methods which mix research functions with supportive or therapeutic functions. For example, Hammersley and Atkinson (1983) have argued that social and intellectual distance must be maintained between researchers and participants to allow proper analytic work to take place. I first became acutely aware of such reservations in 1994 when I submitted a paper based on the material contained in this chapter to an academic journal which specialises in qualitative research. The paper was rejected for publication largely because reviewers felt that counselling and research interviewing were inimical. One reviewer was aghast at the suggestion that these domains might be profitably merged and speculated that I was 'doing this article for shock value'! I drew comfort from the fact that other more illustrious researchers have encountered similar reactions. For example, Ann Oakley (1992: 21) found that her proposal for using 'socially supportive interviewing' in research was criticised by reviewers on the grounds that 'they saw interviewing as interviewing and social support as something quite different'.

A second reviewer of my paper specified exactly what their objections were:

> In counselling, primary therapeutic goals include facilitating clients' insights about their emotions and actions. The goals of research are not ordinarily to increase participants' insights, rather, to elicit participants' descriptions and evaluations of their experiences. The researcher seeks to understand participants' experiences from participants' point of view, not help them make changes in the way they understand their own experiences.

Such concerns about altering participants' accounts and viewpoints rather than simply reflecting them within counselling interviews represent a naïve interpretation of what happens within any interview situation. It has been pointed out, for example, that research interviews are social relationships and are therefore subject to the usual social processes that inhabit any social relationship (Oakley, 1992; Stanley and Wise, 1993). More specifically, it has been noted that participants are often engaged in a process of constructing their identity in research interviews as they produce and reflect upon ideas about themselves (Nicolson, 1994). Thus, being required or permitted to reflect upon the research topic may cause the participants' worldview to be altered in some way (Acker, Barry and Esseveld, 1991). This is quite different from introducing bias in that reflection-based replies represent an inescapable artefact of the interview process. Bias itself – in the form of directing respondents' replies – is no more likely to occur in the research-focused counselling interview than in any other form of in-depth research interview. In the early stages of counselling, person-centred counsellors aim to work non-directively, helping clients to verbalise and organise their experiences without suggesting what their experiences should be. This aim is similar to that of interviewers in research settings. The risk of bias being introduced depends on the skill of the interviewer rather than on the interviewing approach used. These realisations are now resulting in an acknowledgement that research interviews and counselling interviews are not necessarily distinct and that research interviews can be enhanced by the adoption of a counselling approach (King, 1996).

ILLUSTRATING THE COUNSELLING INTERVIEW IN RESEARCH CONTEXTS

The use of the counselling interview within a research context will be illustrated by drawing examples from two studies on sensitive topics which used counselling interviews to collect research data. One examined experiences of AIDS-related bereavement among sixteen gay men who had lost at least one close gay friend or partner to an AIDS-related illness in the past five years (Wright, 1993). The other study investigated the experiences of twenty-two people with terminal illnesses, focusing on experiences of diagnosis and care, strategies for coping and effects on the family (Good, 1992). In each case, the interviewers worked through a set of core questions, the subject matter of which had been determined in advance. However, the exact wording of the questions, their order of presentation and the choice of supplementary questions were left to the discretion of the interviewers, who responded to the issues raised by respondents.

Interactions will be presented which demonstrate the use of the counselling skills of paraphrasing, reflecting and summarising and the conveying of the counselling attributes of empathy, genuineness and unconditional positive regard within the research interviews. It is, however, important to remember that counselling attributes should be a constant feature of the counselling interview – as should the counselling skill of attentive listening – and, as such, they are conveyed incrementally. The illustrative extracts therefore focus on the types of rhetorical strategies that can be used to convey these attributes, although the communication of counselling attributes cannot be reduced to a mere technical skill. It is difficult, though, to convey their gradual construction without presenting transcripts of complete interviews. Due to the overlap between the various counselling skills and counselling attributes, the categories in which the examples are classified are not exclusive, so the same example could potentially fit into more than one category. In the quotations cited, the omission of material is indicated by the use of square brackets.

Paraphrasing

Within the research interview, paraphrasing can be used to check the interviewer's understanding of what the interviewee has said and to spark further elaboration. On hearing the paraphrase, the interviewee can provide feedback on its accuracy. It may also be interpreted as a signal that the interviewer considers the content of the paraphrase to be important and as an invitation to the interviewee to elaborate the points raised. Some of these functions can be discerned in the following example, taken from the AIDS bereavement study. The interaction begins with the interviewee talking about how a friend helped him at the time of his loss:

Interviewee: He's a gay priest and a lot of his work is involved in people dying. And I knew him before and he was with us when Michael died and he was a great support. And I'm not saying – I'm not a religious person but he was just there in the background, you know.

Interviewer: So it wasn't really him doing or saying anything. It was just him being there.

Interviewee: I think so. And people – I think people afterwards too because after it all, after the funeral, that's when it started to really really hit home.

The interviewee then proceeded to elaborate in response to the paraphrase, explaining how others had helped in the days and weeks after the funeral simply by making themselves available and spending time with him.

Paraphrasing can also be used to initiate responses to some of the key research questions. For example, early in one of the AIDS bereavement interviews, when asked where he had obtained support, an interviewee said:

Interviewee: Well, I think my support has come from, OK, from other friends but basically from within because I am very, it's in my nature, um, never to burden anyone else with my problems.

Later, the interviewer came to the question of how the interviewee had coped with AIDS-related bereavement and she followed the question with a paraphrase of his earlier response, as follows:

Interviewer: We all have different ways of coping with difficult events in our lives. In what ways have you coped with your AIDS-related bereavement? You said that you've kept things to yourself, done things in your own way.

Here paraphrasing clarified the question by providing an example of the sort of material that the interviewer wished to explore. As it revisited something that was mentioned earlier in the interview, it also emphasised to the respondent that the interviewer has been listening attentively to what he had been saying.

Paraphrasing was also used to reorient interviewees to the specific research topic. For example, after the same interviewee had spoken of relying on his own resources for support, he proceeded to revisit parts of his account of his house-mate's death. This had already been covered and did not address the question about support that had been posed. However, it was felt that the interviewee would not have followed this path unless he needed to retell his story. The inter-viewer therefore responded with appropriate questions, encouraging elaboration before paraphrasing what he had said previously about his way of coping:

Interviewer: So your way of coping was not to talk to people about it but just to keep it to yourself.

This performed the function of refocusing the interview on the research question and encouraging the interviewee to elaborate what he had previously said.

Reflecting

On many occasions, the affective element of what interviewees said was reflected back to them so that it could be clarified and made explicit for them and so that, as with paraphrasing, they could confirm or correct it and elaborate it. In a straightforward example from an AIDS bereavement interview, one interviewee spoke of how his friend's family did not help while his friend was ill but yet they now tended his grave:

Interviewee: They could have been there for him before he was dead. That is what I would have most wanted. I still see them occasionally at the cemetery. It annoys me that they can go and put flowers on the grave but they couldn't go and see him when he was ill. And it makes me wonder why they couldn't do that for him then, but they can do it now after he has died. Why?
Interviewer: It sounds like you feel quite angry towards them.
Interviewee: Yes I am.

Summarising

While paraphrasing involves restating a particular aspect of what an interviewee has said, summarising draws together the gist of what was said and encapsulates it in a brief statement. This serves a number of functions. Firstly, it emphasises that the interviewer has been listening. Secondly, it again checks that the inter-viewer has correctly understood what has been said and allows the interviewee to correct misunderstandings. For example, one interviewee had offered a general account of his AIDS bereavement experience and, pre-empting a specific question on support, had spoken of how certain other people had supported him. Introducing the specific question, the interviewer summarised these supportive strategies and checked the validity of the summary in this way:

Interviewer: My next question is 'What have they said or done which you have found helpful?'. You have answered that saying that they have been positive and they have accepted you as you are. Would you say that's what you said or not?

Interviewee: Yes, that's it.

A summary can also abstract general principles from concrete experiences offered by the interviewee. The process of data analysis, i.e. of abstracting general themes from the data, can thus begin during the interview. For example, one research question in the AIDS bereavement study concerned how coping with past losses influences coping with more recent losses. In response to this, one interviewee spoke of how, through past experiences of death, he had learned to tell when people were about to die. This meant that he now knew when to summon the person's family and friends to the bedside. On the debit side, he felt he did not have the time needed to mourn each death because there were so many to contend with. The interviewer abstracted the general principles from his responses and summarised thus:

Interviewer: So, on a practical level, you feel it's had a positive influence but on an emotional level, you feel it's meant that you don't give so much time to each one.

The participant agreed with the summary and then expanded upon the effects of multiple loss. In therapeutic terms, the summary clarified the precise nature of the positive (practical) and negative (emotional) implications of past losses for the interviewee. He may then have proceeded to elaborate upon the negative implications in order to engage in cathartic disclosure and formulate a coherent account of these experiences.

To take another example, in the terminal illness interviews, one interviewee offered an account of coping in which she seemed to have coped with her illness not by receiving support from those around her but by supporting them. The interviewer abstracted this from the coping account and summarised it, which elicited a confirmatory response from the interviewee:

Interviewer: But getting back to this business about other people, what seems to be coming over very strongly all the time [   ] is that you tend to be the one who is strong and coping and keeping everyone else going.
Interviewee: Oh yes, there isn't anyone, not really.

This form of analysis is, of course, provisional and represents only the initial stage of analysing qualitative data. It fits with Krueger's (1994) recommendation that the first step in analysis is to summarise the responses given by each person to each question, before identifying potential common themes in these summaries and then testing out these analytic hunches by returning to the data.

One specific form of summary has been termed the 'theme summary' (Nelson-Jones, 1993). This involves introducing something that the person said earlier in order to test whether it links to what they are saying now as part of a recurring theme. Qualitative research sometimes has problems in identifying possible lines of association and causation (Bryman, 1988). The use of the linking summary is one means of achieving this and of checking possible links with the person who is producing the data. For example, one research question in the AIDS bereavement work concerned whether an AIDS-related death was more difficult to deal with than deaths from other causes. One interviewee spoke of the social stigma associated with AIDS and of the relative youth of many of those who have died as a result of AIDS-related illnesses. Earlier, he had noted how families which have suffered an AIDS-related death may maintain that the cause of death was something other than AIDS. The interviewer introduced a summary of this point to check whether or not this might be in some way related to the question under consideration:

Interviewer: And again, you mentioned earlier that families tend to convince themselves that it's not an AIDS-related death.

The interviewee agreed that the link was valid and incorporated this factor into his response to the question.

Empathy

The fostering of counselling attributes often has more to do with nonverbal behaviour and tone of voice than with what is actually said. However, certain interventions will contribute to the development of counselling attributes more explicitly than others. Some examples of these types of interventions are offered, beginning with the communication of empathy, i.e. conveying an understanding of the person's world from their perspective.

In the AIDS bereavement study, one interviewee spoke of how the sister of his best friend who was dying had stayed with him in order to be near her brother. During this time, they became quite close. After the death, he met the sister's husband who was very openly hostile to him, which he found shocking. The interviewee attributed this reaction to the fact that 'he wanted to be with his wife because she was in such a state, but he wasn't'. The interviewer empathised with the interviewee's shock through an emotive summary of the key point of the story in the following interaction:

Interviewer: So at your most vulnerable time . . .
Interviewee: Exactly.
Interviewer: You had somebody expressing their anger, and maybe their guilt as well, at you.
Interviewee: Yes.

The interviewee's affirmative interjections suggested that the interviewer had succeeded in empathically attuning to his feelings. In therapeutic terms, this intervention may have helped to validate the interviewee's reaction to the situation which he described.

Various rhetorical techniques can help to convey an interviewer's empathic response. One such technique involves the interviewer incorporating into their interventions terms or metaphors that were used by interviewees. For example, one interviewee described the process of dealing with an AIDS-related death as being like trying to find your way through long grass to a clearing when you cannot see above the grass. He said:

Interviewee: The grass just seemed to get longer every bloody day and you're trying to see over it and see the clearing. And there's no clearing [. . . .] It felt like I went in and the grass was only an inch high and by the end, it was well over my head. I was out of my depth and I was there alone. And everywhere I turned, there was just grass.

Later, this interviewee revealed that the day before the interview, his new partner had disclosed that he was HIV positive. He commented on how bleak the future looked. The interviewer empathised with him by invoking his previous metaphor in the following interaction:

Interviewee: I don't know how I'm going to prepare for the future because it doesn't seem like this year is going to be any happier than last.
Interviewer: More long grass, do you feel?
Interviewee: Since yesterday, I feel like the grass is growing over my head.

The interviewee's response suggests that the invocation of the 'long grass' metaphor was an appropriate means of communicating an empathic under-standing of his feelings. It also served the functions of affectively linking these experiences with earlier experiences and conveying that the interviewer has been listening carefully.

Genuineness

In a counselling context, the essence of genuineness is said to reside in the counsellor not hiding behind a professional mask but actively engaging in the counselling interaction as a real person, expressing reactions and feelings where appropriate. However, in a research context, the expression of personal opinions or feelings by the interviewer may bias interviewees' responses (unless the inter-viewer's opinions and feelings accord exactly with those of the interviewee). Therefore, the interviewer has to monitor carefully their expression of opinions and feelings or has to devise alternative ways of expressing genuineness.

An example of the interviewer expressing feelings about an interviewee's experiences occurred in the terminal illness study when one interviewee spoke of her experience of poor communication when she accompanied her mother-in-law to hospital. Her account of poor psychological care culminated thus:

Interviewee: One of the doctors said to her 'You've got advanced cancer and it's spread to your bones and we start chemotherapy on Friday. We think your

hair might fall out'. We went out into the patient area and the breast nurse specialist followed us, and, in a room full of people, asked if we were all right. There was nothing, nothing.
Interviewer: It's not easy and there's nobody there. It's this lack of psychological back-up. At times like that, I very much agree with you, it's totally inadequate.

In expressing such feelings, the interviewer appears not as a detached recorder of experiences but as someone who shares and validates the pain of the interviewee. Such an intervention goes some way towards satisfying Oakley's (1981) call for reciprocity in ethical interviewing. As the interviewer's feelings reflect those of the interviewee, they are unlikely to introduce bias.

Interviewers are often perceived as experts in their research topic by interviewees. However, genuineness necessitates the interviewer acknowledging their knowledge but also acknowledging when they require assistance. For example, one interviewee spoke of how others did not know how to react when he told them that he had lost a close friend to AIDS. The interviewer responded:

Interviewer: Do you think the social stigma around AIDS – I'm trying to tease out the social stigma around HIV and AIDS and the social stigma that's still around about gay relationships. Do you think that the social stigma around AIDS – is that because people mistakenly still think that it's a gay disease, or do you think it's because it's AIDS itself?

In this extract, the interviewer acknowledged her expertise by introducing the technical term 'social stigma' and by stating what she was trying to achieve by her questioning, i.e. to determine whether people's reactions to AIDS bereavement experienced by gay men were primarily due to the stigma associated with HIV/AIDS or the stigma associated with gay sexuality. However, the hesitant way in which the explanation is phrased and the positioning of the questions after the question rationale makes the passage appear as a request for help from the interviewee. In this way, the interviewer does not hide behind a façade of detached expertise but seeks the interviewee's assistance in constructing a psychosocial account of his experiences.

Unconditional positive regard

Unconditional positive regard involves accepting and valuing the person as they are rather than as the counsellor/interviewer might want them to be. An identifiable example of this occurred in the AIDS bereavement study during the interview with the person who had experienced the most recent bereavement. At the start of the interview, he expressed a wish to tell his interviewers about the series of events over ten days which preceded his partner's death. However, he was concerned about how long this would take:

Interviewee: When he actually died, that was a tremendous shock. If we had had the time, I would like to have shared the ten days with you but I suspect that when you use the term 'bereavement', you're talking about the period after the death and onwards, rather than the ten days before, which I actually think is very much part of the process.

Interviewer 1: Right, well obviously if you want to talk about that . . .
Interviewee: It's time, um, your time I mean.
Interviewer 1: That's fine.
Interviewee: But the, um, it's very difficult. Most people do not understand. Almost ninety per cent of people I've had contact with have absolutely no understanding of what it's like.
Interviewer 2: But you were able to summarise it to me whenever you were talking to me on the phone. It really came across very clearly what you'd been going through.

The interviewee proceeded to give a very lengthy account of the events that led up to his partner's death. When the interviewee expressed his wish to talk about these events, the interviewers could have responded by focusing the interview on the predetermined questions that they wished to have answered. However, sensing that the interviewee was at a stage where he needed to retell his story about his partner's death, they accepted this. The first interviewer gave him permission to relate his story, despite his concerns about taking up the interviewers' time, and the second actively encouraged him to do so. The message being conveyed here is 'we accept you at the stage that you are now at' instead of wishing that he had moved beyond this stage and hastening him through the interview. The interviewers' acceptance of him was thus not conditional upon his adhering strictly to the interview questions.

THE THERAPEUTIC VALUE OF USING THE COUNSELLING INTERVIEW IN RESEARCH

The hypothesis about the therapeutic effects of incorporating the counselling process into research interviews was explored by asking interviewees in the AIDS bereavement study to comment on how it had felt to take part in the research. All who commented said they had found the interview a positive experience. For example, one interviewee said:

Interviewee: It's benefited me an awful lot really. Just being able to talk about [him]. because there's so much to say and you rarely get the chance to say it. [   ] This is actually the first time I have talked at length about [him] for twelve months really. So it has benefited me a lot.

Although specific evaluative questions were not included in the research on terminal illness, many interviewees spontaneously offered positive feedback on the interview. The following represent a selection of their comments:

Interviewee: I have enjoyed the interview. It was lovely talking to someone who understands.

Interviewee: I wondered how I was going to cope with this, but you've been a help. Just talking helps.

Interviewee: I didn't know [   ] how easy you would be to talk to, so that makes a difference if you're able to communicate with someone, doesn't it?

Of course, there are no comparisons between methods here so it could be that a regular in-depth interview would have elicited the same positive evaluations. However, the use of counselling skills with their emphasis on clarifying, checking and linking responses can only help participants to attain the sort of insights mentioned by the interviewees in the AIDS bereavement study who said:

Interviewee: I thought I'd be totally matter of fact about it but I must admit there's been two or three times [   ] when I started feeling very emotional and I found myself reliving things. And it's partly what's made me realise that I haven't got [   ] it out of my system [   ] and you realise it's still there, right near the surface really, just hidden a bit [   ]. I think you don't realise until you're confronted with it that there's something still underneath there and it's quite strong.

Interviewee: It's only in situations like this that you suddenly realise that there is still a lot going on inside you, of turmoil. That you haven't really got it out of your system at all. You've just put it on the back burner.

If the interview does bring to the fore emotional turmoil that has been placed 'on the back burner', an interviewer who is working within a counselling framework and who has been prepared for the possibility of strong emotional reactions will be better placed to respond constructively to this situation than an interviewer who lacks such skills. However, in the two studies presented here, only one interviewee – who had lost his partner to AIDS only three months previously – became significantly distressed during the interview. The researcher (who was a trainee clinical psychologist) subsequently saw this interviewee for several purely therapeutic sessions. This service was offered to all the interviewees in the study to ensure that any distress arising from participation in the interviews could be dealt with properly. The decision to offer such a service was, however, prompted by the unusual circumstances of the study in that, because of recruitment difficulties, the researcher had to agree to interview anyone who met her inclusion criteria and who wished to participate, regardless of how recently they had experienced their bereavement. Follow-up therapeutic sessions were not offered in the terminal illness study because this was conducted in a hospice where resources were available to help interviewees work through any problematic issues that were stimulated by participation in the interview. Nevertheless, each time the researcher returned to the hospice to conduct further interviews, she visited her previous interviewees to check their well-being and to provide social support. She thus ensured that the research process involved a truly mutual exchange.

PRACTICAL AND ETHICAL ISSUES

The use of counselling interviews in research contexts raises a number of practical and ethical problems. Directors of research on sensitive topics may agree that the counselling interview represents an appropriate data collection tool for their research. Yet, because of time and resource limitations, they may feel that it is appropriate for use only by researchers who already have considerable counselling training and experience. However, it is not necessary to subject researchers to intensive counselling training. The research counselling interview involves only the most basic counselling skills, although more advanced skills can also be usefully employed. Essentially it represents only the initial exploration stage of Egan's (1994) three-stage model of counselling. There is no planning and delivery of therapeutic interventions. The therapeutic value of the interview arises from its clarifying, account-forming and cathartic functions. In order to employ counselling skills in a research interview context, it is therefore not necessary for the researcher to be an accredited counselling psychologist (unless there are particular concerns about the degree of distress the interview is likely to elicit, as outlined above). Generally, it is sufficient for the researcher to have proficiency and confidence in using basic counselling skills and in fostering counselling attributes, together with an ability to confront strong emotional reactions. Such skills can be developed within a relatively short time in an experiential workshop setting (Burnard, 1991). Of course, it is particularly appropriate for reseachers who are qualified or trainee counselling psychologists to use the counselling interview in their research. Such researchers would be well-placed to investigate particularly sensitive topics and could incorporate into their research contract with respondents the offer of a limited number of therapeutic sessions if this should prove necessary. For trainee counselling psychologists, such therapeutic work may help meet their training requirements for client contact time. Whatever the nature of the research contract with respondents, interviewers need to be aware of the limits of what they can offer within a research counselling interview and convey these boundaries to respondents.

It is also necessary to convey clearly to respondents the major distinction between using a counselling interview in a research context and in a therapeutic context when obtaining their consent to participate in the research. In counselling interviews with an exclusively therapeutic focus, the counsellor or counselling psychologist usually guarantees the client confidentiality and assures them that anything they say will not be disclosed to a third party, at least not without the client's consent. Clearly, the research interviewer cannot guarantee confidentiality in this form because they will want to present illustrative excerpts from their data in their research report and, if the report is published, to place it in the public domain. This needs to be explained to respondents. However, this does not mean that anonymity cannot be protected. Respondents should be informed about what will happen to the information that they provide, i.e. how it will be analysed and, if some of their words are chosen for citation in the research report, how their anonymity will be ensured. For example, verbatim quotations may be anonymised by removing the names of people and places and replacing them with generic terms, so 'Dr Jones' in the transcript becomes '[the doctor]' in the quotation cited in the research report. It may be useful to outline plans for disseminating the research report and steps for protecting anonymity on the consent form which respondents sign so that they can provide fully informed consent for their participation.

It should be remembered that, as Lee (1993: 106) has pointed out, 'if the interview can be distressing to the respondent, it can also be stressful for the interviewer'. It has been recommended that those involved in professional counselling receive supervision for their counselling practice from another counsellor (British Association for Counselling, 1990). This allows them to consider the dynamics of the counselling relationships in which they have been involved, to work through and learn from any problems that have been encountered and to obtain professional support. Researchers who are conducting counselling interviews on sensitive topics could also benefit from supervision that fulfils similar functions. Academics or research directors whose students or staff are employing this research method need to be aware that, as well as academic and technical support, students and staff may require social and emotional support. If they are unable to provide this and if their students are not receiving supervision as part of counselling or psychotherapeutic training, they need to investigate how they might develop the necessary skills to fulfil this role or they should consider providing alternative channels of support. If a researcher is working as part of a team. peer support from other researchers may help meet their supervision requirements, but supervisory and support sessions need to be formally time-tabled and organised. Otherwise they may be jettisoned as other research tasks are accorded greater priority. Ultimately, failure to provide adequate supervision and support may be detrimental to the well-being of the researchers (Brannen, 1988).

CONCLUSION

This chapter highlights the ways in which qualitative inquiry and the practice of counselling psychology are closely related and suggests how this relationship can be capitalised upon for research purposes. The experiences of the researchers in the studies of AIDS-related bereavement and terminal illness suggest that if interviewers possess or develop basic counselling skills and use these to convey counselling attributes within the research interview, this can equip them to address sensitive issues with research participants effectively, responsibly and in a way that is beneficial for both parties.

REFERENCES

Acker, J., Barry, K. and Esseveld, J. (1991). Objectivity and truth: problems in doing feminist research. In M. Fonow and J. Cook (eds), *Beyond Methodology: Feminist Scholarship as Lived Research* (pp. 133–153). Bloomington: Indiana University Press.

Brannen, J. (1988). The study of sensitive subjects. *Sociological Review*, 36, 552–563.

Breakwell, G.M. (1995). Interviewing. In G.M. Breakwell, S. Hammond and C. Fife-Schaw (eds), *Research Methods in Psychology* (pp. 230–242). London: Sage.

Brenner, M. (1985). Intensive interviewing. In M. Brenner, J. Brown and D. Canter (eds), *The Research Interview: Uses and Approaches* (pp. 147–162). London: Academic Press.

British Association for Counselling (1990). *Code of Ethics and Practice for Counsellors.* Rugby: British Association for Counselling.

Brown, L.M. and Gilligan, C. (1993). Meeting at the crossroads: women's psychology and girls' development. *Feminism and Psychology*, 3, 11–35.

Bryman, A. (1988). *Quantity and Quality in Social Research.* London: Unwin Hyman.

Burnard, P. (1991). Acquiring minimal counselling skills. *Nursing Standard*, 5(46), 37–39.

Coyle, A. (1995). Discourse analysis. In G.M. Breakwell, S. Hammond and C. Fife-Schaw (eds), *Research Methods in Psychology* (pp. 243–258). London: Sage.

Coyle, A. (1996). Representing gay men with HIV/AIDS. *Feminism and Psychology*, 6, 79–85.

Egan, G. (1994). *The Skilled Helper: A Problem-Management Approach to Helping* (5th edn). Pacific Grove, CA: Brooks/Cole.

Finch, J. (1984). 'It's great to have someone to talk to': the ethics and politics of interviewing women. In C. Bell and H. Roberts (eds), *Social Researching: Politics, Problems, Practice* (pp. 70–87). London: Routledge & Kegan Paul.

Glaser, B.G. and Strauss, A.L. (1967). *The Discovery of Grounded Theory: Strategies for Qualitative Research.* New York: Aldine.

Good, A.M.C. (1992). Psychological issues in terminal illness. Unpublished MSc dissertation: University of Surrey.

Hammersley, M. and Atkinson, P. (1983). *Ethnography: Principles in Practice.* London: Routledge.

Harvey, J.H., Weber, A.L. and Orbuch, T.L. (1990). *Interpersonal Accounts: A Social Psychological Perspective.* Oxford: Basil Blackwell.

Henwood, K.L. and Pidgeon, N.F. (1992). Qualitative research and psychological theorizing. *British Journal of Psychology*, 83, 97–111.

Herth, K. (1990). Fostering hope in terminally ill people. *Journal of Advanced Nursing*, 15. 1250–1259.

King, E. (1996). The use of the self in qualitative research. In J.T.E. Richardson (ed.), *Handbook of Qualitative Research Methods for Psychology and the Social Sciences* (pp. 175–188). Leicester: BPS Books.

Krueger, R.A. (1994). *Focus Groups: A Practical Guide for Applied Research* (2nd edn). Thousand Oaks, CA: Sage.

Lee, R.M. (1993). *Doing Research on Sensitive Topics.* London: Sage.

Lee, R.M. and Renzetti, C.M. (1993). The problems of researching sensitive topics: an overview and introduction. In C.M. Renzetti and R.M. Lee (eds), *Researching Sensitive Topics* (pp. 3–13). Newbury Park, CA: Sage.

Massarik, F. (1981). The interviewing process re-examined. In P. Reason and J. Rowan (eds), *Human Inquiry: A Sourcebook of New Paradigm Research* (pp. 201–206). Chichester: John Wiley.

McNamee, S. and Gergen, K.J. (eds) (1992). *Therapy as Social Construction.* Newbury Park, CA: Sage.

Nelson-Jones, R. (1993). *Practical Counselling and Helping Skills: How to Use the Lifeskills Helping Model* (3rd edn). London: Cassell.

Nicolson, P. (1994). Reflexivity and the experience of the research interview: women's subjectivity in the transition to motherhood. Paper presented at the British Psychological Society London Conference, Institute of Education, London.

Oakley, A. (1981). Interviewing women: a contradiction in terms. In H. Roberts (ed.), *Doing Feminist Research* (pp. 30–61). London: Routledge & Kegan Paul.

Oakley, A. (1992). Getting at the oyster: one of many lessons from the Social Support and Pregnancy Outcome Study. In H. Roberts (ed.), *Women's Health Matters* (pp. 11–32). London: Routledge.

Pidgeon, N. (1996). Grounded theory: theoretical background. In J.T.E. Richardson (ed.), *Handbook of Qualitative Research Methods for Psychology and the Social Sciences* (pp. 75–85). Leicester: BPS Books.

Pidgeon, N. and Henwood, K. (1996). Grounded theory: practical implementation. In J.T.E. Richardson (ed.), *Handbook of Qualitative Research Methods for Psychology and the Social Sciences* (pp. 86–101). Leicester: BPS Books.

Potter, J. and Wetherell, M. (1987). *Discourse and Social Psychology: Beyond Attitudes and Behaviour.* London: Sage.

Roberts, H. (1992). Answering back: the role of respondents in women's health research. In H. Roberts (ed.), *Women's Health Matters* (pp. 176–192). London: Routledge.

Rogers, C.R. (1951). *Client-Centered Therapy.* Boston, MA: Houghton Mifflin.

Stanley, L. and Wise, S. (1993). *Breaking Out Again: Feminist Ontology and Epistemology* (2nd edn). London: Routledge.

Wright, C.M. (1993). Experiences of AIDS-related bereavement among gay men. Unpublished MSc dissertation: University of Surrey.

Chapter 5

Researching the 'therapeutic relationship' in psychoanalysis, counselling psychology and psychotherapy
A qualitative inquiry

Petrūska Clarkson

This chapter reports the methodology of a research project based on and including a review of almost a thousand texts and more than twenty years of learning and supervised practice, as clinician and supervisor in the psychotherapeutic professions, on the nature of the therapeutic relationship. Following a pilot study of five years, the findings are reported in a 165,000-word document which encompasses poetry, personal experience, many textual extracts of theory or therapeutic dialogue, other research reports, theoretical considerations, clinical reflections, syllabus constructions – a postmodernist assemblage which nonetheless attempts coherence, validity and reliability. The findings have also been tested in the field, for example by (a) providing the framework for at least one four-year psychotherapy training course from which the first students have recently graduated by external assessment and (b) an independent psychotherapy accreditation process by a case study submission. It is argued that clinical practice or supervision should be inseparable from research – particularly qualitative research in psychology.

INTRODUCTION

In the psychotherapeutic disciplines there is a *proliferation of different schools* or distinctly identifiable approaches (450 distinct schools according to Corsini, 1984). There are not 450 different ways to do coronary bypass surgery, so why should there be 450 different ways to treat a 'broken heart'? Polkinghorne (1992: 158) puts it this way: 'The large number of theories claiming to have grasped the essentials of psychological functioning provide *prima facie* evidence that no one theory is correct'.

In addition there is the unremitting *inconclusiveness of quantitative empirical evidence* attempting to prove that any one theoretical approach is more effective than another across a broad spectrum of problems (reviewed in Norcross and Goldfried, 1992). It has been said that the current state of psychotherapy outcome research is like the caucus race in *Alice in Wonderland*: 'All have won and all must have prizes'.

Furthermore as Shelef (1994: 1) points out: 'it is important to affirm that it is a researcher's wanting to know, wanting to understand that can be the basis of a research question'. As well as the above questions, I wanted to explore the most frequently found *common factor* associated with the effectiveness of psychotherapy outcome across approaches – the therapeutic relationship.

> Studies have shown that psychotherapists rarely find psychological research relevant for practice, and that they have to build up a second body of knowledge. The practitioners' expert knowledge is dynamic and context dependent; and Polkinghorne [1992] goes on to argue that this largely oral knowledge of practice is in tune with postmodern ideas of knowledge as without foundation, fragmentary and constructed, as well as with the current neopragmatic shift from metaphors of correctness to those of utility (Kvale, 1992: 5).

As a practitioner myself, it occurred to me that perhaps one of the reasons psychotherapy research is often so ambiguous and inconclusive is that it was trying to model itself on the quantative investigatory paradigms of the physical sciences. Indeed Searight (1990) has argued that experimental and quasi experimental methods cannot do justice to describing phenomena such as the therapeutic relationship.

A qualitative investigation into this field promised greater hope and perhaps more illumination. Denzin and Lincoln's 1994 volume contains an excellent overview of the arguments and the scope and value of the field. I also wanted to explore for myself the capacities and limitations of qualitative research which was grounded in the life, liveliness and livelihood of the consulting room instead of in the laboratory rat mazes and high tech psycho-physiological quantative measurements of my first Masters and Doctoral degrees. The research questions of phenomenological research methods would, in the words of Moustakas (1994: 21), 'reflect the interest, involvement and personal commitment of the researcher . . . viewing experience and behaviour as an integrated and inseparable relationship of subject and object and of parts and whole'.

The research questions therefore emerged quite simply: Why are there so many distinct and very different approaches to psychotherapy? Why does the relationship appear to be more important in assessing the effectiveness of psychotherapy than adherence to any of these many approaches? Could it be that these many different approaches are all talking about the therapeutic relationship, but from different universes of discourse or focusing on different aspects of it? Could I find a format for distinguishing such universes of discourses? Could it be small enough to be useful, yet large enough to encompass the whole field? Would it fit the data? Would it fit my experience as person and clinician? Would it work for others?

The core objectives of the investigation were (a) to articulate and experiment with a qualitative research device *to enhance the understanding and effectiveness of clinical practice, teaching and supervision in the psychotherapeutic professions*

(b) in the words of the editor of the journal in which the phase one document (Clarkson, 1990) was piloted, to make

> . . . a careful analysis of the various levels of the psychotherapeutic relationship in an *attempt to find a perspective from which an overview might become possible.* She [Clarkson] . . . offers a way of circumventing the inherent contradictions and incompatibilities that exist *between* different psychotherapies; instead of incompatibilities we have different priorities and emphasis. And this leaves a way open for the beginnings of a possible integration of psychotherapies (Hinshelwood, 1990: 119)

and (c) *to explore a postmodern qualitative research methodology, context and content which was grounded in a moral universe* where issues of values, ethics and the cultural/ecological situatedness of everyone accompanied the investigation instead of maintaining a pretence of objectivity, neutrality, or even authority.

CONCEPTUAL FRAMEWORK

The conceptual framework for this investigation is broadly drawn from the disciplinary fields of psychoanalysis/psychotherapy, psychology and counselling – all the forms of helping through talking. These can be visualised as three overlapping circles . The 'heart' of the study, to use Miles and Huberman's (1994) felicitous phrase, is the *therapeutic relationship* – the focus for 'the case' under investigation in this instance. This case was conceptualised as primarily located in the field of psychotherapy theory, supervision and practice.

The decision to limit and concentrate on the therapeutic relationship (as opposed to other variables such as client–therapist match) is based on extensive evidence from the literature (which was reviewed in both the 1990[1] and 1995[2] documents of this study) as well as personal, clinical and supervisory practice. The exploration and study of other variables in psychotherapy are minimised here except insofar as they impinge on the heart of this case. However, there may of course be other variables equally or better able to explain the existing reported commonalities or contrasts. However, the therapeutic relationship seemed suitable for qualitative investigation and perhaps qualitative investigation would suit the relationship best.

The boundary of this study maintained for the largest part a pragmatic distinctness of the central work of psychotherapists, psychologists and counsellors from the work of other helping relationships, such as those which may be involved in the practice of medicine, pastoral guidance or spiritual healing. These may be alluded to on occasion, but were not studied in depth in this case. Future studies may of course expand or test this project into other areas.

1 The 1990 document is: P. Clarkson (1990) A Multiplicity of Therapeutic Relationships, *British Journal of Psychotherapy*. 7 (2). 148–163.
2 The 1995 document is: P. Clarkson (1995) *The Therapeutic Relationship in Psychoanalysis, Counselling Psychology and Psychotherapy*, London: Whurr.

In 'Toward reflexive methodologies' Gergen and Gergen (1991: 86) have suggested that: 'By taking a reflexively dialogic approach to research, a new form of scientific work can be developed'. Clinicians have often in the past defended their hostility, avoidance and rejection of scientific research on the grounds that the mystery of human relationship cannot be subjected to the analyses of the white coats. I had in the past myself likened it to trying to catch butterflies with tractors. Traditional scientific method has often seemed inappropriate if not damaging to the mystery and elusiveness of the healing human relationship.

However, the new form of scientific work may have, or develop, the capacity to honour both the mystery and its greater appreciation by understanding. Perhaps this dialogic approach to research could become acceptable, even desirable, to clinicians and their co-researchers into the human psyche – their patients. 'The intentional nature of human practices is well captured by *qualitative methods*. There is an acceptance of diverse ways of producing knowledge. . . . also encompassing qualitative methods involving interactive and contextual approaches and including case studies' (Kvale, 1992: 51).

So. the research reported here would have to do with using the metaphor (and reality) of writing as relationship, while engaging in therapeutic relationships, as well as engaging with the writings of others about the nature and range of their understandings of the therapeutic relationship. I would intentionally include many diverse ways of producing knowledge. In this way I specifically began with 'but a provisional stance towards a subject, and progressively elaborate "the nature of the problem" as it is refracted through the intelligibilities of others' (Gergen and Gergen, 1991: 79).

THE QUALITATIVE METHODOLOGY

The study eventually comprised:

(a) The use of my own personal and professional experience as client, teacher and supervisor of psychotherapists (and allied professionals) as locus of the exploration. Instead of an 'objective experimenter' on an object, I would engage from the subjective realities of my ongoing existential situation. This would correspond to Shelef's (1994: 2) *'heuristic incubation'*. The period of my personal and professional engagement with this question is catalogued in several places (including my CV) and spanned at least twenty years, several psychoanalysts and three continents. My background is considered uncommonly wide and thorough in my profession. It is during this period of immersion that I followed a strategy similar to that which is reported by Bamberger and Schon (1991: 187): 'search[ing] for such boundaries without trying to be explicit about the criteria'.

(b) It was expected that the theory would emerge in an inductive manner from this large collection of data. The creation of a research device (Shotter, 1992) or qualitative research tool would follow, through which I would conduct my hermeneutical (as distinct from empirical) investigation into the nature of the therapeutic relationship across schools or approaches. This would consist in the 'generation of categories for understanding human phenomena and the investigation of the interpretation and meaning that people give to the events they experience' (Polkinghorne, 1992: 112). This combination of both *finding* and *making* formed the basis for the formulation and publication of the pilot 1990 document in a major journal of the psychotherapeutic profession.

(c) The publication of the minor pilot project's results (the 1990 document) led to the construction of a training course and further opportunities to test and verify the findings. It included as significant components extracts from authoritative texts, clinical examples, patients' dreams and kinship metaphors.

The abstract and somewhat artificial separation of lived experience and sequentially unfolding research components was intentionally superseded by an alternative qualitative research paradigm (Hoshmand, 1989). What was intended was an engagement with the research problem of both passion and discipline, analysis and holistic appreciation of the phenomena as well as use of the self as 'the instrument by which the research was conducted' (p. 3). The nature of the research question, however, leads to it being an open-ended project. The publication of the major 1995 document will continue the research as readers and reviewers respond, reject, counter, expand or use the material – particularly the theoretical framework presented.

(d) In addition, my own experience of designing training courses, giving international lectures and workshops formulated around issues of the therapeutic relationship would provide me with ongoing and repeated feedback (verification or rejection) on the validity and acceptance of my interpretive framework. I used the 1990 document as the basis for all these experiments with presentation, comprehensibility and acceptance to a wide range of professionals from a wide range of backgrounds and theoretical affiliations.

A general theory should have considerable scope, range and conceptual complexity, and that means also that it will be fairly abstract and have a fair degree of specificity (and so encompass much variability). It necessarily gathers up and helps to integrate what previously have been discrete theories, and elements of theories, that bear on the phenomena you are focused upon (Strauss, 1995: 17).

(e) The research into relationship was furthermore itself conceptualised as relationship.

The major document (published in 1995) would be indeed *as and about* relationship, gleaned from different methods of collecting data including: an inquiry into the field itself; texts from the field and poetics of the consulting room and surveys of research texts and samples of theoretical texts drawn from the experience of others; my own subjective experience and the resonances, reverberations, rejections and rewards it brings; and data from subjects and subjectivity and the larger community of both the discipline and the particular cultural and temporal world within which the study has taken place.

Clandinin and Connelly (1994: 425) also view research itself as about relationship, conducted in relationship and through relationship:

> Personal experience methods inevitably are relationship methods. As researchers, we cannot work with participants without sensing the fundamental human connection among us; nor can we create research texts without imagining a relationship to you, our audience. Voice and signature make it possible for there to be conversations through the texts among participants, researchers, and audiences. It is in the research relationships among participants and researchers, and among researchers and audiences, through research texts that we see the possibility for individual and social change. We see personal experience methods as a way to permit researchers to enter into and participate with the social world in ways that allow the possibility of transformations and growth.

Indeed one can consider the possibility that relationship is at the very heart of the recognition and growth of qualitative methodology because the qualitative research paradigm is based on the interrelatedness of subjects, not the apparently disembodied study of objects by some non-involved value-neutral analytic experimenter. It is centrally concerned with the researcher-researched unit where one can never authentically be peeled off from the other except in abstract compartments. In this sense it is consistent and congruent with the observer–field interdependence which is the particular contribution of quantum physics and the emerging sciences of chaos and complexity which I have discussed elsewhere (Clarkson, 1993). On a macroscopic scale these findings of interrelatedness corroborate the existential validity of the research hypothesis.

Any inquiry into relationship is by the same token research. And if psychotherapy is about relationship, then it must also *be* research in a sense. The fact that the work of the clinic is too frequently left unreflected and unreported in a rigorously reflected qualitative way does not mean that it cannot be done. In the future, responsible clinical practice may require that it does not remain undone. Both supervisors and clinicians need to write in order not only to reflect on their experience, but also to offer it to the community of professionals for their edification, challenge and support. As the 'unexamined life may not be worth living', the unexamined therapy may not be worth doing. As Richardson (1994) has suggested, writing itself is of course a method of inquiry in its own right. And any writing done consistently over a large number of years inevitably has the mark of the researcher upon it.

> All qualitative researchers are philosophers in that 'universal sense in which all human beings . . . are guided by highly abstract principles' [Bateson, 1972: 320]. These principles combine beliefs about ontology (What kind of being is the human being? What is the nature of reality?), epistemology (What is the relationship between the inquirer and the known?), and methodology (How do we know the world, or gain knowledge of it?) [Lincoln and Guba, 1985;

Guba, 1990; Guba and Lincoln, 1994] These beliefs shape how the qualitative researcher sees the world and acts in it. And writing is a primary way of both seeing and acting in the world (Richardson, 1994: 517).

The documents which are some of the products of this research embody both the process and the content of the act of research in the relationship in this theoretical as well as practical way.

> Specifically, poststructuralism suggests two important things to qualitative writers: first, it directs us to understand ourselves reflexively as persons writing from particular positions at specific times; and second, it frees us from trying to write a single text in which everything is said to everyone. Nurturing our own voices releases the censorious hold of 'science writing' on our consciousness, as well as the arrogance it fosters in our psyche. Writing is validated as a method of knowing (Richardson, 1994: 517).

Bor and Watts (1993) wrote that researchers in counselling psychology should conduct their research using a methodology which is congruent with their theoretical framework and approach to counselling and psychotherapy. It is possible to argue that the serious and dedicated writing up of subjective experience. the theories of others and the invention of one's own, the questioning of received wisdom and popular assumptions, the encounter with the other in the consulting room and their words and images, the prose as well as the poetry of healing all form a congruent representation of the work of the clinician supervisor in this field. It is thus my opinion and recommendation that research should be inseparable from supervision or clinical work. This theme is developed elsewhere (Clarkson, 1995; and see also Chapter 1 of this volume).

SAMPLING

Sampling strategies in this qualitative inquiry would (a) focus on maximum variation and (b) be theory based as well as (c) opportunistic after Miles and Huberman (1994). So, in addition to my own experience, data would be solicited from all published and experiential sources allowing maximum variation of samples (within the field of investigation) drawn from the many different approaches to psychotherapy in order to identify important common patterns which I had studied over two decades, was teaching or which came my way, as a result of unexpected discoveries, conversations or references.

> The naturalist is likely to eschew random or representative sampling in favour of purposive or theoretical sampling because he or she thereby increases the scope of range of data exposed (random or representative sampling is likely to suppress more deviant cases) as well as the likelihood that the full array of multiple realitites will be uncovered (Lincoln and Guba, 1985: 4).

It would therefore be theory based in the sense of drawing on all the major theoretical approaches in the field, but also engaged in the initial formulation of theory – at least a theoretical framework for the exploration and utilisation of the therapeutic relationship across approaches and across disciplines.

I attempted to 'abandon the problem of the origin of ideas within the head, and shift concern to the emergence of language within communities' (Gergen and Gergen, 1991: 80) – in this case therapeutic 'schools' or communities – all of whom articulate and speak about the therapeutic relationship in the grammar, idiom and vocabulary of their specific linguistic capacities – thereby creating as all languages do voids – which cannot be spoken – or perhaps even thought.

PROCESS

After this invention phase of research design, Kirk and Miller's (1986) discovery phase followed. However in this study it was inextricably intertwined in a feedback loop fashion with the interpretation or analysis phase in the sense that the information sought and the data collected were constantly subject to analysis and evaluation in terms of the possibility of 'fit' within the framework being tested. (The so-called explanation phase of communication would be contained in the 1995 document.)

The pilot study (the 1990 document) drew from a basis of fifty-eight specific referenced sources. (Later, for the major document, I would use twenty times more sources, a much wider palette of discourses and a more imaginative sampling sieve subjecting some further 1,000 texts (specified in three books and one manuscript) to thematic analysis. As here in the pilot, these would be drawn from an intentionally wide variety of therapeutic communities to reflexive practice and theoretical analysis focused on the importance of 'identifying contrasts between ways of speaking; and identifying points where these ways of speaking overlap' (Banister *et al.*, 1994). I would do this by means of constructing a messy text – substantial enough to have face validity, with requisite variety at least to explore reliability.

Figure 5.1 summarises the entire process to date.

DISCOURSE ANALYSIS

The researched 1995 document can also be presented as a product of discourse analysis or more specifically thematic analysis (Aronson, 1994). I conceive of this in the sense that it is the task of the textual and practical analysis 'to tease apart the discourses that are at work' (Banister *et al.*, 1994: 94). There are of course many possible fruits of such analyses – my intention was to find the smallest number of categories with the largest explanatory potential and the greatest inclusivity of universes of discourse about the therapeutic relationship.

This process has been engaged in a number of different phases – each of which is but a punctuation mark in an ongoing investigation conceived of as a longitudinal study lasting a professional lifetime. So any report can never be the final report, but is only a report on the most recent findings and the methods and

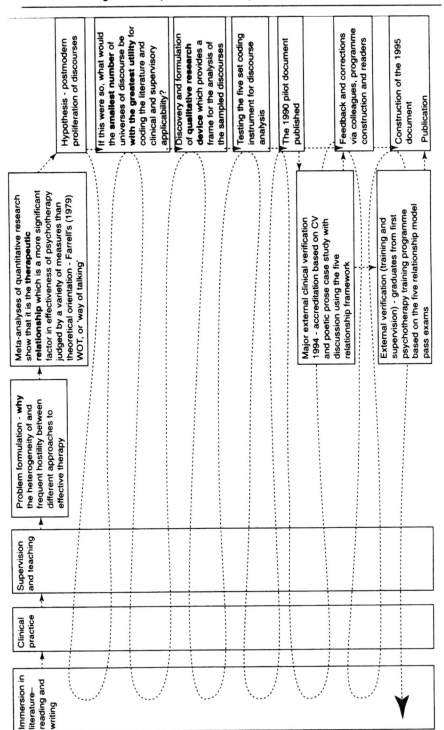

Figure 5.1 Diagrammatic summary of entire research process to date

means of acquiring them. It is intended as the beginning of collegial conversation, not an end.

First there was the thorough exploration of the 'diversity of meaning, the different contradictory ways of speaking that govern what we [as psychotherapists] do (and who we can be)' (Banister *et al.*, 1994: 92). I sought to explore all the major relationship discourses in psychoanalysis, psychotherapy and psychological counselling. This phase is documented primarily by certificates of study, academic and professional recognitions, lecture and workshop notes and the list of publications which preceded it.

Next was the construction of categories – the five relationships – which provided a way of structuring the textual research into a hypothetical sorting matrix. This device actually emerged one evening in my consciousness as a completed Gestalt, suddenly clarifying boundaries between the different kinds of therapeutic relationship about which much is spoken and which indeed I had experienced, both as practitioner/supervisor and as client. The experience constituted the kind of shift of knowing which Shotter (1992: 56) described from knowing by 'looking at' to knowing by being 'in contact, or in touch with'.

The efficacy of this thematic analysis matrix would be assessed by its (1) usefulness in clinical, teaching and supervisory practice as well as actual programme construction and validation; (2) the ease of understanding by novice and experienced practitioners in the field under investigation (the recognition factor); and (3) the adequacy of fit. This is here conceived of as the extent to which it made manageable or comprehensible the multiplicity of perspectives – often contradictory – which are co-existent in the psychotherapeutic literature regarding the 'relationship'.

The 1990 pilot study was launched with the publication of an original paper in a major journal for psychoanalysis and psychotherapy. A first test in this regard was peer review and acceptance by a premier journal in a first world country. 'One of the functions of the text, as of any text, is to bring to life (again for us now as researchers) a network of relationships' (Banister *et al.*, 1994: 117). Verbal and written reports supported the initial formulation and hopefully helped to bring it more to life.

In this case as well, the place of overlap between all forms of psychotherapeutic endeavour seemed to be the central importance of the therapeutic relationship. I hypothesised that the contrasts between the different schools depended on the ways of speaking about this relationship and therefore the different universes of discourse associated with each. This formulation became an early categorisation subjected to constant and rigorous analysis and evaluation.

In this process I identified five primary universes of discourse in the major texts dealing with psychoanalysis, counselling psychology and psychotherapy. The analysis was thematic rather than statistical partly because of the interpreter fluency/rater expertise required. They emerged as themes in the way the solution to a puzzle sometimes emerges clearly but essentially inexplicably from long-term intense engagement with it.

It appeared to me that there are five *kinds* of such relationship which can repeatedly be identified in the extant research and theoretical literature by such a thematic engaged analysis. These are: the working alliance; the transference–countertransference relationship; the developmentally needed or reparative relationship; the person-to-person or real relationship; and the transpersonal relationship. I hypothesised that all five kinds of therapeutic relationship are at least theoretically potentially available in most approaches to therapy and actually aspects of each appear in most of the major approaches studied.

(See the 1995 document for details: this chapter is focused on the methodological issues involved.)

THE CONSTRUCTION OF THE 1995 DOCUMENT BOTH AS RESEARCH RESULT AND RESEARCH QUESTION

The 165,000-word document published in 1995 marks a recent temporary but defined stage post in this research study. It includes case material, poetry, chunks of texts from other writers, ponderings, arguments, conflicts, confusions, juxtapositions and particularly a constant acknowledgement of flux in the field in which it is situated and the contradictions, paradoxes and growth potential of the author.

At least 10 per cent (a tithe) of the text is explicitly engaged in moral/ethical discourse and a section on the inescapability of values in counselling and psychotherapy carries the implicit and explicit acknowledgement that all actions and non-actions (including writing) are *valuing* acts. Throughout this the author and reader are being questioned as well as informed and challenged. It was meant as a messy text.

Marcus (1994: 566) writes that: 'The postmodern premise that there is no possibility of fixed, final, or monologically authoritative meaning has radicalized the critique within anthropology of its own forms of representation by challenging the authority on which they have been based.' I attempted to experiment with this kind of approach as a contribution to the literature of psychotherapy by repeated exercises in construction in the bulk of a chapter in the final 1995 document, often followed by a deconstructive piece disengaging from, challenging or blatantly questioning the foundations upon which the chapter had been constructed. In this way I hoped to invite the reader into serious consideration of opposing viewpoints; the discomfort of theoretical uncertainty; and the excitement of the deconstructive process of individual discovery. An example of this is the chapter in which I write an extensive overview of the literature on the developmentally needed relationship, but the so-called 'counterpoint' piece is concerned with undermining the very notion of the usefulness, credibility or moral defensibility of developmental perspectives in psychoanalysis and psychotherapy.

Marcus (1994: 567) explains at least three justifiable and valid reasons for constructing messy texts:

First, they arise simply from confronting the remarkable space/time compression that defines the conditions of peoples and culture globally. . . . Second, they wrestle with the loss of a credible holism. . . . In messy texts there is a sense of a whole, without evoking totality, that emerges from the research process itself. . . . Third, messy texts are messy because they insist on an open-endedness, an incompleteness, and an uncertainty about how to draw a text/ analysis to a close. Such open-endedness often marks a concern with an ethics of dialogue and partial knowledge that a work is incomplete without critical, and differently positioned, responses to it by its (one hopes) varied readers.

The construction of the five relationship framework provided an analytic tool which is itself a commentary about the multiplicity of co-existing universes of discourse in the field. It certainly is a research device. I am not sure if the five relationship framework constitutes a theory. It may be more of a hypothesis or a framework for complex data analysis.

Collegial feedback has however insisted quite strongly that it is indeed a meta-narrative in its own right (Christoph-Lemke, 1994). In this sense the formulation of the five relationship framework could be a theory (Strauss, 1995) based on the continuous interplay of data and conceptualisation over many years. The theory I was developing became more complex and delineated as I constantly (theoretically and practically) compared the sampled data sources from the body of literature researched one with each other and also in terms of my proposed analytic framework. Exploration of the data yielded sufficient confirmation to use the framework as an ongoing categorisation of universes of discourse relevant to what is generally understood as 'the therapeutic relationship'.

If it is a theory, the five relationship framework is a fairly abstract theory of therapeutic relationships. It gathers up and helps to integrate hundreds of different approaches to psychotherapy, at the same time as being able to encompass much variability. The extent and limitations of this theoretical or pragmatic model as a theory can be further pursued in the future by myself and other researchers.

VERIFICATION PROCESSES

The design and construction of a training course for psychotherapists based on this model would test the theoretical framework as a formula for learning the practice of psychotherapy by externally assessed standards. Although obviously not tightly controlled in the more traditional quantitative mode, the students were indeed engaged as co-researchers testing and using the framework to support their learning and their practice. This is research tested *by application*.

This is partly for Kvale's (1992) suggestion that by discarding a modern legitimation mania, justification of knowledge is replaced by application, with a pragmatic concept of validity. This criterion of validity is particularly applicable in this case where usefulness of the framework is its raison d'être – not its 'truth' per se.

In addition this work was supported by my own personal and professional application of the device or framework in psychotherapy, supervision and organisational consultancy at least over the period of duration of the study. All people in therapy, supervision and training interacted dialogically with me living the material day by day *in* relationship. From them I learnt what made sense, what worked, what didn't. They were my first co-researchers and my best teachers. In another sense all the writers of books and papers in psychology, psychoanalysis and psychotherapy were also my co-researchers as they were reporting on the vagaries and vicissitudes of their researchers and experiences of the therapeutic relationship in their settings and within and relevant to their idiosyncratic theoretical approaches – each in their own individual universe of discourse. Gergen and Gergen (1991: 79) also showed 'the advantages of allowing a multiplicity of voices to speak to the research issues of concern'.

The five relationship model was then subjected to further practical test in the *consulting and lecturing room*, through teaching and in supervision as well as in the construction of a programme based on it. It has been used consistently by myself for at least five years *after* its published formulation and has stood the tests of time, diversity of approaches of clinicians and accessibility and interest to novice as well as very experienced clinicians/supervisors. This is the interweaving of researcher and researched, folding in on the self and out into the practice. 'It is through this spiral movement, through experiencing lived space with others, that the researcher would learn, illuminate, and generate data' (Shelef, 1994: 3). Also of course, test the data.

The first *psychotherapy training programme* which used this framework as its primary integrative shape has recently been completed. Several of the students have been awarded merits or distinctions by an external examining board based on their casework presentations and dissertations. It should be noted that the other staff on the programme I had originally conceptualised and most of the adjunct supervisors were familiar with the model – although each one hopefully brought their own particular uniqueness to its interpretation and implementation. Students would, in the best cases, amplify and diversify according to their proclivities and theoretical and clinical preoccupations. Indeed this is the very form and function of the model as originally intended – to create a theoretical framework within which many different approaches can be articulated, shared and understood without necessarily privileging any one or more as *the* authorised discourse on this theme.

The five relationship framework has been used as a basis for a number of *other courses* in psychology, counselling or psychotherapy. Investigation of these would be a possible future avenue for further research as to whether it can meet multiple interests and needs. I did subject it to evaluation by formulation, programme construction and participant evaluation or publication in peer-reviewed journals in three specific other areas – organisational consultancy, couples therapy and group therapy.

A FURTHER EXTERNAL ACCREDITATION TEST

As a further test of the theory I constructed a case study in prose-poetry with a discussion paper and submitted it as an example of competent clinical psychotherapy to a major psychotherapy accreditation body. (Authorities such as Eisner (1991) have argued before that qualitative research is art, based on connoisseurship and criticism, and accepts the personal, literary and even poetic as valid sources of knowledge.) The five relationship theoretical framework applied to a real client who had been in therapy with me and described in this way was accepted by a UKCP validated body's accreditation board as valid and sufficient (with my CV) to become a member of their organisation. I submit this as further evidence of recognisability of the model as well as one possibility among many to test validity and reliability. It is another aspect of qualitative inquiry which I have not yet seen documented elsewhere.

The final 1995 document exists as the summary transcript of the research process itself including the fact that it is a text of texts as well as containing reflections on its own textuality and situatedness in contemporary postmodernity – particularly as it affects issues of ethics and epistemology. It is currently being presented to the psychotherapeutic community as a book for review and sale. The responses to it will again shape the findings, birth new hypotheses and further the general dialogic relationship with professionals and theoreticians in these fields. This will lead to further refinements and more differentiated small-scale studies which can again continue the research process.

Every day new material emerges which can be incorporated, alternative frameworks are posited, questions, amplifications and reservations are articulated which problematise or valorise certain aspects more than others. Its justification lies in its engagement and the showing of the relationship between text and author, and in making this struggle accessible in this form – an ongoing invitation to reflection, exploration and relationship.

Table 5.1 Summary of method with reference to Lincoln and Guba (1985)

Focus for inquiry	The therapeutic relationship
Fit of paradigm to focus	Amenability to qualitative inquiry
'Fit' of inquiry paradigm to the theory selected to guide the inquiry	Combination of phenomenological (therapy sessions/interviews); heuristic (literature analysis); and ethnographic (study of the texts of different 'tribes' of psychotherapy)
Where and from whom data will be collected	Clients, colleagues, self as client, therapist, supervisor and teacher, major texts, pscyhological literature, trainees, journal and book reviewers, poets and formal accreditation panels
Successive phases of the inquiry	Theoretical and experiential immersion, formulation/discovery of 'categories' based on an impressionistic discourse analysis – the making of the

Table 5.1 continued

Successive phases of the inquiry (*continued*)	qualitative research device, field application, pilot study (1990), incorporation of feedback, training programme construction and implementation, further discourse analysis and much enlarged (diversity and volume) field sampling procedures
Instrumentation	The application of the five relationship framework to the field with the researcher as instrument
Data collection and recording modes	Library retrieval, collegial discussion, extensive reading, ongoing clinical, teaching and supervisory practice; the writing, rewriting and eventual construction of the major document (1995)
Data analysis procedures	Multiple
Logistics	Best left to the imagination – management of a personal and professional clinical/supervisory and teaching life including conferences and workshops in several different countries while consuming large quantities of professional literature as well as writing and rewriting a 165,000-word book
Trustworthiness	The coding frame (five relationships) was repeatedly presented to clients, supervisees and colleagues in order to test whether they could understand the themes and arrive at similar conclusions – for example, to the journal reviewers of the 1990 document and to the twelve senior manuscript reviewers of the 1995 document
	No causal relationship was postulated about the five kinds of therapeutic relationships. The possibility that at least some of the conflicts and misunderstandings in theory and practice between different schools of psychotherapy were attributable to differential prioritisings of different aspects of the therapeutic relationship is by no means proved. However, prolonged engagement (25 years in the field), persistent reported reflections on observation (100+ professional publications) and the checking of multiple sources of data such as my own practice, the descriptions of the practices of my colleagues, 1,000+ texts and other research studies provide at least some evidence for internal validity – to be further explored
	External validity was specifically tested by the external assessment of the first graduates from the programme designed on the basis of this framework and by the submission of a case study in poetic prose as part of an application for membership accreditation by the procedures of a recognised psychotherapy accrediting organisation

A POSTMODERN STUDY?

Finally I would submit that this study has not only been post-modern in the diversity and particularities of its components and its construction drawing from a multiplicity of styles, instances and cultures from different periods and cultures in and around psychotherapy; it has also itself been a product of the postmodern turn in psychology as described and discussed particularly in Kvale's (1992) *Psychology and Postmodernism*. The following table attempts to summarise some other main features.

Table 5.2 Summary of other postmodern features of this inquiry

From	To	Source
Theory	Practice	Shotter, 1992: 59
Theorising	Instructive account	Shotter, 1992: 59
An interest in things	Interest in activities/uses	Shotter, 1992: 59
Preformed 'psychological instruments'	Devised tools	Shotter, 1992: 59
What goes on in the heads of individuals	Sociality/relationship	Shotter, 1992: 59
Reflection as origin	Embeddedness in activity	Shotter, 1992: 59
Reality in language	Social relations in language	Shotter, 1992: 59
Reliance on experience as the basis for understanding the world	A questioning of the social processes of their construction	Shotter, 1992: 59
Investigations based on authoritative foundations	Modes which allow for error correction on the spot	Shotter, 1992: 59
A unitary perspective	Plurality of perspectives	Shotter, 1992: 36
A split of culture into science, morality and art	A rehabilitation of the ethical and aesthetic domains	Shotter, 1992: 36
Quest for extrinsic legitimisation, universality, rationality and commensurability	Intrinsic legitimisation, uniqueness, intuition and quality	After Gergen, 1992: 41

FUTURE RESEARCH

Every day new directions for future research emerge and become clearer. I will mention some here.

1 An investigation of inter-rater reliability of the assessment of therapeutic transactions in terms of which relationship vector is intended or acted upon by extensive and thorough discourse analysis of therapeutic sessions. This will

test or give some indication of the recognisability of the five different kinds of relationship and may facilitate the development of criteria for differentiating them for ease of use in practice, supervision and research.

2 A comparison of the discourse analyses done in such a way within and between different schools or approaches to psychotherapy to explore whether the differences reported in the literature between schools are indeed an artefact of language or social constructions rather than fundamental incompatibilities, as is sometimes believed.

3 A phenomenological exploration into the five relationships – subjective differences, experienced value at different stages or critical incidents of psychotherapy and/or perceived failures or misunderstandings – conducted with therapy clients as active co-researchers.

4 A further exploration and exposition of the perceived affinity of qualitative research paradigms with the models and procedures of chaos and complexity theory as well as with quantum physics. Some implications for psychological research I have already discussed elsewhere (Clarkson, 1993). A small example concerns the fractal iterative nature across scale of, say, the five relationship device (from therapy transcript segment to case study to the whole of the field).

5 A further and much more detailed investigation into the usefulness of this paradigm of research specifically in clinical supervision, building on the initial formulation already published in the 1995 document.

6 According to Rudestam and Newton (1992: 38): 'Because the researcher is regarded as a person who comes to the scene with his or her own operative reality, rather than as a totally detached scientific observer, it becomes vital to understand, acknowledge and share one's own underlying values, assumptions and expectations'. A further exploration of the ethical and moral situatedness of the researcher/clinician/supervisor in psychotherapy is thus indicated. This may involve taking the postmodern works concerning ethics, politics and moral action of, for example, Anderson (1990), Bauman (1993) and Hutcheon (1989), as well as a qualitative investigation into the cultural, social and psychological aspects of bystanding behaviour, into the discursive domain of avowed and enacted values (Clarkson, 1996).

7 Finally to do an equally broad and wide sweep of research writings in psychology/psychoanalysis/psychotherapeutic counselling engaging with the five relationship device in a thematic analysis of the field of research. It would be looking for patterns or clusters of preoccupations in the languages and discourse of researchers in this field which may sort into the relationship categories of (1) the working alliance; (2) the transference/countertransference; (3) the developmentally needed or reparative; (4) the person-to-person; and (5) the transpersonal (or a category for the currently inexplicable).

I can imagine sifting the literature in the nature of a thematic analysis to explore the clarity or ambiguity with which researchers in theory and practice deal with (1) quantitative methods; (2) data distortion and expectancy effects; (3) as learning or educational acts for the researcher and researched; (4) as engagement and dialogue of the kind which qualitative research valorises; or (5) allow place for the ultimately mysterious – even itself again as a kind of research exploring the human quest for knowledge or the end of it where individuality or a separate voice no longer exists. Or as the phenomenologist Merleau-Ponty (1962: 354) phrases it:

> In the experience of dialogue, there is constituted between the other person and myself a common ground; my thought and his are interwoven into a single fabric, my words and those of my interlocutor are called forth by the stage of the discussion, and they are inserted into a shared operation of which neither of us is the creator. We have here a dual being, where the other is for me no longer a mere bit of behaviour in my transcendental field, nor I in his; we are collaborators for each other in consummate reciprocity.

On the other hand, the heuristic device which has proved so useful in this instance may give way to a completely different way of relating to the meta-theoretical analysis of the multitude of practice of research in this field.

TEMPORARY CONCLUSION

This paper discussed and summarised the qualitative methodology which formed the basis for the construction of a researched text documenting the ethnography of textual and applied understandings of 'the relationship' within a theoretical framework drawn from the psychotherapeutic profession.

The research yielded repeatedly and under a variety of conditions five major categories of discourse about the therapeutic relationship. This original theoretical framework has been found to function at least in some cases as a unifying and inclusive framework which allows for the co-existence of multiple perspectives on the therapeutic relationship as well as developments within any one approach. In this sense it reflects a contemporary postmodernist attempt to give validity to all the 'different stories about stories' (Anderson, 1990: 267) which currently constitute the body of knowledge and practice we call psychotherapy. It also allows for future development.

The inquiry is here presented to my scientific community of peers for constructive feedback, suggestions for improvement and perhaps recognition of this kind of approach (as a valid if tentative beginning) of building a more dialogic relationship between the clinic and the academy.

RECOMMENDATIONS

In particular I am suggesting that the practice of the clinic should not be separated from rigorous and constant research. In this way the therapeutic relationship can be returned to itself. For example, a qualitative research project such as a disciplined and methodologically informed case study is not something to be done once for a dissertation or paper – I believe it needs to be conducted with every client, every session, for as long as a clinician/supervisor works professionally.

Inter-rater reliability in assessing between clinician, client and supervisor whether an intervention was effective or not is but one example of such reflexive practice. The analysis of transcripts or disciplined inquiry by means of writing can augment this. The supervisor is then not someone to whom one is in a hierarchical relationship, but becomes someone who acts as a co-worker researching the clinical as well as the supervisory work at every step. The engagement of the client in this process is also to be explored.

In order to accomplish this, it would be necessary for all clinicians to become familiar and at ease with research, particularly the paradigms and disciplines of qualitative inquiry. It is possible that qualitative research is the method of choice for clinicians because it overcomes the sterility and alienation of much quantitative research in its close relationship with the ambiguities, imponderables and unmeasurables of the healing encounter.

It would therefore also be necessary for all supervisors to be skilled in acting as co-researchers in every case or situation brought to disciplined reflection also subjecting their own clinical and supervisory work to investigation – not once or twice in a life time, but all the time. Although there will probably always be important differences in experience, interests and expertise, conjoining the work of *doing and reflection* in this way might even signal the end of the difference between research and clinical supervision in training.

This could potentially be to the benefit of all concerned – not least the clients. Learning with the client in such a way introduces a praxis of the recovery of knowledge which is surely at the very heart of the therapeutic endeavour itself.

Life is achieved by resolving the tension in responsive feeling and creative activity, in which having is not eliminated but is assimilated to being, in which one and another become I and thou; in which science is integrated with metaphysics; in which autonomy (managing my own affairs) is transcended in liberty, which is participation; in which my body and the world with which it is consubstantial and which enlarges and multiplies its powers is the place in which I bear witness to Being; in which I work out my fidelity and my hope and keep myself open, fluid and ready to spend (Marcel, 1952: 66).

REFERENCES

Anderson, W.T. (1990) *Reality Isn't What it Used to Be*, San Francisco: Harper & Row.
Aronson. J.T. (1994) A pragmatic view of thematic analysis, *The Qualitative Report* 2 (1): 1–3.
Bamberger, J. and Schön, D.A. (1991) Learning as reflective conversation with materials, in F. Steier (ed.) *Research and Reflexivity*, 186–209, London: Sage.
Banister. P., Burman, E., Parker. I., Taylor, M. and Tindall, C. (1994) *Qualitative Methods in Psychology – A Research Guide*, Buckingham: Open University Press.

Bateson, G. (1972) *Steps to an Ecology of Mind*, New York: Ballantine.

Bauman, Z. (1993) *Postmodern Ethics*, Oxford: Blackwell.

Bor, R. and Watts, M. (1993) Training counselling psychologists to conduct research, *Counselling Psychology Review* 8 (4): 20–21.

Christoph-Lemke, C. (1994) Personal communication.

Clandinin, D.J. and Connelly, F.M. (1994) Personal experience methods, in N.K. Denzin and Y.S. Lincoln (eds) *Handbook of Qualitative Research* (pp. 413–427), Thousand Oaks, CA: Sage.

Clarkson, P. (1993) New perspectives in counselling and psychotherapy (or adrift in a sea of change), in P. Clarkson, *On Psychotherapy* (pp. 209–232), London: Whurr.

Clarkson, P. (1995) Counselling psychology in Britain – the next decade, *Counselling Psychology Quarterly* 8 (3): 197–204.

Clarkson, P. (1996) *The Bystander (An End to Innocence in Human Relationships?)*, London: Whurr.

Corsini, R. (1984) *Current Psychotherapies*, Itasca, IL: F.E. Peacock.

Denzin, N.K. and Lincoln, Y.S. (eds) (1994) *Handbook of Qualitative Research*, London: Sage.

Eisner, E.W. (1991) *The Enlightened Eye*, New York: Macmillan.

Farrell, B.A. (1979) Work in small groups: some philosophical considerations, in B. Babington Smith and B.A. Farrell (eds) *Training In Small Groups: A Study of Five Groups* (pp. 103–115), Oxford: Pergamon.

Gergen, K.J. and Gergen, M.M., (1991) Toward reflexive methodologies, in F. Steier (ed.) *Research and Reflexivity* (pp. 76–95), London: Sage.

Guba, E.G. (ed.) (1990) *The Paradigm Dialog*, Newbury Park, CA: Sage.

Guba, E.G., and Lincoln, Y.S. (1994). Competing paradigms in qualitative research, In N.K. Denzin and Y.S. Lincoln (eds) *Handbook of Qualitative Research* (pp. 105–117, London: Sage.

Hinshelwood, R.D. (1990) Editorial, *The British Journal of Psychotherapy*, 7 (2): 119.

Hoshmand, L. (1989) Alternative research paradigms: a review and teaching proposal, *The Counselling Psychologist* 17: 3–79.

Hutcheon, L. (1989) *The Politics of Postmodernism*, New York: Routledge.

Kirk, J. and Miller, M.C. (1986) *Reliability and Validity in Qualitative Research*, London: Sage.

Kvale, S. (1992). Postmodern psychology: a contradiction in terms?, in S. Kvale (ed.) *Psychology and Postmodernism* (pp. 31–57), London: Sage.

Lincoln, Y.S. and Guba, E.G. (1985). *Naturalistic Inquiry*, Beverly Hills, CA: Sage.

Marcel, G. (1952) *The Metaphysical Journal* (B. Wall, trans.), London: Rockliff.

Marcus, G.E. (1994). What Comes (just) after 'post'? The case of ethnography, in N.K. Denzin and Y.S. Lincoln (eds) *Handbook of Qualitative Research* (pp. 563–574), Thousand Oaks, CA: Sage.

Merleau-Ponty, M. (1962) *Phenomenology of Perception* (Colin Smith, trans), London: Routledge & Kegan Paul.

Miles, M.B. and Huberman, A.M. (1994) *Qualitative Data Analysis: An Expanded Sourcebook*, London: Sage.

Moustakas, C. (1994) *Phenomenological Research Methods*, London: Sage.

Norcross, J.C. and M.R. Goldfried, M.R. (eds) (1992) *Handbook of Psychotherapy Integration*, New York: Basic Books.

Polkinghorne, D.E. (1992) Postmodern epistemology of practice, in S. Kvale (ed.) *Psychology and Postmodernism* (pp. 146–165), London: Sage.

Richardson, L. (1994) Writing: a method of inquiry, in N. K. Denzin and Y. S. Lincoln (eds) *Handbook of Qualitative Research*, pp. 516–529. Thousand Oaks, CA: Sage.

Rudestam, K.E. and Newton, R.R. (1992) *Surviving your Dissertation: A Comprehensive Guide to Content and Process*. Thousand Oaks, CA: Sage.

Shelef. L.O. (1994) A simple qualitative paradigm: the asking and the telling, *The Qualitative Report* 2 (1): 1–6.

Shotter. J. (1992) 'Getting in touch': The meta-methodology of a postmodern science of mental life, in S. Kvale (ed.) *Psychology and Postmodernism* (pp. 58–73), London: Sage.

Strauss. A. (1995) Notes on the nature and development of general theories, *Qualitative Inquiry* 1 (1): 7–18.

Chapter 6

Cross-cultural issues in counselling psychology practice

A qualitative study of one multicultural training organisation[1]

Petrūska Clarkson and Yuko Nippoda

ABSTRACT

Counsellors' perspectives on how the issues of race and culture affect counselling, psychology and psychotherapy were explored in this phenomenological inquiry by distributing questionnaires to 108 co-researchers – all the staff and students of one multicultural counselling and psychotherapy training organisation. It was left to the participants to choose the terms to describe themselves (within the context of this research) and thirty-one different self-descriptions emerged. Content analysis and frequency measurements were carried out on the data obtained in response to our inquiry about their experience of how the issues of race and culture affect counselling, psychotherapy and psychology. We identified five categories of statements: positive, negative, neutral ('it does not matter'), qualification ('it takes time') and a category we called 'unclear' (for those statements which were not possible to categorise).

Fifty-four per cent of statements concerned the positive influence or effect of cultural/racial issues on their experience, while 22 per cent were negative statements. Both positive and negative statements were then divided into subcategories according to the content of the statements. Six different categories for positive statements emerged: learning/understanding; commonality/individual differences; reparative/healing; positive emotion; experience of enrichment; and overcoming or awareness of prejudice. Four different categories of negative statements were found: experiencing counsellor's errors/mistakes; prejudice/transference; feeling deskilled/competency issues; and inferior/bad feelings. This being a phenomenological study, we did not attempt to make any generalisation. However, it can be said that for the population we studied (which explicitly affirms the value of cultural difference and the integration of transpersonal dimensions with psychological counselling) racial and cultural influences were subjectively experienced distinctly as very positive as well as moderately negative.

1 We would like to acknowledge with gratitude the input, support and encouragement of our colleagues, especially Melanie Johnson, Kristina Scheuffgen, Tessa Adams, Marie Angelo, Zack Eleftheriadou, Sherna Gayara Chatterjee, Garfield Harmon, Vincent Keter, Len Kofler, Zenobia Nadirshaw, Joan Kendall, Rita Cremona, and all our co-researchers.

INTRODUCTION

We consider it impossible to conduct counselling psychology or any of its related activities out of context. That means that *all* therapeutic activities inevitably and inextricably occur within the idiom and the atmosphere, the climate and the background of the cultures which impinge on it. These 'cultures' or what are called 'structures of feeling' can be related to gender, religion, organisation, profession, sexual orientation, class, nationality, country of origin, parts of the country of ancestral origin, language and so on. Any attempt to pay attention to any one of these in particular inevitably highlights the absence of those not studied, not mentioned. Such an effort also risks highlighting some issue from the viewpoint of 'other', at the same time as trying to bridge a gap, and may appear to point out that there are different banks to a river. No wonder complexly motivated silence, professional avoidances and academic neglect characterise these kinds of issues to the extent that indeed we think they do in our professional literature. So, instead of a token mention or a continuing lament about the invisibility of such difficult and sensitive matters in the indexes and the tables of contents of papers and books, as well as in the very texture and structures of our professional disciplines, we bring this tentative attempt at illuminating some integrated research and practice. We look forward to others furthering the work not only in practice and conversation, but also in print.

Britain is increasingly becoming a multiracial society in which professionals are coming into contact with people from a diverse range of cultural and ethnic groups. On many occasions psychologists/counsellors/therapists may find themselves working with people whose culture is substantially different from their own. On this subject, there is not a great deal of information and guidance for the counselling psychologist in our professional literature. This is acknowledged by Ray Woolfe in the *Handbook of Counselling Psychology* (Woolfe and Dryden, 1996: 17): 'The fact that there is no chapter in this book on counselling psychology in a cross-cultural context is in itself indicative of the distance that has yet to be travelled'. McLeod (1993: 118) also suggests that 'The field of cross-cultural counselling has received relatively little attention in the research literature'; while Nadirshaw argues that

> There is an increasing concern amongst [ethnic] groups about the lack of available, accessible, adequate, appropriate and relevant services to black people. The concern is ever greater in black and minority ethnic communities as they remain at the receiving end of little or no services. That includes psychotherapy and counselling services (Nadirshaw, 1992: 257).

Nadirshaw's excellent paper includes a list of some eleven assumptions which, in her view, interfere in the attempts of traditionally trained helping professionals to deliver such services appropriately.

Kenney (1994) suggests, based on his research, that European-American students have more commitment to the counselling process than African-American and Asian international students. But, as Nadirshaw and others point out, there may be many good reasons for such a finding. According to Littlewood (1992: 6) ethnic minorities are predominantly working class and their 'relative poverty as well as discrimination [make] access to time-consuming and costly therapy . . . less available'. Also, some ethnic minorities have a collective society as a cultural background. This may be associated with the notion that it is experienced as a stigma to benefit from therapy services. However, many more people in the world rely on symbolic healing or culturally traditional approaches to personal development than on West European models. Eleftheriadou (1994) also mentions that clients who are unsure about the effectiveness of the 'talking cure' may benefit from the work of somebody from their own ethnic/cultural background whose role is equivalent to that of a counsellor, such as a psychiatrist or spiritual healer.

In counselling, psychology and psychotherapy, too, the theoretical approaches are mainly (if not exclusively) based on White Eurocentric models with little awareness of the influence or inescapable context of ethnicity. This, in itself, as Clarkson has discussed elsewhere (Clarkson, 1996), is oppressive. Helman (1994: 280), too, writes:

> Where patient and therapist come from similar backgrounds, they may share many assumptions about the likely origin, nature and treatment of psychological disorders. However, the proliferation of new 'talk therapies' has meant that, in many cases, the patients may have to *learn* this world view gradually, acquiring with each session a further understanding of the concepts, symbols and vocabulary that comprise it. This can be seen as a form of 'acculturation', whereby they acquire a new mythic world couched, for example, in terms of the Freudian, Jungian, Kleinian or Laingian models. This mythic world, shared eventually by patient and therapist, is often inaccessible to the patient's family or community, who in any case are excluded from the consultation.

Farrell (1979) makes a similar point when he describes how participants are declared 'cured' or 'trained' when they have adopted the WOT (way of talking) of the trainer (or the counselling psychologist).

Anecdotal evidence suggests that most training schools do not pay attention to cultural aspects in ways which satisfy either the trainees on the programmes or the many who apply to come into counselling psychology. (This is irrespective of 'equal opportunities statements' in their literature.) In our experience there are usually only one or two black or Asian people in most professional gatherings (conferences, training courses, etc.); people from a White European background usually predominate.

There are many instances of counselling and psychotherapy sessions which are terminated prematurely because, in the dyad of counsellor/psychotherapist and client from a different culture, the client did not feel understood culturally by the counsellor/psychotherapist. There are probably many which are never even spoken of because the influence of prejudice is out of awareness or because the individuals involved cannot find a way to speak about it. All of us are creatures of one or more cultures – 'structures of feeling'. The notion of culture-free counselling psychology is as implausible as a value-free or neutral counselling (or clinical) psychology (Newnes, 1996).

In this study, we wanted to get closer to how the people concerned perceive the issues of race and culture affecting counselling, psychology and psychotherapy, particularly focusing on the 'culture' of their training school.

AIMS AND OBJECTIVES OF THIS STUDY

Our research population is different from most of the research populations represented in the literature, therefore little can be transferred or generalised. Our intention is more modest: to provide a phenomenological inquiry into the perception of race and cultural issues of a complete group of trainers and staff of a counselling programme. It is a programme dedicated to the valuing of cultural difference, the integration of transpersonal and counselling perspectives. Uncharacteristically, it does not primarily represent 'minority' cultures, but people from all over the world, many who normally live in 'majority cultures' but whom we assume, by virtue of the fact that we inhabit the same planet, have all been touched, in one form or another, by prejudice.

In this project, we were not studying the outcome of therapeutic, psychological counselling or the effectiveness of training in a multicultural environment explicitly committed to the values of appreciation of diversity and integration. Phenomenological research as a particular kind of qualitative research methodology attempts to get close to, if not exactly 'capture', the qualities of human experience, as the humans themselves describe their own subjectivity. According to Moustakas (1994: 21) these aspects are not 'approachable through quantitative approaches'. Our work here does not set out to prove or disprove anything in the ways which can be the important goals of quantitative research.

The case for qualitative research as an adjunct, or alternative but valid and valuable approach, to the study of human experience phenomena is further outlined in many other contemporary sources (Denzin and Lincoln (1994) and Polkinghorne (1992), for example). A recent issue of *Counselling Psychology Review* (February 1996, Vol. 11, No. 1) deals with this subject in depth and some of the papers from this journal are reproduced elsewhere in this book.

It is not very easy to find a chapter regarding cross-cultural issues in the books on counselling psychology and psychotherapy, whereas people talk about theories and perspectives on various approaches and other issues. The current situation in these fields is that cross-cultural issues are secondhand. What hinders people from working on this, even though everybody is in touch with culture and our research shows that most people are concerned about cross-cultural issues?

During the process of writing up this paper, we became aware again of the sensitivity and care-fullness experienced in dealing with this delicate area. History and cultural developments bring about changes in what is considered 'politically correct' and sometimes these attempts at formal control of our collective cultural shadows work paradoxically. We wondered whether the inhibiting effect of such fears may be one of the reasons why so few people work, research or publish their opinions and experiences on issues concerning race and culture? We would hope that all sincere work can be welcomed, improved on and encouraged by all who have an interest in this field.

For the purpose of this research, it is important to be in touch with clients' racial and cultural background, their process and what it means to them. Moreover, D'Ardenne and Mahtani (1989) suggest that it is essential that counselling psychologists and psychotherapists are aware of their own cultural views and biases before dealing with clients' points of view. In his profound chapter, 'Racism and psychotherapy; working with racism in the consulting room: an analytical view', Lennox Thomas (1992) also draws special attention to this kind of awareness when he introduces the therapeutic process of the dyads of the white therapist and the black patient, the black therapist and the white patient, and the black therapist and the black patient.

It is extremely difficult for any form of racism, accrued from a lifetime of socialisation, to be brought to personal awareness, yet this is indeed what needs to take place, so that our practice is not dominated by what can be termed 'societal racism'. In order to work effectively across cultures and with people of different colour, psychotherapists, I would suggest, need first to attend to their own racism, their own prejudices, and their own projections on other racial and cultural groups. Personal attitudes and assumptions need to be re-worked and re-examined (Thomas, 1992: 133–45).

The basic point of counselling and psychotherapy is 'Who am I?' To know and understand oneself, one has to take into account racial and cultural aspects, since race and culture are essential parts of everybody. 'How does it feel to be *you* with *your* race and cultural background?' would be a very important question to ask yourself. Then you can get to know your own process and experience your subjectivity; and then you can search for where you are in terms of other races and cultures.

Psychological counsellors and psychotherapists have many opportunities to see clients from different cultural backgrounds nowadays.

Cultural factors are important to counsellors, and they have the responsibility of learning all they can about the cultural background of their clients. It is too much to ask that they become specialists in all the cultures of the world; it should not be impossible for them, however, to become aware of the range of values and patterns of behavior of which human societies and individuals are capable and to learn as much as they can about the particular ethnic groups that constitute their clientele. Many counsellors have asked themselves what there is in counseling that is universal and what aspects need tailoring to meet the specific needs of specific groups. I see no alternative to developing awareness of both the universals and the cultural particulars. Finally, counselors should never lose sight of the fact that no two individuals are fully identical in their needs, their problems, and their values and goals. We cannot remind ourselves too often that these three approaches – to human beings in general, to members of particular cultural groups, and to the individual in his or her uniqueness – all require our full attention (Klineberg, 1987: 34).

OUR PERSONAL SITUATEDNESS IN RELATION TO THE THEME

In accord with this and the philosophy and procedures of qualitative research, it becomes necessary therefore to indicate our personal situatedness to the themes. One of the reasons the group were willing to participate in the research may be, as a participant wrote (unsolicited) on the questionnaire, because the senior counselling psychologist researcher is well known in this community for her work on bystanding (Clarkson, 1996). Clarkson's interest seeded from personal experience of discrimination, injustice and prejudice from a variety of perspectives as well as growing up in a culture where, for example, the *majority* of the people of the very heterogeneous country were excluded by law from participation in government. Bystanding is more fully contextualised and developed in the book on that particular theme (Clarkson, 1996).

The other co-author is from a homogeneous society. Since coming to this multicultural society in the UK, she has been working on cross-cultural issues, in particular cultural transition (Nippoda, 1993) and transcultural collective psychology. The more she has worked, the more she has realised the complexity and the confusing aspects of the issues. Her views have also changed in various ways during the time – and continue to change. She is developing her own theory and perspectives. This research is part of her ongoing learning process from which she hopes her work in the future will develop and grow.

CONCEPTUAL REALMS AND LITERATURE REVIEW

Because of its scope our study implicates all of psychology – 'being human' – and we looked specifically at the body of work on the themes of race, racism, ethnicity, cross-cultural, transcultural and acultural practice, identity, language, political science and poststructuralism, amongst many others. A thorough overview is left to others more expert than ourselves, since an insistence on its achievement before attempting a study such as this could paralyse individual researchers from even starting a fraction of the task.

Most books and articles on cross-cultural issues focus on how to deal with those issues within a multicultural context, rather than within traditional Eurocentric counselling and psychotherapy models. D'Ardenne and Mahtani (1989) explain how the relationship of ethnicity between therapist/counsellor and client could affect the counselling/therapy process. However, many books which deal with cross-cultural counselling/therapy concentrate on the difference between traditional therapy/counselling and ethnocentric therapy/counselling. They do not tend to pay enormous or detailed attention to how these issues are perceived and experienced by people from all kinds of cultural backgrounds.

Transference can be used in a different way depending on the approaches. D'Ardenne and Mahtani (1989) introduce Smith's (1985: 79) description about transference in a transcultural setting. They write:

> For our purposes [transcultural counselling] 'transference' may be defined as the attitudes and feelings placed by the client on to the counsellor in the therapeutic relationship. In our own experience, 'transference' has an additional dimension. Clients who have had a lifetime of cultural and racial prejudice will bring the scars of these experiences to the relationship.

Thomas (1992: 136) also explains that 'It is the therapist's task to recognise and explore pathological fit along racial lines in the transference. This, of course, is not easy when the countertransference is also powerfully bent on enactment'.

There is little research in cross-cultural counselling, as noted by Lowenstein (1987: 41): 'There has been virtually no research on the subject of intercultural counseling in Great Britain'. Perhaps the best overview is contained in Kareem and Littlewood (1992) to which all readers are referred. It explores themes, interpretations and practice, and includes case examples for teaching and group discussion, inserting quantitative research results in intercultural context. Moorhouse (1992: 98), in her review of past research and the project at Nafsiyat Intercultural Therapy Centre, comes to the conclusion that 'the view that black and ethnic minority people cannot benefit from formal therapy is wrong. The research also suggests, albeit with small numbers, that people who show severe symptoms as determined by conventional rating scales may benefit from psychotherapy'. At the 1994 conference of the Transcultural Counselling/ Psychotherapy Forum held at Goldsmiths College, University of London, it was reported by Nafsiyat that 'Research (a research project funded by the DHSS) left many questions unanswered. Further research is necessary' (Adams, 1996: 40).

Other attempts have been sporadic and are not very well known. Eleftheriadou (1994: 79) mentions that 'We do need further cross-cultural research in all the social science disciplines and more integration of the information. Because research has been done within different disciplines, there has not yet been synthesis of all the information obtained'. Where there is research which we have not found, this paper will hopefully act as a call to interested organisations and people to share such research, compare findings and perhaps collaborate on further projects.

In 1989 Acharyya *et al.* found that 'the subtle differences of experience and response [of second- or third-generation immigrants] have yet to be studied' (Moorhouse, 1992: 86). Our interest was not in prescription, but in the *description* of their experience; in fleshing out in words the *experience* of these people (and not primarily in generalisation from this population to a wider one by means of 'objective scientism'). However, speculation in order to generate hypotheses for future research is to be welcomed – as is any serious effort to increase our understanding in this most complex and sensitive area which affects every single one of us – all the time. It is, however, unlikely that a more racially and culturally heterogeneous group on one counselling programme of this size in Britain could be found – and perhaps even elsewhere. The commonality between the participants – if any – was an explicit commitment to multicultural appreciation and the integration of transpersonal concerns with personal growth and development, values which prioritise growth and the richness of diversity and difference.

In our research we have focused on phenomenological experience of race and culture. Everybody is unique and has different experiences. Conventional researches focus on how therapists/counsellors use diagnoses for ethnic minorities, what kind of interventions would be appropriate or suitable for ethnic minorities, or the outcome of the therapy/counselling. In other words, many research projects focus on the ways in which practitioners deal differently with ethnic minorities compared to white European clients. Of course, it is not appropriate to use the same approaches and interventions with everybody, and practitioners have to pay attention to cultural differences. However, when we were doing this research, somebody said that they are not an ethnic minority; in their culture and society, they are an ethnic majority. We gathered the impression that the phrase 'ethnic minority' and the idea of 'how to deal with ethnic minorities' can perhaps contribute to, as well as ameliorate, the marginalisation and isolation of people to whom, for good or ill, or a mixture of intentions, such nominations are applied.

COMPARISON WITH NADIRSHAW (1992)

Nadirshaw focuses on how traditional Eurocentric therapists/counsellors perceive the issues of ethnic minorities and ways of dealing with such a clientele. Nadirshaw makes several recommendations for good practice which includes examining the relevance of culture in the therapeutic process and the conduct of therapy within the cultural context, although she stresses the acceptance of different value systems and the development of cultural sensitivity. She quotes the findings of Fernando (1991) which showed that expert knowledge about a culture alone does not necessarily lead to successful therapeutic outcomes. Nadirshaw mentions the importance of setting, non-verbal facility, ability to read emotions from other cultures, the necessity of taking into account the transference toward the very therapeutic process itself, contextual familiarity, 'ability to be sympathetic to the oppressed position of the client and create positions of equal power and control', the ideal of having worked through the counsellor's own racist attitudes, beliefs and prejudices and the culturally different influences of gender, the perception of the therapist/counsellor, and the goals and tasks.

A thorough assessment of how the combined effects of deprivation, disadvantage and racism impinge on the client's personality and identity needs to be undertaken. . . . Imposition of therapist's views about such matters (i.e. labelling, categorizing and classifying) should be avoided and the practice of therapy/counselling in a non-judgemental, non-oppressive manner should be endorsed (Nadirshaw, 1992: 260).

Finally, Nadirshaw (1992: 260) recommends appropriate and relevant training courses, such as the one run by Nafsiyat, as 'models that mainstream training counselling courses could learn from'. Her research is a call to people who could afford to think about other ways than the current ones. Although our research talks about the current situation of the issues, our focus was different from Nadirshaw's. We have focused on the subjective experience of the counselling trainees and on how the issues of race and culture affect counselling/psychotherapy as a whole, rather than on how to deal with clients from ethnic minority groups. In this research we wanted to assess people's perception of issues of race and culture.

METHODOLOGY

Quantitative and qualitative research

This is phenomenological research; it relies on the subjective, phenomenological experience of people, and not their objectification. This research tries to represent these views as assumption-free as possible, although we of course acknowledge that assumptions are always present. By presenting them to colleagues before and after publication such explicit and implicit assumptions can at least be brought overtly into discussion and mutual exploration. The report of such responses is intended as another, future phase of the current research project. However, since we also employed figure and percentage analysis of the descriptions of subjective experience in terms of categorisation, it can be said that we also employed quantitative methods to work with and communicate about our data.

Selection of participants

Many organisations were approached when we were seeking institutes which would be willing and able to participate in the research project. We formally contacted some thirty-two likely organisations for their co-operation in the distribution of the questionnaire. Forty-four completed questionnaires were returned, mostly from people who described themselves as white Europeans.

Only one organisation responded favourably within our time frame with a substantial number of replies – 108. Forty-five of these were from white European cultural backgrounds and sixty from black or Asian cultural backgrounds. It so happened that it was a counselling training organisation where people from thirty nationalities, speaking an even larger number of languages, were in full-time training with trainers, many supervisors and psychotherapists, from a wide range of cultural backgrounds. We think it would be rare in Britain to find a training organisation of this size with such a diversity of cultural backgrounds.

All the people in this organisation have been exposed to counselling or counselling variants such as growth groups, personal effectiveness facilitation, spiritual direction, psychotherapy from UKCP registered psychotherapists or psychotherapeutic counselling psychology for short or long periods. Anonymity was respected in this questionnaire in order to facilitate free descriptions of the participants, and some of the participants received a draft of the final paper to which they could freely add comments. This allowed for triangulation (Barker, Pistrang and Elliott, 1994: 81) of our research results.

For the purposes of this study we have not factor analysed the specifics of these types or periods of experience because our interest at this stage was in (a) how people may describe themselves in terms of race and culture, and (b) how they may think or feel about issues of race and culture that affect counselling and psychotherapy. It was enough that 98 per cent had some experience (and the 2 per cent who did not report it, we assume, knowing their general history, would probably have had experiences similar to counselling – for example, in preparation to come on the course). The second question was thus a kind of screening device and not further analysed for the purposes of this research at this stage.

INSTRUMENTATION

The short questionnaire used for this inquiry consisted of three sentences to be completed freely by each participant. They were given some twenty minutes to complete it after which all questionnaires were handed in to the senior researcher.

The three questions were as follows:

1 I would describe myself as —— (For example, Black, Asian, Afro-Caribbean, White European, etc.)

2 (a) My experience of counselling, psychology and psychotherapy is —— (For example, I have been in counselling or psychotherapy with an Asian counsellor or Black or White Irish psychotherapist for —— many years.)

  (b) I have been the counsellor, psychologist or psychotherapist of —— (For example, Asian, Afro-Jamaican, White European or British clients, etc. for —— months during and/or after training – whatever applies to you.)

3 In my experience/opinion, issues of race and culture affect counselling, psychology and psychotherapy in the following ways ——

This research questionnaire was not designed with pre-made boxes or specifically pre-packaged categories within which people had to 'insert' themselves. The richness of the data obtained in this way supported the open-ended nature of our research questionnaire design – even though from a quantitative view certain 'facts' may be hidden or obscured.

Method of analysis

We collected and typed up the answers from the whole survey. We sub-divided the answers to the three questions by scissoring. Each question had its own section. The first question was divided into the categories of ethnicity which the participants used to describe themselves. The result is shown in Table 6.1. p. 106).

In the second question, we could only pick up the counsellor and client pairings of those who indicated both their own ethnic origin and that of their counsellors. We divided the counsellors and clients into three categories: White, Black and Asian/Indian, and checked the pairing patterns in order to extract the percentage of the pairings. Nonparametric measures of association (Phi co-efficient and Cramer's V) were employed to estimate the significance of these relationships.

The answers to the third question were divided into 322 statements. At first we put them into five themed categories: positive statements, negative statements, neutral (issues do not matter), qualification, and unclear. Qualification here means, similar to its definition in the *Shorter Oxford English Dictionary* (1973), 'to modify in some respect'.

We furthermore put positive statements into six categories of themes: learning/understanding; commonality/individual differences; reparative/healing; positive emotion; experience of enrichment; and overcoming or awareness of prejudice. We also put negative statements into four categories: experiencing counsellor's errors/mistakes; prejudice/transference; feeling deskilled/competency issues; and inferior/bad feelings.

In order to attempt some measure of inter-rater reliability, we categorised the statements separately on three separate occasions, by three different raters, from three different ethnic groups: British Afro-Caribbean, White South African and Oriental Japanese. After that, we compared our categorisation. On negatives, we had five disagreements, one of which was unclear. On positives, we had no disagreements but two were unclear. Then we counted the number of the statements in each category and found that the percentage inter-rater reliability was 91 per cent.

RESULTS

(1) The identities of the trainee counsellors in Question 1 are described by themselves in at least thirty-one different ways (see Table 6.1).
(2) In Question 2, because of the nature of the question, we did not get sufficient data at this stage of our study. The advantage and purpose of the style of the question was to get each participant's own description; the disadvantage was that we lost other kinds of data. (This can be rectified and followed up in future.)
(3) To Question 3, we received 174 answers of positive statements, seventy-one of negative statements, twenty-nine neutral comments (the issues of race and

culture do not matter), twenty-five unclear answers and twenty-three statements of qualification (see Figure 6.1).

The percentages of the five main categories are:

- Positive statements: 54 per cent;
- Negative statements: 22 per cent;
- Neutral comments (e.g. that the issue of race does not matter): 9 per cent;
- Unclear: 8 per cent;
- Qualification: 7 per cent.

Table 6.1 Self-descriptions of trainee counsellors (obtained from replies to Question 1)

White European	22	Multicultural, Anglo Irish roots	1
Asian	20	Irish woman	1
Black African	16	White American USA male	1
African	11	North USA Caucasian	1
European	4	Irish Catholic	1
White Irish European	3	Irish	1
Black	3	Human being European	1
White	2	Brown Indian	1
European White Male	2	Asian male	1
Black South African	2	Asian Indian	1
White South African	2	British Context White	1
Black coloured human being	2	Human being with brown skin	1
(As above) with intellect and will	1	A person	1
White European Italian	1	A person who relates to persons	1
Indian Black	1	Child of God	1
White European Female	1		

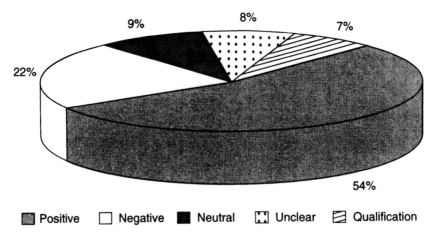

Figure 6.1 Pie diagram to show categories of replies according to percentage

Table 6.2 Subdivision of positive and negative responses

Positives
Learning/understanding	44
Commonality/individual differences	35
Overcoming or awareness of prejudice	31
Reparative/healing	29
Positive emotion	20
Experience of enrichment	15

Negatives
Inferior/bad feelings	24
Prejudice/transference	22
Experiencing counsellor's errors/mistakes	17
Feeling de-skilled/competency issues	8

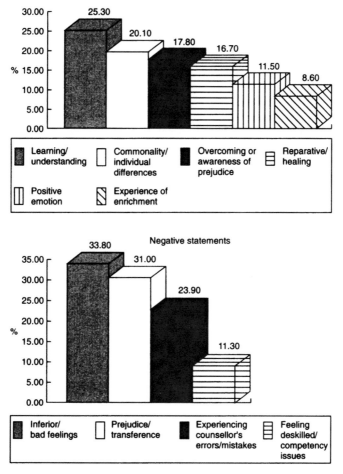

Figure 6.2 Graph to show positive and negative statements according to percentage

DISCUSSION OF RESULTS

In respect to Question 1, there are some distinctive patterns. Half of the categories (sixteen out of thirty-one) and more than half of the statements (sixty-one out of 108) referred to skin colour. Eighteen people explained their nationalities: three Indians, nine Europeans, two Americans and four South Africans. Black people did not enter their nationalities at all, except the South Africans. What does that mean? According to one of the assumptions which Nadirshaw (1992) lists, traditional therapists/counsellors might believe and act as if 'Black communities (Asians, Afro-Caribbeans) represent homogeneous groups, sharing a common culture and heritage, without acknowledging the diversity that exists within each of these groups'. Our findings may indicate that she may be correct about this. However, this obviously does not mean that the black community lacks consciousness of diversity and a sense of nationality in other contexts.

There were not many people who described themselves as just a human being or person without mentioning race and national identities; it seems to be important for most people to describe race and cultural aspects in order to describe themselves. (People show high awareness of race and cultural identity within themselves.)

In respect to Question 3, as can be seen in Figure 6.1, we divided the responses into five categories of statements. We found many kinds of answers but there were some similarities and we categorised them in accordance with the individual's subjective perception.

Five main categories (Figure 6.1)

Positive

This pertains to the experience, through the issues of race and culture, brought about by some kind of change for the individual in a positive way. They have learned something new, experienced different things, and broadened their points of view, thus overcoming past hurt or becoming aware of their own process.

Negative

This indicates that their experience of the effect of race and cultural issues was that of a negative effect on counselling and psychology – feelings of failure, incompetence, anger from prejudice, and so on.

Unclear

The responses in this category showed that the individual acknowledged some kind of effect from the issues of race and culture, but was unable clearly and precisely to articulate what that effect might be. Since we did not personally interview many of the participants (yet), we had to understand what was meant from the sentences; some were ambiguous or did not give the detail to make it clear whether the intended meaning was positive *or* negative – or may have implied both. For example, 'issues of race have affected me greatly when it comes to other races' and 'issues of race have affected my experience because we have different racial backgrounds'. Other statements explained how, but they did not give a sense of evaluation – for instance, 'spiritually', 'socially', 'politically', 'psychologically' or 'economically'. However, every statement in this category suggests that the issues of race and culture have *affected* their counselling and psychotherapy .

Qualification

The replies in this category did not give an immediate reaction of effect from the experience but they spoke of a feeling that it had affected them and that, as time goes by, things become better. Also, some mentioned the language barriers and how after some time this might give positive effect. For example, 'It took me some time to trust her because of her colour'; 'An initial fear that I might not be understood in my own context'; 'I would open up gradually and share more as trust builds'; and 'I was most affected by a racist client in that I struggled to remain "Rogerian" and yet was empathic to his mugging that reinforced his stereotypical beliefs'. Hence, it is not to say the experiences were positive straightaway, and indeed there maybe some limitation to the degree of positiveness.

Neutral or 'it does not matter'

This category denotes that basically the participants did not think that the issues of race and culture affected them. A few participants commented that 'Race does not matter', 'Not the colour or race' and 'Issues of race did not arise'. However, others stated, 'I am also aware of the commonality of human experience irrespective of race and culture', and 'Human experience is the best teacher so I need to accept and respect persons rather than race and culture'. They focused more on the commonality of human beings no matter how different the race and culture. They may be denying, ignoring or minimising the cultural issues first maybe in order to stress the commonality. Of course, it should not be assumed that therefore other aspects were not implied or perhaps taken for granted within the context. However, the raters wished to err in the direction of not 'reading into' the statements and refraining from imposing spurious assumptions on the categorisation which all three of us (from our very different backgrounds) could not easily agree about. This neutral category is therefore *different* from the sub-category of commonality *and* individual differences in the positive category, and we will explain this difference later.

As a whole, from the research, 91 per cent of the statements showed that there was some effect from the experience of issues of race and culture. Of course the very fact that we asked the question shaped the consciousness of people's responses. Although the difficulties with using either or both these terms are understood, these are the terms which featured in conversation with participants as well as in the professional literature and the acronyms of groups committed to improvements within such universes of discourse and practice.

Sub-categories of positive statements

We divided the positive statements into six categories, as previously discussed (see Table 6.2). The percentages are shown in Figure 6.2.

Learning/understanding

In their replies in this category, the participants raised points about learning something about their own culture as well as other cultures, about their own limitation, and about acceptance of people from other cultures. For example, 'I have better understandings of the good and bad things in my own culture as a result'; 'Issues of race have made me aware how we need each other in order to survive. Whites had always been paternalistic towards us blacks but I have discovered little by little how I have to affirm myself in this White-dominated world. I really think the only way is to accept that these racial differences are in themselves a richness that has to be appreciated. Each race has to learn from the other. It has made me aware that we all need self-criticism'; '[Certain cultural beliefs] are not absolutes and can be changed depending on how much a person has allowed themselves to know about and their willingness to change their ideas which they may hold due to lack of true knowledge about it'; and 'Only coming into this multicultural setting have I been able to put a more clear and balanced view on my perception of different cultures'.

Commonality/individual differences

We kept these themes together in one category. We judged from the statements that the participants came to respect people from other cultures as human beings with their difference and their uniqueness. For example, 'We all have feelings and emotions', 'and begin to appreciate their uniqueness', 'Having been here and experiencing different cultures and races, I found out that all of us (whether black or white or brown or whatnot) we do have needs, problems, strengths, good and bad points'. Also, compared to 'neutral' or 'it does not matter' in the main categories, the statements here tell that as a result of experience through race and cultural issues, the participants have realised that human beings have a commonality no matter how great the cultural differences, and yet everybody is different and unique. These participants have accepted that these issues affect them – 'I have learned to appreciate the people for who they are', 'I have learned to look at the human being' – and statements in this section on the whole had a different feel to them from those in the 'neutral' or 'it does not matter' category. Oerter (1996) addresses this theme and acknowledges that individuals across cultures have commonalities in physical and psychological aspects.

Reparative/healing

The replies in this category showed that many people addressed how they have been healed from the experience of race and culture issues. 'Most of the fear on how to face White people was cleared during these sessions'; 'They have helped me to deal with past hurts coming from friction with people of other races'; 'the issue of race has affected myself in the sense I overcome the complex of inferiority I had'. Some mentioned a sense of freedom: 'l was freed'; or healing: 'My experience of counselling is that I have been healed!'; pride: 'to consider myself as good as other different races and appreciate my racial belonging'. It is the element of reparation, the experience of a therapeutic healing, that separates this section from the *Learning and Understanding* category, which fundamentally seemed to have to do more with knowledge.

Positive emotion

Here the responses were a description of how positively the participants felt about the whole process of race and cultural issues in terms of emotion or affect. They used terms and phrases such as: 'openness', 'tolerance', 'free', 'good and happy because I felt there is nothing wrong with my culture', and 'live life fully in order to enjoy the here and now'. These responses focused on feelings like, 'I did not feel threatened'; 'Sometimes it was very touching and very meaningful . . . in the way of relationship'. Though they may contain an element of healing, we felt that because these statements did not specifically mention the individual's past experience in comparison with the present situation and describe how the individual had changed, they should be in a separate category.

Experience of enrichment

Contrary to much of the writing in this field which tends to focus on the problems and the problematique, along with an acknowledgement of negative experience in this group (see below), there was also a prominent theme of 'enrichment'. Here are some examples: 'Cross-cultural has greatly broadened and enriched my experience'; 'Issues of race have sometimes given me the joy of entering a wider world'; 'Helped me to grow'; 'I really think the only way is to accept that these racial differences are in themselves a richness that has to be appreciated'; and 'In general I was enriched by being with persons of different cultures and race'.

Overcoming or awareness of prejudice

In cultural issues, it is common for people to have prejudices. In an extensive discussion of the theoretical and psychoanalytic components (Clarkson, 1993), I discussed how the root of transference is 'to carry across' and how in that sense it is usually a necessary component of all learning – anticipation based on previous learning. It is only when prejudice or anticipation becomes rigid and not capable of changing in the light of updated information or new experiences that it can be said to be 'neurotic', prejudiced, unhelpful or damaging. On the positive side, the responses of this inquiry which we categorised as 'overcoming or awareness of prejudice' described something about becoming aware of, and dealing with, their own prejudice: 'For the first time I became aware of my prejudice'; 'They have helped me deal with my racial prejudice'; and 'as part of the training I had to work through my prejudice'. It sounds as though they have gained realisation in order to go forward. How the effects of prejudice and racism were healed or overcome therapeutically through the counselling process in this setting may be the subject of another in depth study in future. The very fact that the element of prejudice was addressed in the negative statements, too, opens possibilities for comparison and learning.

Sub-categories of negative statements

We divided the negative statements into four categories, as previously discussed (see Table 6.2). The percentages are shown in Figure 6.2.

Experiencing counsellor's errors/mistakes

The responses here showed how difficult people find it to deal with people from different cultures and that notwithstanding the best of intentions negative experiences do occur. Failure to open up because of the cultural difference on both sides makes the relationship artificial and difficult: 'Over-sensitivity to accommodate the cultural differences has led to an artificiality in the sessions' and 'lack of freedom of speech at times'. Some people mentioned 'authentic' Europeans and colluding black people. Others focused on the power issue: 'Working with a European counsellor I felt I was playing the '"Yes father"/ victim role of conformism', and 'a victim role because the counsellors acted a domineering role'. Holloway (1995) explains the power issues in the supervisory relationship. She cites the research of McRoy *et al.* (1986) on cross-cultural issues in supervision which found that, although supervisees perceive the supervisors as sensitive to cultural issues, they find it difficult to talk about these issues openly. On the whole, statements indicated that issues of race and culture, as experienced by our respondents, created some difficulties, errors and even failures in counselling on a number of occasions.

Prejudice/transference

These statements contained awareness of the participants' own experience of racism and prejudice during counselling sessions, and their feelings of not being understood: 'I experience injustice in putting people in colours, since there is prejudice and stereotype'. Some people mentioned how prejudice and racism affected the therapy relationship. 'Taking for granted that the person comes from a completely different background has caused some embarrassment at times'; and 'Racism has affected my relationship in that she could not understand some patterns of my behaviour'. They mention their own racism and prejudice, too: 'On an occasion or two, my prejudice blocked my [relationship or] understanding of the issue'; 'I am sure I would have been prejudiced if counselling across the colour'.

Lack of understanding, due to prejudice, could lead to feelings of anger or bitterness: 'The racism has affected me to a certain level, that I have not been able to express myself fully in case the other people did not understand me or made a judgement on me'; 'The feelings of bitterness because of sufferings due to racism', and 'I feel angry when I hear the prejudices of the Europeans about Africans'. These statements indicate that experiences of blockage in counselling relationships may be due to racism and prejudice. The way in which collective prejudices become sedimented as individual transference is well established. In our research we came upon two statements of transference and countertransference which, in view of the common usage of the term, we sense as intrinsically negative: 'I still experience transference and countertransference of my past bad experience' and 'I feel countertransference from my counsellor'.

Feeling deskilled/competency issues

The statements in which experiences of feeling or being deskilled and lacking competency arose did not specifically mention mistakes in counselling but, because of the sensitivity of the issues experienced by the participants, their statements seem to reflect that they felt deskilled and incompetent. For example: 'I feel incompetent even if I have experienced counselling people'; 'I was not in a position to give the correct empathy when counselling the other person'; '[Issues of race and culture] crop up in the nitty gritty of everyday relationship. I often catch myself being critical/impatient'; and 'This has led me to develop a lot of defence mechanisms in order to survive in this world'.

The counsellors were also criticised on what sounded like skills and competency issues: 'Black brought dreams which White did not fully understand'; 'my issues could have been better dealt with by an African who wouldn't have difficulties in getting what I was saying' as well as 'sometimes I feel like I'm being humiliated and over-inquired'.

Inferior/bad feelings

These are potentially overlapping with the above category, but we separated general bad and inferior feeling statements from those which seem to refer more to the counselling process. This category contains statements of 'feeling inferior', 'feeling oppressed', 'feeling small among other races' and 'exploited'. One participant 'worries about fundamentalism' and for others, the whole experience of race and cultural issues means something bad for them: 'I have been sure white people would not understand my issues as a black person'.

COMPARISONS

More than half of the people in this survey told us that they had had *positive* experiences through these issues, rather than negative. It is possible that the very exposure in a training setting to so many cultures (some thirty languages, twenty-three nationalities) develops or helps to develop a more positive mindset in staff and trainees than is produced in xenophobic or predominantly unicultural organisational or national cultures. Certainly it has been found that one of the primary functions of stereotypes is to preserve the social distance (Taijfel, 1981) and thus to resist the acknowledgement of relationship.

This finding can of course not be directly compared, but it can be considered in the context of the research of Sutter and McCaul (1993). They found that respondents with more social contact with immigrants, as well as those who had positive experiences with immigrants, tended to score higher on the tolerance measure which they developed and tested. Proximity and acquaintanceship are documented as important in changing attitude (Krech, Crutchfield and Ballachey, 1962).

The category of statements which is included under both positive and negative headings is *prejudice*. However, the content of the statements was understood to be different. In the positive statements, the participants indicate that the *awareness of prejudice* was a significant experience for them. However, these responses did not give details of any personal change. More information about the individual's feelings and the affects in the counselling process were given in the *negative* category: for example, 'However, even though this happened, I still experience transference and countertransference from my past bad experience'.

Comparing other sub-categories of positives and negatives, the positives mentioned more about what they gained through the experience and thus implied a therapeutic process; however, in the negatives, there were many statements regarding counsellors' qualities or abilities. On the whole, we found that quite a large number of people feel that the issues of race/racism and culture affect counselling in ways which they experience as positive. This predominance is enhanced when positive statements including qualification are added on. The presence of negative statements with an authentic ring to them could indicate that these statements of positive experiences and value should be taken at least equally seriously in our receipt of this report.

Implications for the practice of psychotherapeutic psychological counselling

There is no study of which we are aware for direct comparison (a) involving this variety of racial and cultural backgrounds; (b) a counselling/psychotherapy training institution; (c) so explicitly concerned with the integration of counselling and transpersonal dimensions to be utilised in many different countries of the world.

The literature reviewed does not deal in depth with many of the issues raised and space prohibits much further discussion here. However, we would draw attention to the kind of fit between the 're-search' we have engaged in here and our search to resonate to the experiences of our co-researchers in this project as different from the ideals and paradigms of psychological research which espouse 'the heuristics of suspicion', privilege objectivity, accept the possibility of neutrality in the researchers and disqualify responsible involvement (Banister, Burman, Parker, Taylor and Tindall, 1994). The kind of phenomenological approach which we have begun to approximate here questions not only traditional quantitative academic psychological research with its factor analyses and null hypotheses, but in particular questions the ideological substructures which support, sustain and reward compliance with such Northern Eurocentric models. We wanted to know: What's it like for you? rather than: What is or is not the case to what percentage of probability? in order to reliably and validly generalise from this particular to the rest of the world.

If we have achieved only a possibility of an awareness of a variety of points of view and multiplicities of experience, and some beginnings of ways to reflect seriously on these, the effort has been worthwhile. Helms (1989) reviewed and compared papers by several authors on racial identity counselling which implicate various degrees of Eurocentrism. One of the most important Eurocentric values is considered to be dualistic thinking. We have attempted to conduct this research in a way which allows for multiple perspectives – the possibility of doing many different kinds of research – quantitative, qualitative, interview, immersion, phenomenological, observational, action research, etc. We believe space needs to be created now for non-binary systems of human experience and that Ani (1994) puts the case best:

> The main cultural force that dictated the creation of the myth [of 'objectivity' and the 'uses of scientism'] and supported its continuance was the fact that it provided pseudoscientific support for the imposition of European ideology. . . . 'Knowing' and 'understanding' then become more humanly and existentially meaningful than what has been meant by 'scientific knowledge' – defined Eurocentrically (p. 518).

It leads as well to the questioning of the 'scientific character' of *any* information gathering and its subsequent interpretation. Maquet concludes that subjectivity is encountered *throughout* the 'scientific process'. He attempts to redefine the concept of 'objectivity'. Conventionally, in keeping with Platonic epistemology, it meant 'conformity with the object' and independence from the subject. But, says Maquet, 'the content of knowledge is never entirely independent; rather it is the result of the meeting of the subject and the object' [Maquet, 1964: 54]. This, he says, is true of 'scientific knowledge' generally, for there is always the possibility of different perspectives. Maquet suggests therefore that the only requisite for 'objectivity' be that one's observations and conclusions are partly determined by the object; elimination of the subject is *not* necessary (pp. 516–517).

The implications of Maquet's proposed redefinition are radical in the context of the European *utamawazo*. A change that the phenomenologists have been attempting to effect for over a century. It would mean a complete break from the epistemology that is based on the idea and methodology of 'objectification'. on which the total separation of 'subject' and 'object' – of the 'knower' from the 'known' – is predicated. Ultimately the implications of a radical change in the definition of knowledge or 'what it means to know' are not only a change in epistemological methodology, but a change in the European conception of the self, with corresponding changes in the conception of 'other' and behavior towards others as well. If the traditional mode of European science – 'objectification' – loses its position of primacy on their scale of values, the redefinition of the culture itself theoretically becomes possible (p. 517).

Of course in the space of one chapter we can only discuss a small number of facets, but we have attempted to be open to discovery rather than prove or disprove a null hypothesis. Research in the latter paradigm is considered very valuable indeed. However, it needs to be considered along with all the other known and possible paradigms in reflecting on, understanding and being 'touched' by others – epistemologically, academically and philosophically.

FUTURE RESEARCH

We could explore these issues further using the results of this research. What we could think of for the future research is to obtain more detailed descriptions of the participants' subjective experiences and the processes involved. In addition, we could compare the differences between and among self-defined cultural groups. The purpose would be to challenge and inform the current situation where many counselling schools do not pay adequately *experienced* attention to cultural issues, although most people are conscious of these issues. (When attention is paid to these issues, it is in one-sided or simplistic ways which do not always honour the complexity of our multicultural situatedness in the world.)

Probably our most important result indicates that people's experience of counselling and psychotherapy could become more positive than negative by experiencing a multicultural environment. Lago (1996: 154) explains that

The link between research and training is obviously an important relationship, where research can inform trainees and they in their turn may be stimulated towards new research. Research is also required on the efficacy of the training process itself in producing knowledgeable, aware and skilled counsellors.

Recognising the limits of our present contributions, we would like to refer our readers to the many excellent volumes of work cited in our reference list, particularly the key recommendations for multiculturally skilled counsellors as collated by Sue *et al.*(1992).

REFERENCES

Acharyya, S., Moorhouse, S., Kareen, J. and Littlewood, R. (1989) Nafsiyat: a psychotherapy centre for ethnic minorities, *Psychiatric Bulletin* 13: 358–60.

Adams, T. (ed.) (1996) *Transcultural Counselling/Psychotherapy Forum. Symposium – Psychotherapy and Black Identity: Addressing the Debate. 22 October 1994*, London: Goldsmiths College, University of London.

Ani, M. (1994) *Yurugu: An African-Centred Critique of European Cultural Thought and Behavior*, Trenton: Africa World Press.

Banister, P., Burman, E., Parker, I., Taylor, M. and Tindall, C. (1994) *Qualitative Methods in Psychology: A Research Guide*, Buckingham: Open University Press.

Barker, C., Pistrang, N. and Elliott, R. (1994) *Research Methods in Clinical and Counselling Psychology*, Chichester: John Wiley.

Clarkson, P. (1993) *On Psychotherapy*, London: Whurr.

Clarkson, P. (1996) *The Bystander (An End to Innocence in Human Relationships?)*, London: Whurr.

D'Ardenne, P. and Mahtani, A. (1989) *Transcultural Counselling in Action*, London: Sage.

Denzin, N. and Lincoln, Y. (eds) (1994) *Handbook of Qualitative Research*, London: Sage.

Eleftheriadou, Z. (1994) *Transcultural Counselling*, London: Central Books.

Farrell, B.A. (1979) Work in small groups: some philosophical considerations, in B. Babington Smith and B.A. Farrell (eds), *Training In Small Groups: A Study of Five Groups*, pp. 103–115, Oxford: Pergamon.

Fernando, S. (1991) *Mental Health, Race and Culture*, London: Macmillan/MIND Publications.

Helman, C.G. (1994) *Culture, Health and Illness* (3rd edn), Oxford: Butterworth-Heinemann.

Helms, J.E. (1989) Eurocentrism strikes in strange ways and in unusual places, *Counselling Psychologist* 17 (4): 643–647.

Holloway, E. (1995) *Clinical Supervision: A Systems Approach*, Thousand Oaks, CA: Sage.

Kareem, J. and Littlewood, R. (1992) *Intercultural Therapy – Themes, Interpretations and Practice*, Oxford: Blackwell Scientific Publications.

Kenney, G.E. (1994) Multicultural investigation of counselling expectation and preferences, *Journal of College Student Psychotherapy* 9 (1): 21–39.

Klineberg, O. (1987) The social psychology of cross-cultural counseling, in P. Pedersen (ed.) *Handbook of Cross-Cultural Counseling and Therapy*, pp. 29–35, New York: Praeger.

Krech, D., Crutchfield, R.S., and Ballachey, W.L. (1962) *Individual in Society: A Textbook of Social Psychology*, San Francisco: McGraw-Hill.

Lago, C. (1996) *Race, Culture and Counselling*, London: Open University Press.

Littlewood, R. (1992) Towards an intercultural therapy, in J. Kareem and R. Littlewood (eds) *Intercultural Therapy – Themes, Interpretations and Practice*, pp. 3–13, Oxford: Blackwell Scientific Publications.

Lowenstein, L.F. (1987) Cross-cultural research in relation to counseling in Great Britain, in P. Pedersen (ed.) *Handbook of Cross-Cultural Counseling and Therapy*, pp. 37–44, New York: Praeger.

Maquet, J. (1964) Objectivity in anthropology, *Current Anthropology* 5 (1): 50–60.

McLeod, J. (1993) *An Introduction to Counselling*, Buckingham: Open University Press.

McRoy, R.G., Freeman, E.M., Logan, S.L. and Blackmon, B. (1986) Cross-cultural field supervision: implications for social work education, *Journal of Social Work Education* 22: 50–56.

Moorhouse, S. (1992) Quantitative research in intercultural therapy: some methodological considerations, in J. Kareem and R. Littlewood (eds) *Intercultural Therapy – Themes, Interpretations and Practice*, pp. 83–98, Oxford: Blackwell Scientific Publications.

Moustakas, C. (1994) *Phenomenological Research Methods*, Thousand Oaks, CA: Sage.

Nadirshaw, Z. (1992) Theory and practice: brief report – therapeutic practice in multi-racial Britain, *Counselling Psychology Quarterly* 5 (3): 257–261.

Newnes, C. (1996) For the development of counselling psychology and its values, *Clinical Psychology Forum* 95: 29–34.

Nippoda, Y. (1993) Cross-cultural counselling and personal development in another culture: how the Japanese adapt to Britain. Unpublished MA dissertation, Keele University.

Oerter, R. (1996) Are there universals and why? A reply to Minoura and Weisz *et al. Culture and Psychology*, 2 (2): 203–209.

Polkinghorne, D.E. (1992) Postmodern Epistemology of Practice, in S. Kvale (ed.) *Psychology and Postmodernism*, pp. 146–165, London: Sage.

Smith, E.M.J. (1985) Ethnic minorities: life stress, social support and mental health issues, *Counseling Psychologist* 13 (4): 537–579.

Sue, D.W., Arrendondo, P. and McDavis, R.J. (1992) Multicultural counseling competencies and standards: a call to the profession, *Journal of Counseling and Development* 70: 477–486.

Sutter, J.A. and McCaul, E.J. (1993) Issues in cross-cultural counseling: an examination of the meaning and dimensions of tolerance, *International Journal for the Advancement of Counselling* 16 (1): 3–18.

Taijfel, H. (1981) *Human Groups and Social Categories. Studies in Social Psychology*, Cambridge: Cambridge University Press.

Thomas, L. (1992) Racism and psychotherapy: working with racism in the consulting room: an analytical view, in J. Kareem and R. Littlewood (eds), *Intercultural Therapy – Themes, Interpretations and Practice*, pp. 133–145, Oxford: Blackwell Scientific Publications.

Woolfe, R. and Dryden, W. (eds) (1996) *Handbook of Counselling Psychology*, London: Sage.

Chapter 7

Psychological counselling in primary health care

A review[1]

Linda Papadopoulos and Robert Bor

INTRODUCTION

The incorporation of counselling as a distinct therapeutic process within the medical setting has raised questions with regard to issues of appropriateness, confidentiality, accountability, cost and effectiveness. As many as one-third of problems seen in primary care settings are psychological in nature, and research has shown that people with psychosocial problems are treated more often by general practitioners (GPs) than they are within psychiatric or social services (Shepherd, Cooper, Brown and Kalton, 1966; Blacker and Clare, 1987; RCGP, 1973). When taking into account the busy nature of the general practice setting, it becomes evident that GPs will find it very difficult to handle cases of this nature alone. It is important, therefore, to examine how best to organise and/or equip the primary care team to manage psychological problems, and how resources can be utilised to supplement and support the primary care team (Corney and Jenkins, 1993). Recent literature in the field reflects the rapid development of counselling in the primary health care field, the practice of counselling psychology in general medicine and the addition of counsellors as part of the primary health care team in the UK (e.g. Corney, 1992; Higgs and Dammers, 1992; Paykel, 1990; Thompson, Schwankovsky and Pitts, 1993; Boot *et al.*, 1994; Waseem, 1993). A number of studies have highlighted benefits, problems and possibilities for the future of counselling in primary health care. Most research can be categorised under one of five main headings: liaison between the counsellor and other professionals; evaluation of treatment in primary care and patient satisfaction; general practitioners' ability to counsel; family therapy in general practice; and problems with referrals. This chapter reviews this literature and identifies certain gaps in current research which may need to be addressed.

1 This chapter is based on a paper which appeared in *Counselling Psychology Quarterly*, 1995, 8 (4), 291–303. We acknowledge and appreciate the editor's and publisher's permission to use this material.

LIAISON BETWEEN THE COUNSELLOR AND OTHER PROFESSIONALS

The entry of the counsellor into the general practice medical setting may be viewed as a welcome development by those who favour holistic and non-medical approaches to the treatment of psychological and emotional problems along- side conventional medical approaches. However, the novelty of a counselling service within a medical service poses problems with regard to the professional relationships between members of the service and may be underscored by the ideological discrepancies between professions. Hierarchical structures, archaic assumptions and vocational stereotyping may underlie the working relationships of the members of the multi-disciplinary health team and these factors can foster poor communication and occupational rivalry between team members (East, 1995).

By virtue of their training, medical doctors and counsellors interact with the patient[2] and deal with his/her presenting problem from different perspec- tives. GPs tend to work within the conventional biomedical model which is pri- marily concerned with the symptomatology of the patient. Symptoms are analysed and clustered together in order to form a diagnosis and the patient may then be diagnosed as suffering from a particular illness for which the physician may prescribe a treatment. Taylor (1991) argues that the patient is most often treated in the medical model as a 'victim' of an external event or misfortune for which he/she holds little or no personal control or responsibil- ity. She states that this ideology is in strong contrast to the model used by many counsellors. The patient–counsellor relationship is seen as a collaborative one and not necessarily one in which a 'cure' is handed down by an expert pro- fessional. Rather than giving advice, medication or reassurance, counsellors encourage the patient to participate more actively in the treatment and healing process.

Wilson and Wilson (1985) discuss their experience of liaison with GPs, describing how difficulties can arise especially through slow development of communication and consequent misunderstandings between themselves as counsellors and the doctors. The authors suggest that problems occur because GPs and counsellors have different expectations, both of each other and of their relationship with their patients. In his paper on counselling in general practice, Gray (1988) suggests that difficulties often arise when attempting to establish a *modus vivendi* between general practitioners and other health care professionals with different backgrounds and styles of working. The author suggests that in order successfully to integrate the counsellor into the primary care team, careful preparation should be undertaken. Physicians and counsellors may have to learn to *speak each other's language* and more frequent team meetings may be needed to facilitate a good understanding of each other's views. They will need to

---

2 The term 'patient' is used in preference to 'client' because of the settings in which the authors work. This is not to suggest that the person seen for counselling is necessarily physically ill.

negotiate referrals, working practices and boundaries, among other issues. In their experience working in a GP practice, family therapists Graham and his colleagues (1993) state that the different language and ideas used when discussing cases can cause irritation to other members of the primary care team. Even the use of the term 'client' in place of 'patient' causes disagreements symbolic of wider discrepancies in approaches to health care and caring for patients. Although discrepancies such as these may pose problems in the working relationships of GPs and counsellors, the literature suggests these are not insurmountable and that doctors who have been exposed to counselling practices usually encourage the use of psychological approaches to counselling.

Setting up a counselling service in a medical setting has implications not only for the doctor–counsellor relationship, but also on patterns of referral to other mental health specialists. In their review of a family therapy clinic established in a general practice in London, Graham et al. (1993) described an audit of referrals and suggested that physicians were reasonably equipped to deal with various family problems often without the need of a referral. The audit also showed that since the establishment of the clinic, referrals for family problems and children's behaviour problems to outside agencies had decreased considerably. In their study of thirty-five GPs, nine counsellors and ninety-nine counselled patients, Waydenfield and Waydenfield (1980) reported that physicians greatly valued the direct access to counsellors without having to go through the referral system. Results of the study also showed that following counselling, doctor–patient communication improved and there was less pressure to prescribe drugs. Further, there was evidence to suggest that scepticism surrounding counselling quickly faded as knowledge of the counselling process grew, and the efficacy of its results became known. A recent study by Fletcher et al. (1995) examined the relationship between the provision of counselling and the prescribing of antidepressants, hypnotics and anxiolytics in general practice. The results of the study suggested that the provision of counselling services in general practice was not associated with lower prescription rates of psychotropic drugs. Indeed, the results suggested that the highest quantity and costs related to antidepressant medication were incurred in those practices where a counsellor was employed directly by a practice.

However these results need to be viewed in light of certain methodological shortcomings of the study. Firstly, as the authors themselves point out, counselling intensity was measured in terms of availability of a counsellor to the practice and may not therefore have reflected the uptake of counselling in each individual practice. Secondly, the definition that the authors used to define the term 'counsellor' was vague and could not therefore account for possible discrepancies in terms of qualifications and experience between counsellors. Thirdly, the fact that more antidepressants appeared to be prescribed in cases where there was a practice-based counsellor could be related to the fact that practice-based counsellors often accumulate long waiting lists, thus prompting GPs to prescribe psychotropic medication to patients while they are waiting.

This may be particularly relevant in the case of depressed patients who may be perceived by GPs as posing a threat to themselves.

The presence of a counsellor in a primary health team can not only benefit individual patients seen by the counsellor but can also benefit the health care team as a whole. Time may need to be invested by the counsellor in supporting other practice members who want to develop their own counselling skills, and in helping GPs to refine their counselling and assessment skills so as to enable them to recognise patients that present with psychological problems and make the necessary referrals. Corney and Jenkins (1993) suggest that the development of a practice protocol or guidelines within the primary care service may facilitate better referral systems and greater support between group members. The development of guidelines for the employment of counsellors in primary care and the establishment of skills and training standards will allow for the evaluation of skills that counsellors bring to the primary health care setting and for the exploration of different modes of practice.

EVALUATION OF PSYCHOLOGICAL TREATMENT IN PRIMARY CARE AND PATIENT SATISFACTION

Research into the efficacy of counselling in medical settings is a particularly important issue. Counsellors need to demonstrate that a significant contribution to the assessment, treatment and healing process can be made and that the service represents value for money in an era of shrinking health budgets and dwindling resources (East, 1995). The main reasons why evaluative studies of the effectiveness of counselling in general practice are essential are described by Corney and Jenkins (1993). The authors point out that given the constraints of time and resources it is essential to focus on those patients who will benefit most from counselling, and evaluative studies should be involved in identifying such patients. They also suggest that since there is such a wide range and diversity of therapies being used in the primary care setting, evaluative studies need to examine which of these benefit the patient most. In terms of counsellor training, it is recommended that the level of skill that is necessary for effective counselling to occur be examined. Finally, the authors suggest that since it is a common finding that there is greater variance in outcome in treated clients than in untreated controls, this may indicate that some individuals could actually be harmed by therapy; evaluative studies should aim to investigate this more closely. Several outcome studies will be considered in this section and the methodology used to conduct these studies will also be discussed.

The evaluation of psychological treatment in primary care has been examined in a number of studies: for example, Crossley, Myers and Wilkinson (1992); Earll and Kincey (1982); Trepka and Griffiths (1987); and Boot et al. (1994). Outcome studies of psychological treatment have often been criticised with regard to their methodology, sampling procedures and dependent measures. Trepka and Griffiths (1987) argue that there are limitations in the evaluation of psychological treatment, and results of many studies fail to give an accurate picture of the value of psychological treatment in general practice. They suggest that trials of specific intervention techniques with appropriate subgroups are more accurate than are attempts to measure treatment effects of referral cohorts, since the latter reveal little about treatment effectiveness and tend to highlight instances of patient drop outs, and those patients who do not benefit from treatment.

In their assessment of psychological care in general practice, Crossely, Myers and Wilkinson (1992) undertook a prospective study using the General Health Questionnaire, in an attempt to overcome the methodological difficulties that are often associated with the assessment of psychological treatments. Through the use of structured methods for the evaluation of diagnosis, management within consultation and the development of predetermined defined measures to evaluate management, the authors attempted to pilot a method of assessing psychological care by general practitioners. The results of the study suggested that through the use of pre-consultation inquiry (the General Health Questionnaire) and a quantifiable case specific index, assessment of psychological care in general practice is feasible despite the difficulties with regard to standardisation of diagnostic terms and optimum management.

The General Health Questionnaire was used in a study by Boot et al. (1994) to evaluate the short-term impact of counselling in general practice. Their paper described the findings of a randomised controlled trial where patients who had received advice for acute psychological problems (e.g. relationship difficulties, anxiety, depression) from their GPs were compared with those who had received counselling from qualified counsellors in primary care settings. Data were collected from both patients and GPs on two occasions, prior to either counselling or GP advice and again six weeks after the initial consultation. Results showed that the group which had received counselling from a 'qualified' counsellor exhibited greater improvement as measured by the General Health Questionnaire than did the group that had been counselled by their GP. The researchers also pointed out that significantly fewer of those counselled were referred to psychiatrists or clinical psychologists or were prescribed psychoactive medication. In addition, patients who were counselled were more likely to report satisfaction with treatment and that they were coping better.

A study of patients' intentions in primary care (Salmon, Sharma, Valori and Bellinger, 1994) examined the relationship between presenting problems and intentions of patients when visiting a GP surgery. The researchers undertook a series of three studies; in the first a specially devised symptom checklist was used to form component-based scales on which patients' physical symptoms were scored. Results from this study revealed that although physical symptoms were unrelated to intentions, the degree of psychological symptoms correlated with the motivation for support from the physician. In the second study findings from study one were replicated. The new variable integrated into the second study examined the amount of support the patients had from their family and friends and looked at whether or not this correlated with the amount of support sought from the GP. Results demonstrated that there was no correlation between the amount of support received from the social and familial networks and the desire for support sought from the GP. Finally, in the third study, GPs were asked to complete a simple evaluation form after each consultation for each patient they had seen. Results indicated that doctors were able to identify which patients wanted support but were insensitive to other intentions. The authors suggest that a technique where the intentions of patients may be quantified will facilitate formal investigation of issues surrounding primary care consultations.

Most patients who are offered counselling or therapy in a primary care setting are often only seen for a limited number of sessions. Thus, researchers have attempted to examine the efficacy of short clinical contact therapy. Blakey, Sinclair and Taylor (1994) undertook such a study and examined the effect of short-term therapy on a hundred patients referred by GPs to a psychology department over one year. Patients were offered two interviews for assessment and a follow-up session at three months. The results of the study showed a significantly high number of patients reporting satisfaction with the therapy received. Patients were also asked to what extent they felt that their problems had been solved following intervention. Interestingly, the results suggest that there was a difference between the number of patients who thought their problems had been resolved following counselling contact and the number of those who felt more competent to deal with their problems after therapy (the latter being the significantly larger group). This may indicate that patients may not always be looking for a magical cure or quick fix in therapy, but rather may be seeking the skills and support to be able to deal with life stresses, and an opportunity to talk to a professional about their difficulties.

An important issue that should be considered when interpreting efficacy and outcome studies of counselling in primary health care is that generally these tend to assume that the variable of 'counsellor' is a 'constant'. This is far from reality. As Sibbald et al. (1993) found in their study, there is wide diversity in skills, practice and training among counsellors working in general practice, including a sizeable proportion with no training at all. In a national study commissioned by the British Association of Counsellors (BAC) to examine how counsellors working in primary care settings were trained, recruited, selected and inducted, Breakwell (1987) found that there was a wide diversity of definitions of counselling among the district health authorities that took part in the study; indeed of all those employed in primary care settings only clinical psychologists were expected to have counselling qualifications before being appointed. Other counselling staff members had a counselling *element* identified in their role and usually had only received brief, voluntary training.

There is a necessity for evaluative studies to examine training needs, competence and skill levels required by counsellors in medical settings. MIND recommends the establishment of a compulsory published register of counsellors and psychotherapists which lists the code of ethics to which they adhere in order to deal with ethics and complaints procedures (Wood, 1993). Academic institutions and professional bodies have also recognised the need for increased professionalisation and recognition for counsellors in primary care settings. Five postgraduate courses in Counselling in Primary Health Care were set up in 1995 in universities in the UK. These are sponsored by the Counselling in Primary Care Trust which has taken a lead in developing training for primary care counsellors (East, 1995). Advances such as this will have the potential to strengthen and broaden the knowledge base that exists in the field of counselling in primary health care and will also contribute to research and evaluative studies in this field.

CAN GENERAL PRACTITIONERS COUNSEL?

It has been suggested that general practitioners are in an excellent position to counsel their patients when they present with psychosocial problems. However, although many physicians use counselling skills during consultations, few have received any formal training in counselling. This distinction between having counselling skills and *being* a counsellor is one that should be addressed in the field of primary health care counselling. Bor, Miller and Goldman (1992) explain that most health care professionals, be they trained in nursing, medicine or other allied professions, counsel through the course of their work. They interact with patients clarifying treatment options, helping in adjustment to new situations and discussing unwelcome circumstances. Professional counsellors, however, most often have advanced training in counselling, family therapy or psychotherapy, and some are trained in other disciplines such as social work, nursing or clinical/counselling psychology. Unlike GPs who use counselling *skills*, these professionals are trained to use the counselling *process* to help patients resolve their issues and problems.

The concept of GPs counselling their patients was explored extensively by Michael Balint (1964) who used his psychoanalytic training to help GPs better understand their patients' needs, and to make more insightful responses to their patients' presenting problems. He described techniques for listening, interpreting and understanding both doctor's and patient's transference. However, although Balint's work has profoundly influenced the way physicians are trained today, treatment is still mostly symptom-focused and doctor-led (Graham *et al.*, 1993), rather than a more collaborative encounter between doctor and patient (Seaburn *et al.*, 1993).

Rowland, Irving and Maynard (1989) discuss the problems that GPs face when counselling and the benefits of professional counsellors in GP surgeries. They argue that, by virtue of their training, the way in which doctors conceptualise and attempt to deal with their patients' problems is in stark contrast to the counselling relationship/procedure, which attempts to help the patient to deal with his/her difficulties through skills such as problem clarification, understanding, summarising and confrontation rather than through advice giving. The function of the counselling process is for the clients to be helped to discover solutions for themselves, and with the aid of the counsellor to clarify and resolve difficulties. Whereas counselling attempts to foster independent decision-making in clients, patients may experience feelings of dependency on their doctor. It has been suggested that these feelings of dependency may stem from the fact that having been patients since childhood, the 'unfinished business' of childhood may get projected onto the physician–patient relationship (Gill, 1978).

Arborelius and Bremberg (1994) investigated how doctors discuss lifestyle issues with their patients and examined video-recorded consultations in general practice. Issues discussed included diet, exercise, alcohol intake and smoking. The results suggested that both short and lengthy advice sequences were of similar structure. The tactics that physicians used to influence patients' behaviours included condemnations of the behaviour in question and persuasion to change. These authors suggest that there is a lack of adequate skills regarding lifestyle counselling among GPs. This is attributed to the possibility that many physicians doubt the efficacy of their counselling skills, and do not believe that counselling will lead to behaviour change. It may also be the case that the doctors involved in the study believed that successful counselling resulted in patients being recruited to share their own views about lifestyle and health risks. In a recent study, Howe (1996) interviewed nineteen GPs regarding their own perceptions of the influences on their performance as detectors of psychological distress. Results of the study suggested that GPs were aware of many of the factors which influenced detection of psychological distress. Indeed, the majority of GPs acknowledged their actions to be crucial in the process of detection. However, whereas previous studies have emphasised skills and training as the factors which best predict GP performance in terms of detection of psychological distress (Gask et al., 1987), the GPs in this study tended to perceive the problem as being one of time and energy to use the skills they already possessed. This study suggests that GPs may indeed perceive a choice as to whether or not they will attempt to gather evidence of psychological distress during a consultation.

Rowland et al. (1989) suggested that although the outcome of patient care is likely to be improved if patients are actively involved in their treatment, the relationship between the doctor and patient is unlikely to reflect that of counsellor and counsellee, since the GP will need to give practical help and advice which would be inappropriate to some aspects of the counselling relationship. In addition, patients' expectations of their doctors may also be an obstacle in the counselling process. Patients who present with somatic complaints usually expect somatic diagnosis (i.e. an indication that something physiological is the cause of their ailment) and may resist a treatment or cure that only involves talking. Indeed, they may feel that the physician has not done his/her job adequately unless they leave with a prescription. There may be an expectation on the patient's part that the physician would rather hear about physical symptoms than emotional or psychological problems.

An important consideration for GPs who counsel is the use of time in a busy clinic setting. On average, a consultation with a physician lasts six minutes, whereas a counselling session lasts between thirty and fifty minutes. GPs may not be able to offer patients the same time available to counsellors when attempting to be psychotherapeutic. There can also be many practical constraints for physicians who want to counsel, including interruptions by staff and telephone and the risk of being overheard outside the consultation room (Rowland *et al.*, 1989). Furthermore, it is unlikely that most doctors will be able to satisfy the demands of their patients for therapeutic counselling without adversely affecting the time needed for clinical work since no additional payment is received for time spent counselling (Rowland and Hurd 1991).

McLeod (1987) suggests that although many general practitioners may be interested in their patients' psychological problems, others may not be and therefore it is likely that patients of non-psychologically orientated physicians may benefit from the presence of a counsellor. In a study of counselling in general practice, Rowland and Irving (1984) found that the presence of a trained counsellor within the general practice setting facilitated physicians' work with patients, which in turn led to the early identification of patients' difficulties, to fewer inappropriate referrals, to a decrease in consultation times and to a reduction in the prescription of drugs. If GPs are to delegate the task of counselling to other members of the health care team, they will have to do so with a clear understanding of their fellow professional's skills and capabilities. This should include knowledge of the content of counselling training the person has had, so as to avoid any uncertainty with regard to the limitations and abilities of that person in carrying out his/her role as a counsellor (Sheppard, 1993).

FAMILY THERAPY AND GENERAL PRACTICE

Counsellors who work in primary care settings approach the patient and his/her problem from different perspectives depending on the therapeutic model from which they work. Cognitive therapy, analytic psychotherapy, non-directive counselling and family therapy have all been used to counsel people in primary care settings (East, 1995). Recent literature has focused on the contribution of family therapy in general practice not only because GPs often have to take into account family issues, but also because the systemic approach used by many family therapists can be used to understand and manage the complex dynamics in the patient–family–GP–counsellor constellation (Bor and Miller, 1991). As Doherty and Campbell (1987: 46) have pointed out:

> Family therapists have expertise in systems theory, family dynamics, and promoting behaviour changes – skills that can be invaluable in these settings. Increasingly, family therapists are being trained to deal with health related problems and are collaborating with other health professionals. . . . [We] believe that the most effective approach to health promotion and risk reduction requires this kind of collaboration.

Family therapy is based on the premise that families are systems and that problems will either improve or persist depending on the way the members of the system behave and interact with each other. Therefore, causes and cures are not located within a particular person but within the relationships between family members (Markus *et al.*, 1991; Seaburn *et al.*, 1993; Senior, 1994). The family's impact on health, and vice versa, is also relevant with regard to adjustment and coping with illness. It is therefore important that in certain cases family members become involved in the counselling process, since it is almost inevitable that they will be involved in the patient's illness experience. This section will examine some of the literature on family therapy in general practice.

Collaboration between physicians and family therapists has gained attention both in the primary care and in the family therapy literature (McDaniel, Hepworth and Doherty 1992). In their paper on family therapy in general practice Seaburn *et al.* (1993) highlight several important factors that arise when working within the primary care setting, including the importance of language used within a multi-disciplinary team. They argue that medical language tends to be more concrete in nature than the language of counselling or therapy which may be theoretical and imprecise. Since physicians often need to discuss patients' cases with counsellors, the authors suggest 'translating language' into specific and concrete terms. The relationship between physicians and their patients is mostly punctuated by a brief period of treatment, where help is sought out only during acute exacerbations of problems. Since the relationship with the family physician is usually ongoing, counsellors may run into patients in the waiting room before medical visits or may hear about their progress through physicians who provide their health care. This type of relationship is therefore different from that of a counsellor working in an agency or private practice, as there is less potential for contact with the counsellor outside of sessions. In the primary care setting, contact may take place after therapy has ended although Seaburn *et al.* (1993) view this as advantageous as it enhances ongoing collaboration even when patient and family are not engaged in counselling, thus enabling more effective intervention at times of crisis.

Dym and Berman (1986) propose that the family physician collaborate with the family therapist to develop a primary health care team. A similar view is held by Seaburn and colleagues (1993), who suggest that the family therapist and the primary care physician should be the centre of the primary health care network. They assert that an important role of the family therapist in the networking process is to encourage the collaboration of the different members of the health care team, a concept now well advanced in many settings in the USA. Senior (1994) discussed the development of a family planning clinic within a group general practice. The author explained that a strong motivating factor for setting up the clinic was the fact that many referrals to secondary services within the health care system failed to materialize. He speculated that this may have been due to the fact that some families felt uncomfortable with the prospect of having to see a therapist, and that this could be overcome by being able to seek help at the familiar setting of their local GP surgery. Perhaps the role of the counsellor in the primary care setting is not only to deal with patients directly, but also to facilitate communication between doctors and their patients, through discussion with team members (Bor, Miller and Goldman, 1992).

Graham and colleagues (1993) undertook a four-year review of a family therapy clinic in a general practice in London. Initially the therapeutic style used was described by the team as being influenced by their training in family therapy and their work in specialist clinics. Over time, however, the team modified their structural/strategic approach, and a more narrative style of therapy was adopted. Indeed conversations between therapists and GPs were often held in the presence of the family and even included the family in the conversation.

PROBLEMS WITH REFERRALS

The concept of the referring person within the context of systemic family therapy is discussed in a classic paper by Palazzoli and colleagues (1980) and has important implications for counselling in primary care. The paper describes the person that refers the family to therapy as occupying 'a nodal homeostatic position in that family' (Palazzoli *et al.*, 1980: 3). The authors assert that it is important to ascertain the present position of the referring person in the family group, and whether or not that person has become involved to the extent that they might have been inducted into the dynamics of the family. They point out that among others, family physicians and pediatricians are particularly susceptible to becoming homeostatic influences on the family or systemic problems.

The potential problem of the referring person is clearly an issue with regard to the primary care setting where family physicians might have known and become an integral part of the family life of patients over many years. Stewart, Valentine and Amudson (1991) discuss the difficulties in defining presenting problems in therapy and how these can be affected by the therapist, the family and the referring person. They warn against 'premature certainty' on the part of the therapist especially where the referrer's views guide interviewing and assessment procedures of therapy. The definition of the problem may then come about through a collaborative effort on the part of the family and the therapist, involving a stance of co-operation rather than competition. Whether or not counsellors working in primary care settings choose to work with families, they are constantly confronted with problems which affect and can be dealt with in the wider system, including the patient's family, the GP and the practice among others.

CONCLUSION

This chapter has attempted to outline some of the issues that have been addressed in recent psychological and medical literature on counselling in primary health care. It is by no means an exhaustive review since the field of primary care is very rich in both the diversity and originality of ideas. If we are to move towards a greater acceptance and recognition of both the value and the efficacy of primary care counselling, ongoing evaluation should become an essential component in the setting up and development of counselling services. This will ensure that counselling services achieve and maintain high standards of practice. There is also a need for Family Health Service Authorities (FHSAs) to provide resources for evaluating counselling services so as to ensure that these remain viable and accessible (Corney and Jenkins, 1993).

It is imperative that training standards be established which reflect the competency of those who counsel in primary care settings. At present, counsellors working in primary care settings may come from a variety of training backgrounds, ranging from those with little training or who offer a few hours of unsupervised counselling each week, to a range of professionals including counsellors, social workers, psychiatrists and psychologists with advanced training. This has obvious implications for the evaluation of counselling services and should be taken into account not only by those conducting research in these settings but also by those who employ counsellors. Employment of untrained counsellors can no longer be justified on any account. The British Association of Counsellors' guidelines on employment highlight the need to clarify the role and function of counsellors, especially those in fundholding general practices, in the light of changes in mental health services (East, 1995). Training should include theory, skills, supervision and practice so as to provide counsellors with the well-balanced knowledge base that this role requires (Corney and Jenkins, 1993).

The counsellor's role within the primary care setting is potentially diverse, and it is important therefore that GPs, counsellors and FHSAs clarify the responsibilities and obligations of counsellors. Particular attention should be paid to the benefits not only for the patient, but also for his/her family and to other members of the health care team. As part of a multi-disciplinary team primary health care counsellors are bound to come across 'cultural' and 'language' difficulties when communicating with other team members, and it is perhaps most appropriate that as experts in relationships, counsellors address any problems of this nature with colleagues in a supportive and empathic way. The provision of counselling should also help our colleagues to improve their therapeutic skills for dealing with patients who present with emotional or psychological issues or problems. Primary care counselling is an exciting and fast-expanding field that will be at the forefront of health care in the 1990s and beyond as health care resources are improved in GP settings. An opportunity now exists to develop and promote effective, responsive, ethical and creative counselling practice in primary care settings.

GUIDLINES FOR PSYCHOLOGICAL COUNSELLING IN PRIMARY CARE

• Psychological counselling in primary care is usually brief. This does not mean that it is diluted. Brief therapy has been shown to be effective and can be intensive.

- Attend as much to the client's resources, coping abilities and strengths, as to their problems.
- Refer to other professionals and specialists where appropriate, such as psychiatrists, clinical psychologists and psychotherapists.
- Discuss with professional colleagues how feedback will be given to them and which feedback they will find helpful.
- Discuss practical issues such as the number of sessions available, note keeping, secretarial support, use of consulting rooms and so on before starting counselling.
- Respect professional differences, and be mindful of different languages and jargon used.
- Pay as much attention to your relationship with your colleagues as with your clients.

REFERENCES

Arborelius, E. and Bremberg. S. (1994) Prevention in practice. How do general practitioners discuss lifestyle issues with their patients? *Patient and Education Counselling*, 23. 23–31.

Balint. M. (1964). *The Doctor, the Patient and the Illness* (2nd edn). London: Pitman.

Blacker. C.V.R. and Clare, A.W. (1987) Depressive disorder in primary care. *British Journal of Psychiatry*, 150, 3–51.

Blakey. R., Sinclair J. and Taylor R. (1994). Patient satisfaction with short clinical psychology contact. *Clinical Psychology Forum*, July, 13–15.

Boot. D.. Gillies, P., Fenelon, J., Reubin, R., Wilkins, M. and Gray, P. (1994). Evaluation of the short term impact of counselling in general practice. *Patient and Education Counselling*, 24 , 79–89.

Bor. R. and Miller, R. (1991). *Internal Consultations in Health Care Settings*. London: Karnac.

Bor. R.. Miller, R. and Goldman, E. (1992). *Theory and Practice of HIV Counselling*. London: Cassell.

Breakwell, G.M. (1987). Mapping counselling in the non-primary sector of the NHS. Unpublished report for BAC.

Corney. R. (1992). The effectiveness of counselling in general practice. *International Review of Psychiatry*, 4. 331–337.

Corney, R. and Jenkins R. (1993). *Counselling in General Practice*. London: Routledge.

Crossley. D., Myers, M.P. and Wilkinson, G. (1992). Assessment of psychological care in general practice. *British Medical Journal*, 305,1333–1336.

Doherty, W.J. and Campbell, T.L. (1987). *Families and Health*. Beverly Hills, CA: Sage.

Dym. B. and Berman, S. (1986). The primary health care team: family physician and family therapist in joint practice. *Family Systems Medicine*, 4, 9–21.

Earll. L. and Kincey, J. (1982). Clinical psychology in general practice: a six year study of consulting patterns for psychosocial problems. *Journal of the Royal College of General Practitioners*, 32. 32–37.

East. P. (1995a) *Counselling in Primary Health Care*. London: Open University Press.

East. P. (1995b). *Counselling in Medical Settings*. Milton Keynes: Open University Press.

Fletcher. J., Fahey, T. and McWilliam, J. (1995). Relationship between the provision of counselling and the prescribing of antidepressants, hypnotics and anxiolytics in general practice. *British Journal of General Practice*, 45, 467–469.

Gask, L., McGrath, G., Goldberg, D. and Millar, T. (1987). Improving the psychiatric skills of established general practitioners: evaluation of group teaching. *Medical Education*, 21, 362–368.

Gill, C. (1978). Counselling in general practice. *Counselling News*, 23, 10–11.

Graham, H., Senior, R., Lazarus, M., Mayer, R. and Asen K. (1992). Family therapy in general practice: views of referrers and clients. *British Journal of General Practice*, 42, 25–28.

Graham, H., Senior, R., Dukes, S., Lazarus, M. and Mayer, R. (1993). The introduction of family therapy to British general practice. *Family Systems Medicine*, 11, 363–373.

Gray, D.P. (1988). Counsellors in General Practice. *Journal of the Royal College of General Practitioners*, 38, February, 50–51.

Higgs, R. and Dammers J. (1992). Ethical issues in counselling and health in primary care. *British Journal of Guidance and Counselling*, 20, 27–38.

Howe, A. (1996). 'I know what to do, but it's not possible to do it' – general practitioners' perceptions of their ability to detect psychological distress. *Family Practice*, 13 (2), 127–132.

Markus, A.C., Parkes, M.C., Tomson, P. and Johnston, M. (1991). *Psychological Problems in Medical Practice*. Oxford: Oxford University Press.

McDaniel, S., Hepworth, J. and Doherty, W. (1992). *Medical Family Therapy – A Biopsychosocial Approach to Families with Health Problems*. New York: Basic Books.

McLeod, J.M. (1987). *The Work of Counsellors in General Practice. Occasional Paper 37*. London: Royal College of General Practitioners.

Palazzoli, M.S., Boscolo, L., Cecchin, G. and Prata, G. (1980) The problem of the referring person. *Journal of Marital and Family Therapy*, 6, 3–9.

Paykel, E. (1990). Innovations in mental health care in the primary care system. *Mental Health Care Delivery: Innovations, Impediments and Implementation*. Cambridge: Cambridge University Press.

RCGP (Royal College of General Practitioners) (1973). Present status and future needs of general practice. *Journal of the Royal College of General Practitioners*, Reports on general practice No.16.

Rowland, N. and Hurd, J. (1991). *Counselling in General Practice: A Guide for Counsellors*. British Association for Counselling. Counselling in Medical Settings Division 1991.

Rowland, N. and Irving, J. (1984). Towards a rationalization of counselling in general practice. *Journal of the Royal College of General Practitioners*, 34, 685–687.

Rowland N., Irving, J. and Maynard, A. (1989). Can general practitioners counsel? *Journal of the Royal College of General Practitioners*, 39, 118–120.

Salmon, P., Sharma, N., Valori, R. and Bellinger, N. (1994). Patients' intentions in primary care: relationships to physical and psychological symptoms, and their perception by general practitioners. *Social Science and Medicine*, 38, 585–592.

Seaburn, D., Gawinski, B., Harp, J., McDaniel, S., Waxman, D. and Shields, C. (1993). Family systems therapy in a primary care medical setting: the Rochester experience. *Journal of Marital and Family Therapy*, 19, 177–190.

Senior, R. (1994). Family therapy in general practice: 'We have a clinic here on Friday afternoon . . .' *Journal of Family Therapy*, 16, 313–317.

Sheppard, J. (1993). The clinical task. In M. Pringle (ed.) *Change and Teamwork in Primary Care*. London: BMJ Publishing Group.

Shepherd, M., Cooper, B., Brown, A.C and Kalton, G.W. (1966). *Psychiatric Illness in General Practice*. London: Oxford University Press.

Sibbald, B., Addington-Hall, J., Brennman, D. and Freeling, P. (1993). Counsellors in English and Welsh general practices: their nature and distribution. *British Medical Journal*, 306, 29–33.

Stewart, K., Valentine LaNae and Amudson, J. (1991). The battle for definition the problem with (the problem). *Journal of Strategic and Systemic Therapies*, 10, 21–31.

Taylor, S.E. (1991). *Health Psychology* (2nd edn). New York: McGraw Hill.

Thompson, S.C., Schwankovsky, L.P. and Pitts, J. (1993). Counselling patients to make lifestyle changes: the role of physician self efficacy, training and beliefs about causes. *Family Practice*, 10, 70–75.

Trepka. C. and Griffiths, T. (1987). Evaluation of psychological treatment in primary care. *Journal of the Royal College of General Practitioners*, 37, 215–217.

Waseem, A. (1993). The ethnomedical model as a conceptual tool for counselling in health care decision-making. *British Journal of Guidance and Counselling*, 21, 8–19.

Waydenfield, D., and Waydenfield, S.W. (1980) Counselling in General Practice. *Journal of the Royal College of General Practitioners*, 30, 671–677.

Wilson, S. and Wilson K. (1985). Close encounters in general practice: experiences of a psychotherapy liaison team. *British Journal of Psychiatry*, 146, 277–281.

Wood. D. (1993). *Wordswordswordswords, the Power of Words: Uses and Abuses of Talking Treatments*. London: Mind Publications.

Chapter 8

Therapeutic factors in group psychotherapy

Jorge Ribeiro

INTRODUCTION

General considerations

It is difficult to define what psychotherapeutic factors are:

1 because of the intricate relation with complex and different compounds from human experience;
2 because of the many different names they have which we use to express them, such as therapeutic factors, cure factors, cure mechanisms, changing mechanisms. Different names for the same thing of course create confusion;
3 since literature talks about 175 factors, grouped in nine or twelve factors;
4 because as we work with scales and questionnaires about feelings and emotions, the evaluations from the patients will be, necessarily, subjective. Besides, many factors influence the result from the patient depending on therapeutic factors: the duration of the therapy, the level of the functioning of the person or type of group, the ideology of the therapist, besides the fact that these factors are interrelated. They do not occur or function separately.

'Despite these limitations, the speech from the patients is a rich and immeasurable source of information. Besides, it is their experience, and the more we move away from the experience, the more inaccurate are our conclusions'.[1]

Yalom goes on to comment:

I don't speak from a nihilist position, but, on the other hand, I believe that the nature of our principles is so rich, complex and highly subjective that this makes an inapplicable scientific methodology. So, I doubt that a psychotherapy scientific research will ever have that certainty to which we aspire, and we need to learn to effectively accept that uncertainty. We have to listen to what the patient says; we have to consider the best experience available from the questioning of the clinical observation; and finally, we have to develop a therapy, designed to offer the high flexibility required to face the endless possibilities of human problems.[2]

Definition of problems

The concept of therapeutic factors is still developing, because of its complexity. This development involves different processes, some of them very clear, some of them very confusing when they are interrelated; so we can have the same process which is both therapeutic and antitherapeutic, depending on the circumstances. The interrelation of factors creates a new complexity, due to the difficulty in distinguishing the elements of its definition.

With these considerations in mind, I present two definitions: one more descriptive and the other more dynamic. The therapeutic factor 'is a group therapy element which helps to improve the condition of the patient and is dependent on the actions of the group therapist, on the other members of the group and on the patient him/herself'.[3] It is a mechanism, through which the whole group, consciously and unconsciously, provokes changes, inter- or intrapsychic, in its members. This mechanism's effects are to benefit their members, although it can accidentally produce secondary negative effects, depending on how and when it is experienced. That is why there is a necessity to study the therapeutic factors and their results all together, to observe the extent to which these mechanisms can be, indeed, cure mechanisms. As these therapeutic factors are processes that the group is experiencing, it is essential to study the theory of group process and then see how the changes occur.

The definition problem is a vital process because, until we do define the aim of our study, it will be very difficult to know where we stand, what materials to use, what methodology to follow, and which results to trust. The main point of how the therapeutic factor functions is misunderstood. For instance, is the fact that it is a coherent group important? Is it 'the possibility of either the self-recognition or the capacity of fully opening oneself that provides the personal information?'.[4] Another important point is that the therapeutic factors belong to the same levels, and are organised in different ways depending on how they were caused, but as a whole, they amount to the same thing.

The therapeutic factors involve three different areas: emotional, cognitive and operational. Some of them are called, with reference to the therapist, for example, *guidance and instillation of hope*; with reference to the group, *universality* and *cohesion*; with reference to the patient, *self-disclosure*, *altruism*, *catharsis*; and some are interrelated, for example *interpersonal learning* and *vicarious learning*.

These points, in general, are the main topics we shall study in this project. The more complex they are, the more essential it becomes to make an effort clearly to understand their nature, to see how they work.

METHODOLOGY – PROCEEDINGS

Individuals and their composition

We worked with four groups (1988–90), organised in the following way:

Group I

All the individuals were undergraduate students from the course of Experimental Psychology, University of Sussex, England. Four men and four women, 25–40 years old, with different academic backgrounds. Only one had been in therapy before. The group had twenty-five weekly sessions, two hours each session.

Group II

All the participants were therapists from different backgrounds and they are now in a course for Gestalt therapist training, at a psychotherapy institute in London. They are five men and five women, 30–45 years old. Some of them have already practised the psychotherapist profession for some years. The average period spent in this group is three-and-a-half years. Our study covered eighteen sessions at the end of the therapy, as our group was getting smaller. Sessions were two hours each, one per week.

Group III

All the individuals had different educational backgrounds, and all of them were full-time undergraduate students from the University of Brasilia, Brazil – four men and four women, 20–25 years old. There were thirty sessions, two hours each per week. None of them had been in therapy before. All of them were single.

Group IV

All had different professions. This group was essentially therapeutic, without academic purposes. There two men and eight women, 35–50 years old. Some of them were married with children. This group was in a kind of weekly workshop of sixteen hours each. We agreed to have four weekend workshops of sixteen hours each. The workshop started on Friday, in the evening, and finished on Sunday at midday. This group was from Newhaven, England.

Some final observations about the composition of the groups: except for Group III, where all the participants were single, the other groups were made up of people of varied marital status: they were married, single, divorcees, with children, and others. With reference to the kind of problem, we could describe them as neurotic or existentialist problems, which affect behaviour. None of them was a psychotic. The researcher was, at the same time, the therapist in Groups I and III; in Groups II and IV he was an observer who merely intervened when he was addressed by the group.

Instruments

We used three instruments:

1 *An individual questionnaire about therapeutic self-evaluation (ITSEQ)*

This questionnaire is divided into two kinds of factors:

i Interpsychic or psychosocial therapeutic factors. These factors are nine in number. They refer to group processes, as the group is seen as a psychosocial entity, although factors 4, 5 and 6 are also related to the individual, as an individual linked to feelings and emotions (see Table 8.1, p. 139);
ii Intrapsychic therapeutic factors. S.H. Foulkes used to call these factors analytic factors. These six factors are linked to the unconscious behaviour of the individual in the group, and also reflect the group's unconscious (see Table 8.1).

The ITSEQ has a scale of seven points. After each session, participants filled in the questionnaire, indicating from 1 to 7 the value given to each item (1 for low presence, 7 for high presence).

At the end of each session, they wrote down statements referring to the feelings and emotions they experienced during the session in the same questionnaire. This information is very important because it helps us to understand the real sense of value given to the item and its relation with other items, and with the whole; and it helps to inform about the running of the session that day.

Also with the scale, participants received a sheet of paper with the definitions of factors to help them memorise the meanings and to ensure that their answers were correct. In the first three sessions, there was a big argument about the sense of the definitions, where to change words or choose better terms to express the concepts seen, trying to make them understandable in terms of their specific psychological meaning.

We wanted to be sure that participants knew what they were responding to.

2 *Content analysis of every session*

Each session was written and recorded. Using some methodology techniques of content analysis and principles from the theory of group process, we identified the main dynamic processes of the group as a whole and also of the participants in that specific session. Hence, we could better understand the affirmations that the participants made, with the marks that they had given in that session. We tried to understand the correlation between the pieces of information and the correlation between the group process and the therapeutic factors, pointed out by the group.

Another important process that we are developing as a new technique is to place all the pieces of information that a participant has given during all the twenty-eight sessions one after the other in order to perceive, in a longitudinal linear process, his/her individual progress in the group environment. By doing this, we hope to understand better how the individual process occurs in the group process and how the group as a whole is affected by this individual process. This is more evident when only a single item took up either most or all of the session and the group gave high marks to some of the therapeutic factors.

3 *Final therapeutic questionnaire*

This questionnaire has six open questions. Some items are related to the effectiveness and to the power of the help expressed by the factors; some are related to the results of the therapy (see Appendix 8.1, p. 155).

This questionnaire is very useful, because it allows the participant to see his/her own therapeutic process retrospectively, to see his/her process not as fragmented, but as a whole, as it happened in every session. The questionnaire gives us an *a posteriori* vision, an X ray, from the group process as a whole and lets us distinguish the group process as it is itself, the result and, consequently, lets us distinguish which processes were more effective and which ones helped more in the changing process.

RESULTS

Our results give us a real and complex source of information. One piece of information, which may be one of the most important, consists in showing the different cultures, developed in each group, in a very didactic and clear way. Besides, it is evident that some results are surprisingly similar, regardless of the therapist's style, the composition or the character of the group (weekly sessions or workshops).

The final order of the weekly results from the four groups is presented in Table 8.1.

In the four groups, the psychotherapeutic factor is the one with the highest mark and catharsis with the lowest mark, except for the Group IV, where catharsis comes second to last. If we observe the SD in the four groups with reference to Factor 9 (psychotherapist), we can see that all the groups' results are more or less the same, which is indicative of the feelings and emotions linked to that factor. It must be underlined that in Group IV, whose modality is that of the workshop (weekend groups), the participants are in a high level of agreement about their perception in what is said in Factor 9 (psychotherapist) (SD 57), although there are not other correlations in this group between the psychotherapeutic factor

Table 8.1 Final order of the weekly results from the four groups

	Group I			Group II			Group III			Group IV		
	X	SD	Final order	X	SD	Final order	X	SD	Final order	X	SD	Final order
Therapeutic factors												
1 Motivation	5.56	1.92	5	6.82	1.47	3	5.04	2.20	5	6.80	1.35	3
2 Permission to speak	5.75	1.83	3	7.22	1.04	2	5.90	1.93	2	6.42	1.44	6
3 Acceptance	5.79	1.62	2	6.58	1.45	4	5.57	1.86	3	6.69	1.28	4
4 Corrective emotional experience	4.95	1.80	8	5.88	1.84	6	4.29	2.08	8	6.15	1.91	9
5 Catharsis	4.43	1.96	9	4.56	2.14	9	3.96	2.01	9	6.28	1.81	8
6 Vicarious learning	4.96	1.97	7	4.92	2.02	8	4.50	2.05	7	6.46	1.52	5
7 Self-disclosure	5.55	1.75	6	6.17	1.62	5	5.36	2.07	4	6.84	1.22	2
8 Guidance	5.57	1.57	4	5.74	1.92	7	4.78	2.21	6	6.36	1.72	7
9 Psychotherapist	6.27	1.50	1	7.29	1.06	1	6.47	1.75	1	7.61	0.57	1
Therapeutic intrapsychic factors												
1a Anxiety	5.38	1.82	2	3.54	1.82	4	4.06	2.15	2	5.92	1.87	1
2a Resistance	4.79	1.83	5	3.31	1.44	5	3.61	1.82	5	5.15	1.99	5
3a Silence	4.51	2.03	6	3.10	1.66	6	4.06	2.03	3	4.88	1.84	6
4a Regression	4.84	2.03	3	4.18	1.91	2	3.04	1.62	6	5.56	1.85	3
5a Identification	5.65	1.77	1	4.99	1.72	1	4.34	1.91	1	5.88	1.76	2
6a Transference	4.80	2.02	4	4.10	1.81	3	3.62	1.88	4	5.52	1.83	4

SD = standard deviation

and another factors (Table 8.5, p. 145). Factor 5 (catharsis) and 4 (corrective emotional experience) scores are lowest. The SD informs us that groups have difficulties in perceiving, in the same way, what is happening with reference to these factors. This could be explained because of the difficulty of operation, in quantitative terms, through a definition of what these factors are themselves, and through an experience in which one is personally involved.

In Table 8.1, we can also observe, between the intrapsychic factors, that Factor 2a (resistance) presents the same classification in the four groups and the Factor 5a (identification) has the same classification in Groups I, II, III, except for IV, where it appears in second place, with Factor 1a (anxiety) in first place. This seems to be congruent, as a high level of group identification should produce in the group a low level of resistance, although this fact does not represent significant correlations. In Group II, identification has a small correlation with vicarious learning, p = 0.54. (p = < 0.10) (Table 8.5). It is interesting to observe that the anxiety factor, in the intrapsychic therapeutic factors, scores highest in Group IV, confirming the general opinion that the weekend workshops are, generally, more anxiety-inducing.

Still looking at Table 8.1, in Group IV, we can see that self-disclosure (Factor 7) comes in second place and that anxiety (Factor 1a) comes first. What does this mean? If we look at Table 8.5, we see that the correlation between resistance and silence is p = 0.66 (p = < 0.05), and that between silence and self-disclosure is p = 0.56 (p = < 0.10). Thus we can understand the reason for anxiety in group IV. Since the correlation between acceptance and self-disclosure in Group IV is p = 0.66 (p = < 0.05), it seems that silence takes over and becomes resistance, when the members of the group do not feel themselves accepted, they become insecure, and consequently they do not talk.

Table 8.2 shows clearly the level of effectiveness and helping potential that the factors have. The responses from the four groups were organised one close to each other, following a decreasing order of importance. The first three most quoted were considered of high effectiveness and help, the medium three of medium effectiveness and help, and the last three of less effectiveness and help.

In Table 8.1, we have a quantitative order, the result of the scoring in every session. In Table 8.2, we have a qualitative order, the result of what was understood to be most important. The literature does not say anything about psychotherapist, motivation or permission to speak as proper cure factors but as a changing condition, mainly the latter two. I will come back to this distinction later, because I consider it more confusing than enlightening. If we accept that distinction, self-disclosure and acceptance appear to be the most effective and helpful factors in the cure process. Actually, if we look at Table 8.5, acceptance and self-disclosure have a consistent correlation in Group I, p = 0.64 (p = < 0.05), and in Group IV (p = 0.66). In Group III it is moderately consistent p = 0.60 (p = < 0.10).

Table 8.2 suggests a link between identification and anxiety. It seems as if

Table 8.2 Overall rank of the final mean for each group

Level	Group I	Group II	Group III	Group IV
Effectiveness and helping potential	The nine psychosocial therapeutic factors			
High	Therapist Acceptance Permission to speak	Therapist Acceptance Motivation	Therapist Acceptance Permission to speak	Therapist Self-disclosure Motivation
Medium	Self-disclosure Motivation Guidance	Self-disclosure Permission to speak Corrective emotional experience	Self-disclosure Motivation Guidance	Acceptance Vicarious learning Permission to speak
Low	Vicarious learning Corrective emotional experience Catharsis	Vicarious learning Guidance Catharsis	Vicarious learning Corrective emotional experience Catharsis	Guidance Catharsis Corrective emotional experience
Presence	Intrapsychic therapeutic factors			
High	Identification Anxiety	Identification Regression	Identification Anxiety	Anxiety Identification
Moderate	Regression Transference	Anxiety Transference	Silence Transference	Regression Transference
Low	Resistance Silence	Resistance Silence	Resistance Regression	Resistance Silence

there were a close relationship between identification, transference, resistance and anxiety, although these relationships are still not defined clearly. Thinking clinically, when we look at Table 8.4 (p. 144), we see that in Group I, identification is either highly present or six participants, in the same group, consider it highly curable (that means that it has the power or action to cure), whilst anxiety, although highly present, is not related to the cure process. In that way, resistance is seen as curable by two participants, in Group II. Therefore, I think anxiety is a process that belongs to the true nature of the group, in itself, whilst identification, transference and resistance emerge as cure processes within the anxiety process.

The results in Table 8.3 are part of the questions asked in 'the final questionnaire'. The group was asked to look retrospectively at the whole process of therapy, that is, to look backwards and see the process as a whole, and again, to mark all the factors from the point of view of effectiveness and helpfulness.

Table 8.3 Rating of the efficacy and helpfulness of the psychosocial psychotherapeutic factors in the opinion of the group in its last session

		Factors	Group I (6 persons)	Group II (9 persons)	Group IV (9 persons)	
High	1	Motivation	4	7	4	3*
	2	Permission to speak	2	2	2	2
	3	Acceptance	2	2	2	3
	4	Corrective emotional experience	3	3	6	2
	5	Catharsis	3	1	3	–
	6	Vicarious learning	1	–	2	1
	7	Self-disclosure	2	–	3	1
	8	Guidance	–	3	2	3
	9	Therapist	1	9	4	3
Medium	1	Motivation	2	2	–	1
	2	Permission to speak	2	4	–	2
	3	Acceptance	–	6	–	2
	4	Corrective emotional experience	3	5	–	3
	5	Catharsis	2	4	–	2
	6	Vicarious learning	2	1	–	3
	7	Self-disclosure	2	3	–	2
	8	Guidance	2	2	–	2
	9	Therapist	3	–	–	1
Low	1	Motivation	–	–	–	1
	2	Permission to speak	2	3	–	2
	3	Acceptance	4	1	–	1
	4	Corrective emotional experience	–	1	–	1
	5	Catharsis	1	4	–	4
	6	Vicarious learning	3	8	–	2
	7	Self-disclosure	2	6	–	3
	8	Guidance	4	4	–	1
	9	Therapist	2	–	–	2

* New classification, 6 months later, with just 6 members.

The table shows that, when the group looks back at its process, they modify their perception of what happened and its meaning. This task was not requested from Group III.

The three groups' position is completely different now. I see that this request for a new evaluation of the factors was made in the last session of each group, in this way: Looking back at your process as a whole, how would you classify the same factors today? It was requested that they order all the factors according to their importance. Now Group II merely keeps the same position, and, in Group I, only one member still considers the psychotherapist to be the most curative of the factors.

In Table 8.1, the corrective emotional experience factor comes in last place in Group IV, and, in Table 8.3, six members indicate that the same factor is the most effective and the one that helped most. It is well known that weekend groups are considered, sometimes, a little bit aggressive because they show their strong and uncontrolled emotions which would be exposed in corrective emotional experience factor. At first glance, the group disqualify the situation, perhaps because of embarrassment of having their feelings exposed without control, going beyond their limits, involuntarily. At the end of the therapy, looking at the same data and the same emotions more objectively, the group tends to classify them in a more positive way, as very important and efficient in the cure help process. That which was considered as a psychosocial group process is now felt as incorporated and personal.

Finally, six months later, there is another change in the perception of the same phenomenon. Only two people appreciate it as highly effective and helpful; three with medium power, so it goes back again to the first classification. Perhaps here the participants express either an academic position or a didactic result. Because of the lack of information in the same group six months after it ends, it becomes more difficult to understand this.

Table 8.4 deals with intrapsychic therapeutic factors. The group was asked to say how these mechanisms were present and how far they could be seen as cure mechanisms. Here it is also a retrospective evaluation of the group process, because they were asked only when they were present during the sessions. As can be observed, identification was highly present in Group I, and six people in the same group thought that identification has a high cure power, while transference was highly present in Group II, and seven people thought that transference has a high cure power. Anxiety and silence are not cure mechanisms like the rest, although it is important to observe their function to the same degree in the group process. Both are considered to have a moderate cure power in both groups.

The correlations in Table 8.5 show clearly the different cultures developed in each group. It is interesting to observe that the highest correlations are in Group IV, which is the model from weekend groups, called commonly the weekend workshops, which seems to confirm the idea, already general, that these groups experience more intensely all the processes that happen there.

The correlations in level $p = < 0.10$ merely indicate the tendencies of different factors, and although they are not totally trustworthy, we can observe in which direction they tend to go, as self-disclosure and acceptance, catharsis and corrective emotional experience, catharsis and vicarious learning.

DISCUSSION AND CONCLUSION

First of all, I would remind you that I did not work with many of the present factors or factors related to current literature. As a Foulkesian group orientation therapist, I was aware of a number of group phenomena, some of them identified by Foulkes, and others by me. I published two essays in the magazine *Group*

Table 8.4 Presence and efficacy in Groups I, II and IV

Level	Factors	Group rating of the presence of the six intrapsychic factors			Factors	Group rating of the healing value of the six intrapsychic factors		
		Group I (6 persons)	Group II (9 persons)	Group IV (9 persons)		Group I (6 persons)	Group II (9 persons)	Group IV (6 persons)
High presence	Anxiety	4	3	5	Anxiety	1	1	3*
	Resistance	1	1	1	Resistance	2	3	2
	Silence	1	2	2	Silence	—	—	2
	Regression	1	4	5	Regression	3	3	3
	Identification	4	2	2	Identification	6	4	1
	Transference	1	6	3	Transference	—	7	1
Moderate presence	Anxiety	1	4	—	Anxiety	4	3	—
	Resistance	1	3	—	Resistance	1	1	3
	Silence	3	5	—	Silence	3	6	2
	Regression	4	2	—	Regression	1	4	3
	Identification	1	1	—	Identification	—	2	3
	Transference	2	3	—	Transference	3	2	1
Low presence	Anxiety	1	2	—	Anxiety	1	5	3
	Resistance	4	5	—	Resistance	3	5	1
	Silence	2	2	—	Silence	3	3	2
	Regression	1	3	—	Regression	2	2	—
	Identification	1	6	—	Identification	—	3	2
	Transference	3	—	—	Transference	3	—	4

*New classification, 6 months later, with just 6 members.

Table 8.5 Correlation between therapeutic factors in the four groups

Factors	Group I	Group II	Group III	Group IV
Therapist and guidance	0.74**	–	–	–
Therapist and acceptance	0.60**	0.53**	–	–
Therapist and self-disclosure	–	–	0.55**	–
Therapist and permission to speak	–	0.52**	–	–
Acceptance and self-disclosure	0.64*	–	0.60**	0.66*
Acceptance and permission to speak	0.55*	–	–	–
Acceptance and guidance	–	0.56*	–	–
Catharsis and corrective emotional experience	0.56**	0.58**	0.67*	0.57**
Catharsis and vicarious learning	–	0.58*	–	0.66**
Catharsis and motivation	–	–	0.55**	–
Self-disclosure and guidance	0.59**	–	–	–
Self-disclosure and silence	–	–	–	0.56**
Motivation and permission to speak	0.61*	0.56**	–	–
Motivation and corrective emotional experience	0.56**	–	–	–
Motivation and guidance	–	–	–	0.74*
Vicarious learning and guidance	–	0.54**	–	–
Vicarious learning and corrective emotional experience	–	–	–	0.60*
Vicarious learning and identification	–	0.54**	–	–
Resistance and silence	–	–	–	0.66*
Transference and identification	0.53**	–	–	–

* $p < 0.05$
** $p < 0.10$

Analysis, where I called these phenomena 'Cure Helping Agents and Cure Psychodynamic Mechanisms'.[5] In this context, I think it is essential to start first by talking about the distinction between therapeutic factors and changing conditions, and then to follow with the discussion.

Bloch and Crouch[6] talk about this distinction which I consider more confusing than enlightening. Once it is difficult to have a formal and material definition of 'cure factor', it becomes complex to make distinctions with reference to the cure factors, as they belong to different fields. Friedman[7] talks about the belonging of therapeutic factors to four different areas. Although they happen in groups, their origin, their source, comes from different causes and processes. Not only do they come from different causes, but there are also different names for the same processes. These different names cause confusion: for instance, vicarious learning, identification and therapy observer are commonly used to refer to each other, although I realise that this relates to the complexity of human experience which cannot be contained in just one name or process. I prefer not to make a distinction between some processes that are cure factors and others that are changing conditions: for instance, group cohesion and acceptance.

If we look at the group as a whole, as either a resource or a system, all factors can be 'cure factors' or 'changing conditions', depending on the point of view of the process considered. As an individual, all factors are related to the participant as 'changing conditions'. that is, one cannot change if one is not motivated, if one does not accept oneself and others, if one did not try to accept oneself, to self-reveal oneself, if one did not pay attention to others, trying to understand oneself and others. As a group, as a whole self revealing itself, motivated, in catharsis, learning through the interaction, accepting itself – all these factors became a changing strength for the participant and thus became therapeutic factors and cure mechanisms. Then, I see the fulfilment of necessities in the coming together of human beings. From this perspective, the group is the main cure power. Experiencing the group processes in action, they are the cure mechanisms, because they have a huge transformational power. When they are accepted with more or less intensity, they become conditions of changing and cure.

Having in mind these comments, I go on with my discussion and conclusion.

Table 8.1

Table 8.1 (p. 139) gives us a general vision of all the processes for the four groups. Differences are seen as different paths followed by the groups. Bearing in mind that each group is different in its composition and its necessities, they also experience the changing process at a different pace and intensity.

The order of classification of factors expresses the kind of necessities and movement of each group. This shows group necessities and group wishes in that direction. I agree with Bloch and Crouch[8] and Yalom[9] when they state that what happens with the individual also happens with the group with reference to the scoring for certain factors that resemble the necessities of the individual and the group. Participants tend to score highly on those factors that represent their necessities better or that represent the experiences they are going through. The psychotherapist factor has the highest mark, even though the therapist is also the researcher in the group itself. I agree with Truax's[10] – opinion that the therapist is the most powerful therapeutic factor. Catharsis and corrective emotional experience occupy the last places, that is, they have got the lowest marks. My appreciation of this result is that, when the therapist works mainly in the 'here and now', s/he does not facilitate these processes that, in a way, belong mainly to the past. In the case of these four groups, therapists were strongly based in phenomenology.

The factor classification order shows the different stages and necessities of each group. Acceptance, for instance, comes in second place in Group I, because, as they are the only group with a time limit imposed, they feel the necessity of being sure of themselves through acceptance, and then they go on to the following stage of permission to speak. This hurry makes them anxious (anxiety comes in the second place), and they need explanation, which appears as the fourth factor. Motivation comes in fifth place, which does not surprise us, because, as they are an undergraduate psychology student group, they had said that they would like to experience two stages: to know what the group process is and how it happens, and to be in it. This information makes sense if we observe the classification order of the intrapsychic therapeutic factors, where identification is in first place, followed by anxiety and regression. So, we can affirm that Group I went through a deep process of therapy, as there is a good correspondence and balance between the cure factors and the intrapsychic ones. Some important observations about Group III: the SD of this group is the highest of all groups. This group did not homogeneously see what was going on and had also a different understanding of the process in course. This different perception comes, I think, from the extra group elements. In this group, the limits between the therapist and the participants, between participants and participants were not clear. The therapist had been lecturer and supervisor of some participants, and some of them had been colleagues in some subjects, while others were close friends, outside the group. Privacy was not taken into account, and this was the real atmosphere in the group.

These changing roles do not help to develop an effective process, it causes confusion and perturbation in the meetings. The parameters are completely permeable, different forms of acting out come up mainly from confluence and retroflection.

Table 8.2

Self-disclosure and acceptance emerge as the most effective and helpful factors, if we think of permission to speak and motivation not as factors but as changing conditions. On the other hand, catharsis and corrective emotional experience appear as the less effective and helpful.

When somebody is working phenomenologically, s/he becomes more conscious of the fact of the here and now, becomes more conscious of his/her own consciousness and keeps his/her power in a more conscious way. Following this line of thought, working in the here and now, the participant keeps under control his acceptance and self-disclosure, because these factors are more intellectual than physical. This did not occur with catharsis and corrective emotional experience which are more present. The unconscious is under pressure of physical processes and the participant's capacity of control decreases with a strong emotional experience.

Looking at the intrapsychic therapeutic factors, we see that identification and anxiety are highly present, or that they make us consider that acceptance and self-disclosure are experienced as difficult processes and that the group therapist should be careful to facilitate the emergence of these factors in the first moments or stages of the group.

Table 8.3

The data obtained in Tables 8.1 and 8.2 are the results from the weekly applications of questionnaires; Table 8.3 shows the results from the only evaluation which happened at the end of the therapy sessions, in the very last session, just before the termination of the groups, except for Group II whose end was scheduled for July 1990. In relation to Table 8.3, the participants were asked to try to see the therapeutic process as a whole, after the twenty-five sessions, and, again, to mark it, now with the feeling that the factor had been effective and very useful throughout the therapy. As we can see, the marking or the order of factors in this final evaluation is different from the classification obtained with the weekly marking immediately after each session. For instance, in Table 8.3, self-disclosure and acceptance do not appear more highly effective in Groups I and II than moderately effective in Groups I, II, III. Only Group II, with an average group existence of nearly three-and-a-half years, keeps the psychotherapist as the most effective and helpful factor in the cure process.

Why is Group II so consistent in relation to the psychotherapist? I can provide some answers:

1 the therapist is really a powerful and effective participant;
2 there is a huge dependency on the therapist;
3 from the psychoanalytic point of view, the longer the group goes on, the more the therapist becomes an introject of love that ends up keeping the group together, working to prevent its division. Introjection and confluence can be the base of this third hypothesis.

Six months after Group IV had answered the final questionnaire, I asked them, again, to do a reclassification of the therapeutic factors. Immediately, again, they modified their understanding of their therapeutic process: for instance, the corrective emotional experience factor, that had six positive responses in the second evaluation, now had only two. This indicates that with the passing of time, either the introjected therapeutic learning is seen differently with respect to the way it was experienced and the factors assume different values and significance, or that with the passing of time, the experienced process becomes a reality integrated in the individual and it is seen as more distant and difficult to classify.

I agree with Bloch and Crouch,[11] trying to understand the difference of reliability of the responses, when participants answer them after the session and when they answer them after a period of time: 'the respondent thinks with reference to a restricted period of time, relatively brief (for instance, 3 sessions), which allows him to remember all the important things that happened during those sessions more easily, and also, more accurately. On the other hand, if he tries to remember a selection of events of something which happened a couple of weeks or months ago, it is very likely that he will not remember clearly'. This fact would explain the change in the evaluation opinion when this is done months later.

Table 8.4

Table 8.4 is very significant, because it shows how a factor that was highly present can also be a cure factor. Anxiety, for instance, is highly present in Group I, but it does not appear with a high cure power, only moderate. It is important to remember that Group I is a group formed by undergraduate students of psychology. This result throws into relief the function of the anxiety in group therapy. High anxiety or no anxiety (Group IV and Group II, Table 8.1) suggests the necessity of a deep understanding with reference to the group process and the relationship between the therapist and the participants. Moderate anxiety seems to be a good sign that the cure process is possible. When there is no anxiety, it seems to me that there is not a real cure process either.

Identification, transference and regression are types of process that seem to be related to each other. Although some Gestalt therapists say that they do not work with transference, or through it, transference is always present, at least, according to our understanding. Identification and transference are seen, respectively, as highly curative by the participants (Group I and II). These processes seem to happen independently of the techniques, but are dependent on the attitude and behaviour of the therapist, as well as the attitude of the group members. These processes are essentially human existential; they belong to the intimate, to the deepest part of the human being and occur in a high or low proportion, independently of the therapeutic method used.

In Group IV, we see that identification and transference are not substantially present. Why? Let us remember that this group was a weekend one, which used to meet every three months, although the participants were the same. Could it be that frequency of the sessions, like the weekly ones, is needed to create and keep these processes? Could it be that three-monthly groups, according to their nature, could not create and keep stable links that generate these relationships? Taking into account the responses of six members of this group, six months after the application of the first questionnaire, only one member sees transference and identification as highly present. It seems that with the passing of time, there is also a passing of links.

Reviewing Table 8.1, Group I is not a resistant group, but the most anxious one of all. It seems that they do not feel free and secure in that group. On the other hand, in Group II, anxiety comes in fourth place, nearly non-existent. Links here are very strong which facilitate good introjections. Identification and transference processes are essential for the development of the group and their members, and the encouragement of the cure process.

These mechanisms are seen analytically as resistance forms for the cure process. The Gestalt therapy sees them as perturbations in the contact limit. It may be that anxiety is an unconscious movement that hastens the process of going from the symbolic to the real, characteristic of projective identification.

When the data are organised, identification is more present as a form of avoiding anxiety. When the group becomes more familiar, transference takes over from anxiety.

Table 8.5

Table 8.5 shows us the correlations between the four groups. I accept $p = < 0.10$ only as an indicative of a tendency. For instance, catharsis, although seen as unimportant and ineffective (Group II), is the one most related to corrective emotional experience, which makes sense.

It is very difficult to define how independent these factors are from each other, at least in the results. I believe it does not present a problem to my definitions, because they emerge and remain in a very fluid field, where it is difficult to establish limits through the operation of such definitions.

Through these correlations we can see a group, in a vertical cut, in its here and now, as an instantaneous image. We can also see more easily the culture of each group. These factor correlations, in each group, are a kind of therapeutic existentialist movement. Through them, we can see the different levels of the group stages like a proceedings or interventions indicator and like a process source which provides didactic information of combinations of echoes from the most intense processes experienced by the group.

We are trying to understand the basic processes from these four groups and the cure processes experienced by them, so it is important to relate the inter- and intrapsychic factors experienced by the group. Nevertheless it is a scale which seeks to quantify feelings, some of them with a nature more unconscious than conscious; we have to accept the participants' perceptions as fundamentally correct and true.

In the final analysis of the data (which explains the cure process), the information from the order of the factor classification will be first considered also with the researcher's knowledge about the process and the history of each group. In this sense, Group II, although similar to the rest of the groups in many respects, is qualitatively different in basic items, as for instance, anxiety. It is important to remember that the average life of Group II is about three-and-a-half years, which probably alters the group behaviour.

These observations are valid and consistent due to the fact that the groups are well developed, which can be appreciated by the evaluation of the final questionnaire. We can state that these sources reflect the process studied by each group in search of its change, realisation of its power, well-being and cure.

FINAL ANALYSIS OF THE CHANGING PROCESS

The multidirectional identification process works as the most present mechanism. There is a permanent *mirror*-reaction, through which the group elements are seen by each other and they relearn to read, to modify their fixation process of the neurotic behaviour and to fulfil their necessities. This identification process involves an introjection movement with reference to the projection, in relation to each group member, to the therapist and to the group as a whole. Perhaps we could state that a group that cannot achieve a high level of identification will have also difficulties in becoming fully involved in the healing relationship.

We should still verify if there is a correlation between a high level of identification and a low level of resistance, as happened in these groups. Anxiety plays an important role in the cure changing process. The identification process seems to increase anxiety, instead of reducing it, when it places the individual against his own problem, projected onto another, forcing him/her to face the confrontation and possible solutions, which increases anxiety. Besides, we can also say that a high level of anxiety does not provoke necessarily a high level of resistance. In this context, resistance and anxiety are together as complementary functions of different levels of the individual and the group. A high level of anxiety decreases the level of resistance.

This duplicate identification process and anxiety pushes the group unconscious towards a regressive dimension, in a kind of search for an understanding of what has been experienced. Well-being or otherwise is obvious in a group situation. To retreat means to go the origins, to look for the origins, to experience the origins. In this context, neglect occurs and then the transference process comes up as an

Table 8.6 Final sum of the factors order in the four groups

Factors	Psychosocial therapeutic factors		
1	Therapist	1	4
2	Permission to speak	2	13
3	Acceptance	3	13
4	Motivation	4	16
5	Self-disclosure	5	17
6	Guidance	6	24
7	Vicarious learning	7	27
8	Corrective emotional experience	8	31
9	Catharsis	9	35
Factors A	Intrapsychic therapeutic factors		
1	Identification	1	5
2	Anxiety	2	9
3	Regression	3	14
4	Transference	4	15
5	Resistance	5	20
6	Silence	6	21

unconscious solution for this neglect, when the invisible turns into visible because of the transference. The transference works as a guarantee, albeit provisional, of the fact of being in contact, ending with the rejection sensation, common in a regression situation.

Taking into account the group process as a whole, it is as well to remember that a balanced relationship between intra- and interpsychic factors helps in the understanding of how these groups work.

Interpsychic factors

Groups agree systematically and consistently that the psychotherapist is an essential element in the changing process. Unlike the intrapsychic factors, where identification is the most effective factor, provoking other factors, here the psychotherapist is a helping agent for the different processes. Table 8.5 gives us an idea of how the changing process initially revolves around the therapist. In different levels, the psychotherapist is related to guidance, acceptance, self-disclosure and permission to speak. In a second stage, self-disclosure and guidance, acceptance, guidance and permission to speak are interrelated. This indicates that in these groups, the changing process happens based on the therapist, who is the irradiation centre of energy, which is caught by the group and transformed into a changing process, and cure factors, which are experienced in a different way by each participant.

The changing process happens basically on two levels: individual intrapsychic and group interpsychic. Perhaps we could add a third level that has elements with processes in both levels that are Factors 4, 5, 6.

From the point of view of the interpsychic factors, it seems as if permission to speak, having the chance to talk freely without obstacles, causes the rest of the processes. Self-disclosure and explanation, acceptance, and permission to speak are correlated among themselves. There are indications that the process of change occurs through the therapist, who is transformed at the centre of this energy – as is the group, which experiences the process of change through the various curative factors.

In the case of the four groups here, motivation appears as a process, the consequence of 'being able to talk' and of 'feeling accepted'. Motivation appears as a process of elaboration in and for the therapy based, above all, in the previous process of acceptance. The process of elaboration of the acceptance is the pivot of the comprehension of others' processes.

Thus the process of acceptance antecedes the one of motivation. The definition of motivation involves an element of group inclusion, of being really involved, and an intimate contact with the inner and exterior worlds which leads naturally to the process of self-disclosure. This self-disclosure is not just another social process of being able to talk and exchange information or experiences, but it is based in self-change, it is something profound, and it depends on the basic acceptance of the 'I'. This self-disclosure occurs not to provoke a change but *because of* a profound change that already has taken place. It is a celebration of the person's own simplicity, of his or her own found singularity; it is something that is felt as belonging, essentially, to that particular person, something that cannot be stolen or adulterated. To be open oneself, without borders, healthfully, seems to be the signal of a mature and irrevocable victory.

Although the explanation is done by the therapist, it also occurs through the members of the group. Explanation, unlike the other factors, is not exactly a process; it is something that occurs externally, but which is provoked internally. It is not clear if explanation is essential to the evolutionary process of the group, even though the therapist, who usually is the one who explains most, is the essential element in the healthful development of the group. Explanation showed itself to be correlated to the psychotherapist in Group I p =74 (p < 0.05) (the only group whose members had not participated previously in any form of therapy). However, no significant correlation was found in the other groups. Yalom says that clients pay little attention to what the therapist says, but that they do pay attention to *the way* he/she says things. Also, clients have a tendency to attribute the success of the therapy not to the group, but to elements external to the process.[12] Perhaps these factors help us to understand better that what the therapist does in explaining is not as important as what he/she *is as a person*.

The last three factors, vicarious learning, corrective emotional experience and catharsis, have many elements in common, and the latter two have more unconscious elements than vicarious learning, at least according to the proposed definitions. These three mechanisms bring an idea of re-experiencing conflicts, sorrows, anxieties, in a real way and not completely under control. These sensations, these processes, happen at an unconscious level as a response to a present situation which evokes such experiences. The difference is that, originally, the processes which generated the symptoms will happen without proof or will happen under pressure of significative forces from which one could not escape, such as, for instance, the familiar pressure on the child. In the group, these conflicts emerge under the auspices of a loving and free environment amongst individuals and, mainly, the therapist.

The group relive their experiences, now trying the other side of the coin, hidden, not experienced before, which is expressed by an environment which facilitates free expression, without censorship and looking for the lost originality and creation of the real self. The group patiently attends the creation of a new creature, through the sorrow, the feelings caused by power, violence, and a distant past, apparently forgotten.

Unlike the intrapsychic factors which are the individual experiences in group, these three interpsychic factors (4, 5 and 6) are forms of group reactions, experienced by the individual. In this sense, it seems more difficult for the individual to be completely conscious of his/her dimensions and possibilities.

These three classified factors, as the last ones with reference to the effectiveness and capacity of helping, raise challenging questions.

1 Does the fact of not creating a situation which helps the emergence of these phenomena belong to the group process?
2 Are the phenomenologic approaches (in this case Gestalt therapy) less orientated to the emergence of these processes due to the fact of being in the here and now?
3 Would a course of psychotherapy, in the strict sense of the term, be more characterised by the presence of these factors whilst their absence or their near absence would characterise the process more as a social therapy, although the cure process happens in the same way?
4 Would the presence of these factors be more related to the therapist's style than to his/her theoretical approach?

Although these processes had happened on many occasions in all the groups and had been commented upon by the participants as 'important and deep', some members of the four groups considered them to be the least efficient and helpful. Why? Perhaps because the group atmosphere is not the ideal place for them due to fear, resistance, fear of the loss of control. Perhaps it is because, as they approach unconscious layers, they are not perceived immediately as efficient and active by the group, and it is difficult to classify them on a more conscious level of experience. Perhaps it is because of the fact that the rest of the factors are more group-oriented and the others more internal, less frequent and, as they are less visibly present, that they are seen as less effective and active by the group members. All these questions should be studied more deeply, because their theoretical approach can determine better the nature of the therapeutic process and clarify the utility of different approaches and the important role of the therapist. I believe that the explanation of these theoretical questions can be very helpful in the process of group psychotherapy, in the explanation of the change concept and how to facilitate or not this change in the group.

Taking into account this comparative study, I present some important conclusions to develop the group process and to inform about the training theory.

1 Each group forms its own different culture. There is not a model. Therapeutic factors occur in a different way in each group.
2 Some factors are more present, effective and are more helpful than others, in different group stages.
3 Factors that have a higher classification than others express the participants' different requirements in a clear and perhaps urgent way.
4 The classification order of factors is a profile of the individual process and of each group. A posteriori, this order indicates the direction followed by the individual in his/her cure search or development and also the process followed by the group as a whole. The participant tends to classify this as the most important factor, the one that expresses his/her requirements best.
5 The classification order of factors can express the grade of the participant's necessities, his/her opinion about which factor is more efficient in the cure development or which factor is going to facilitate the process.

6 These factors are interdependent and work as a sub-system of a bigger system which is the group. They emerge or disappear depending on the basic group necessities, regardless of sex, age or educational level of the members.

7 In the four groups, the therapist was considered as the most important factor. S/he was considered the most valuable cure factor, regardless of her/his style or the fact that s/he was the researcher. In these four groups, the therapists were highly experienced individuals. It only remains to find out if this factor would have been considered the most relevant if the therapist had not been such a recognised expert. This raises the question: is it the real necessity of the group that makes the therapist be the principal factor?

APPENDIX 8.1: THE FINAL QUESTIONNAIRE

1 How long have you been in the group?
2 What kind of changes in your life can you see as a direct effect on your process of being in group psychotherapy?
3 Choose three from the nine (1–2–3–4–5–6–7–8–9) psychotherapeutic factors which helped or have helped you more in this group?
4 Choose two from the six (1–2–3–4–5–6) intrapsychic factors which have really worked in your psychotherapy, being really present.
5 Do you believe that your main aim in being in group psychotherapy was achieved?
6 Would you please say something that you feel is relevant in your psycho-therapeutic process.

NOTES

1 Yalom (1985) p. 5.
2 Ibid., pp. 71–72.
3 Bloch and Crouch (1985), p. 4.
4 Ibid., p. X.
5 Ribeiro (1978; 1979).
6 Bloch and Crouch (1985), pp. 5, 6, 103, 122; Yalom (1985), p. 71.
7 Friedman (1989), p. 60.
8 Bloch and Crouch (1985), p. 234.
9 Yalom (1985), p. 111.
10 C. B. Truax, in Friedman (1989), pp. 87–88.
11 Bloch and Crouch (1985), p. 272.
12 Friedman (1989), p. 166.

REFERENCES

Bloch. S. and Crouch, E. (1985) *Therapeutic Factors in Group Psychotherapy*, Oxford: Oxford Medical.
Friedman, W.H. (1989) *Practical Group Therapy*, London: Jossey-Bass.
Ribeiro, J.P. (1978) 'Psychotherapeutic cure facilitation agents in group analysis: a Foulkesian approach', *Group Analysis* XI: 203–207.

Ribeiro J.P. (1979) 'Psychodynamic cure mechanisms in group analysis: a Foulkesian approach', *Group Analysis* XII: 114–117.

Slipp. S. (ed.) (1982) *Curative Factors in Dynamic Psychotherapy*, London: McGraw-Hill.

Smith. P.B. (1980) *Group Process*, London: Harper & Row.

Yalom. I.D. (1985) *The Theory and Practice of Group Psychotherapy* (3rd edn), New York: Basic Books.

Chapter 9

Transformational research

John Rowan

For many people, research is a forbidding word, bringing up all sorts of pictures of tables, charts, diagrams and statistics. But in the last thirty years there have been two revolutions in our thinking about research, and I think that a third revolution is on the way. All real revolutions start off by negating what went before; but they also incorporate much of what went before, now seen and experienced differently (Kuhn, 1962).

The first revolution was the advent of qualitative research in the 1960s. The new thing about qualitative research was that it denied the necessity of going on to quantitative verification. Instead of a pilot study involving ten people followed by a major study of a thousand people, we have an entire study consisting of interviews with thirty people. It was not until the 1970s, however, that qualitative research began to appear in the official texts and journals. A slightly later American text includes the following:

> Participant observation, content analysis, formal and informal interviewing, videotaping, the discovery and use of unobtrusive measures, life history construction, archival data surveys, historical analysis, and various formal sociologies such as dramaturgic analysis, frame analysis, ethnomethodology, and conversational analysis are but a few examples of some very different substantive and procedural approaches falling under the qualitative research label (Van Maanen *et al.*, 1982: 15).

A British book of the same period focuses on four main methods: depth interviews, group interviews, participant observation and projective techniques (Walker, 1985: 4).

The second revolution was the advent of new paradigm research in the 1970s. Again there had been many precursors to this, but it was only in 1977, after a conference of the Association for Humanistic Psychology, that the New Paradigm Research Group was set up in this country. Similar things were happening in other countries, too, in Norway, the USA, in Tanzania, in India, in Canada, in Scandinavia and so on (Reason and Rowan, 1981). This went much further in the direction of being non-alienating research. It pointed out that qualitative research was totally controlled by the researchers. It was a one-way sucking out of information from the people involved in it, for the benefit of the sponsor, who very often was a commercial firm only interested in its own concerns. The people involved in a piece of qualitative research quickly picked up what the researchers were really interested in, and gave them that. For example, in all the qualitative research I was involved in or heard about in the 1960s and 70s no one ever mentioned feminism, even though it was a major concern for at least some of the thousands of women being questioned.

So new paradigm research tried to do better than that, and to involve the people being researched much more deeply. We talked about doing research *with* people, rather than *on* people, and Peter Reason and I edited a book called *Human Inquiry* in 1981 which brought a lot of this work together in one place. We tried to recruit people for any research study we carried out who would be genuinely interested in and benefited by the results. Some of us called it 'collaborative inquiry', and there is now a newsletter with this title which comes out regularly from Peter Reason at Bath University.* This is a very exciting approach which is still spreading worldwide, and which is particularly suitable for work in developing countries who would find other forms of research hard to accept and easy to subvert. For some further material on this see for example Lincoln and Guba (1985) and Berg and Smith (1988).

But now I think a third revolution may be on the way, and it is this that I want to concentrate on here. It is a form of research which goes beyond being non-alienating and thinks in terms of genuine transformation. Not so much involving the people being studied, but more like *being* the people studied. The barrier between researcher and subject, which had been eroded a good deal in collaborative research, disappears altogether at times. Before going into the details of that, let me set the scene a bit more by saying where this is coming from.

FOUR LEVELS OF CONSCIOUSNESS

Table 9.1 shows some interesting details about the process of psychospiritual development. According to Ken Wilber (1995) we are all on a psychospiritual path of development, which has on it a number of different way stations. Starting with the earliest ones which go from life in the womb up through birth and infancy into childhood and adolescence, we pick up the story in early adulthood.

It can be seen that column 1 is all about ordinary everyday consciousness, which most of us adopt most of the time. There are few surprises as our eyes go down the column. Qualitative research, as we have described it above, comes fully in column 1. (So does quantitative research, but we are not talking about that at the moment.) This first column is dominated completely by the ego of the researcher. It is the researcher's values and interests which are paramount here, even when there is an attempt to reach out more to the people being studied.

---

* Ceased publication in 1997.

Table 9.1 A comparison of four positions in personal development

	1	2	3	4
Wilber level	Persona/ shadow	Centaur	Subtle self	Causal self
Rowan position	Mental ego	Real self	Soul	Spirit
Self	I am defined by others	I define who I am	I am defined by the Other(s)	I am not defined
Motivation	Need	Choice	Allowing	Surrender
Personal goal	Adjustment	Self-actualisation	Contacting	Union
Social goal	Socialisation	Liberation	Extending	Salvation
Process	Healing – ego building	Development – ego-extending	Opening – ego-reduction	Enlightenment
Traditional role of helper	Physician/ analyst	Growth facilitator	Advanced guide	Priest(ess)/ sage
Representative approaches	Hospital treatment Chemotherapy Psycho-analysis Directive Behaviour modification Cognitive-behavioural Some TA Crisis work RET Brief therapy	Primal integration Gestalt therapy Open encounter Psychodrama Neo-Freudians Bodywork therapies Some TA Person-centred Co-counselling T-groups	Psycho-synthesis Some Jungians Some pagans Transpersonal Voice dialogue Some Wicca or magic Kabbalah Some astrology Some Tantra Shamanism	Mystical Buddhism Raja Yoga Taoism Monasticism Da Love Ananda Christian mysticism Sufi Goddess mystics Some Judaism Advaita
Focus	Individual and group	Group and individual	Supportive community	Ideal community
Representative names	Freud Ellis Meichenbaum Beck Eysenck Skinner Lazarus Watzlawick Wessler Haley	Maslow Rogers Mahrer Perls Lowen Schutz Moreno Stevens Argyris Bugental	Jung Hillman Starhawk Assagioli Gordon-Brown Mary Watkins Jean Houston Bolen Grof Boorstein	Eckhart Shankara Dante Tauler Suso Ruysbroeck Nagarjuna Lao Tzu George Fox Julian of Norwich
Research methods	Qualitative	Collaborative	Transformative	Meditation
Questions	Dare you face the challenge of the unconscious?	Dare you face the challenge of freedom?	Dare you face the loss of your boundaries?	Dare you face the loss of all your symbols?
Key issues	Acceptability, respect	Autonomy, authenticity	Openness, vision	Devotion, commitment

Collaborative research, which is one of the forms of new paradigm research (Reason and Rowan, 1981), comes mainly in column 2. It is a classically humanistic approach, where there is an emphasis on honesty, truth and authenticity. Alienation is systematically and consistently fought against and critiqued. There is a social conscience as to what projects are taken on. But there is a clear distinction between who the researcher is and who the subject is, even though they are much more intimately related than in the previous forms of research.

Column 3 is less familiar and may require some thought. In this chapter we shall try and examine it in some detail, under the heading of transformational research. Here we are questioning the whole necessity for boundaries and the reality of separation. This approach says that we are essentially spiritual beings in a spiritual universe, that humans ultimately seek meaning within their activities, and that creative living is necessary for both psychological and spiritual growth (May, 1991). Mythology and storytelling are valued and worked with, and there is some emphasis on ecological vision and planetary consciousness (Gomes and Kanne, 1995).

Just to say something about column 4, at this level we cannot do research, because our interests have drifted so much away from any kind of instrumentality. So I am proposing to ignore column 4 in this particular context, although I think it is true that work at the level of column 3 is much helped if the people involved have an experience and an appreciation of the nourishment which can be obtained from their own involvement in meditation and other activities which belong in column 4.

CASE EXAMPLE

So with this much as background and context, let us now look at an example of this approach in action. John Heron carried out a piece of research on altered states of consciousness (Tart, 1990) which brings out the way in which these things work out in practice. One of the first points which Heron makes is that the researchers must share in the experience. He says:

> It makes sense for ASC researchers to be involved in the altered states they are studying, if they want to generate appropriate categories of understanding and methods of inquiry. It is unsound to map an unknown country by never visiting it yourself, and by trying to make sense of the reports of others who have visited it. (Heron, 1988: 182)

This means that the research becomes at the same time a training in entry into and use of altered states. Here we get the theme of initiation (Whiteman, 1986). The researchers need to be initiated into the quality and depth of the altered states they wish to study. This point is also made by Sheila McClelland: 'there was a sense that we could only learn, develop and hone these skills by launching into action. Paradoxically, the skills needed to start out are precisely those which engagement in the inquiry actually develop' (McClelland, 1994: 114).

This research was carried out in a five-day workshop with twenty participants located at the CAER centre in Cornwall. The altered state it was decided by the group to study was that where we are at one and the same time in everyday physical reality and aware of and paying attention to another non-physical reality, a subtle energy world of presences and powers that is somehow within and around the physical world.

The first round used ritual as the method of getting in touch with non-ordinary reality (fully described in Heron, 1988). As a result of this ritual, three people obtained what seemed to them to be instructions for how to proceed further. These seeming instructions were then used for the second round. We must hurry past the intriguing details of all this, which is a pity, because they have much to say about the concepts of alignment and attunement which we shall be talking about later on. In the third round everyone practised noticing extrasensory impressions at the very edge of the ordinary physical visual field. In the fourth round the group first found the spot in the garden where the birds flocked (this was one of the instructions from round one) and then filed into the *fogou* – an underground cave used in prehistoric times for religious ceremonies. Some strong impressions and impacts came from these activities.

Out of all these experiences five things emerged: (1) streaming of energy in and out of the energy field of the physical body; (2) visions of faces and symbolic objects; (3) a felt sense of presences, and of their energies and activities, in the other reality within certain areas of physical space; (4) a sense of the numinous, the holy; and (5) emotional uplift. The group then got worried as to the status of these experiences. Were they genuine altered states of consciousness, putting the participants in touch with non-ordinary reality, or were they, on the other hand, evidence of a massive consensus collusion which had created a set of shared illusions? It seemed important to have some way of telling which was which.

There were two further rounds which introduced more material again, and tremendous energy and involvement were released, but let us stop there with this account. John Heron says:

> One of the major difficulties with ASC research is that there is a tendency to come not quite fully back from an altered state, and so to fall short of sufficient critical discrimination, in an ordinary state, about what was really going on. (Heron, 1988: 192)

Yet one of the most interesting findings of this research was that there were six criteria which, when taken all together, could in principle distinguish between true and false impressions.

1 *Agreement* Two or more persons have the same or similar impressions of the other reality.
2 *Heterogeneity* Very different sorts of impressions of the other reality, which occur both simultaneously and serially, in the same person and in several persons, are compatible.

3 *Synchronicity* Impressions of the other reality occur simultaneously to two or more persons, and are meaningful to them in the same or a similar way.

4 *Spontaneity* Impressions of the other reality often come unexpected and unbidden: are often surprising in their content; and the recipient did not want or intend to produce them in the way in which they occurred.

5 *Independence* Impressions of the other reality have a life of their own and are not amenable to manipulation and interference.

6 *Spatial reference* Impressions of the other reality have reference to locations in a subtle and inwardly extensive space that is somehow *within* physical space.

You might like to consider whether these criteria could validate the existence of UFO abductions, extra-sensory perception, angelic presences, mystical experiences and so forth. Such experiences have of course been studied much more in recent years, as for example in the work of Stanislav and Christina Grof (Grof and Grof, 1990).

Heron makes the point that although the research was transformational, and although the content was at least partly within the subtle realm, and although the participants did manage and control a good deal of the research process, it falls short of the full promise of transformational research in two respects. One was that the five-day format was set by John Heron, without any kind of consultation with the prospective participants, and the other was that it was John Heron who wrote up the report, all by himself. Hence, though it was in large measure non-alienating research, there were still elements of alienation involved in it. Let us have a closer look at this question of alienation.

THE RESEARCH CYCLE

If we look at a representation of the basic standard research cycle (Figure 9.1), we can see that it has a very definite form, with some unavoidable stages within it. The full details and justification of it are given in my chapter in *Human Inquiry* (Rowan, 1981).

As you will see, we normally start over on the left-hand side, just being. We are working happily away in our field, when some disturbance arises. It may be negative, in that we have to solve some problem in order to survive; or it may be positive, in that we see an opportunity and take it. There are many possibilities as to why we should need to take action. But when we do so, the first thing we do is to get more information. This is the phase I have called thinking. During this stage we are taking in material and processing it, in order to find whether there is some answer already, so that we do not need to do research. We survey the literature, we make telephone calls, we pick people's brains, we keep our antennae out, we lay ourselves open to receiving ideas and information.

At a certain point, we stop doing that and start inventing a Project. Projects are very important: Sartre once said that people are known by their projects.

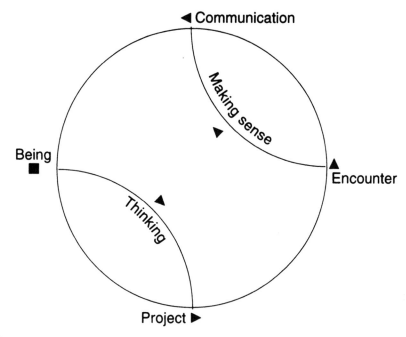

Figure 9.1 The cycle model

A project is a plan of action, a statement that if we do this, we shall get the answers we need. We may revise the project, scrap the project and start again. amend the project in the light of advice from experienced people in the field. and so on. The project may be invented by one person, or be the result of much consultation with a number of people, but it has to be a plan of some kind. Ian Cunningham (1988) has pointed out that in certain cases we should talk about general preparation rather than a formal project. In one case he produced sixty-one pages of notes for ideas on a particular project, and in the end rejected almost all of them; but he says that they were nonetheless valuable as preparation. as they forced him to think through the ideas and test them out.

But at a certain point. we need to abandon planning and actually get out into the field and do something. Here comes the encounter with reality. Here comes the test of all our planning and plotting. We open ourselves up to the possibility of disconfirmation. We lay ourselves open to the possibility of learning something, genuinely and for ourselves. And there is a paradox here: the more planning we have done. the more spontaneous we can be in responding to the needs of the new situation as it presents itself.

Again. at a certain point the involvement has to stop. We have to stand back and assess where we have got to, and bring all the results together, and make sense of them. Some of this is done by contemplation and soaking ourselves in the data, and some of it is done by thinking and analysing and systematising the results obtained. We may do it on our own, or as part of a research group, or with the participants in the research itself.

And eventually we arrive at something communicable, and we put it out in some form. We write or co-write a report, we go on television, we speak to journalists, we go on chat shows, whatever seems to be appropriate and possible. This is the stage of communication . And when we have delivered ourselves of all we have to say, we go back to being again, in our field, as before but not as before. Once more around the spiral.

Now that we have this general schema for what research is, we can use it in an interesting way. Suppose we represent alienation by a dotted line, and non-alienation by a solid line. And suppose that we represent the researcher by the circle, and the people whose experience is being studied by a line making some sort of contact with the circle. Then pure basic research, quantitative empirical research, would appear as shown in Figure 9.2.

The circle represents the researcher being alienated and role-bound, and the line represents the subject meeting the researcher, only at a tangent, at the point of encounter, or in other words only during the experiment or observation or survey. Figure 9.3 shows another style of research, called existential research.

Here the solidity of the line means that neither the researcher nor the subject is alienated, but the two only meet even now at one point on the cycle. The researcher is genuinely open to the subject, and is setting or making use of a situation in which the subject is genuinely open to the researcher, but is not

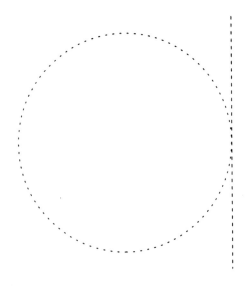

Figure 9.2 Representation of basic empirical research

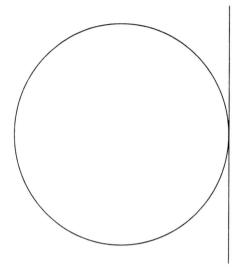

Figure 9.3 Representation of existential research

otherwise involving the subject in the whole research process. This is the kind of work which Charles Hampden-Turner (1976) has done, in his work with ex-addicts in the Delancey Street operation, which John Enright (1970) has done in his work with ex-addicts at Synanon, and which I myself (Rowan, 1976) have done in my work on the Tavistock Group.

So it is possible to show alienation and non-alienation quite clearly in these diagrams . What it is also possible to show, in a different way, is the extent of the involvement between researcher and subject. Figure 9.4 represents action research (Sanford, 1981), intervention research (Argyris, 1971) and personal construct research (Fransella, 1972).

Here the dashed line indicates that there is no direct compulsion to be alienated. The degree of alienation is allowed to vary, depending on the people involved and the social context. But the crucial difference is that the research subjects are also involved in the project stage and the communication stage. This means that they are involved in planning the research, and also involved in the final interpretation of what the research outcomes meant.

It can now be seen that there are two ways in which we can move away from basic empirical research: one is to decrease the amount of alienation, and the other is to involve the subject at more points on the cycle. Moving on now to new paradigm research, we can say that it does both of these things: it decreases the amount of alienation and it also involves the subjects at more points on the cycle (Figure 9.5).

The being and thinking points may sometimes be involved, but this is rare and does not seem to be essential. This is the kind of research which has been carried

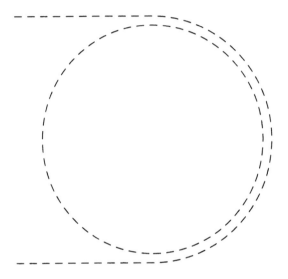

Figure 9.4 Representation of action research, intervention research and personal construct research

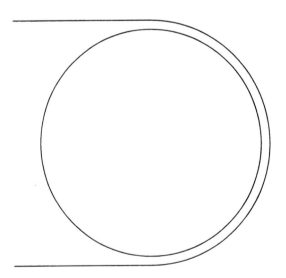

Figure 9.5 Representation of participatory research, collaborative research, experiential research and endogenous research

out by Bud Hall (1975, 1978) in his many participatory projects, Max Elden (1981) in his work on bank employees, and Magoroh Maruyama (1981) in his work with prisoners. It is sometimes called experiential research, sometimes endogenous research and sometimes collaborative research.

If we now use this kind of analysis to look at the John Heron research on altered states of consciousness we met earlier, the resulting diagram looks like Figure 9.6.

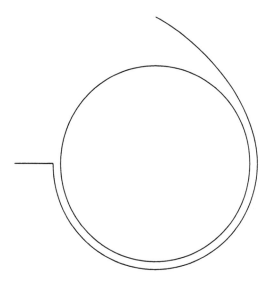

Figure 9.6 Representation of John Heron ASC research

This is taken from Peter Reason's (1988) reflections on the research, which he put together afterwards. It can be seen that this goes a long way towards the holistic ideal which we have been approaching all the time.

One of the most striking things about research done in this way is the amount of energy released. This is why it seems fitting to call it a high-energy type of research. What is more, energy seems to be released as each point on the cycle is left behind. This seems to have to do with the much higher degree of involvement and commitment required of the investigator. The researcher is in touch at several levels, not just the one level favoured at the mechanistic end of the continuum.

If we now ask what is the difference between transformative research and collaborative research, we can perhaps express it as shown in Figure 9.7.

Here the distinction between researcher and subject has disappeared altogether. But is this possible? It is certainly rare – I have not been able to find any fully realised examples. Some certainly come close; think of Freud's own self-analysis as revealed in his book *The Interpretation of Dreams*. Here the researcher and the subject went round the cycle many times, and real discoveries

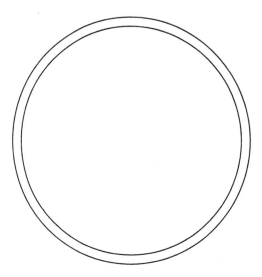

Figure 9.7 Representation of transformational research

were made in this way. But perhaps it is too easy if the researcher and the subject are the same person: how about if they are different people?

STORYTELLING AS RESEARCH

One interesting approach to research which follows these lines is storytelling as inquiry. as used by Peter Reason and Peter Hawkins. They investigated male–female relations in a mixed group by asking each participant to write a story involving a male–female interaction. Then, instead of discussing or analysing the stories, other participants replied to the stories by telling another story of their own. These responses took the form of replies, echoes, re-creations and reflections.

A reply is 'my reaction to your story': an expressive way of giving shape to the feelings and ideas arising while listening to the story. An echo is 'your theme in my story': here the listeners make a sharing response, of telling their own stories on the same theme. A re-creation is 'your story as re-created by me': here the listeners take the story and re-shape it into another form, finding their own way of telling the tale. This could be a poem, a fairy tale, or some other kind of story. It may stay at the same level as the original, or move toward the mythic or archetypal level. And a reflection is 'my story about your story': essentially the reflection involves standing further back, pondering on the story and its meaning.

What they found was that instead of simply obtaining data on male–female relationships and interactions, they were moving towards the deeper meanings of these things. They say:

Once we begin to inquire into the origins of meaning we begin to enter the paradoxical realms of transpersonal and spiritual knowing. In a holistic view of knowing, matter, mind and spirit interpenetrate: we have moved beyond the unreformed materialism of orthodox inquiry, and we need now to integrate a knowing from spirit (psyche, soul) with our existential human inquiry. A science of persons is inadequate without a knowing from soul. (Reason and Hawkin, 1988: 97)

This was a short workshop, only extending over two days, but it seems that the promise is there of something which could be used very effectively in various forms of heuristic and hermeneutic research, where the emphasis is on exploring meaning rather than obtaining generalisable results. The work of Michael Meade (1993) is not formal research, but could easily be turned in this direction, and I personally find it quite inspiring.

My own opinion is that all these people are very much in line with the contribution of feminism to this kind of thinking. I think of Ann Oakley (1981) and Janet Finch (1981) as having been some of the first in the field, with their contributions on the problems connected with the interviewing of women. I might add that more recently there has been a very interesting book edited by Erica Burman (1990) which makes a definite connection between feminism and new paradigm research. It appears that in the last few years, feminist research has taken up these new ideas and found them to be more relevant to their concerns. For example, Jan Burns says:

Furthermore, as new paradigm research becomes more acceptable women must fight for the acknowledgement that feminist psychology deserves in this development. As Reason and Rowan point out, many women have been doing new paradigm research for a long time with little recognition and credibility. Only now that it has been given a different name and taken under the more credible umbrella of new paradigm research has it become acceptable. Thus, feminist psychology should be recognised as not only participating in, but as being one of the leading influences of this changing paradigm within the social sciences (Burns, 1990: 161).

Some feminists go further than this. in outlining a specifically feminist approach. For example, Maria Mies (1983) has set out specific criteria for feminist research. They agree with the view of Sue Wilkinson (1986) that 'A female perspective is to be regarded as central to the research, not as an additional or comparative viewpoint'. It is interesting to note that the Reason and Hawkins research was about gender. and that the Meade approach is clearly from a masculine standpoint . There seems to be something here about gender taking us to the cutting edge of research in some way. Perhaps race is another site where this sort of thing is going to happen. as Gill Aitken (1996) suggests. An important point made by Wilkinson is that feminist research entails a critical evaluation of the research process itself – one of the main tenets of all these new approaches. Ann

Phoenix (1990), however, makes the point that there is no unitary feminist methodology to which all feminists have to subscribe.

SOME THEMES

Let us now try to draw together some of the threads, and make some general points about a transformational approach. Themes which I think emerge from all the data and need to be thought about are nine in number. In terms of our original four-column chart, this is now all about column 3. Let us look at them one by one.

(1) The first is balance. This means balancing the active with the receptive, the intellectual with the emotional, the body with the soul, the tough with the tender, and doing justice both to the male and the female. This is not a one-sided and partial approach – it embraces opposites in what is for some a confusing and paradoxical way. This is very much the thinking found in the Tao Te Ching, which is so characteristic of the transpersonal approach. A good critical edition comes from Ellen Cheng (1989).

(2) One of the typical concepts is 'alignment'. Transformational research requires vision. A clear and timely vision catalyses alignment. Alignment is a condition in which people operate as if they were part of an integrated whole. It is exemplified in that level of teamwork which characterises exceptional sports teams, theatre groups and chamber ensembles. When a high degree of it develops among members of a team committed to a shared vision, the individuals' sense of relationship and even their concept of self may shift. In a team of people committed to research, it channels high energy and creates excitement and drive, as we saw earlier, in connection with the Heron research and the Reason and Hawkins research.

(3) Another idea is 'attunement', defined as a resonance or harmony among the parts of the system, and between the parts and the whole. As the concept of alignment speaks to us of *will*, so that of attunement calls up the mysterious operations of *love* in organisations: the sense of empathy, understanding, caring, nurturance and mutual support. Attunement is quiet and soft, receptive to the subtle energies which bind us to one another and to nature. There is a good description of this and the previous concept in a pioneering piece by Roger Harrison (1984) in the context of management generally. Doing transformational research can stir up powerful emotions, and mutual support is crucial in such a case. Anyone doing this type of research (e.g. Traylen, 1994) needs to look to their own emotional competence and the way in which it is to be supported.

(4) Another concept is 'empowerment'. This word had been used before, mainly by humanistic people in the sense of self-actualization – that is, self-empowerment. But the new twist here is the emphasis on mutual empowerment. Where there is empowerment, 'people at all levels feel directly responsible for results, are continually learning and developing their skills, feel the trust to share their best ideas, and work together in teams that contain not one, but many,

leaders' (Jaffe and Scott, 1993: 140). This has particular implications for women
in eroding the invisible barriers that tend to keep them in mundane organisational
roles. With mutual empowerment people support each other rather than trying
to put each other down. This again makes us think of the connection with feminism.

(5) We talk about intuition freely in this work, and encourage the development
of intuition quite consciously and deliberately. But it is important to realise that
intuition is a form of knowledge which is distinct from propositional knowledge,
practical knowledge and experiential knowledge. New paradigm research pointed
out that propositional knowledge is not enough, and that it is also not enough
to add practical knowledge: experiential knowledge is important too. But transformational research adds that intuitive knowledge is necessary in addition to
these as an essential condition.

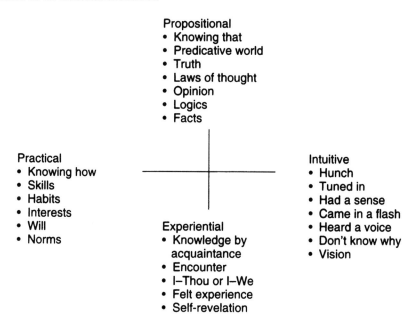

Figure 9.8 Types of knowledge

We can see from Figure 9.8 how similar these ideas are to the conventional
Jungian layout of the four functions, and there are some interesting thoughts we
might pursue along these lines.

(6) An important phrase to remember is 'co-creation'. This goes beyond the
familiar notions of competition and co-operation, and speaks of a way of being
which enables new ideas and new ways of working to emerge out of personal
experience. 'Co-creation combines the best of competition and co-operation with
a balance between goal and process orientation' (Joba, Maynard and Ray, 1993:
55). In research terms we come across many examples of this in the books we
have looked at in this chapter.

(7) Another thought is summed up in the phrase 'planetary consciousness'. Everything done in the research is related to this higher (or deeper) purpose. If we find on reflection that there is no longer joy in the struggle, that we are burning ourselves out in the effort, that we are no longer energised by what we do. then that may be a signal that it is time to move on to a new vision of what we are doing. Perhaps we have lost touch with our purpose on this planet. And perhaps the direction of effort needs to change to reflect what is happening. This gives us a much more ecological consciousness in what we do – we become conscious of the side-effects of our actions. Transpersonal ecology (Fox, 1995) is now an important discipline, and research has to take it into account. This represents a change in our horizons.

(8) This approach says that we are essentially spiritual beings in a spiritual universe, that humans ultimately seek meaning in their lives, and that creativity is necessary for both psychological and spiritual growth. It represents a trans-personal approach to research, insisting on its location in a much wider context of time and place. This involves transformative changes in the fundamental nature of the research effort: it is about giving research a new kind of vision and mission. As Peter Reason and Peter Hawkins say: 'We need to find a way to acknowledge both the independent meaning-making of the authentically autonomous human being and the universal patterns to which we all belong' (Reason and Hawkins, 1988: 97).

(9) A transformative approach to research goes beyond Aristotelian logic (A is A. A is not not-A, nothing can be A and not-A at the same time), and starts to be interested in dialectical logic, process logic, many-valued logic, fuzzy logic and so forth – all sorts of variations which show that Aristotelian logic is a choice. not an inevitable law of thought. (The Boolean logic which underlies most computer programs is based on the Aristotelian model.)

When we are working from the transpersonal position of column 3 it makes sense to say that A is never simply A, and that if it were it could never change. It is only because A is not simply A that it has within it the potentiality for change. And it is research which can often reveal the potential for change lying within a given situation. Perhaps not every researcher realises that they are denying Aristotelian logic every time they work for real change, but this is one of the many instances of where we are working transpersonally without even realising it.

CONCLUSION

Research can be exciting stuff, which changes the consciousness and the lives of those taking part. If we let it move into these transpersonal ranges, it can be an inspiring source of movement into a new world.

Counselling psychology, with its emphasis on the importance of scientific research, has a big part to play in developing the styles of research which can go beyond the crippling paradigms of the past. We can be involved in a radical questioning of science, and can take on board the expanded notions of science spelt out in this chapter and in such key texts as Mitroff and Kilmann (1978), which show so well how limited most accounts of science are.

It was of course Ian Mitroff (1974) who showed that the 'storybook image of science' given in so many psychology textbooks bore very little resemblance to the actual work of researchers in the hard sciences. He produced a list of eleven 'conventional norms' and their corresponding 'counter norms' in science, and showed by careful research that it was the counter norms which were used in practice by hard scientists. Thus, for example, conventional norm No. 1 was 'Faith in rationality': the corresponding counter norm was 'Faith in rationality and nonrationality'. Conventional norm No. 2 was 'Emotional neutrality as an instrumental condition for the achievement of rationality': the corresponding counter norm was 'Emotional commitment as an instrumental condition for the achievement of rationality'. This was not even an attempt at improving notions of science: it was simply an account of what went on as distinguished from what was supposed to be going on.

Similarly in psychology it is important to distinguish between what we do and what the texts say we are supposed to be doing. We shall then find that what we are doing is far from the ideals laid out in the texts, and quite possibly nearer to the ideas we have been encountering in this chapter. The aim here has been to lay out a coherent picture of the third revolution in research methodology: but it may turn out to be a picture of what is actually going on today in counselling psychology, as distinguished from what is supposed to be going on.

REFERENCES

Aitken, Gill (1996) 'The covert disallowing and discrediting of qualitative research', *Changes* 14 (3), 2–198.

Argyris, Chris (1971) *Intervention Theory and Method: A Behavioural Science View*, Reading: Addison-Wesley.

Berg, David N. and Smith, Kenwyn K. (1988) *The Self in Social Inquiry*, Newbury Park: Sage.

Burman, Erica (ed.) (1990) *Feminists and Psychological Practice*, London: Sage.

Burns, Jan (1990) 'Women organizing within psychology: 2' in Erica Burman (ed.) *Feminists and Psychological Practice*, London: Sage.

Cunningham, Ian (1988) 'Interactive holistic research: researching self-managed learning' in P. Reason (ed.) *Human Inquiry in Action*, London: Sage.

Elden, Max (1981) 'Sharing the research work: participative research and its role demands' in P. Reason and J. Rowan (eds) *Human Inquiry: A Sourcebook of New Paradigm Research*, Chichester: Wiley.

Enright, John (1970) 'Awareness training in the mental health professions' in J. Fagan and I.L. Shepherd (eds) *Gestalt Therapy Now*, Palo Alto: Science and Behavior Books.

Finch, Janet (1981) 'It's great to have someone to talk to: the ethics and politics of interviewing women' in Helen Roberts (ed.) *Doing Feminist Research*, London: Routledge.

Fox, Warwick (1995) *Toward a Transpersonal Ecology*, Foxhole: Resurgence.

Fransella, Fay (1972) *Personal Change and Reconstruction*, New York: Academic Press.

Gomes, Mary and Kanner, Alan A. (1995) *Ecopsychology*, San Francisco: Sierra Club.

Grof, Christina and Grof, Stanislav (1990) *The Stormy Search for the Self*, Los Angeles: Jeremy Tarcher.

Hall, Bud (1975) 'Participatory research: an approach for change', *Convergence: International Journal of Adult Education* 8 (2) 24–32.

Hall, Bud (1978) 'Notes on the development of the concept of participatory research in an international context', *International Journal of University Adult Education* 17 (1).

Hampden-Turner, Charles (1976) *Sane Asylum*, San Francisco: San Francisco Book Co.

Harrison, R. (1984) 'Leadership and strategy for a new age' in J. Adams (ed.) *Transforming Work*, Alexandria: Mile River Press.

Heron, John (1988) 'Impressions of the other reality: a co-operative inquiry into altered states of consciousness' in P. Reason (ed.) *Human Inquiry In Action*, London: Sage.

Jaffe, Dennis T. and Scott, Cynthia D. (1993) 'Building a committed workplace: an empowered organization as a competitive advantage' in M. Ray and A. Rinzler (eds) *The New Paradigm in Business*, Los Angeles: Jeremy Tarcher.

Joba, Cynthia, Maynard, Herman Bryant and Ray, Michael (1993) 'Competition, cooperation and co-creation: insights from the World Business Academy' in M. Ray and A. Rinzler (eds) *The New Paradigm in Business*, Los Angeles: Jeremy Tarcher.

Kuhn, T (1962) *The Structure of Scientific Revolutions*, Chicago: University of Chicago Press.

Lincoln, Yvonna S. and Guba, Egon G. (1985) *Naturalistic Inquiry*, Beverly Hills: Sage.

Maruyama, Magoroh (1981) 'Endogenous research: the prison project' in P. Reason and J. Rowan (eds) *Human Inquiry: A Sourcebook of New Paradigm Research*, Chichester: Wiley.

May, Rollo (1991) *The Cry for Myth*, London: Souvenir Press.

McClelland, Sheila (1994) 'The art of science with clients' in H. Payne (ed.) *Handbook of Inquiry in the Arts Therapies*, London: Jessica Kingsley.

Meade, Michael (1993) *Men and the water of life: initiation and the tempering of men*, San Francisco: Harper San Francisco.

Mies, Maria (1983) 'Towards a methodology for feminist research' in G. Bowles and R.D. Klein (eds) *Theories of Women's Studies*, London: Routledge.

Mitroff, Ian I. (1974) *The Subjective Side of Science*, Amsterdam: Elsevier.

Mitroff, Ian I. and Kilmann, Ralph H. (1978) *Methodological Approaches to Social Science*, San Francisco: Jossey-Bass.

Oakley, Ann (1981) 'Interviewing women: a contradiction in terms' in Helen Roberts (ed.) *Doing Feminist Research*, London: Routledge.

Phoenix, Ann (1990) 'Social research in the context of feminist psychology' in Erica Burman (ed.) *Feminists and Psychological Practice*, London: Sage.

Reason, Peter (1988) 'Reflections' in P. Reason (ed.) *Human Inquiry in Action*, London: Sage.

Reason, Peter and Hawkins, Peter (1988) 'Storytelling as inquiry' in P. Reason (ed.) *Human Inquiry in Action*, London: Sage.

Reason, Peter and Rowan, John (eds) (1981) *Human Inquiry: A Sourcebook of New Paradigm Research*, Chichester: Wiley.

Rowan, John (1976) *The Power of the Group*, London: Davis-Poynter.

Rowan, John (1981) 'A dialectical paradigm for research' in P. Reason and J. Rowan (eds) *Human Inquiry: A Sourcebook of New Paradigm Research*, Chichester: Wiley.

Sanford, Nevitt (1981) 'A model for action research' in P. Reason and J. Rowan (eds) *Human Inquiry: A Sourcebook of New Paradigm Research*, Chichester: Wiley.

Tart, Charles T. (1990) *Altered States of Consciousness* (3rd edn) San Francisco: Harper San Francisco.

Traylen, Hilary (1994) 'Confronting hidden agendas: co-operative inquiry with health visitors' in P. Reason (ed.) *Participation in Human Inquiry*, London: Sage.

Van Maanen, John, Dabbs, James, M. and Faulkner, Robert R. (1982) *Varieties of Qualitative Research*, Beverly Hills: Sage.

Walker, Robert (1985) 'An introduction to applied qualitative research' in R. Walker (ed.) (1985) *Applied Qualitative Research*, Aldershot: Gower Press.

Whiteman, J.H.M. (1986) 'The mystical way and habitualization of mystical states' in B.J. Wolman and M. Ullman (eds) *Handbook of States of Consciousness*, New York: Van Nostrand Reinhold.

Wilber, Ken (1995) *Sex, Ecology, Spirituality*, Boston: Shambhala.

Wilkinson, S. (ed.) (1986) *Feminist Social Psychology: Developing Theory and Practice*, Milton Keynes: Open University Press.

Part II

Counselling psychology research and practice: some professional dimensions

Investigating the learning experiences of counsellors in training

A research question

Helen Cowie and Annemarie Salm et al.

INTRODUCTION

This discussion arose from a very practical research problem – how to do a systematic analysis of interview data gathered from a sample of counsellors in training. In order to find a solution, we turned to colleagues in the School of Psychology and Counselling at the Roehampton Institute, London. Some of those who contributed to this discussion are counselling psychologists, some are not. But the ensuing debate (which is ongoing) raised issues which go far beyond the immediate problems of one research project. We found that we were inevitably drawn into the debate about the relative merits of quantitative and qualitative research methods, and the appropriateness or otherwise of different research paradigms for the study of personal experiences and meanings.

The ideas which were generated during the dialogue are, we believe, of general interest to those counselling psychologists who would like to engage in research. The scene is set by Martin Glachan who, in Section 1 'Balancing the qualitative and the quantitative in counselling psychology research', argues that, in the attempt to gain insights into the complexities of human experience, counselling psychologists should not be too hasty in abandoning traditional research methods in favour of new paradigms. He demonstrates that the dialogue among the different strands of research is a constructive and healthy one.

In Section 2, we see this viewpoint put to the test. Annemarie Salm, who is investigating the impact on the professional and personal lives of those who embark on a course of training in counselling, describes how she has attempted to access the processes of change which are experienced by trainees by interviewing them at critical points during their course. Previous research had isolated particular aspects of training, for example the impact of personal therapy on the counsellor's sense of self, or the link between skills training and supervision on practice. But this was largely done retrospectively. By contrast, Annemarie Salm's research looks more immediately at the interaction of factors which contribute to a trainee's ongoing and developing sense of competence and skill as a counsellor. Yet this person-centred approach to the issue in itself generated problems. What was the most appropriate method for analysing the wealth of interview material which had been gathered? Was grounded theory more useful than discourse analysis? Would it be worthwhile to attempt a content analysis of the data? Would it be better to treat each participant as a unique case study? In her section, 'The research question: significant learning experiences in counselling training – a longitudinal study', she presents some of the dilemmas faced by researchers who wish to retain the uniqueness of individual response while at the same time making wider generalisations about a particular population – in this case counsellors in training.

In Section 3, 'Illuminative case studies: a solution', Helen Cowie and Annemarie Salm consider the use of the case study method in deepening our understanding of the processes of change experienced by trainees over time. They argue that the case study method has immediate appeal to practitioners because it captures the distinctive issues which are of importance to each participant at different points in time during the course. Furthermore, if the method is carried out rigorously, it can enable researchers to test interpretations against evidence drawn from a series of different case studies, so providing systematic evidence to strengthen interpretations and predictions.

In Section 4, 'Content analysis of qualitative data', Regina Pauli and Diane Bray suggest another possible method. They argue that, although content analysis is firmly grounded in a traditional positivist framework, nevertheless it offers important perspectives on qualitative data. For example, it provides a systematic framework for describing the content of what the participants said in answer to the interview questions. In the present study, this would refer to the learning experiences which each trainee counsellor identified as being significant to them. Again, content analysis of the data could provide evidence to support a particular model. Here, it could be used to test the hypothesis, proposed by previous researchers, that there are certain developmental stages which trainees go through as they learn about counselling. Finally, content analysis could also chart changes in trainees' perceptions of a course over time and, for example, link these to factors, such as reasons, personal and professional, for engaging in counsellor training in the first place.

In Section 5, 'Grounded theory: a potential methodology', Jean O'Callaghan discusses how grounded theory might be used by the researcher to capture the lived experience of counsellors in training. This model, she argues, is particularly appropriate since it is 'grounded' in the experiences and personal accounts of the participants in the study and yet at the same time offers a systematic procedure for analysis. Jean O'Callaghan shows how the researcher 'inspects' the data through a series of coding strategies which gradually refine the meanings expressed by the participants. The method is challenging since, at each stage of the analysis, the researcher must wrestle with the problem of the interpretation of meaning. Thus there is a tension between capturing the account of the experience in the words of the participant on the one hand, and actively constructing new perspectives and understandings. She illustrates this process by considering how Salm might use grounded theory to make sense of an extract from one of the interviews.

Paul Dickerson, in Section 6 'Discourse analysis: a possible solution', provides both a theoretical framework and a practical method for exploring Salm's data. The article sketches out the social constructionist philosophy of discourse analysis which differs from the 'realist' perspectives which have tended to be prevalent in most quantitative and qualitative approaches. It also highlights the way in which discourse analysis encourages the researcher to focus on the participants' *construction* of reality (in this case their experience of training) and the specific dialogic context in which the constructions are produced. An analysis of one piece of text provides some contrasts with grounded theory and usefully illustrates how the researcher might begin to apply this approach.

Annemarie Salm, in Section 7, reviews the issues which have been raised and discussed in the context of her own research study. She goes beyond her own immediate concerns to identify issues which are of importance to all counselling psychologists who wish to engage in research in this emerging field.

Finally Jamie Moran, in Section 8, 'Eros and Hermes', argues passionately that, since counselling psychology research is largely concerned with capturing meanings, the new paradigm wave offers a uniquely appropriate way of coming to understand human experience. By contrast with Martin Glachan's plea for openness to both quantitative and qualitative research methods, Moran comes down firmly on the side of the new paradigm. The debate continues!

SECTION 1

BALANCING THE QUALITATIVE AND THE QUANTITATIVE IN COUNSELLING PSYCHOLOGY RESEARCH*

The use of qualitative approaches in psychology's repertoire of research tools has a long history. However, for a large part of this history qualitative data collection has often been portrayed as the poor relation or used as an adjunct to the main quantitative data analysis. The implication was that quantitative data were more powerful and reflected a more rigorous (and by implication more scientific) approach to the study of human affairs. However, in more recent times there has been a clear shift by many in psychology to take a more conciliatory role to qualitative approaches (see the special edition of *The Psychologist*, March, 1995) and some have come to argue for their exclusive use. This change of attitude has been particularly evident in areas of professional social practice such as counselling, community and health psychology.

While the greater acceptance of qualitative methods is to be welcomed it brings with it the danger that some may abandon the use of quantitative methods on philosophical or epistemological grounds (which I will dispute) or even worse that it permits researchers, who lack confidence with numerical data, the opportunity to avoid complex statistical analysis (Wise, 1985). In agreement with some others (Bryman, 1988; Denzin and Lincoln, 1994) I would argue that there is clearly a place for both approaches even in such areas as counselling practice and that researchers should be well versed in both and be aware of their different strengths and weaknesses.

The argument that there are epistemological or philosophical reasons for not using quantitative methods is often based on a disillusionment with empiricism and the assumptions on which traditional experimentation was based. Essentially the argument is that methods, whose origins lie in traditional sciences such as physics and chemistry, are not appropriate to understanding the complex nature of human experience. The empiricist tradition is based on the assumption that there is a reality which has some objective order and can be described and understood by investigation. The aim is to search for what many regard as 'illusory', universal laws through the observations of an objective experimenter whose role is to design the study and rationally manage the data. The experimenter supposedly remains aloof and in no way influences the data which are collected.

A further complaint against this type of approach is that the experimenter determines what is to be measured and how this will occur. In other words s/he already claims to know a lot about the phenomenon being studied prior to data collection. For some it is as if the data have already been cooked before the work begins so that the research does not clarify the issue but distorts it from the

---

* Martin Glachan. School of Psychology and Counselling, Roehampton Institute. London.

outset. In other words, the findings you get are only as good as what you have decided to measure in the study. The qualitative argument is essentially: Don't let pre-selected measures determine the outcome; let individuals speak for themselves.

There is a further and more fundamental aspect to this debate. This concerns what should constitute the key issues of psychological investigation. The argument is that empirical work largely deals with that which is directly observable and fails to get below the surface to the actual human experience. This argument is commonly evident in the designing of counselling research. Much qualitative work is based on a constructivist epistemology which does not look for general laws but for socially constructed meanings which, it is believed, cannot be accessed by numerical data. Lincoln and Guba (1985) have argued that qualitative approaches allow the researcher to be more sensitive to the multiple interpretations which individuals may make of experiences in an attempt to gain some sense of meaning. Within this context it has been argued that we need to throw out the old empirical assumptions and start again with a 'new paradigm'. The aim is to research a new area (meaning) in a new way (qualitatively).

I find a lot of this argument attractive. In particular the notion that 'reality' is not simply directly observable and that universal laws governing human functioning are not going to be found. Furthermore, the idea that the meanings we create for ourselves should be a key topic for psychological investigation also appears to be valid. However, some meanings may be able to be shared (at least in part) and do not always have to be idiosyncratic to each individual. The attempt to share our experiences is common in everyday life as well as in professional settings such as a counselling context. In this regard I believe that quantitative methodologies as well as qualitative approaches offer us a way of gaining insight into shared meanings and shared experiences. I do not agree with those who suggest that we should drop quantitative methodologies and work exclusively in the qualitative domain.

There are five major arguments which support this view.

1 There are many valid psychological research questions not specifically concerned with meaning which can be investigated quantitatively. For example a study of the effectiveness of different teaching approaches to students' examination performance. Even in the study of counselling psychology, there is no reason why different counselling approaches or different counsellors could not be evaluated in terms of client experience using well-designed rating scales. In the academic world we use numerical ratings to assess student work and these numbers represent to examiners qualitative differences in the quality of student work. Thus where such schemes can be agreed by those using them, numerical data can reflect agreed meanings among examiners and if desired among researchers and professionals.

2 Most qualitative work depends on verbal or written material of some kind. This type of data may be fine when working with adolescents and adults but

becomes problematic when dealing with infants and young children or with those with some linguistic disability such as autism. These are groups who potentially could be of interest both to counselling psychologists and to researchers. They raise many valid research concerns and qualitative methods may not always be appropriate for investigating these.

3 Those who argue that only qualitative methodologies can give us insight into 'under the surface' phenomena are probably misguided. For example, there is a large body of work in developmental psychology which has used experimental techniques to investigate young children's theories of mind (Astington *et al.*, 1988; Wellman, 1990). This work has produced many valuable insights into how young children conceptualise and respond to the often hidden mental states of others (beliefs, attitudes, desires, emotions, etc.).

4 The empirical philosophy which has been used to characterise quantitative approaches does not apply to large numbers of people who adopt these approaches. Quantitative methodologies have developed over the years in an attempt to reflect the complexity of human phenomena. Many multi-variate approaches have been developed (e.g. factor analysis, regression analysis, discriminant analysis, etc.) which can consider multiple aspects of complex phenomena and how they relate to each other. This type of approach usually produces patterns and models of association rather than absolute causal laws. They can be used in the investigation of highly complex phenomena of relevance to counsellors such as the impact divorce has on different people or the long-term effects of family violence.

5 The methodologies used in qualitative approaches also have inbuilt weaknesses which means that they do not offer a 'holy grail' for psychology's future even when considering the study of meaning. It is these weaknesses which I will now address.

Sometimes I hear students saying that they wish to use a qualitative approach in their research. Behind this statement often lies a misconception: namely that there is a consensus about how to do qualitative work. There is in fact no obvious consensus among qualitative researchers about the paradigm to be used nor about how the analysis of the data should be managed. There are a number of approaches around including grounded theory, phenomenological approaches, critical theory, naturalistic/ethnographic approaches, discourse analysis and the high context approach, among many others. Each of these approaches starts with different assumptions and would manage the same data in somewhat different ways.

For example, phenomenological traditions differ from grounded theory in that their emphasis is on describing the phenomena under investigation as closely as possible rather than on discovering emerging theories. Furthermore, many individuals who use some form of discourse analysis would emphasise the constructive and functional role of language (e.g. Harré and Gillet, 1994). They would argue against language as a 'transparent' medium reflecting 'real' thoughts and 'real' experience; rather language is seen to provide the place at which our sense of reality is given some form and meaning. A particular concern may be why a particular formulation is offered at a particular point in time and in that particular context. Such an approach would differ fundamentally from a researcher who treats the linguistic content of an interview as offering relatively direct and unambiguous insight into an individual's construction of their experience.

In contrast to traditional empirical research the researcher in qualitative work is usually viewed as an integral part of the process of gathering and interpreting information rather than an objective reporter of underlying facts. This view of the active role of the researcher has evolved within the qualitative tradition. For example, the earliest proponents of grounded theory argued that theory would simply emerge from the data (Glasner and Strauss, 1967). However, later researchers have argued for a more constructivist view of grounded theory in which the researchers acknowledge the personal perspective from which they analyse their data (Charmaz, 1990).

From this perspective, researchers form part of the context of the research, bringing with them their own personal interests and values, their own personal experience and their own personal philosophical stance. These will inform the constructions which they impose on the data collected. From this perspective it could be argued that the researcher should have much in common with the participants (e.g. gender, social class, ethnic background, key life experiences, etc.) if they are going to be able accurately to represent the meanings they impose on the subject populations' experiences. A researcher from a very different background may interpret the language used from a very different perspective and would be more likely to misconstrue the intended meaning. Again it should be noted that many who advocate the use of discourse analysis would not see this as a problem as they do not view language as offering a direct route to understanding personal experiences.

Perhaps surprisingly, these concerns do have some parallels in experimental work which has also acknowledged the influential role of the researcher. Rosenthal (1966) argued that experimenter expectancies can directly influence the performance of subjects. This can occur in a wide variety of experimental contexts including laboratory studies, person perception studies, learning studies and even inkblot test studies. While some have argued that experimenter effects have been overstated (Christensen, 1980) few would deny that they can influence subjects. Kazdin (1980) called them 'unintentional expectancy effects' because the researcher may unconsciously influence a subject through a range of subtle verbal and non-verbal behaviours. Also expectancy effects can evolve during the investigation. An observer may identify a pattern of behaviour in another which sets up an expectation that future observations will reveal similar patterns.

In the area of developmental psychology it has long been acknowledged that young children are highly sensitive to various parameters of the context of an experiment and vary their responses accordingly (Donaldson, 1978; Light, 1986).

Specifically the problem lies in the conversation between adult researcher and child subject who may not have shared meanings about the task being carried out. Again, the adult experimenter forms an important and influential aspect of the research context. These findings again suggest that both quantitative and qualitative researchers have to face up to the problems of context effects. The role of the researcher may be generally construed in different ways by many with a preference for a qualitative or quantitative approach but in either case it remains problematic.

Issues of this sort have led to considerable debate between qualitative researchers concerning the reliability and validity of the findings they produce. Broadly speaking, reliability of data reflects whether or not similar findings would be obtained at different times or in different contexts or with different researchers. Validity refers to whether or not the methods used to study a phenomenon actually do assess that phenomenon. These concepts are key issues in most quantitative methodologies and are given a very high priority in such research. A key question is whether or not we can depend on the findings obtained to give us more than a personal anecdotal account of the researcher's view of that being studied. In fact for many it is this rigour which sets psychology apart as a discipline attempting to understand human experience. It has been argued that these are highly problematic issues in the domain of qualitative research (Henwood and Pidgeon, 1992).

Once again there is no consensus among those adopting qualitative approaches concerning these issues. Some have suggested that they are not relevant to qualitative research on philosophical grounds. They suggest that if we were to adopt criteria of reliability and validity then this would suggest that there is some truth or reality waiting to be described. This could be construed as reminiscent of the assumptions of the traditional empirical tradition which many New Paradigm researchers wish to leave behind. Others have been more concerned about reliability and specifically about leaving the data analysis solely in the hands of a single researcher as it may lay the work open to criticisms of its subjective or even anecdotal nature. As a result some qualitative researchers have used second researchers to give some measure of inter-rater reliability. Others have taken their analysis back to their participant population in order to get some respondent validation. This, however, has also been questioned due to the inescapable discourse power between the experimenter and the participant. Thus the participant may find it difficult to question the construction of the psychologist.

Lincoln and Guba (1985) have preferred to replace previous measures of generalisability with the notion of 'transferability'. This reflects concern that responses may vary in different contexts and assesses how consistent findings are in similar contexts but not necessarily across contexts. Finally, it should also be noted that some researchers use qualitative approaches in more traditional ways (Green, 1995). In this approach qualitative data can be used to supplement and even validate established quantitative measures. Such a process can involve the content analysis of interview protocols, coding and inter-rater reliability checks followed by some statistical analysis usually involving frequencies and chi square tests. In this way qualitative data can be converted into some numerical form. What is clear is that different individuals are using qualitative approaches in quite different ways and maintain fundamentally dissimilar attitudes to concerns about reliability and validity.

Given these limitations and unresolved conflicts within the qualitative domain there is a need to view the potential of qualitative methods with some caution. They do offer a set of positive alternatives to more quantitative approaches but should not be viewed as a replacement for them. Minimally they have a clear role where theory is non-existent or as a complementary supplement to quantitative data. Furthermore they offer valuable approaches when investigating issues of personal experience and the meaning these hold for individuals. However, the debates about which qualitative paradigm should drive data analysis, the role of the researcher, the impact of context on personal reporting, the extent to which language may or may not act as a transparent medium reflecting thought and the issues of reliability and validity are ongoing. Given these concerns I believe that there is a place for both qualitative and quantitative approaches in the endeavour to gain insight into human experience. Both areas continue to develop and will attempt to overcome some of the problems they face. For example, the continuing development of multi-variate quantitative approaches to analyse complex human phenomena offers highly valuable research tools which could be particularly useful in many areas of counselling psychology research. I would support the pragmatic approach to research which advocates that the method adopted in any research study should be that which is best suited to the question under investigation (Bryman, 1988). To start with the methodology before the question is, I believe, to be uncritical of the limitations which all approaches possess. I believe we should welcome qualitative methodologies. However, we should not abandon quantitative approaches, because of their flaws, to replace them with new methods and paradigms which are equally flawed.

References

Astington, J.W., Harris, P.L. and Olson, D.R. (1988). *Developing Theories of Mind*, New York: Cambridge University Press.

Bryman, A. (1988). *Quantity and Quality in Social Research*, London: Unwin Hyman.

Charmaz, C. (1990). Discovering chronic illness: using grounded theory. *Social Science and Medicine*, 30, 1161–1172.

Christensen, L.B. (1980). *Experimental Methodology* (2nd edn), Boston: Allyn & Bacon.

Donaldson, M. (1978). *Children's Minds*, London: Fontana Press.

Denzin, N.K. and Lincoln, Y.S. (1994). *Handbook of Qualitative Research*, London: Sage.

Glasner, B.G. and Strauss, A.L. (1967). *The Discovery of Grounded Theory: Strategies for Qualitative Research*, New York: Aldine.

Green, A. (1995). Verbal protocol analysis. *The Psychologist*, 8, 126–129.

Harré, R. and Gillett, G. (1994). *The Discursive Mind*, London: Sage.

Henwood, K.L. and Pidgeon, N.F. (1992). Qualitative research and psychological theorising. *British Journal of Psychology*, 83, 83–111.

Kazdin, A.E. (1980). *Research Design in Clinical Psychology*, New York: Harper & Row.

Light, P. (1986). Context, conservation and conversation. In M. Richards and P. Light (eds) *Children of Social Worlds*, Cambridge: Polity Press.

Lincoln, Y.S. and Guba, E.G. (1985). *Naturalistic Enquiry*, Beverley Hills: Sage.

Rosenthal, R. (1966). *Experimenter Effects in Behavioral Research*, New York: Meredith.

Wellman, H.M. (1990). *The Child's Theory of Mind*, Cambridge, MA: MIT Press.

Wise, S.L. (1985). The development and validation of a scale measuring attitudes towards statistics, *Educational and Psychological Measurement*, 45, 401–405.

SECTION 2

THE RESEARCH QUESTION: SIGNIFICANT LEARNING EXPERIENCE IN COUNSELLING TRAINING – A LONGITUDINAL STUDY*

The question addressed in this study is how counselling trainees – students on one of our postgraduate courses – experience their learning and what they find are significant learning experiences in relation to their developing competence as a counsellor. The course, like many others, consists of various components: (1) theory related to counselling; (2) counselling practice which includes skills training and supervised client work; and (3) personal development which includes individual therapy and experiential groups. I was interested to see how students perceive these various components contributing to their learning as counsellors.

In the literature, some global models of counselling/psychotherapy training have been presented, for instance conceptualising it as a 'journey' (Goldberg, 1988). or a developmental process (Ralph, 1980; Norcross and Guy, 1989); other research looked at certain aspects like ego development and changes in the way trainees process information about clients (Borders *et al.*, 1986; Borders and Fong. 1989; Cummings *et al.*, 1990), or the role of personal therapy (a range of publications, more recently for instance Norcross, 1990; Wheeler, 1991; Macaskill and Macaskill, 1992). Some studies try to investigate the effectiveness of training components like skills training (e.g. Kivlighan, 1989) and personal therapy (Beutler *et al.* 1986, MacDevitt 1987; Wheeler, 1991), in relation to the therapy process and outcome.

The link between counsellor/therapist training and effectiveness with clients is based on the assumption that training increases competence and competence is what creates successful outcomes. Competence is therefore the mediator between training and effectiveness with clients, and the research into the role of 'therapist variables' in successful treatment addresses one side of the equation (for a review eg Beutler *et al.*, 1994). Strupp *et al.* (1988) relate the concept of competence and the research to the context of training, pointing out that it is a complex concept, which includes many facets and can be assessed in various ways.

However, in my study the focus is not on the development of competence from an objective perspective, but from the experience of the trainees: how do they conceptualise competence and what contributes to its development? It is assumed that changes in what they perceive as competent and of their own competence are part of the learning process, as suggested by the model developed by Ralph (1980) on the basis of a qualitative study.

Of all the previous research in the field of counselling/psychotherapy training,

*Annemarie Salm. School of Psychology and Counselling, Roehampton Institute. London.

Ralph's (1980) study comes closest to what I am interested in. He interviewed thirty-six trainees and eight of their supervisors about the process of training. The analysis of these interviews – using a grounded theory approach, according to the author – led to the development of a model of training. Learning psycho-therapy is described as a developmental process in four stages characterised by 'conceptual milestones' which represent radical changes in the way trainees conceptualise what they are doing:

1 *Learning the role of a psychotherapist as a non-directive expert.* This means coming to terms with ideas of having to be the expert on the one hand and using an open-ended, unstructured approach on the other. Successful resolution is achieved by abandoning the commonsensical role of the expert and letting go of the need to control, structure, and do something for the client.

2 *Patient-centred and content-centred way of working.* The focus is on the understanding of the content of the session and the client's experiences brought into it. At that stage, trainees tend to adopt a theoretical approach within the non-directive framework. The Rogerian approach is particularly popular, prob-ably because it provides the right level of manageable complexity/simplicity. It provides sufficient theoretical back-up to allow the trainees to trust that they are doing something beneficial, without burdening them with complex concepts that they find difficult to deal with in practice. On the other hand, psychodynamically oriented trainees at this stage were often found to assume that it is their task to 'solve the riddle of the person's life', like detectives, and to hand this insight back to the client who would use it in some straightforward and linear way.

3 *Discovery of psychotherapy as an interpersonal process.* This involves the feelings and reactions of both client and therapist; an awareness of the *metacontent* of the session, i.e. the feelings that emerged in the relationship between them during that session. Whereas previously these undercurrents have been regarded as not belonging to therapy or rather interfering with the process, they become now a central aspect of the work. Often this develop-ment seemed to be initiated in supervision by the supervisor.

4 *Increased understanding and use of the therapist's own feelings.* This is based on an increased sense of confidence and self-esteem, in particular a greater trust in their own emotional reactions as a source of information, and being able to use their own sensitivities and intuitions. Along with this comes being more comfortable with own limitations, own doubts, and clients' criticisms. Own experience in therapy as a client was seen as contributing in various ways to arriving at this stage.

Ralph concludes by referring to these changes as a facet of ego development, in terms of lasting changes in the way the therapists view themselves and their clients, a change in schemata. These changes tend to occur slowly – since schemata are resistant to change – and through exposure to experiences that are more complex than the existing structures can handle, i.e. in this case, when they have been found to be insufficient to organise the perceptions of the therapeutic process and to act within it.

This model is only one example of a number of stage models used to describe the professional development of therapists. For an overview of similar models see Skovholt and Ronnestad (1992). All of these appear more or less plausible and provide a potentially useful way of looking at the process of learning psychotherapy.

However, the empirical basis often remains obscure. Although Ralph (1980) for instance claims to have used a systematic method – grounded theory – to analyse the interviews, the presentation of the results appears rather anecdotal, and it is not clear how far his data actually support the developmental model he puts forward. Furthermore, trainees were asked retrospectively about their views and experiences of their training.

The experiences of students while they are learning and their current and changing perspectives on the learning process have not been studied, with a view to training as a whole. This is what I am investigating. The focus of my study is not on the outcome or effectiveness of the training, but on the process from the students' perspectives: what the students perceive or construct as significant learning experiences, how they perceive their own development, and how that changes during training.

Very often, the decision to train as a counsellor takes place in a context of life change and search for self-fulfilment. Students' motivation for training, their background, and the way they came into counselling, will shape their expectations from the course and the way they perceive the various components of the course. For example, there seems to be a group of students with a strong focus on the process of personal growth, who regard their training as part of their general development, and other students with a more pragmatic focus on career development and more specific outcomes such as enhancing their skills, or obtaining a recognised qualification. Do these expectations change and how are they related to the way the students perceive their learning?

Interviews with a small number of volunteers were repeatedly conducted at various times: in the first weeks of the course, in the second term and at the end of the course. A further interview took place a year after they had completed the course, in order to see how they perceive the impact of the course on their current practice and their lives.

These interviews are conducted in a semi-structured way. Centred around a few open-ended questions, I used a facilitative style to encourage reflection and exploration of personal experiences. The first question was how the student got into counselling and why did they choose that particular course. When this area was sufficiently covered, I moved on to ask about their learning on the course, starting with: 'What experiences on the course, so far, were significant to you. Where did you feel you learned something, or something clicked or changed?' After this, I checked all the components of the course and asked the student what they felt they had learned from them. I tried to focus on the learning in relation to the development of counselling competence rather than general learning. But it was sometimes very difficult, particularly when I asked about personal development, for example: 'What did you learn from the experiential group?' All kinds of things came up what they learned for themselves, but when I asked 'How does it help you to become a better counsellor?' – then it became more difficult.

All four interviews centred around significant learning experiences and the course components. The last interview also included a retrospective evaluation of the meaning of the course in the student's life, which can be linked to the exploration of the student's motivation and background in the first interview.

There are various research methods dealing with these kinds of interview data. What have these approaches to offer? What kind of approach is most appropriate for my research questions? What kinds of answers do they generate? Is it what I want to know? And there is the additional question of how to deal with repeated interviews and change over time.

All this is tied in with my deep-down concerns: Is what I'm doing worthwhile? What kind of information does it generate? How can I find an order in the variety of unique views and experiences, which reflect the way students construct their world at that particular time of the interview and under the particular circumstances of being interviewed by a member of staff at the institutions where they are learning? What do their experiences tell about counselling training in general and how can I adequately, satisfactorily extract the essence of their accounts and translate it into something that is meaningful, stimulating, worth telling others about? And what will really come out of it that will justify the money and the time that goes into it? What is the best way of using that material to justify the effort?

In the following articles I collaborate with five colleagues to examine four distinctive research approaches to the analysis of the kinds of qualitative data which I have been gathering.

References

Beutler, L.E., Machado, P.P.P. and Neufeldt, S.A. (1994). Therapist variables. In A.E. Bergin and S.L. Garfield (eds) *Handbook of Psychotherapy and Behaviour Change* (4th edn). New York: Wiley.

Borders, L.D., Fong, M.L. and Niemeyer, G.J. (1986). Counseling students' level of ego development and perceptions of clients. *Counselor Education and Supervision*, 26, 36–49.

Borders, L.D. and Fong, M.L. (1989). Ego development and counseling ability during training. *Counselor Education and Supervision*, 29, 71–83.

Cummings, A.L., Hallberg, E.T., Martin, J., Slemon, A. and Heibett, R. (1990). Implications of counsellor conceptualisations for counsellor education. *Counsellor Education and Supervision*, 30, 120–134.

Goldberg, C. (1988). *On Being a Psychotherapist: The Journey of the Healer*. New York: Gardner Press.

Kivlighan, D.M. (1989). Changes in counselor interventions and response modes and in client reactions and session evaluation after training. *Journal of Counseling Psychology*, 36 (4), 471–476.

Macaskill, N. and Macaskill. A. (1992). Psychotherapists-in-training evaluate their personal therapy: results of a UK survey. *British Journal of Psychotherapy*, 9(2), 133–138.

MacDevitt, J.W. (1987): Therapists' personal therapy and professional self-awareness. *Psychotherapy*, 24(4), 693–703.

Norcross. J.C. (1990) Personal therapy for therapists: one solution. 96th Annual Meeting of the American Psychological Association: The hazards of the psychotherapeutic practice for the clinician (1988, Atlanta, Georgia).

Norcross. J.C. and Guy, J.D. (1989) Ten therapists: the process of becoming and being. In: W. Dryden and L. Spurling (eds) On *Becoming a Psychotherapist*. London: Tavistock/Routledge.

Norcross. J.C., Strausser-Kirtland, D.J. and Missar, C.D. (1988). The processes and outcomes of psychotherapists' personal treatment experiences. *Psychotherapy*, 25, 36–43.

Ralph. N. (1980): Learning psychotherapy: a developmental perspective. *Psychiatry*, 43, 243–250.

Skovholt, T.M. and Ronnestad. M.H. (1992). *The Evolving Professional Self. Stages and Themes in Therapist and Counsellor Development*, New York: Wiley.

Strupp. H.H., Butler, S.F. and Rosser, C.L. (1988): Training in psychodynamic therapy. *Journal of Consulting and Clinical Psychology*, 56(5), 689–695.

Wheeler. S. (1991). Personal therapy: an essential aspect of counsellor training, or a distraction from focusing on the client? *International Journal for the Advancement of Counselling*, 14(3) ,193–202.

SECTION 3

ILLUMINATIVE CASE STUDIES: A SOLUTION*

The intensive study of one case has played an important part in the development of theory and practice. The case study can investigate one distinctive approach in therapy (Hobson, 1985), the possibility of intervening to compensate for the effects of extreme neglect on young children (Koluchova, 1972), emotional survival despite lack of parenting (Freud and Dann, 1951), the identification of factors which facilitate and barriers which impede the implementation of co-operative group work in the school community (Cowie and Rudduck, 1988), to mention but a few examples. It may refer to detailed reports by one entity, for example, a class of students, a course or an organisation, drawing evidence from a wide variety of sources of information. Case studies have immense potential for capturing meaningful characteristics of a person, a real-life event or a social system in context. Typically, the case study researcher observes the acts of an individual unit – a person, a family or group, or a larger community or organisation. The researcher probes and analyses intensively the many aspects which contribute to the identity of this unit and, as a result, is able to formulate generalisations about the wider population to which this unit belongs. The investigator has a unique opportunity to remain open to aspects and events as they emerge, to record accounts and narratives in the participants' own words, to gain rich inside perspectives and to draw on observational insights based on experience and understanding of the particular issue. Furthermore, as Coolican (1990) points out, the case study may provide evidence of an outstanding phenomenon, rarely encountered, which may direct research into new, uncharted areas.

Practitioners have always seen the value of case study material in illuminating their understanding of issues in the field, and, in fact, much of their knowledge is based on theory which evolved out of case study research (e.g. Freud). But the wider research community has tended to remain aloof.

Research psychologists have traditionally viewed the case study as a rather unscientific, unsystematic method whose value at most might lie in its role as a pilot for more rigorous work. Too often the procedures are not specified. Therapists in particular seem to have difficulty in separating evidence from conjecture, and do not always address alternative explanations. The major barrier to the acceptance of the case study as a research method has been the problem of generalising from one instance to a wider population.

Recently, however, there has been a shift in some psychologists' attitudes towards the case study (Wells, 1987; Mendelson, 1992). They point out that, while individual cases cannot represent typical children or families, samples are also not representative, based as they are in a particular geographical region, in

*Helen Cowie and Annemarie Salm. School of Psychology and Counselling. Roehampton Institute, London.

a particular social group or at a particular point in time. Yin (1994) argues that both case studies and samples in traditional experiments can be generalised analytically to theory. From this perspective, the well-conducted case study can generate new hypotheses and research questions. Interpretations made on the basis of one case study can be tested against evidence drawn from subsequent case studies, so several possible perspectives can be viewed and reviewed in the process. This is especially true when the researcher uses a range of sources of evidence and takes care to adopt systematic research procedures. Techniques include observation, interviews, the use of documents and records.

The case study has the great advantage that it is flexible enough to adapt to real-life situations and can focus on processes of development and change over time. Questions to be considered might include:

- Are these questions answerable?
- Can you collect data on them?
- How should the questions be reviewed in the light of interactions with the person or persons involved in the study?
- Should the researcher be a participant or a non-participant observer?

In designing a case study Robson (1993) writes that the researcher needs:

- a conceptual framework;
- a set of research questions;
- a sampling strategy;
- to decide on methods and instruments for data collection.

He also suggests that the researcher need not have all of these in a fully developed form at the start of study since work on the design can continue after it has started. It is essential that the researcher should have an inquiring mind and be flexible and observant. The researcher should be sensitive to what participants are saying and be disposed to respond to documents and other types of evidence. The researcher also needs to be able to capture moods and emotions which underlie spoken and written words.

Illuminative case studies can really bring an investigation to life. For example, Cowie, Smith, Boulton and Laver (1994) used case studies to deepen understanding of the ways in which different children responded cooperatively or aggressively in relation to one another. Using sociometric measures, they identified children who bully, children who are victimised, children who are left out, children who are rejected and children who are popular. Once they had identified these children through peer nominations, they carried out in-depth interviews with selected individuals, tape-recorded them in groups and observed them over a period of time; they also obtained evidence from teacher reports. These case studies gave useful insights into how a child might engage in bullying behaviour, become a victim or be proactive in helping their peers, the impact of parenting styles on the emergence of bully–victim relationships, perceptions of self by those who bully. peer perceptions of children who bully and who are victimised, teacher perceptions in the class and in the playground. Through video-recordings at different points in the school year, the researchers discovered the particular contexts in which children were most likely to behave aggressively or co-operatively. The evidence came from a variety of sources, so building up a picture of particular individuals which could then in turn be checked against similar vignettes of children in a systematic way.

With regard to the present research, the case study could take one of two forms.

First, the researcher could carry out case studies of the two diploma courses which are the focus of her research – the Diploma in Psychological Counselling and the Diploma in Humanistic Counselling. Here she would gather evidence from the course validation documents, such as reading lists and programme booklets, students' experiences at different points in the course, interviews with tutors, experiential group facilitators and supervisors, self-reflections on the part of students, evaluations and self-assessments, and the researchers' observations of the two courses in action. Each diploma has a distinctive rationale and is rooted in a particular model of counselling. She would try to discover how different people involved in each course actually construe it and how their constructions change over time. For example, one of the issues which Annemarie Salm wishes to explore concerns the philosophy of a counselling course and how that is expressed in practice. One student actually said in an interview: 'I have a couple of friends who are in very self-motivated courses. No input. And you spend half the first year deciding on the curriculum and the agenda and arguing with one another, which seemed totally silly to me'. This person would like to have structure to her course, an issue which could be explored in the context of the diploma in Humanistic Counselling where there is an explicit rationale that the course is student-centred and where there is a deliberate emphasis on giving students the opportunity to negotiate the structure and content of their own course. One research question could then focus on difference in the student-learning practices of the two diplomas.

Second, the researcher could do case studies of individual students in order to illuminate the different reasons which underlie a person's decision to apply for a place on a counselling course, or the different processes of change which participants in a counselling course experience.

Two potential groups of people on counselling courses have already been mentioned – those who have a strong focus on personal development and those whose focus is more on career or professional qualification. In order to explore this facet of her research, Salm could select for a study a student who has identified strong personal reasons for studying counselling in order to answer existential questions, perhaps precipitated by a personal crisis, about the meaning and purpose of his or her own life, as the example from one interview indicates:

How did I get into counselling? Well, actually I got to a stage in the career where I had achieved the goals that I went in with and all of a sudden I realised that those being out of the way, there was nothing left for me to do other than carry on. . . . I looked at it and thought, 'I've got another 30 years of working life', and I felt that I wanted to do something that I could see as useful but also something that I could see as being fulfilling.

Another student with a focus on personal development, who does not want to become a full counsellor but develop her skills with people in her work, describes the development of her interest in counselling as the discovery of a 'so far hidden' part of herself: 'I suppose doing this job with numbers had been a way of blocking a side of me off, suppressing a side of me that I wasn't at that time ready to get in touch with'. A different approach to the training is represented by a student who felt she needed a career change for more pragmatic reasons: ' . . . and I decided because I am nursing, it is physically very exhausting, and as I am getting older I feel I would like to do something else now, other than carry on nursing'.

A fourth student may be characterised by conflict between personal values and the move towards counselling as a career change:

I was looking for a career change. . . . Counselling kept coming up as an option and I kept rejecting it . . . I had a couple of friends who were in therapy and it didn't appear to be doing them any good, just superficially. And I think I come from quite a political background and, particularly in the 70s there had been these two diverging ideologies. One was more about society and one more about self . . . I don't know what finally decided me to give it a try.

The same person later says:

I can't see myself being a private counsellor. . . . For almost 20 years I have been paid by a Local Authority to do the job. I've never been paid by the individuals who get my services. And I feel happier doing that . . . most of my clients are poor and I don't like the idea of people having to be able to pay for me.

The case studies could follow these four people over the duration of the course to see how each changed and whether each realised her goals. The case studies would be based on interviews and on other observations during the course.

These examples demonstrate how important it is that the researcher selects a critical case and is meticulous in defining the concepts which are to be used. Concepts can be further clarified by drawing on experience, discussing with fellow researchers and practitioners in the field and by reviewing the literature on the topic under investigation. Yin (1994) also recommends that draft reports of each case study should be given to participants for their commentary and review so encouraging a process of mutual collaboration in the research venture and ensuring that their unique perspectives are captured.

When carried out in a systematic way, the case study can enable both practitioner and researcher to come to a deeper understanding of the processes of change over time. The case study, we argue here, is appealing to practitioners because of the rich insights which it offers and because it highlights what is unique about the person or the event being studied. At the same time, if it is carried out systematically and with rigour, it can be useful to the researcher in illuminating key issues in the area of investigation. Thus the case study has the potential to help heal the too frequent rift between academic research and clinical practice.

References

Coolican, H. (1990). *Research Methods and Statistics in Psychology*, London: Hodder & Stoughton.

Cowie, H. and Rudduck, J. (1988). *School and Classroom Studies*, London: BP Education.

Cowie, H., Smith, P.K., Boulton, M. and Laver, R. (1994). *Cooperations in the Multiethnic Classroom*, London: David Fulton.

Freud, A. and Dann, S. (1951). An experiment in group upbringing, *The Psychoanalytic Study of the Child*, VI, 127–169.

Hobson, R. (1985). *Forms of Feeling*, London: Tavistock.

Koluchova, J. (1972). Severe deprivation in twins: a case study. In A.M. Clarke and A.D.B. Clarke (eds) *Early Experience: Myth and Evidence*, London: Open Books.

Mendelson, M. (1992). Let's teach case methods to developmental students, *Society for Research in Child Development Newsletter*, 12–13 Feb.

Robson, C. (1993). *Real World Research*, Oxford: Blackwell.

Wells, K. (1987). Scientific issues in the conduct of case-studies, *Journal of Child Psychology and Psychiatry*, 28 (6), 783–790.

Yin, R. (1994). *Case Study Research*, Thousand Oaks, CA: Sage.

SECTION 4

CONTENT ANALYSIS OF QUALITATIVE DATA*

Content analysis is perhaps the most 'traditional' approach to the analysis of verbal qualitative data. Although this approach is firmly rooted in the positivist framework of quantitative methods in psychology with all its inherent philosophical problems, we believe it has something to offer when faced with the analysis of rich interview data. There are some psychologically valid research questions posed by such data that can be addressed in a more quantitative manner without necessarily compromising the richness of the data. In addition, the relatively recent emergence of multivariate data analysis methods can facilitate descriptive analysis of such quantifications. In this section we will outline a brief methodological description of content analysis followed by three approaches to qualitative interview data in which content analysis is used to address a variety of research questions.

Methodological issues

Content analysis is a method for the study of communications which permits the analysis of rich verbal data in a systematic, objective and quantitative manner. Early authoritative discussions of this method were provided by Berelson and Holsti (1954) and Holsti (1968). More recent discussions of the method include Krippendorf (1980) and Brewer and Hunter (1989). The aim of content analysis is to extract units of meaning from the verbal data in a manner which permits the quantification of the material in terms of frequency of occurrence of certain categories. The method is extremely flexible in its application. Different research questions may, for example, require different units of analysis or different coding categories. The researcher can decide how to divide up the material in the manner most appropriate to the research question. The relationship between content analysis and other methods has been explored in more detail by Markoff, Shapiro and Weitman (1974) and more recently by Brewer and Hunter (1989).

On a practical level, there are essentially two steps in content analysis. Firstly, the transcribed verbal material is divided into units of meaning resulting in 'objects' in a systematic manner. Units of meaning can be words, phrases, sentences or themes. Depending on the purpose of the analysis, units of meaning of different size may be appropriate. The second step is to form categories according to which the content of the transcripts can be quantified. Categories can be either formed on an *a priori* basis, i.e. the researcher determines categories of interest possibly based on previous research, or they can be emergent categories, which are directly derived from the contents of the transcripts. Objects are then assigned to their appropriate categories. The simplest way of

*Regina Pauli and Diane Bray. School of Psychology and Counselling. Roehampton Institute, London.

deriving quantifications from this procedure is to count the number of objects which have been assigned to each category, i.e. to extract a frequency count.

One of the advantages of using a structured systematic approach such as content analysis is the possibility of assessing the reliability and validity of such analysis, thus objectifying the analysis beyond the subjectivity of the individual researcher. Thus the identification of units of meaning and the assignment of objects to categories can be independently performed by two or more individuals. Reliability of a particular content analysis can then be assessed in terms of agreement between the two classifications. Statistics such as Cohen's Kappa (Howell, 1992) may be employed to estimate the degree of agreement between two judges taking into account chance agreement. Validity of the analysis largely derives from the validity of the categories employed in addressing the research questions of interest, and the extent to which the data are actually captured by the categories.

Three approaches to interview data using content analysis

In the context of the present data there are a number of ways in which content analysis may be used to inform with respect to a number of different research questions. The longitudinal nature of the data provides an opportunity to investigate not only what is important to students in their counselling training but also what is important at different points in time. The process of developing counselling competency may thus be inferred directly from the students' own perspective. The central research question relates to the significance of learning experiences as perceived or constructed by students. This could be approached from one of three angles. Firstly, content analysis could be used to examine emergent categories resulting from exhaustive coding of the data. This would result in a complete picture of students' perceptions of counselling training, rather as a grounded theory approach might be expected to. Secondly, categories may be derived from previous literature in order to examine whether previous models of the learning process during counselling training are borne out in students' own perception over time. Ralph's (1980) model may be a good starting point here since this presents a developmental model of students' own conceptions. Thirdly, content analysis could be used more specifically in relation to certain variables of interest, for example, motivation for entering counselling training in relation to how certain elements of the training are perceived. Each of these approaches is outlined in more detail in relation to the research questions asked in the first part of this section.

1 What learning experiences do counselling trainees experience as significant during training?

Content analysis could be used simply to describe the contents of interviews in a systematic way. In this application all the units of meaning would be classified into a category and new categories emerging from the data would be created until the content was exhaustively categorised. On a practical level, the goals of this 'open coding' type of analysis would be similar to that of a grounded theory approach, since the aim is to identify common themes and to provide a general description of the rich contents of the interview data. The final presentation of the data would be in terms of frequency of occurrence of certain motives or themes common to most transcripts. This is particularly valuable if there are quite a number of different interviews, because information is obtained about experiences of counselling training as well as whether these are common experiences for many trainees or whether particular experiences are quite idiosyncratic.

2 Is Ralph's (1980) developmental theory of counselling training supported by students' changing ideas as evident from the present transcripts?

Since there is some previous research literature, which gives us some idea about the processes we might expect to discover in the current data, it may make sense to develop a set of *a priori* categories deriving from such research. The aim here is to provide supporting evidence for a previously proposed theory. In the case of the present data, Ralph's (1980) developmental theory of learning counselling is a particularly suitable candidate. Categories for content analysis in this application would need to capture as fully as possible the four stages described by Ralph. Taking his first conceptual milestone as an example it is clear that at least two categories relating to expertise would be required, one relating to the student's experiences of the burden of being an expert and the other relating to experiences of abandoning the expertise approach in favour of a more non-directive approach. It would be expected that the frequency of remarks relating to the former category would be higher in the initial interview than in the later ones, whereas the opposite should be true for the latter category. This hypothesis can simply be tested using the chi-square statistic. This represents a relatively crude attempt at testing Ralph's model, however, and a more sensitive approach might be to identify sections of the transcripts which relate to his four 'conceptual milestones' and use open coding on those sections to elucidate the actual processes experienced by students in relation to these milestones.

3 Do experiences of certain course elements change over time and is this influenced by students' prior motivations for entering counselling training?

In this third approach, content analysis would be used to 'measure' (i.e. quantify) certain variables of interest. One particular focus of interest of the present research is how students' experience of training changes over time. One way of approaching this question is to analyse the content of the interviews in relation to what is said about particular course elements. Since individuals were interviewed on three occasions throughout the course it is possible to cross-classify the experiences relating to course elements at different times in the course, thus arriving at a rows times columns contingency table. Such data can be analysed in a descriptive manner by a multidimensional scaling technique known as correspondence analysis (Weller and Romney, 1990).

In order to illustrate how such an analysis might be done and how the results are presented, we have conducted a crude content analysis of one student's three interview transcripts. For this purpose we simply counted the frequency of units of meaning (in this case sentences) relating to particular course elements. Specifically, we recorded the frequency of sentences relating to experiential groups, the student's own therapy and the student's client work for each of the three interviews resulting in the contingency table presented as Table 10.1.

Table 10.1 Frequency with which course components are mentioned at three points of time during counselling training

	Time 1	Time 2	Time 3
Experiential group	91	69	36
Own therapy	30	8	12
Client work	38	30	57

Correspondence analysis is an exploratory metric scaling technique which permits the simultaneous representation of interview times and experiences in a two-dimensional space, thus providing a direct visual description of the association between the two variables. The closer two points appear graphically in the plot the closer the respective categories are associated with each other. The correspondence analysis plot for the present data is shown in Figure 10.1. It is clear from this that during the first interview, both self-analysis and experiential groups are of importance whereas client work is not a concern closely associated with this stage in the training. The second interview is most closely associated with experiential group experience, whereas towards the end of training client work becomes very much more important to the student.

This analysis is a very crude example of how content analysis can be used in conjunction with multidimensional scaling techniques in order to present quantitatively based descriptions of data which are nevertheless intuitively appealing. In this example, we assumed that the extent to which someone talked about a particular learning experience is equivalent to how important this experience is for them. In order to do the data justice, though, finer discriminations would need to be made. It would, for example, be possible to use separate categories for positive and negative experiences. This approach is also useful for examining individual differences. Thus it would be possible to examine the plots of individuals who entered counselling for different reasons to see how they experience different aspects of the course at different times in their training.

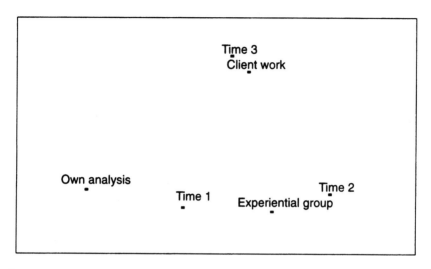

Figure 10.1 Correspondence analysis plot showing importance of different course elements at different times

Conclusions

The purpose of this section was to give a flavour of the multiple applications of content analysis and associated statistical techniques to the qualitative data under discussion here. This implies that we have not even attempted to give an authoritative account of any of these approaches. Although content analysis and multidimensional scaling techniques are firmly rooted in the positivist framework, we do not feel that any conclusions reached from such analysis are necessarily 'objectively' true; rather we feel they provide rich descriptions of qualitative-rich data.

References

Berelson. B. and Holsti. O. (1954). Content analysis. In G. Lindzey (ed.) *The Handbook of Social Psychology*, vol. 1, Reading, MA: Addison-Wesley.

Brewer. J. and Hunter. A. (1989). *Multimethod Research. A Synthesis of Styles*, Newbury Park. CA: Sage.

Holsti. O. (1968). Content analysis. In G. Lindzey and E. Aronson (eds) *The Handbook of Social Psychology*, vol. 2 (2nd edn), Reading, MA: Addison-Wesley.

Howell. D.C. (1992). *Statistical Methods for Psychology* (3rd ed), Belmont, CA: Duxbury Press.

Krippendorf. K. (1980). *Content Analysis: An Introduction to its Methodology*, Newbury Park. CA: Sage.

Markoff. J., Shapiro. G. and Weitman. S. (1974). Toward the integration of content analysis and general methodology. In D. Heise (ed.) *Sociological Methodology 1975*, San Francisco: Jossey-Bass.

Weller. S. and Romney. A.K. (1990). *Metric Scaling*, Newbury Park. CA: Sage.

SECTION 5

GROUNDED THEORY: A POTENTIAL METHODOLOGY*

The central question of this research is concerned with how counsellor trainees experience and perceive aspects of their training in developing competence as counsellors. The researcher, Annemarie Salm, has expressed dissatisfaction with existing theories of counsellor training and a wish to find a more satisfactory model which is sensitive to the 'lived experience' of trainees. Grounded theory as a distinct methodology for developing theory that is grounded in data systematically gathered and analysed by distinct coding procedures may offer an appropriate mode of inquiry. The kinds of theories that are developed using grounded theory, Strauss and Corbin (1994) acknowledge are interpretations made from given perspectives as adopted by a researcher who needs to remain open to the essentially provisional character of every theory. Given the essentially interpretative and provisional nature of such findings from this method of inquiry, it is proposed in this section briefly to outline what is involved in using grounded theory and then to explore some of the implications of this approach in relation to the present research proposal.

What is grounded theory?

There are two distinct meanings associated with the term 'grounded theory' when referring to the original work of Glaser and Strauss (1967). Firstly it suggests the notion of grounding theory in experiences, accounts and distinct contexts. As a qualitative paradigm it focuses on the search for meaning and understanding to build innovative theory rather than on abstract universal laws. Henwood and Pidgeon (1995) would also agree that there is a need in human science research to be sensitive to participants' own understandings as seen from their local frames of reference or from inside their own socially situated phenomenal worlds. Secondly, the term is used to describe a method. This involves specific analytic strategies formulated for handling and making sense of initially ill-structured qualitative data. A basic proposal of Glaser and Strauss (1967) is that researchers should engage in the close inspection and analysis of such qualitative material, both generating emergent theory and extending this through further, theoretically driven sampling. Using grounded theory, the researcher strives for coherence and theory building by exploring the data through a series of coding strategies which first closely examines the data by 'breaking down' interview transcripts into distinct units of meaning which are labelled by the researcher to create concepts. These concepts are initially clustered into descriptive categories representing the phenomena discerned. The categories are then re-evaluated for their interrelationships or meaningful

* Jean O'Callaghan. School of Psychology and Counselling, Roehampton Institute. London.

associations and through a series of analytical steps are gradually subsumed into superordinate categories or one underlying core category which suggests an emergent theory.

Different perspectives in using grounded theory

From this brief summary of the coding process it is clear that theory just doesn't emerge of its own accord but the researcher's ability to analyse the data sensitively and insightfully is required. At each stage of the coding process the dilemmas of interpretation are evident, although how this is dealt with depends on how one conceptualises the method. As grounded theory has been used over the years, different uses of it have emerged which reflect tensions in philosophical definitions of the approach. It was originally devised by Glaser and Strauss (1967) as a response to a perceived crisis in theory development in sociology where, like in psychology, the main methods employed were in the hypothetico-deductive domain. In contrast grounded theory uses an inductive approach which is generally characterised as the formulation of general laws from particular instances of the phenomenon of research interest.

It is accepted that the use of an inductive approach has its own problems, one important dilemma being the meaning-making process involved in this kind of propositional thinking, i.e. deriving laws or theories from unstructured data. Rennie *et al.* (1988) acknowledge that 'inferencing is vital because without it the investigator is awash in a sea of facts'.

In some uses of grounded theory there is a temptation to avoid this dilemma by adopting a realist stance, naively assuming that the researcher can inductively capture the 'real' experiences recounted by participants and present them 'objectively' without exploration of possible sources of contextual or interpretative influence.

In more recent uses of the method the dilemmas of interpretative processes are being acknowledged and investigators such as Henwood and Pidgeon (1995) suggest the adoption of a constructivist perspective as a more insightful use of grounded theory. According to this perspective, inquiry is always context bound and 'facts' are viewed as both theory-laden and value-laden. Knowledge is seen as actively constructed with meanings of 'existence' only relevant to an experiential world. So there is not a concern with the discovery of an ontological 'real' world but only a focus on how people construct knowledge within an individual and social context. Descriptions of experiences by participants are not independent of language or mental abstractions (Gergen, 1995). Additionally the nature of the inquirer and the inquired-into is in itself interactive and self-influencing (Gale, 1993).

Awareness of this perspective highlights the tensions between the striving to find emergent theory by use of distinct coding strategies while remaining honest and vigilant about the many interpretative processes influencing what is eventually found. Henwood and Pidgeon (1994) explore such tensions in the various uses of the method and they suggest that there seems to be a simultaneous commitment to, on the one hand, realism (inductively reflecting participants' accounts and naturalistic contexts) and, on the other, constructivism, which includes actively encouraging the researcher in the creative and interpretative process of generating new understandings and theory.

Charmaz (1990) demonstrates such tensions in her research on the psychological effects of chronic illness, which may offer a useful perspective for the present research. She initially had prior expectations that she would find 'an inevitable spiral of decline' in patients' accounts of their experiences. Having elicited and analysed their accounts, her attention turned to the study of their motivations and struggles for a positively valued sense of self, which she developed into a hierarchical theory of preferred identities. In this way she was able to suggest an explanation of the continuing achievement of a valued conception of self which the participants showed even facing further debilitation. Here Charmaz illustrates how her interpretative perspective shifted in appreciating different aspects of the data. She advocates that the researcher needs to have a perspective from which to seek and actively to build analyses. This perspective she suggests could include awareness of substantive interests guiding the questions asked, a sense of philosophical stance or school of thought which provides a store of sensitizing concepts and one's personal experiences, priorities and values. Such a conscious awareness of the various influences operative in the interpretative process allows the researcher to distinguish between what is known and what is being discovered in the meaning-making process. Charmaz essentially reinforces Glaser and Strauss' original claim that the researcher does not approach the data as a tabula rasa (1967: 3) and also suggests the full use of the 'flip flop' process between data and interpretation noted by Henwood and Pidgeon (1992).

The researcher's perspective

Given the interpretative processes going on at each stage of using grounded theory. how can the researcher 'take care' of such processes so that prior knowledge as well as idiosyncratic biases will be screened out in the meaning-making process? Rennie et al. (1988) claim that grounded researchers generally avoid reading pertinent literature until the investigation is finished. But this 'blankness' is not always possible when researchers are working in a domain in which they are experts. The present researcher, as an academic, has substantive knowledge of the theoretical and research literature on counsellor training and development which could influence what she focuses on in different ways. Given an insightful approach, she will be aware not only of what her prior knowledge may quickly endorse as important in the data but also of what she might miss because of such an agenda.

Annemarie Salm may also have her own 'implicit theory' of what aspects of training best facilitate the development of competent counsellors formed from her own experiences of training as a therapist as well as her present professional perspective as a trainer of counsellors on other courses. These influences could be an analytical resource in providing a possible philosophical stance for making sense of the data, if fully acknowledged and addressed. One way of addressing this is resonant of the 'flip flop' strategy mentioned above, where the researcher consciously 'brackets' out prior knowledge and personal agendas and strives to look at the data freshly, almost naively. Then in a separate viewing brings 'theoretical sensitivity' and prior experience to bear on the meaningfulness of the data. This process reflects the constant comparative method endorsed by grounded theorists.

Other forms of possible subjectivity include the cultural meaning systems which inform and link participants' and the researcher's understandings and which are interrelated with the assumption of a shared and common use of language when talking about the activities of counselling and training. Rennie *et al.* (1988) note that the absence of external criteria makes it impossible to validate the truth value of individual verbal reports that are evaluated through these procedures. Yet, the use of the constant comparative method to demonstrate that different individuals say the same thing increases the credibility of individual accounts.

Analytic strategies and procedures

The following extract from one interview provides some material from which we can consider some of the interpretative processes involved in examining the data:

P: It's the supervision sessions, I find, in a way the highlight of the week. I feel very close to the other two people in the supervision sessions and I learn a lot from them and the supervision as well. And I think it's – certainly much more than the experiential group – it's the place where I feel I can be most honest. It feels quite a supportive and encouraging atmosphere. So I think that's a very strong part of the course for me.

R: Because you are getting confidence as a counsellor?

P: And relaxing enough to rely on my intuition, on my feelings. Whereas in a way on the other parts of the course you are again fitting into a certain image, or something that's expected of you. Although I don't think the experiential group should be like that but I think it is at the moment. But in the supervision it feels much more open and safe. Very safe and uncritical and very constructive in the feedback and the ideas that I get from other people – very encouraging and yes, safe.

Open coding

Strauss and Corbin (1990) have defined this first stage of analysis as 'the process of breaking down, conceptualising and categorising data'. This essentially involves close examination of the text for distinct 'units of meaning' which are derived from what is descriptively evident and what is inferred by the researcher's interpretation of tacit meanings. These units of meaning are labelled as concepts, using language deemed appropriate by the researcher to be eventually grouped into as many 'open coded categories' as possible. From this brief overview it is evident that these analytic processes involve decisions and choices about meaning which the researcher cannot avoid, and may be vulnerable to idiosyncratic inferences. Rather than requiring the consensus of other co-researchers or the participants themselves in inter-rater reliability of agreed definitions of categories, grounded theory offers a number of strategies to allow the researcher to appreciate the possible meanings in the data.

Theoretical sensitivity

The researcher needs to be sensitive to theoretical issues when scrutinising the data. For example, on first inspection of this extract, it might suggest a sense of this participant's evaluative comments on different components of the course, supervision being valued as 'safe' learning and by inference, the experiential group being 'unsafe'. At face value, this might indicate that certain components of the course are well conducted and others less so, which could be explored further if evident in the transcripts of other participants.

From a more theoretically 'informed' perspective the researcher from her knowledge of object relations theory might be interested in the ways in which this participant uses the term 'safe'. This could suggest a split in perception between global evaluations of 'all good and safe, I can be myself' versus 'all bad, unsafe. I need to present an expected image'. In theoretical terms this splitting may be seen as a way of coping employed by this trainee when confronted with a 'difficult' learning experience, even though she shows awareness that it shouldn't be like this: 'Although I don't think the experiential group should be like that but I think it is at the moment'.

This is just one example of how a theoretical perspective may influence the emerging theory in terms of the perceived significance of trainees' personal development through the various learning experiences of the course.

Making constant comparisons

This strategy allows comparative analysis of the data within each participant's comments, which in this research will be possible across a time span of three interviews. It will be interesting to see how this participant evaluates the experiential group in subsequent interviews, if she has changed in her appraisal maybe then the researcher can infer that her comments are more significant in the context of her own personal development.

Yet comparison across participants is also necessary. As mentioned earlier, if a number of trainees had complained about the experiential group feeling threatening or 'unsafe', then it would be important to explore the possible meanings – maybe the stage of training; maybe the group facilitator, etc. Here wider contextual influences may be considered more influential.

Theoretical sampling

This allows consideration of wider information, extending the research to explore new cases, where new data are likely to clarify emergent theory. Given the above dilemma, the researcher might want to compare the perceptions of trainees on other courses in relation to their feelings about experiential groups at this particular stage of the training, being guided by such findings to pursue further or abandon this line of inquiry.

Making memos

Throughout the process, the researcher is advised constantly to make notes about particular hunches, partial inferences, even exploratory discussions about the data. This reinforces a trust in the process of meaning-making and allows opportunities to manage the chaos and confusion at different stages of analysis by enabling the researcher to be confident in using these strategies for reflexively working through issues.

Subsequent coding procedures

The next stage of Axial Coding asks the researcher to appreciate these open-coded categories in terms of their dynamic interrelationships, constructing a coherent matrix of associations. This again requires the researcher's confidence in the meaning-making process while remaining open to reappraisal.

The final stage of Selective Coding subsumes the data further into a coherent 'core category' or underlying dynamic which the researcher has to discern and justify as the basis of an emergent 'theory'.

Evaluation of findings

In using each of these coding procedures, there is the obvious temptation to adhere to analytic suggestions as, for example, given by Strauss and Corbin (1990) which may further encourage a realist approach of adopting this formula/ recipe to access an emergent theory.

The danger of reification is especially possible at the Selective Coding stage where there may be an assumption of a core essence or truth and the need to come to closure in the interpretative process. Honestly acknowledging any variation in the data, i.e. issues that don't fit neatly with the theory construed, helps to maintain the sense that one has developed one frame of understanding this data from many possibilities, so the theory generated isn't necessarily all inclusive. This raises the question. What significance have the findings from this type of inquiry?

It has been established throughout this paper in agreement with Strauss and Corbin (1994) that theories generated from grounded theory are interpretations made from given perspectives as adopted or researched by researchers and are therefore fallible. Yet this is not to deny that judgements can be made about the soundness or probable usefulness of them. How can we establish the validity or 'goodness' of this research?

The difficulty of establishing such criteria is acknowledged by Henwood and Pidgeon (1995) who suggest that given the constructivist approach two considerations are possibly more helpful in assessing grounded theory research and can be applied to the present study.

Firstly, what rhetorical power might this study have in persuading others concerned with counsellor training of its insightfulness? This will depend on a range of criteria from the design of the study, the range of sampling as well as the clarity and coherence of the discourse used to present the findings. The second consideration of generativity – how this study might facilitate further research – is of crucial importance in locating the contributions of these findings to the ongoing debates in this domain of inquiry. The more honest this researcher is in revealing her interpretative processes as well as the contextual constraints of the study, the more fully the theory presented can guide ways forward for future research.

This essentially places the findings of grounded theory in a relativist position which is possibly a more honest and useful place. Rather than finding the definitive theory, here is a theory to stimulate further research in the ongoing generation of knowledge about counsellor training.

References

Charmaz. C. (1990). Discovering chronic illness: using grounded theory, *Social Science and Medicine*, 30, 1161–1172.

Charmaz. C. (1995). Grounded theory. In J.A. Smith, R. Harre and L. Van Langenhove (eds) *Rethinking Methods in Psychology*, London: Sage.

Denzin. N.K. and Lincoln. Y.S. (eds) (1994). *Handbook of Qualitative Research*, Thousand Oaks, CA: Sage.

Gale. J. (1993). A field guide to qualitative inquiry and its clinical relevance. *Contemporary Family Therapy*. 15 (1), 73–91.

Gergen. K.J. (1995). The social constructionist movement in modern psychology *American Psychologist*, 40, 266–275

Glaser. B.G. and Strauss, A.L. (1967). *The Discovery of Grounded Theory: Strategies for Qualitative Research*. New York: Aldine.

Guba. E.G. (ed) (1990). *The Paradigm Dialog*, Newbury Park: Sage.

Henwood, K. and Pidgeon. N. (1994) Beyond the qualitative paradigm: a framework for introducing diversity within qualitative psychology. *Journal of Community and Applied Social Psychology*, 4 (4), 225–38.

Henwood. K. and Pidgeon. N. (1995) Grounded theory and psychological research. *The Psychologist*, 8 (3).

Henwood, K. and Pidgeon, N. (1992). Qualitative research and psychological theorising. *British Journal of Psychology*, 83–111.

Lincoln, Y.S. and Guba, E.G. (1985). *Naturalistic Inquiry*, Beverley Hills, CA: Sage.

Rennie, D.L., Phillips, J.R. and Quartaro G.K. (1988). Grounded theory: a promising approach to conceptualization in psychology? *Canadian Psychology*, 29 (2), 139–150.

Strauss, A.L. and Corbin, J. (1990). *Basics of Qualitative Research: Grounded Theory Procedures and Techniques*, Newbury Park, CA: Sage.

Strauss, A.L. and Corbin, J. (1994) Grounded theory methodology: an overview. In N.K. Denzin and Y. Lincoln (eds) *Handbook of Qualitative Research*, Thousand Oaks, CA: Sage.

SECTION 6

DISCOURSE ANALYSIS: A POSSIBLE SOLUTION*

One of the joys of exploring the interview data outlined above is the range of different perspectives which can be brought to bear upon them. Thus unlike experimental results whose interpretation is constrained by the initial guiding hypothesis, the interview transcripts are amenable to a variety of analyses which may address, develop or challenge the concerns which prompted the research. The particular discourse analytic approach which I seek to outline may well develop and challenge some of the initial interests behind the research, in particular it questions the notion of using the interview transcripts to 'get at' or refer to something outside of the text itself such as inner mental states. Instead discourse analysis encourages us to pay close attention to the detail and context of the discourse and to be sensitive to the constructive and functional aspects of the interview dialogue.

Most discourse analytic work tends not to use interview generated data, instead (like conversation analysis with which it considerably overlaps) there is a preference for 'everyday' or 'naturally occurring' data (Atkinson and Heritage, 1984; Drew and Heritage, (1992). For discourse analysis this 'everyday data' would include not only oral interaction (the main focus for conversation analysis) but also monologues and written texts. However discourse analysis can still provide a refreshing perspective upon the present interview generated data. In particular it conceptualises interviewees' accounts not as accurate reports upon inner mental attitudes or prior behaviour but as constructs which build versions of the world and which accomplish certain functions. Thus an interviewee's answer to a question about how they came to choose the diploma course at Roehampton is not seen as a window to their internal attitudes and motivations or to some external web of previous actions and activities but instead as a language-based construction of reality, worthy of analysis in its own right. In dealing with constructions of reality discourse analysis pays particular attention both to *what versions of the world are being produced* and to *what sorts of implications or functions they may have* (Silverman, 1992; Dickerson, in press, a). The functions of a piece of discourse could be thought of in terms of locally situated interactional moves such as warranting a claim (Wooffitt, 1992; Dickerson, in press b) or in terms of more diffuse ideological implications which could include maintaining culturally shared ideas about selfhood (Fairclough, 1992; Fowler, 1991; Sampson, 1993).

In order to grasp the distinctive perspective which discourse analysis offers it is worth considering its philosophical assumptions, in particular its commitment to constructionism, an approach which stresses the problems with knowing 'reality as it is' and which considers the way in which we deal with versions or constructions of reality in our everyday lives. The constructionist perspective

has drawn upon the diverse domains of semiotics, structuralism and post-struc-
turalism, each of which has considered with different nuances the relationship
between language and the 'reality' to which it appears to refer (De Saussure
(cited in Potter and Wetherell, 1987); Bakhtin (cited in Morson, 1986 and Morris,
1994; Barthes (1973); Foucault, 1970, 1983; Derrida (cited in Kamuf, 1991)).
Developing these themes constructionism has provided a perspective which
questions the notion that language simply and unproblematically refers to 'real'
entities lying somehow outside of language itself (Shotter and Gergen, 1989;
Shotter, 1992; Gergen, 1985, 1989; Sampson, 1993). In this way constructionism
challenges the idea that language is or can be merely a 'window on the world',
a neutral medium which can allow us unproblematically to see the 'real' determi-
nate experiences and activities lurking behind it. Indeed from the constructionist
perspective, if language is at all like a window on the world, it might be better
considered as similar to the window in Magritte's *La Lunette d'approche* (1963)
which contains in its glass the skyscape we might have expected 'really' to exist
behind it. Alternatively language could be seen as sharing certain features of a
stained-glass window whose colours and shapes give a meaningful form to the
light which flows through it. This metaphor resonates with Fowler's conceptualisation of language: 'language is not a clear window but a refracting, structuring
medium' (1991: 10).

Discourse analysis develops these constructionist ideas by focusing on actual
utterances, that is language in use (which De Saussure categorised and dismissed
as 'parole'), rather than language as merely an abstract system of possibilities
(Potter and Wetherell, 1987). This focus on language in use is one of the ways
in which discourse analysis 'puts to work' the rather abstract philosophical ideas
of constructionism. Through exploring actual instances of language usage we can
start to consider the words uttered (in an interview, for example), as *versions or
constructions* of reality and pay close attention to the particular construction
of reality which is produced within a specific context. Such careful analyses of
'constructions in context' may begin to elucidate the interpersonal or ideological
functions of the constructions being analysed, that is what the constructions do
at a micro or macro level; they may also serve to clarify some of the distinctive
features and implications of the constructions such as the resources through
which people construct self.

In order to take apart the constructions offered in a piece of discourse it is
useful to draw in varying degrees upon a range of analytic resources, four of
which are briefly considered here.

First there is the text itself. The text acts as a resource against which any claims
can be carefully interrogated. Indeed the text may also point to its own discursive
features, perhaps most obviously in the case of contradiction or variation which
Potter and Wetherell (1987) highlight as a major resource for exploring the
constructed aspects of discourse. Thus where an interviewee seems to contradict
themselves we could consider why different versions of their decision to do the
diploma at Roehampton are given at different points in the text.

Second, previous literature may also play an important part in analysis, enabling us to be sensitive to particular features of the text. Thus previous literature may sensitise us to particular aspects of speech such as pauses or interruptions or perhaps the deployment of figures of speech such as metaphors, clichés or idiomatic formulations. In addition to highlighting features of speech, previous literature may also may heighten our attention to some of the functions towards which factual accounts orientate such as accounting for previous behaviour or warranting of the claims made.

A third resource which serves to explicate the distinctive features of particular constructions is the 'analytic imagination'. When contemplating the features of a given construction, it is worth considering 'How else could this be formulated?'. By questioning constructions in this way we can start to see what is distinctive about the particular version of reality which is produced at any given point in the text.

Our intuitive or tacit skills as members of a linguistic community could be considered a fourth resource. Our implicit awareness of the manner in which language operates is in many ways the most powerful tool we have for exploring the distinctive features of a given piece of discourse: because in our everyday lives we use language to do things we are intuitively aware of the ways in which language can be deployed to accomplish particular things in interaction. Thus, for example, we do not need to read Atkinson and Heritage (1984) in order to recognise that the long pause which followed our request for help signals some sort of problem! Such intuitive skills may draw our attention to particular aspects of the text with a sense that 'something interesting is going on'. The challenge, however, is developing with precision what may begin as simply vague hunches.

In this way discourse analysis is perhaps best seen as a particular type of informed reading of a given discourse. Thus unlike certain versions of grounded theory for example (Strauss and Corbin, 1990), discourse analysis does not offer a clearly specified methodology. This, as Billig (1988) notes, need not be a weakness; instead it could be argued that discourse analysis is not trying to use a formulaic methodology to reify its findings and that what may be thought of as its 'looseness' actually places a premium on the diverse and unformulaic nature of scholarship. However, discourse analysis does provide a particular stance towards the text which interrogates the versions of the world or constructions of reality which are produced using, amongst others, the resources which were sketched out above.

In order to get a flavour of some of the sorts of insights which discourse analysis may offer regarding this particular set of interview transcripts it is worth considering one possible focus using examples drawn from the current transcripts. Whilst the following does not constitute anything like a complete analysis it may serve to illustrate one particular point of departure which could be followed up, by continuing to draw upon the text, previous literature, the analytic imagination and intuitive language skills.

The following extract provides some material from which we can begin to consider the contextually embedded nature of constructions. It is worth noting that the extract which is available here has been presented using familiar conventions which 'tidy up' many of the hesitations and overlaps naturally occurring when we speak. Some analytic perspectives, particularly those informed by conversation analysis, insist on transcriptions which painstakingly detail pauses, interruptions, overlaps, emphasis, speed of delivery and shifts in intonation (Atkinson and Heritage, 1984; Drew, 1992). Such details have the advantage of enabling us to see a wide range of different things which are being accomplished within a given conversational exchange – thus a long pause following a request may signal some form of problem which would be missed if we followed convention and decided not to transcribe it. However, whilst incomplete the present transcripts still enable us to make some interesting observations about the fluid and situated nature of identity talk.

Extract one

IR: Have you, before you started the course, have you already worked as a counsellor?

IE: No. I mean, I've in fact even as we speak, one of the problems I've had is actually finding a placement which is only now becoming to come together. There's been a lot of hard work to do that. So in a sense it has increased the risk factor. And that has been a cause of a lot of personal anxiety for the first few weeks of the course. But it, er, the same time it has been an exciting part of it. It's that sort of area that the risk is a sort of excitement. Because there is a certain loss of control where you just have to follow your gut feeling and instincts on certain things. So, no, before this I'd never had any direct counselling experience – not in a formal counselling relationship. But it's interesting that when you start focusing in on things you do start seeing those patterns and I can actually understand where I sort of gave up on the caring side where I became a career person. And in a sense I'm picking it up again I think. And that side of my character and my development, perhaps was on hold for a while.

IR: You mean, not the caring side?

IE: No, the caring side. Not so much on hold, just sort of pushed down a little bit because it's very difficult to – I'm not suggesting you can't be a caring person in a profession, but you become very blinkered and rather insensitive to what's going on around you, I think. So, as I say, I feel that side – now I've found a little bit that I'd forgotten was there really. It's the choice I'm making in terms of what I want to develop and the baggage I want to discard.

Exploring the contextually embedded nature of constructions

1 'Anxiety' or 'excitement'

Within the extract presented above the interviewee constructs their problems in finding a placement as being both 'a cause of a lot of personal anxiety' and 'exciting'. If we were attempting to use the transcripts to get at 'how students experienced difficulties in finding placements' this section might present problems. Some approaches may seek to determine whether the student primarily experienced anxiety or excitement. Following such an approach may entail finding a device which appears to overcome the dilemma such as investigating which emotional experience is referred to most frequently or focusing on the experience which the interviewee finally arrives at (in this case excitement). Alternatively we might code the response as revealing both emotions, anxiety and excitement. Both of these approaches are fraught with problems. Simply prioritising one construction, whether anxiety or excitement, does not do justice to the complexity of the text where the experience has been constructed as both anxiety provoking and exciting. Likewise simply deciding that the interviewee has experienced two emotions, anxiety and excitement, could be seen as contextually insensitive, as it ignores or at least sees as irrelevant the way in which one construction is offered first (anxiety), then another (excitement) and that this is followed by an attempt to integrate the two ('the risk is a sort of excitement').

The discourse analytic perspective enables us to consider that the root experience could be put together or constructed in a number of different ways; the labels 'anxiety' and 'exciting' are just two means of making sense of what may be an ambiguous experience. In this way anxiety and excitement are seen as frameworks through which the interviewee's experience is made sense of rather than reports upon two discrete, pre-defined emotions. A closer analysis could be made in which the detail of the interaction is considered, thus we could consider the way in which the interviewee issued the construction of 'exciting' after their earlier constructions of 'the risk factor' and 'a lot of personal anxiety' seemed, according to the transcripts, to evoke little response from the interviewee. In this way constructions of experience could be seen as making sense of self in the midst of 'pulling off' the interview interaction.

2 'On hold' or 'pushed down'

A similar openness can be detected in the interviewee's construction of what had happened to the 'caring' side of themselves whilst they were pursuing their career (prior to commencing the diploma). At first the interviewee suggests that 'that side of my character and my development, perhaps was on hold for a while'. Subsequently this is revised 'Not so much on hold, just sort of pushed down a little bit'.

Some qualitative approaches, such as certain versions of grounded theory, would perhaps see both formulations 'on hold' and 'pushed down' as so semantically similar that they could be grouped together under some generic category heading. However such categories could be seen as rather arbitrary as they conceal rather than explore the nuances of textual detail. From a discourse analytic perspective the distinction between 'on hold' and 'pushed down' is worthy of note precisely because it is treated as important by the interviewee (Wooffitt, 1992). Thus the interviewee reveals a dissatisfaction with their earlier formulation 'on hold' and instead offers 'pushed down'. This could be seen as a reformulation which orientates towards the interviewer's pursuit of her question (Silverman, 1987). The first construction which the interviewee produced evoked a query; 'You mean, not the caring side?' The second version of what happened to the caring side seems to orientate to the possibility that 'on hold' may have been read negatively. Thus constructing the caring side as 'just sort of pushed down a little bit' very much implies that the caring side, whilst not fully flourishing, was certainly present.

Although it is possible to interpret the above sequence in terms of impression management – that the interviewee is attempting to 'pull off' a presentable (and in this case 'caring') self, for the interviewer – discourse analysis would suggest that this might only form half of the picture. In other words from a discourse analytic stance perhaps the interviewee is in the business of constructing their experience, not just for an observing other but also for themselves. Thus as Shotter's account of the work of Bakhtin and Billig argues 'many of our "inner" mental activities are only given form at the time of their expression, in a moment by moment process' (1992: 11). From this perspective the interviewee can be seen as constructing self for, within and through the interaction in hand. That is the interviewee orientates to the specific turn by turn context of the unfolding interview and yet that very exchange of utterances provides the linguistic resources out of which the meaning of experiences and self can be (at least momentarily) given a meaning or fixed.

An important implication of the interactional focus which has been adopted here is that the interviewer is very much part of the analysis. This does not mean that discourse analysis advocates some rigid guidelines regarding what the interviewer must or must not do to avoid influencing the process. On the contrary discourse analysis suggests that the interviewer cannot possibly avoid shaping the interaction. The interviewer's utterances, minimal responses (mmm, yes, ahh) and silences are all important because these aspects of speech are important and orientated to as such in everyday conversations, (Atkinson and Heritage, 1984). If for example the interviewee's accounts of a particular experience were greeted with silence in a conversation with friends they might reasonably conclude that there was some problem, ambiguity or disagreement with what they have said. Discourse (and conversation) analysis encourages us to recognise that interviewees do not suddenly lose their intuitive sense of conversational dynamics just because we happen to call a particular sort of conversation an 'interview'.

The important point from a discourse analytic point of view then is not to control the interviewer's utterances but rather to take them into account in the analysis.

Summary

This brief outline has merely hinted at the sorts of issues attended to by one specific form of discourse analysis. In particular the version of discourse analysis outlined here adopts a rather 'micro' perspective exploring the deployment of language in terms of accomplishing the changing interactional requirements of the interview. It is possible to suggest that whilst our conversational exchanges certainly do attend to such 'micro' concerns they also draw upon culturally available linguistic resources and thus unavoidably engage with wider social and ideological processes (Fairclough, 1992; Fowler, 1991; Dickerson, 1995).

The constructionist aspect of discourse analysis exemplified in the current section could be seen as problematic. If constructionism precludes us from looking beyond or behind the text of talk (to the realm of 'actual' experiences, intentions and emotions) then we could question its usefulness. This concern can be partially addressed by considering that what discourse analysis offers is not so much a tool to get at empirical truths but rather a different way of conceptualising talk, or in Silverman's (1992) terms 'a new perspective'. This new perspective challenges us to understand talk not as revealing hidden essences but rather as the very medium through which we build up (or construct) our social realities.

Such a conception can offer a position from which to question or rethink research methodology, counselling practice and even our own identities. Discourse analysis challenges research which attempts to fix down meaning; the quest for certainty is replaced by a reflexive humility borne in the recognition that we are only ever dealing with *versions of* reality. It also offers the opportunity to reconstrue therapeutic practice, encouraging practitioners to attend to the possibilities afforded a recognition of what Gergen and Kaye (1992: 182) call *'semiosis'* or 'the forging of meaning in the context of collaborative discourse'. Finally, discourse analysis enables us to reconceptualize identities of self and others not as *fixed essences* but as ideologically and interpersonally *situated constructions*, from which movement to other alternatives is possible (Sampson, 1993). For constructionists trying to use language to look beyond language is like attempting to see the landscape behind a stained-glass window. By misfocusing in this way we are left trying to make sense of nebulous shadows and in so doing we miss the meaning and beauty right in front of us. Instead constructionists stay with the surface of language, indeed its contradiction and fluidity can inspire us acting as a reminder of its emancipatory potential.

References

Atkinson, J.M. and Heritage, J. (eds) (1984). *Structures of Social Action: Studies in Conversation Analysis.* Cambridge: Cambridge University Press.

Barthes. R. (1973). *Mythologies*, London: Paladin.

Billig. M. (1988). Methodology and scholarship in understanding ideological explanation. In C. Antaki (ed.) *Analysing Everyday Explanation: A Casebook of Methods*, London: Sage.

Dickerson, P. (1995). Let me tell us who I am: the multifaceted nature of the construction of self. Paper given at the First International Conference on *Understanding the Social World: Towards an Integrative Approach*. Huddersfield, July.

Dickerson, P. (in press, a). 'Let me tell us who I am'; the discursive construction of viewer identity, *European Journal of Communication*, 11 (1).

Dickerson, P. (in press, b). 'It's not just me who's saying this': the deployment of cited others in televized political discourse'. *British Journal of Social Psychology*.

Drew. P. and Heritage, J. (1992). *Talk at Work*, Cambridge: Cambridge University Press.

Fairclough, N. (1992). *Discourse and Social Change*, Cambridge: Polity Press.

Foucault. M. (1970). *The Order of Things*, London: Routledge.

Foucault. M. (1983). *This is Not a Pipe*, Berkeley and Los Angeles: University of California Press.

Fowler. R. (1991). *Language in the News; Discourse and Ideology in the Press*, London: Routledge.

Gergen. K.J. (1985). The Social Constructionist Movement in modern psychology. *American Psychologist*, 40. 266–275.

Gergen, K.J. (1989). Social psychology and the wrong revolution. *European Journal of Social Psychology*, 19, 463–484.

Gergen. K.J. and Kaye. J. (1992). Beyond narrative in the negotiation of therapeutic meaning. In S. McNamee and K.J. Gergen (eds) *Therapy as Social Construction*, London: Sage.

Kamuf. P. (ed.) (1991). *A Derrida Reader: Between the Blinds*, Hemel Hempstead: Harvester Wheatsheaf.

Morris. P. (1994) (ed.). *The Bakhtin Reader; Selected Writings of Bakhtin, Medvedev and Voloshinov*, London: Edward Arnold.

Morson. G.S. (1986). *Bakhtin; Essays and Dialogues on his Work*. Chicago: University of Chicago Press.

Potter. J. and Wetherell. M. (1987). *Discourse and Social Psychology: Beyond Attitudes and Behaviour*, London: Sage.

Sampson. E.E. (1993) *Celebrating the Other; A Dialogic Account of Human Nature*. Hemel Hempstead: Harvester Wheatsheaf.

Shotter. J. (1992). Bakhtin & Billig; monological versus dialogical practices. *American Behavioural Scientist*, 36 (1), 8–21.

Shotter. J. (1995). In conversation: joint action, shared intentionality and ethics. *Theory and Psychology*, 5 (1), 49–73.

Shotter. J. and Gergen. K.J. (eds) (1989). *Texts of Identity*, London: Sage.

Silverman. D. (1987). *Communication and Medical Practice*, London: Sage.

Silverman. D. (1992). *Interpreting Qualitative Data; Methods of Analysing Talk, Text and Interaction*. London: Sage.

Strauss. A. and Corbin. J. (1990). *Basics of Qualitative Research: A Grounded Theory Approach*. London: Sage.

Wetherell. M. and Potter. J. (1988). Discourse analysis and interpretative repertoires. In C. Antaki (ed.) *Analysing Everyday Explanation: A Casebook of Methods*, London: Sage.

Wooffitt. R. (1992). *Telling Tales of the Unexpected: The Organization of Factual Discourse*. Hemel Hempstead: Harvester Wheatsheaf.

SECTION 7

COMMENTARY*

In evaluating what these four approaches have to offer in order to make sense of the interview material, I asked myself some questions. Do I feel committed to one particular philosophy which would prescribe a certain approach and exclude others? In which way does each approach help me to find an answer to what I want to know? What is the potential of each approach to analyse longitudinal data?

While valuing the discussion about philosophical underpinnings of research methods and finding it important and stimulating, I feel unable to marry myself to any particular view to the exclusion of others. I would see myself as something like a constructivist in a pragmatic sense in that all these methods are ways to make sense of reality, and none captures a simple kind of truth, all have their inherent limitations.

Having had a strong education in quantitative research, I share many of Martin Glachan's concerns about the limitations of qualitative research, in particular concerns about reliability. Similarly, I do not see a reason why we should not use statistical methods and technology where information is to be processed in a more complex numerical way. For instance, categories generated by grounded theory analysis could be numbered and processed by methods described in the chapter on content analysis. Being sceptical of subjective factors in the process of generating and naming categories rather than seeing it as an advantage, it appeals to me to have a measure of inter-rater reliability: at the least it gives some indication of how far someone else can follow my thoughts. Another possibility that is being pursued is to have a set of interview data analysed by two independent researchers, both using grounded theory.

Discourse analysis offers an approach that makes a lot of sense for someone concerned with the subtle interpersonal processes in counselling. The awareness of the way in which meaning is generated in the context of the interaction is part of a counsellor's competence. The distinction between process and content implies that the ideas generated and expressed from moment to moment are 'overdetermined' in the sense that they serve a range of functions in the inter-action, and the attempt to express some inner reality is not the only one. However, I wonder whether the method of discourse analysis may overemphasise the process and disregard too much of the content.

The longitudinal nature of the interview data introduces another level of complexity that these approaches may be more or less able to address. Having started with a grounded theory analysis across the interviewees at each point in time, it soon became clear that there was an increasing divergence of themes which made it difficult to subsume the material under common themes unless one

---

* Annemarie Salm, School of Psychology and Counselling, Roehampton Institute, London.

chose very broad and rather meaningless categories. Instead, we are looking now at each individual's material over the four points in time, which also makes more sense in terms of training as a developmental process. As a result we will have in fact a number of case studies which may illustrate certain types of development. On the other hand, correspondence analysis or other forms of multidimensional scaling may help to identify basic patterns of change which we would not become aware of with the bare eye.

Following this discussion, it is planned to experiment with all the four methods under consideration and to compare the results. The exploration of the merits and limitations of each approach will continue within this process. Purists may be appalled by this pragmatic-eclectic approach, but I learn through trying out.

SECTION 8

EROS AND HERMES: THE TWIN PILLARS OF THE 'NEW PARADIGM' OF QUALITATIVE RESEARCH IN PSYCHOLOGY*

My thesis in this section is that the New Paradigm of qualitative methods of research is a recovery of Greek categories of thought, and a rejection of Latin and Anglo-Saxon categories. My claim is that the New Paradigm not only sees the primary phenomenon of human psychology as that of 'meaning', but more importantly, conceives of this meaning in a fashion that is Greek. The difference in worldview can be evoked in the contrast between terms like 'intuitive, insightful, tacit, interior depth, empathic, metaphorical' which are all part of the workings of the Greek 'reason', and terms like 'logical, inferential, explicit, exterior surface, analytical, literal' which are all part of the workings of the Latin and Anglo-Saxon 'intellect'. What, then, is this Greek approach?

The Greek background

The New Paradigm often begins its philosophical critique, and rejection, of the Old Paradigm of positivist-inspired empiricism, by presenting an argument that there are only two basic conceptions of reality 'Naive Realism' and 'Constructivism', respectively.

Naive Realism proposes a single kind of reality, namely that which we all observe and thus can codify in an agreed way. This reality presents, therefore, clear-cut 'facts'. For purposes of subsequent investigation, the task is to explain the observed regularities and frequencies of occurrence of those facts.

Constructivism, by contrast, points out that in regard to the 'reality' of human beings, the most difficult thing is to get an agreed statement of the publicly observable 'facts'. For example, is the phenomenon of homosexuality biological, familial, social, sociological – or a political act? One of many ways that human beings differ from natural objects is that what can be observed on our surface does not exhaust the reality of what is present; therefore our surface is inherently ambiguous. There are multiple possible 'realities' because the phenomena are inherently imprecise.

There is a third position possible, 'Metaphysical Realism', which is quite different from Naive Realism. In the psychological literature it is sometimes called Critical Realism, but my preferred term for it is Synergistic Realism. Though this position says that the New Paradigm can profit from Constructivism, it is essentially on a different track. Though it agrees that the 'surface' of psychological phenomena cannot be taken as anything like a full indication of what lies beyond, or behind, or within, that surface, it reads this surface as

* Jamie Moran. School of Psychology and Counselling, Roehampton Institute. London.

a metaphor of what lies inside it (see Romanyshyn, 1982). Hence, if we treat psychological phenomena as transparent or window-like in their very ambiguity, such that the shapes and colours on the window are opaque when seen only from the outside, but light up and have a new sense when seen from the inside, then we can pass through the surface's ill-defined nature to some more interior 'reality' beyond it, which uses it to convey itself.

This has a bearing on the relation between qualitative and quantitative approaches to research. I do not see these methods as necessarily forever pitted against one another in an either/or choice. But, it does seem that they are actually researching different 'things'. Since quantitative methods in psychology were 'borrowed' from the natural sciences, where they had been used to study natural objects, *psychological* phenomena were essentially seen as object-like and their *meaning* was often missed. In short, quantitative methods have imposed a very truncated 'conception' upon meaning that either leaves out some of its most important properties, or distort those that they deal with.

The mysterious, the intelligible and the sensible

The ancient Greeks had an integrative vision of the entire universe. Their ontology recognised three interpenetrating kinds of realities, 'spirit', 'soul' and 'body'. The Greek philosophical tradition called them 'the Mysterious', 'the Intelligible' and 'the Sensible'. Of the Mysterious, one can have experience, lived experience, but not knowledge in any procedural sense (though mystical theologies, teaching stories and other paradoxical and allusive sayings may point to the existence of that area, without trying to pin it down). The Mysterious cannot really be researched, though its presence in human beings and indeed in Nature may be glimpsed. The Sensible refers not just to that which we pick up through the senses, but that which is inherently and, by definition, predictable and regular because it is 'external'. The Sensible is, therefore, a kind of baseline. It grounds meaning. It creates what might be called a boundary condition, within which meaning's powers are situated, as a sort of outer limit. Material processes are, at least in part, part of the Sensible order, in so far as they follow its constraints. But this does not imply that other aspects of the material world might not be open to other orders, beyond the Sensible.

The Intelligible lies in between the Mysterious and the Sensible and is affected by both. It is *inspired* by the Mysterious, and it is *confronted* by the Sensible. But the Intelligible is the order of meaning *sui generis*, as a reality of its own kind. My main thesis is that *qualitative research is, as a whole, and despite the various different types, an investigation into what the ancient Greeks would have called the Intelligible*. The Intelligible and the Sensible constitute two different orders of being, two different ontologies, but what concerns us here is to stress that, as such, they also constitute two different orders of perception and understanding and knowledge.

Because of its 'intelligibility', meaning can be unpacked and rendered more clear to our understanding, but as Polyani (1967) demonstrates in his notion of 'tacitness' and Penrose (1990) demonstrates in his parallel notion of 'non-computability', intelligibility does not deny that meaning, as such, is non-analysable and non-reducible to anything more primitive than itself. It certainly cannot be derived from the Sensible order, and all attempts to so derive it end, when properly scrutinised, in manifest absurdity. Whatever we do with meaning, by way of breaking it up or recombining it, draws upon a meaning that is already there, already coherent, already able to be formulated in various ways because it has some inherent form.

The notion that meaning is Intelligible also goes with a very different notion of why we do research and what research is for. Quantitative research, because its natural home has thus far been in the Sensible and thus has been concerned with the rules or causal mechanisms of things, has very often gone with a desire for control. Through that kind of knowledge we do get immense control over the outer world, but as the ecological crisis has shown, such knowledge has its limits in even the Sensible domain, for by trying to exercise total control over Nature we seem to have done harm as well.

But why are we interested in and what might draw us to the realm of the Intelligible? Do we seek control over it? The ancient Greek answer to this is very surprising. They say what motivates our interest in knowing the interior of things is that this interior gives the exterior its beauty. This is not 'curiosity' but what the Greeks call 'eros'. Eros is the quality that animates things from the inside: when we see things through eros, we do not just see them outwardly, but we see the life, the feeling, the passion, the imagination, the intuition, that indwells them and radiates outwardly. Indeed, it is through eros that the Intelligibility hidden inside the Sensible order of outer appearance and behaviour 'speaks' to us: something that is inside things is brought to life and comes through their outside. *So, the notion is that eros draws us to the inner animating principles, for it is these that have beauty and are good, and which when conveyed through the metaphor of the outer, transmute the latter into an expression of meaning, a 'face' rather than just a uni-dimensional, predictable surface.* Thus, the Greek view on why we are drawn to research is because things – especially human beings but Nature also – have a kind of poetic quality of beauty which speaks of some kind of worth, or value, or goodness, of ultimate meaningfulness that indwells things and which we should like to know, by drawing it out more. Research is, therefore, not in order to obtain some causal blueprint that would enable us to control human psychology, but is in order to make more clear the worth and value, the beauty, of the meanings we rest in and use, and thus to raise the question of whether this is the best way to use meaning, or could its potentialities and enormous possibilities not be better used? Meaning is like a mansion of many rooms wherein we dwell, but where we go into and know only one or two of those rooms.

But there is a second side to eros which is very crucial to what is being proposed here about meaning, and this is the notion that with eros you end up in a form of knowing things which is communion with them, or communication with them. Because, what draws us into the interior of things is the life, the power, the intelligence, in that interior; but this signifies that meaning is 'alive' in us, and that in knowing this with *our* life we participate in *their* life. In ancient Greece the faculty that knows is not only the insightful, perceptive 'nous', which has the intelligence needed to understand meaning's hinterland, but more ultimately, the desiring faculty touched by eros. It is the desiring faculty that actually, at the end of the day, is led to real knowledge. By eros, according to ancient Greek thought, we are drawn out of self and able to enter into participation with the inner meaning of what is other to us, the 'knowledge' of God, the knowledge of Nature, and the knowledge of human beings.

This summary of the Greek philosophical background which underpins the New Paradigm, helps us understand three key concepts – *dialogue*, *understanding* and *truth* – which I address in turn.

Dialogue

The New Paradigm literature emphasises dialogue and co-operation. This is what differentiates, for example, qualitative interviewing, and all the skills and abilities and intuitive and empathic techniques that go with it, from other, quantitative, approaches. Far from being soft-headed niceness that fails to exert any control over what is being researched, dialogue of the research process, and thus of the researcher's role in that process, has a much bigger philosophical rationale.

In human beings, the hidden part of us, our inner, could hide itself from the scrutiny of the outside. Maybe there are very good reasons, which we do not grasp, why most of meaning is not on display. Maybe these reasons are involved in why it is that our words, our actions, our images, only partly reveal the inside, and do not just representationally report what's on the inside. Yet they are metaphors in some way and windows in some way. But the real point is, if you want to understand a relation, you have to respect that relation, and share in it. You cannot destroy a relation in the very act of researching it. The necessity for dialogue arises out of the fact that meaning is a person's relation to that which is significant to them, and only by entering relation with them do we honour this fact and therefore induce them to reveal more of that significance. It is a bit like the story of the Little Prince where the fox says to him, 'I will let you tame me, but only through friendship. But if you simply want to put me in a box and destroy the inner me – in effect if you simply want to destroy what is meaningful by putting its intelligibility in a box of the sensible – then I will remain wild'. And so 'taming', which is a metaphor for getting to know someone better, has to be seen as an act of friendship. It has to be seen as co-operative, and that means that qualitative research stands or falls by how much the dialogue works.

Understanding

In the New Paradigm literature there are many interesting attempts to provide a description of the nature of meaning as a domain, or what Harre (1993) calls a 'world', for purposes of further study. These stem from diverse traditions, such as Phenomenology, Existential-Phenomenology, Symbolic Interactionism and Discursive Psychology, and many more, including more recently Narrative Psychology (see Polkinghorne, 1988; Smith *et al.*, 1995). Such traditions allow us to point up many different levels of meaning, such as the personal, the social, the cultural; many different expressions of meaning, such as experience, action and reflection; and many different components of meaning, such as the meaningful situation and what is at stake in that situation for those who are in it. As Bolton (1991: 110) puts this point, 'human nature . . . exists as concern about its own possibility'.

To see what happens when the goal of research becomes to explain, but not understand, meaning, one only has to turn to the pages of standard cognitive psychology texts, where one will be confronted by quite a small grasp of what meaning is or what interpretive activities in human beings are (see Still and Costall, 1991). 'Cognitive theory rests upon the mistake of taking one form of knowing – abstraction – as the model for all knowing' Bolton (1982b; 1991: 109).

When we are dealing with entities that only have tangible existence, and thus are part of the Sensible order, we are on safe ground in imputing to them no greater meaningfulness than that they are governed by rules that cause their appearance and behaviour. In this situation, all the logic of quantitative research makes sense, because what we are doing in that research is second guessing something that has no power to relate, and therefore something with which we cannot dialogue. It has no interior with which to disclose itself and therefore enter into erotic participation with our interior. So it is appropriate we have hypotheses about an entity that is 'mute', it is appropriate that we make predictions. It is appropriate that we test these predictions in very controlled ways. But when we encounter another human being, we are confronted not by the alien-ness of a mute thing, but by a presence. And this presence shares with us the whole metaphoric logic of being able to convey what is interior in some exterior way.

Thus we do not have to second guess that presence because we can just *ask* it. 'Are you willing to disclose yourself?' We can enter dialogue with the interiority of another human being, from our own interiority, and we can use the means we have for expressing this interior-to-interior contact, through language, gesture or imagery.

Of course, because there is a gap in leaping from inner to outer, or vice versa, interpretation occurs. This implicates Hermes, the god of inspired intelligence, or perceptive leaps. It is just here that I think neither Naive Realism – the notion we can just directly grasp meaning in a formulation without any gap arising between its 'meta' and 'physical' levels, nor Constructivism – the notion that we make the meaning what we will in interpreting it, are really helpful. There is a leap, but the Hermeneutic movement is not arbitrary, though it is tricky: Hermes was also the Trickster. He enlightens and fools us by turns. Meaning is 'tricky' because, in its innerness and depth, it is something very different from its forms and figures of expression, and we must honour that. We must not try to reduce meaning, in its core and essence, to its expression; we must leave the difference between the meta and the physical levels of the metaphor. Like Ricour (1984–6), I believe that good interpretations do uncover something real, in the domain of meaning, but I grant that this remains tricky. It is an indirect knowing, not a direct.

Intelligibility, then, can be described as threefold. Operating through the eros of communion in already shared interiority, its hermeneutics imply three levels or processes: (1) meaning itself, (2) the understanding of that meaning, (3) the intelligence needed to understand that meaning, an intelligence that is *rational* in the Greek sense of being able to see 'in', perceptively and incisively, an intelligence that can 'read between the lines'; as contrasted with the sort of intelligence that has heretofore dominated the natural sciences and been (inappropriately) transferred into psychology, an intelligence that is *intellectual* in the Latin and Anglo-Saxon sense, of being stuck with the literal, and only able to use inference and analysis to try to demonstrate what mechanically 'runs' that literalness. When something has intelligibility, it has meaning, and that meaning can be understood by those who employ the right kind of intelligence to understand it. This is an intelligence characterised by the dynamics of the gods Eros and Hermes.

Truth

Truth is probably one of the more disputed notions in the New Paradigm literature. It is clear that delving into meaning cannot produce knowledge which has to meet the criteria of Naive Realism's 'Empiricist' notion of truth, e.g. the so-called 'Correspondence Theory of Truth'. But this might suggest that qualitative research is not concerned with any kind of truth whatever. Is that so? There seems disquiet, and a lot of confusion, on the issue.

Some people, like Lincoln and Guba, think that the problem can be resolved simply by arguing that there are different sorts of warrants for the claims to knowledge of qualitative research. Other people by-pass that whole quandary of having to say 'Well, there are just alternative or different kinds of warrants in qualitative research', by saying, 'Well, this kind of research isn't about warrants. It is rich in meaning, but is not concerned with trying to establish truth'.

It is a standard critique of the notion of truth in quantitative research that, by fixing itself only on the tangible/external/mechanical, it basically has to assume that Nature is uniform over time and space and thus to decontextualise. But this rules out that people are not uniform over time: they actually change. And that people are not uniform over space: context is all. Equally problematic is the reliance on stable orderliness when, like the weather system, meaning is also chaotic and fluid, not just stable; or the reliance on frequencies and central statistical tendencies, when what occurs infrequently may be more important in meaning than what always happens and where the rare and unusual is as indicative of meaning as the average or norm. Since the Empiricist conception of truth seems tied to a logic of experimentation that forces on meaning properties that are foreign to it, it has to be a very different kind of truth that is relevant to meaning.

As we have seen, the Greek term for truth means something like 'un-hiddenness' or 'un-forgottenness'. Heidegger called this truth 'a clearing in being'. a point at which that which is shared but deep comes forth from its 'ground' within things and, as it were, takes on a 'face'. Something that we do not see, or see only very partially, is suddenly disclosed to our gaze in a fuller fashion. From a Greek perspective, the sheer perception of truth may well be not just pre-linguistic, but pre-gestural and pre-imaginal; this perception is not limited to, and certainly not constituted by, the linguistic or other symbolic figures that may seek to aid its disclosure. Thus Heidegger (1971), in a very Greek vein, disputes the extremes of Constructivism when he argues that language – and Susan Langer has argued the same for gesture and image – is not just an arbitrary construction, but – as with gesture and image – has a more organic connection to what it un-hides and un-forgets. Hence he calls language, and the same can be said of gesture and image, a 'house of being'.

Be that as it may, there is a clear implication to this kind of truth. The warrants here are not external, but internal. The disclosure of what is true cannot be proved by appeal to external evidence, thus it must just be referred back to the domain out of which it has come in order to see if its coming 'rings true' of that domain.

Conclusion

The Greek notion of meaning is that it is intelligible, if we use a certain sort of inspired collaborative (Eros) and hermeneutic (Hermes) intelligence to see 'in' to its hidden, tacit structures, dynamics and qualities. But a certain kind of intellectualism that has dominated Western culture at least since 500 AD, and has grown especially powerful in the last 500 years, lacks the Greek way of being intelligent by recourse to empathic communion and understanding; rather, it sticks to the surface, and only reads the surface. It treats that surface not as a window, a metaphor, that opens out into an ever broadening and deepening network of meaning below its surface, but as a literal surface, treating it as a set of defined facts to be counted and collated, so inferences can be drawn about what produces their surface regularity. This keeps meaning imprisoned in a surface conception of it that misses all its depth and breadth, and its creative power. Meaning is *simultaneously* non-graspable if we remain stuck on the surface, e.g. it is 'intangible' or 'imperceptible to the outer touch', but it is 'seeable' if we let ourselves use its own interior nature and interior powers to show themselves to our gaze: *it is intelligible, though it is not sensible.* Western intellectualism refuses to see the intangible in terms proper to its own nature and power; it insists in confining all seeing merely to the surface. But Greek intelligence tells us we can see that which is unseeable by surface terms of reference: we can picture and comprehend it in and through our intelligence.

Hence what all New Paradigm qualitative methods share is that all are researching the intelligibility of meaning by resort to a certain type of collaborative/interpretive intelligence *that can work with that intelligibility, by getting insight into it.* It is just this insight into the depth and breadth, and the tacit and holistic expanse of meaning, that the surface analysis of intellectualism cannot obtain.

However, it does not follow from this that the New Paradigm of qualitative research is a holy grail that will solve all problems of researching human beings. There is no such grail, for any approach has the advantages and limitations of its own paradigmatic ontology, epistemology and methodology. All knowledge is mediated by human assumptions and leaps into the dark; no knowledge is direct. The goal of 'proven certainty' in regard to scientific knowledge of human beings is a total non-runner. However, it would be claimed that the Greekness of the New Paradigm's approach towards meaning is a step closer to this crucial phenomenon – which is 'the' phenomenon – of human psychology than that taken by the Old Paradigm of Positivist-inspired Empiricism, which used experimentation and quantification only to investigate a presumed rulefulness, mechanical predictableness, logical formalism and causal determinism, that meaning does not have. or if it has, has only in the least significant, surface part of its metaphorical depths.

It remains to be seen, for the future, if experimentation and quantification can, as procedures, free themselves from their previous 'world', and be adapted to become of more use in exploring the world of meaning. One of the advantages of grasping the New Paradigm's Greekness is that of challenging us to realise just how unique, how different, meaning is as a phenomenon to the phenomena we are familiar with from the natural sciences. The Greeks grasped the difference between the meta-physical and the physical, and developed (Erotically collaborative and Hermeneutically incisive) procedures for looking 'in' to the former through the latter. Their perspective invites us to realise that all knowledge is ultimately a metaphor about the metaphorical, and thus that it deals in 'rational possibility' rather than 'proven certainty'. Oddly enough, it is when we are cautious and humble about our accuracy that we are most likely to be accurate. Whilst it is human to be stuck on the surface of things, and to trudge along at only that level, it is also human to be inspired and to leap into what lies beyond it. We are using a key power of meaning when we try to understand meaning. That, though not guaranteed, makes sense and is feasible. Maybe we cannot ask for more.

References

Bolton. N. (1982). Forms of thought. In G. Underwood, (ed.) *Aspects of Consciousness*, vol. 3, London: Academic Press.

Bolton. N. (1991). Cognitivism: a phenomenological critique. In A: Still and A. Costall (eds) *Against Cognitivism*, New York: Harvester Press.

Harre. R. (1993). Reappraising social psychology: rules, roles, and rhetoric. *The Psychologist*, January, 24–28.

Heidegger, M. (1971). *Poetry, Language, Thought*, New York: Harper & Row.

Langer. S. (1951). *Philosophy in a New Key: A Study in the Symbolism of Reason*, New York: Harvard University Press.

Penrose. R. (1990). *The Emperor's New Mind, Concerning Computers, Minds, and the Laws of Physics*, London: Vintage.

Polkinghorne, D.E. (1988). *Narrative Knowing and the Human Sciences*, New York: State University of New York Press.

Polyani. M. (1967) *The Tacit Dimension*, London: Routledge & Kegan Paul.

Polyani. M. and Prosch, H. (1977). *Meaning*, Chicago and London: University of Chicago Press.

Ricour. P. (1984–1986). *Time and Narrative* (2 vols), translated by K. McLaughlin and D. Pellauer. Chicago: Chicago University Press.

Romanyshyn, R.D. (1982). *Psychological Life: From Science to Metaphor*, Austin: University of Texas Press.

Smith. J.A., Harre, R. and Langenhove, L.V. (eds) (1995). *Rethinking Psychology*, London: Sage.

Still. A. and Costall, A. (eds) (1991). *Against Cognitivism*, New York: Harvester Press.

Texts that might serve as an introduction to Greek ontological philosophy are as follows

Cornford, F.M. (1967). *The Unwritten Philosophy*, Cambridge: Cambridge University Press.

Thurnberg. L. (1985). *Man and the Cosmos*, Crestwood, NY: St Vladamir's Seminary Press.

Chapter 11

Chartered counselling psychology qualification by the independent route and the role of the training co-ordinator

A little research

Petrūska Clarkson

INTRODUCTION

This chapter considers some aspects of counselling psychology concerning the role of the training co-ordinator of qualification by the independent route based on a small study and drawing on previous work, not finally to delineate, regularise or legislate, but to continue and encourage the continuation of this professional conversation in our discipline.

It may also be useful to refer to the following works: Clarkson (1994a, 1995a and Chapter 1 of this volume) and Woolfe and Dryden (1996).

THE CONTEXT

Counselling psychology has been a British Psychological Society (BPS) Division for about three years. One of the exciting options built into the several routes possible to become eligible for being accorded chartered psychologist status is the 'independent route' which is more fully described in the BPS guidelines. Essentially it means that candidates have alternatives to taught Masters or taught PhD programmes in counselling psychology as offered by accredited courses and that they can in principle customise a legitimate training for themselves providing they meet the BPS criteria, as laid down in the regulations, for becoming chartered counselling psychologists.

In my experience, the independent route tends to suit more mature, independent-minded individual professionals who already have considerable experience in the field and are willing and able to direct themselves and intelligently and responsibly use the direction of others from a number of different sources in a coherent way. One of the pivotal roles in the design of the training plan (which must be approved by the BPS) towards Part I and/or Part II of the BPS Counselling Psychology Diploma Examination is that of the training co-ordinator. Although this role and its responsibilities are still in flux and in the process of development and fine-tuning, it is basically concerned with the responsibility of acting as a *consultant* to the candidate, usually over the whole period of their professional preparation, to enable them to achieve their professional goals in counselling psychology most efficiently and effectively.

It is different in its responsibilities from the roles of supervisor, personal psychological counsellor or trainer/teacher/educator/course or experiential workshop provider, although they may have similar functions from time to time. It is important to note that the professionals in all these cases are ideally qualified senior chartered counselling psychologists with the appropriate expertise in the relevant areas. There are times and places for exceptions to work with professionals who are not psychologically trained, but these have to be negotiated with the BPS and agreed in the training plan. Hopefully this will only have to happen until there are enough chartered counselling psychologists with the specific expertise needed to service the needs of the profession across Britain.

The BPS Board of Examiners made a decision to hold a special all-day meeting for chartered counselling psychologists interested in and/or involved in being training co-ordinators to discuss, explore and research this role and function in the development of our profession on 4 June 1996. As part of the work of this day, twenty-six answer sheets were collected after the small discussion groups focused on discussing the four fictional case examples Pat Didsbury had provided after her talk based on her experience as training co-ordinator. These case examples are outlined in Table 11.1.

METHOD

Talks by Ray Woolfe on 'routes to becoming a chartered counselling psychologist', Sandy Gaskins on 'the experience of being an independent counselling psychology diploma exam candidate' and Pat Didsbury on her 'experience of acting as a training co-ordinator' were followed by some small group discussions. All the potential training co-ordinators (chartered counselling psychologists) present were asked to write down the criteria they individually had used in thinking through decisions they would make or would have made in response to the four fictional case examples (provided by Pat Didsbury) in terms of developing or consulting about potential training plans for the respective candidates. The intention was to surface or make overt as far as possible the criteria for such decision making in an effort to clarify the task and role of the training co-ordinator and the profession itself.

Twenty-six questionnaires were returned. They were subjected to a simple frequency analysis based on nomination – the number of times certain concepts occurred in the protocols. Usually the statements were kept as they were written, but divided for categorisation into meaningful segments. The analysis was checked and further processed by another rater.

Subsequently the data were clustered by hand into ten categories to facilitate discussion and comparison. It would be quite possible and even desirable for myself and/or others to make further analyses of the data in future. Since this was meant to be a 'little' research, only some of the categories are explored in more detail. Further inquiry, exploration and research can perhaps be done at the next day meeting of training co-ordinators.

Table 11.1 Four fictional case examples (provided by Pat Didsbury)

Candidate A

GBR five years ago. Many courses in counselling – all of short duration (weekends, summer schools, day workshops, etc.). The courses attended are of various orientations and none has a supervised practice element. As far as can be ascertained, none of the courses has included any form of marked or examined work. Candidate A is currently working in private practice with a small caseload and has recently begun monthly supervision (one hour per month). When asked 'What orientation do you use with your clients?', Candidate A replied 'A bit of everything'.

Candidate B

Currently working as a Health Visitor. Mid-30s. Has just completed a BSc with the Open University and has completed a counselling module on the course. Has now applied for GBR. Tells Co-ordinator of Training that 'All work in the caring professions is counselling'. Wants to do the diploma by the independent route and continue in present job, but does not know how to begin or where to start. Candidate B is also requesting prior accreditation of learning for the work done on the degree.

Candidate C

GBR several years ago and already working in the NHS as a counsellor. Has completed a certificate in counselling and a diploma in counselling – both in person-centred. Has done supervised practice, case studies and process reports as part of diploma course. Currently in weekly supervision at work.

Candidate D

GBR several years ago and currently working as a counsellor within an organisation. Has completed a diploma in person-centred counselling plus a further diploma in psychodynamic. Currently seeing about fifteen clients per week and receiving supervision twice monthly for one-and-a-half hours. Candidate D has done many experiential workshops focused on various special applications such as marital work, eating issues, psychosexual work, etc. Candidate D undertook personal therapy throughout the second diploma training.

DISCUSSION OF SOME RESULTS

It appears to me that much of the above is self-explanatory and can be used to generate further research or hopefully further discussion, debate and exploration. There is obviously much to be discussed about this data, not the least whether it can be said to be representative at all. However, I would like to highlight some issues of interest or concern to me in view of the emergence and development of the discipline and profession of counselling psychology.

Extensive research has found few, if any, differences in terms of effectiveness among different approaches to psychotherapy (Mahoney, Norcross, Prochaska and Missar, 1989; Norcross and Newman, 1992; Lambert, 1992; Glass, Victor and Arnkoff, 1993; Arnkoff, Victor and Glass, 1993). The meta-analyses mostly fail to show any difference between different forms of treatment, no matter how

Table 11.2 Record of results of study

Category A: Co-ordinator's self		Category B: Checking/verification		Category C: Important factors to do with candidate's experience or study	
Co-ordinator's own		Checking/verification		Diversity/versatility	2
resources	1	of documentation	1	Breadth of experience	1
Logic	1	References	2	Breadth of study	1
Intuition	1	Selection	1	Depth of experience	5
My own values	1	Encourage	1	Depth of study/study	6
Contract	2	Dissuade	1	Lack of clarity	
My own feelings –		Who taught by?	3	(presumably to be	
not wanting to		Who supervised by?		improved)	1
promote self-interest	1	(include checking		Applied work in	
To be fair	1	their credentials)	6	range of situations	1
Not to be a snob	1	Look at placement	1	Consolidation of	
Not to exclude		Viva discussion to		previous learning	1
diverse individuals	1	explore levels of			
		understanding	1		
		Level reached in the			
		process?	1		
		Dipping in or adding			
		gradually to integrate?	1		
		Discussing choices			
		about filling gaps	1		

Category D: Personal qualities of candidates					
Potential for change		Personal growth and		Understanding	1
and learning	1	development	2	Joining	1
Self-direction	1	Work on themselves		Empathy	1
Understanding	2	and self-awareness	4	Personal background	
Personal philosophy	1	Aspiration/goals	8	learning	1
Planning	1	Grasp of reality	1	Age (maturity)	1
Ability to negotiate	1	Personal qualities/		Academic suitability	4
An awareness of		formation/personal		Previous education	
problems	1	suitability	11	may facilitate written	
Motivation	7	Narrowness		work	1
		(presumably to be		An awareness of	
		avoided)	1	politics	1

Category E: Practicalities and resource implications		Category F: Evaluation and assessment		Category G: Use of external criteria	
Availability and		How can we		Other people's	
accessibility of		evaluate practice		agreement on good,	
training facilities	1	by written work?	1	bad, appropriate	
Applied lectures	1	Exam	5	or adequate	2

continued . . .

Financial resources	2	Assessment/ evaluation	5	External – level of chartering/yardstick of diploma	6
Health	1	Audio/video tapes	1		
Time	2	Ethics	5		
Family	1	Gatekeeper	2		
Effort	1				
Work context	1				

Category H: *Separate elements* *of diploma*		*Category I:* *Important factors* *concerning reflection* *and critical ability*		*Category J: Use* *of disciplinary* *nomination*	
Theory/models/ orientations/ school/approaches	31	Continuing exploration into the human condition as to continue to gain understanding	1	Counselling	46
Courses/training/ what is studied	28			Therapy	10
Work/experience	25			Counselling psychology	9
Supervision/ supervised practice	24	'Ability to reflect meaningfully on training already taken and/or write about or show some evidence of application of learning'	1	Psychology	4
Research	11				
Practice	8				
Case study	7				
Process reports	6				
Skills/competence	3	Evaluating the impact of interventions	1		
Essay/written work	2	Evaluating evidence for observation/case notes	1		
Academic	1				
Work log	1	'Ability to criticise constructively academic theory, research and practice'	1		
Workshops	1	'Does candidate get links between client work and personal therapy?'	1		

different in philosophy, e.g. psychodynamic or behavioural, or how different the procedures, e.g. group or individual, and no matter what the disorder being treated (Seligman, 1995; Russell, 1995). This lack of appreciable condition treatment interactions is confirmed by a much smaller number of well-controlled comparative studies (e.g. Sloane, Staples, Cristol, Yorkston and Whipple, 1975). The only exception to the apparently non-specific effects of psychotherapy is the slightly greater success of behavioural methods in treating obsessions and phobias. But even they can be treated with almost equal success by other methods. The lack of specificity is also shown by the comparative effectiveness of many treatments which are neither psychodynamic nor behavioural nor indeed psychological in any sense (Prioleau, Murdock and Brody, 1983).

So the last category J – use of disciplinary nomination first

'Therapy' and 'counselling psychology' are mentioned respectively ten and nine times in these protocols. If 'psychology' mentioned on its own is added to the category of counselling psychology it is still only thirteen times that the distinguishing name is used in the discussion of the criteria for co-ordinating the training of future members of this profession. Of course it is done within a context in which counselling psychology is assumed as the primary universe of discourse. However, given the disciplinary demarcation debates and the implications of terminology, rhetoric and nomination for the establishment of disciplinary acceptance, structures and ideology, it appears that these potential co-ordinators of training at least do not write (talk?) using the nomenclature of our primary profession, but those of the ancillary and different disciplines namely 'therapy' (ten mentions) and 'counselling' (forty-six mentions separately from psychology!).

Psychology (with or without being called counselling psychology) is thus mentioned thirteen times, whereas the professions of therapy and counselling together are mentioned fifty-six times. The implication of this finding is that extreme care needs to be taken in differentiating counselling psychology as a discipline based in psychology from the professions of therapy and/or counselling (which are of course themselves often conflated).

Omission of using the appropriate and accurate disciplinary nomination may also go some way towards explaining the difficulty sometimes experienced in differentiating counselling psychology from these disciplines. We should seriously in practice, as well as in discussion, separate out therapy and counselling conducted by *non-psychologists*, from the psychotherapeutic and counselling work conducted by *psychologists* who base themselves in the terminology, epistemology, values and methods of practice and inquiry of psychology as a discipline and a profession.

As Dryden (1996: xi) pointed out there is 'a problem in the way counsellors and psychotherapists are trained. If the research–practice divide is to be traversed, then research, skills training and supervised clinical practice need to be far more closely integrated on training courses than they are at present'. If counselling psychology is to establish itself as a discipline, we need to think and refer to it as a discipline in its own right separately and independently from the ancillary although overlapping professions of psychotherapy/analysis or counselling. Our teaching, supervised practice and personal psychological or psychotherapeutic psychological counselling needs to reflect this differentiation as a natural and widespread way of talking, thinking and writing otherwise the confusion will most likely perpetuate and aggravate. In this way it may be possible to define and develop both our discipline as well as the competence and confidence of our professionals in themselves and their work – not necessarily in competition with counselling and psychotherapy, but separate and distinct because of (a) being based *on academic psychology alongside practical counselling or psychotherapy skills*; (b) being based on *empirical research* of the client and the counselling and psychotherapy process; and (c) being based on *formal psychological inquiry*, also from the interpersonal relationships between practitioners and their clients. Let us look at these briefly in turn.

First, *academic psychology* has a knowledge base developed not on the authority of theory, where counselling and psychotherapy are integrated into a psychological knowledge and research base, but on research methodology and critical analysis. However, the GBR (as its BPS recognised standard) is the central, most important and non-negotiable requirement for entry into training into this profession. The centrality of psychology as discipline is thus crucial and considered to be the basis for all our work.

Second, *empirical research* of the client and the counselling process is based not on the acceptance or compliance with theory, but on the empirical evidence of research or inquiry into research. This of course includes quantitative as well as qualitative methods of investigating our work. It should also include explorations into the foundations of our work and how we have constructed those foundations. Empirical knowledge is knowledge based on experience which can be contrasted with 'knowledge' based on belief or adherence to ideology. Insofar as psychology is vulnerable to the unaware importation of values and the minimisation of the role of the experimenter (whether counselling psychologist or neurophysiologist), these vulnerabilities are always also open to question, discussion and debate (Newnes, 1996). In psychotherapy it is not unknown for practitioners to be excluded purely for disagreements on principle or questioning of the status quo.

Third, *psychological inquiry* mandates not only the methods and kinds of research, but also of course includes inquiry into methods of knowing or inquiry including the questioning and investigation into the very processes of inquiry. Inquiry means questioning. Research means to search and search again. The questioning scientist-practitioner model is the disciplinary paradigm, not the adherence to unproven or unexamined theory or orientation which is more often the case in psychotherapy or counselling for example.

It is therefore a matter for attention if not concern that theory/models/orientations are mentioned thirty-one times in this study, whereas research only eleven times. Training/courses/study are mentioned at least twenty-eight times (if categories are kept very narrow), whereas the ability critically to reflect is alluded to in only six statements, if these are interpreted quite broadly – the reader can judge the fairness of this notion for themselves from the data under category D. However, it is indeed one of the few things which we know about psychotherapeutic counselling that theory/approach or school appear not to differentiate effective psychotherapy (see literature review in Clarkson, 1995a, 1994b).

Category items such as 'understanding' may have imbedded in them some notions of questioning, critique, ability to evaluate research, critical awareness, ability to compare and contrast, capacity to question foundational assumptions, underlying and implicit values, the epistemology and methodology not only of the knowledge and practice, but of the discipline itself, but I think that would be pushing it.

The counselling psychologist Polkinghorne's (1992) examination of the epistemology that explicitly informs most of the theoretical systems shows that

> they were conceived prior to the developments of cognitive science and its constructivist implications. Freud and Jung wrote as if they were providing descriptions that accurately reflected the actual inner workings of the psyche; Rogers, as if he were describing the actual operations of a substantial self; and Skinner, as if the mechanisms of learning he presented were precise descriptions of real human dynamics. Within a postmodern epistemology, these systems are reinterpreted as models of metaphors that can serve as heuristic devices or as possible cognitive templates for organising client experiences (Polkinghorne, 1992: 155).

The adoption of a professionally defensible practice of theoretical questioning, testing, evaluation and constant review with practitioner research as the norm, should make it much more difficult (or interesting) to work with theoretical 'schools' of psychotherapy. This is the promise and the exciting and valuable achievement to be made possible by counselling psychologists of the next generation.

Omissions

There are of course many concepts or notions which, for all kinds of reasons, are conspicuous by their absence. These are the two which are significant to me now; there may be many more which may be significant to others and can be discussed in future publications.

1 *Awareness of cultural context and imbedded values*

The single mention of 'political awareness', 'context' and the absence of mention of the influence and effects of culture, race, gender, class and all the other factors which have been shown to impinge on the provision of therapeutic help or mental health provision in so many studies are also of concern to me. Our *Zeitgeist* has been described as postmodern and some awareness of 'therapy as social construction' (McNamee and Gergen, 1992) or the observer/experimenter bias effects in psychology seems to be worryingly absent, while 'theory/study/courses/models/approaches' is so well represented. Some representative sources on racism and culturality are Van Dijk (1987); Nardirshaw (1992); Pontoretto and Casas (1991); and Eleftheriadou (1994); and on gender there is Gergen (1994); Goolishian and Anderson (1987); Hare-Mustin (1983); Howell and Bayes (1981); and Widiger and Settle (1987). There is a full though general engagement with this issue in Clarkson (1996a) where many other references will be found, as well as the highly relevant piece 'A socio-cultural context for psychotherapy' (pp. 157–162).

2 The absence of mention of the importance of the relationship

Since this is one of the very few facts relatively undisputed in the research, it would seem vital explicitly to include it within this universe of discourse.

Psychological research (Norcross, 1986) shows that theoretical differences between 'schools or approaches' are far less important in terms of successful outcome of counselling or psychotherapy than the quality of the *relationship* between counsellor and client and certain client characteristics, including motivation for change and the willingness to take responsibility for their part in the process.

A wealth of studies (Luborsky, Crits-Christoph, Alexander, Margolis and Cohen, 1983; O'Malley, Suh & Strupp, 1983; Bergin and Lambert, 1978; Tichenor and Hill, 1989) has demonstrated that it is the relationship between the client and psychotherapist, more than any other factor, which determines the effectiveness of psychotherapy. That is, success in psychotherapy can best be predicted by the attributes of the patient, psychotherapist and their particular relationship (Norcross and Goldfried, 1992; Frank, 1979; Hynan, 1981).

The relationship is therefore consistently being shown in research investigations as more significant than theoretical orientation. Therefore, it makes sense to investigate this factor which appears to be of such overarching importance in statistical comparison of outcome studies, subjective reports and clinical evaluation approaches (Clarkson, 1995b). If indeed the psychotherapeutic relationship is one of the most, if not the most, important factors in successful psychotherapy, counselling psychology would be training in the *intentional* use of relationship based not only on the research, but also on a research mentality, one which privileges questions instead of answers, and investigation into the ideological and cultural bases of our epistemologies as much as in the knowledge base accrued so far in psychology as it applies to our field.

In conclusion, I would like to reiterate that, if we are talking about counselling psychology and not just counselling or therapy by non-psychologists,

> the practice of the clinic should not be separated from rigorous and constant research borne from and bearing theory. . . . It would therefore also be necessary for all professional supervisors to be skilled in acting as co-researchers in every case or situation brought to disciplined reflection – also subjecting their own clinical and supervisory work to investigation. This may need to be done – not once or twice in a life time, but all the time. Although there will probably always be important differences in experience, interests and expertise, conjoining the work of *doing and reflection* in this way might even begin to signal the end of the difference between research and clinical supervision in training [and practice]. This could potentially be to the benefit of all

concerned – not least the clients. Learning with the client in such a way introduces a praxis of the recovery of knowledge which is surely at the very heart of the therapeutic endeavour itself (Clarkson, 1995a: 204).

REFERENCES

Arnkoff. D. B., Victor, B. J. and Glass, C. G. (1993) 'Empirical research on factors in psychotherapeutic change', in G. Stricker and J. R. Gold (eds) *Comprehensive Handbook of Psychotherapy Integration* (pp. 27–42), New York: Plenum.

Bergin. A. E. and Lambert, M. J. (1978) 'The evaluation of therapeutic outcomes', in S. L. Garfield and A. E. Bergin (eds) *Handbook of Psychotherapy and Behavior Change* (2nd edn), New York: Wiley.

Clarkson, P. (1994a) 'The nature and range of psychotherapy', in P. Clarkson and M. Pokorny (eds) *Handbook of Psychotherapy*, pp. 3–27, London: Routledge.

Clarkson. P. (1994b) 'After schoolism', presented at the World Psychotherapy Conference in Vienna, 1996. (Copy available from PHYSIS, 12 North Common Road, London W5 2QB.)

Clarkson, P. (1995a) 'Counselling psychology in Britain – the next decade', *Counselling Psychology Quarterly* 8 (3): 197–204.

Clarkson. P. (1995b) *The Therapeutic Relationship: in Psychoanalysis, Counselling Psychology and Psychotherapy*, London: Whurr.

Clarkson. P. (1996a) *The Bystander (An End to Innocence in Human Relationships?)*, London: Whurr.

Didsbury, P. (1997) 'Some thoughts on the role of co-ordinator of training: a personal view'. *Counselling Psychology Review* 12, 2: 63.

Dryden. W. (1996) *Research in Counselling and Psychotherapy – Practical Applications*, London: Sage.

Eleftheriadou, Z. (1994) *Transcultural Counselling*, London: Central Books.

Frank. J. D. (1979) 'The present status of outcome studies', *Journal of Consulting and Clinical Psychology* 47: 310–316.

Gaskins. S. (1997) 'A tale of excitement and confusion: independent candidates undertaking the BPS Diploma in Counselling Psychology', *Counselling Psychology Review* 12. 2: 66–9.

Gergen. M. (1994) 'Free will and psychotherapy: complaints of the draughtsmen's daughters'. *Journal of Theoretical and Philosophical Psychology* 14 (1): 13–24.

Glass. C. G., Victor, B. J. and Arnkoff, D. B. (1993) 'Empirical research on integrative and eclectic psychotherapies', in G. Stricker and J. R. Gold (eds) *Comprehensive Handbook of Psychotherapy Integration* (pp. 9–23), New York: Plenum.

Goolishian, H. and Anderson. H. (1987) 'Language systems and therapy: an evolving idea'. *Psychotherapy: Theory, Research and Practice* 24: 529–538.

Hare-Mustin, R. T. (1983) 'An appraisal of the relationship of women and psychotherapy: 80 years after the case of Dora', *American Psychologist* 38: 593–601.

Howell. E. and Bayes, M. (eds) (1981) *Women and Mental Health*, New York: Basic Books.

Hynan. M. T. (1981) 'On the advantages of assuming that the techniques of psychotherapy are ineffective', *Psychotherapy: Theory, Research and Practice* 18: 11–13.

Lambert, M. J. (1992) 'Psychotherapy outcome research: implications for integrative and eclectic therapists', in J. C. Norcross and M. R. Goldfried (eds) *Handbook of Psychotherapy Integration* (pp. 94–129), New York: Basic Books.

Luborsky. L. Crits-Christoph. P.. Alexander, L., Margolis, M. and Cohen, M. (1983) 'Two helping alliance methods of predicting outcomes of psychotherapy', *Journal of Nervous and Mental Disease* 171: 480–491.

Mahoney, M. J., Norcross, J. C., Prochaska J. O. and Missar, C. D. (1989) 'Psychological development and optimal psychotherapy: converging perspectives among clinical psychologists', *Journal of Integrative and Eclectic Psychotherapy* 8: 251–263.

McNamee, S. and Gergen, K. J. (1992) *Therapy as Social Construction*, London: Sage.

Nadirshaw, Z. (1992) 'Theory and practice: Brief report, therapeutic practice in multi-racial Britain', *Counselling Psychology Quarterly* 5 (3): 257–261.

Newnes, C. (1996) 'Values in clinical psychology', delivered at British Psychological Society Conference.

Norcross, J. C. (ed.) (1986) *Handbook of Eclectic Psychotherapy*, New York: Brunner/Mazel.

Norcross, J. C. and Goldfried, M. R. (eds) (1992) *Handbook of Psychotherapy Integration*, New York: Basic Books.

Norcross, J. C. and Newman, C. F. (1992) 'Psychotherapy integration: setting the context', in J. C. Norcross and M. R. Goldfried (eds) *Handbook of Psychotherapy Integration* (pp. 3–45), New York: Basic Books.

O'Malley, S. S., Suh, C. S. and Strupp, H. H. (1983) 'The Vanderbilt Psychotherapy Process Scale: a report on the scale development and a process-outcome study', *Journal of Consulting and Clinical Psychology* 51: 581–586.

Polkinghorne, D. E. (1992) 'Postmodern epistemology of practice', in S. Kvale (ed.) *Psychology and Postmodernism* (pp. 146–165), London: Sage.

Pontoretto, J. and Casas, J. M. (1991) *Handbook of Racial/Ethnic Minority Counselling Research*, Springfield, IL: Thomas.

Prioleau, L., Murdock, M. and Brody, N. (1983) 'An analysis of psychotherapy versus placebo studies', *The Behavioral and Brain Sciences* 6: 275–310.

Russell, R. (1995) 'What works in psychotherapy when it does work?' *Changes* 13 (3): 213–218.

Seligman, M. E. P. (1995) 'The effectiveness of psychotherapy', *American Psychologist* 50 (12): 965–974.

Sloane, R. B., Staples, R. F., Cristol, A. H., Yorkston, N. J. and Whipple, K. (1975) *Psychotherapy versus Behavior Therapy*, Cambridge, MA: Harvard University Press.

Tichenor, V. and Hill, C. E. (1989) 'A comparison of six measures of working alliance', *Psychotherapy*, 26: 195–199.

Van Dijk, T. A. (1987) *Communicating Racism*, Newbury Park, CA: Sage.

Widiger, T. A. and Settle, S. E. (1987) 'Broverman et al. revisited: an artifactual sex bias', *Journal of Personality and Social Psychology* 53: 463–46.

Woolfe, R. and Dryden, W. (1996) *Handbook of Counselling Psychology*, London: Sage.

Chapter 12

Learning through Inquiry (the Dierotao[1] programme at PHYSIS)

Petrūska Clarkson

Be patient toward all that is unsolved in your heart and try to love the *questions themselves* like locked rooms and like books that are written in a very foreign tongue. Do not now seek the answers, which cannot be given you because you would not be able to live them. And the point is, to live everything. *Live* the questions now. Perhaps you will then gradually, without noticing it, live along some distant day into the answer.

(Rainer Maria Rilke, 1993: 35)

INTRODUCTION

This paper is a 'fractal' (Mandelbrot, 1974) of an educational research concept attempting to specify some of the assumptions, conceptual frameworks, methodology. sampling and selection criteria, analysis of discourse and verification procedures with recommendations for its conduct and evaluation. It is concerned with the professional *education* ('leading forth from within') of psychologists, psychotherapists, supervisors and organisational consultants, the *application of qualitative research* as ongoing practice in all clinical, supervisory and systemic/ organisational work and the necessity for ongoing *exploration of cultural and ethical situatedness* in what has been described as 'the postmodern condition'.

In the psychotherapeutic disciplines (cognate to psychotherapeutic counselling psychology) there is a *proliferation of different schools* or distinctly identifiable approaches (450 distinct schools according to Corsini, 1984). Amongst others, Norcross and Goldfried (1992) reviewed the literature extensively to demonstrate there the unremitting *inconclusiveness of quantitative empirical evidence* attempting to prove that any one theoretical approach is more effective than another across a broad spectrum of problems – and this applies to any one of the twenty-seven different integrative psychotherapeutic approaches as well! It has been said that the current state of psychotherapy outcome research is like the

---

1 Dierotao or *dierutau* is an ancient Greek word which means 'learning by inquiry'. It is also the name of the educational structure or programme at The Centre for Independent Qualitative Research at PHYSIS. 12 North Common Road. London W5 2QB.

caucus race in *Alice in Wonderland*: 'All have won and all must have prizes'. Polkinghorne (1992: 158) concluded, 'The large number of theories claiming to have grasped the essentials of psychological functioning provide prima facie evidence that no one theory is correct'. In fact, it seems reasonably well-established that theoretical orientation, whether singular or plural, has little if anything to do with the effectiveness of the psychotherapy, however measured. The same may be said for organisational interventions.

It seems vitally important to pay attention to such facts if psychotherapy or psychology training, consultancy or education are at all to be reflective of the current state of the art (science?) and to equip practitioners and supervisors to deal effectively and authentically with the postmodern challenges facing these professions. Yet most, if not all, 'trainings' in these professions are predicated on learning one of these theories – or an 'integration' of these approaches. Whether the 'integration' or the 'incorporation of the pure approach' has been successful usually determines whether the practitioner or supervisor will become 'accredited' or 'recognised'.

As Farrell (1979) pointed out, this avoids the uncomfortable philosophical issue that the participants or 'trainees' or workshop participants are considered to be 'cured' or 'trained' or 'analysed' or 'qualified' by one single criterion – they have adopted the WOT or 'way of talking' of the leaders, governing bodies, examination boards and others of perceived status or power. Mowbray (1995) also persuasively sets out many of the other major arguments in his book, *The Case Against Psychotherapy Registration*.

As a designer and senior co-writer of many successful national, internally and externally accredited courses, prototype academic taught Masters syllabuses and other learning structures in counselling, psychology, supervision and psychotherapy which have been widely copied, adapted or simply hijacked (sometimes without acknowledgement), this is obviously of concern to me. There will probably always be a necessity for taught courses to cater for the needs of some individuals. However, in every case my original intention was to open the field or discipline to ongoing inquiry, challenge and continuous development of complexity, autonomy and integrity. In almost every case, the experiences of many students (and my own) have raised serious doubts as to whether such an intention could be manifested – but particularly whether it could be sustained in professions where the 'bureaucratisation of sadism', the institutionalisation of petty politics on economic grounds and the fear of lawsuits (brought by one's colleagues or one's clients) on dubiously interpreted ethical grounds have become an uncomfortably familiar ambiance. In 1993 Samuels already said that 'one of the things that depresses me about the UKCP is that we have to listen to men and women of the psyche talking like bloody bankers!' (p. 321). And that was before NVQs . . .

It occurred to me that perhaps one of the reasons psychotherapy research is often so ambiguous and inconclusive as well as the fact that there seems to be a virtual absence of research in the training of psychotherapists and supervisors is that it was trying to model itself on the quantitative investigatory paradigms of the old physical sciences. Indeed Searight (1990) has argued that experimental and quasi-experimental methods cannot do justice to describing phenomena such as the therapeutic relationship. After all, 'to know is to possess ways and means of acting and thinking to allow one to attain the goals one happens to have chosen' (Von Glasersfeld, 1991: 16). A qualitative investigation into this field promised greater hope and perhaps more illumination. Furthermore, by 'inquiring into inquiry' the kind of self-reflective process which I believe should be at the heart of these endeavours could be honoured once more. Certainly it could bear open-minded exploration and perhaps again serve the goals of discovery and experimentation when dissenting voices will not be ostracised or ignored.

The Denzin and Lincoln (1994a) volume contains an excellent overview of the arguments in favour of and the scope and value of the field of qualitative research. I took into account that this would require some 'unlearning' or disengagement from conventional learning structures and some of the taken-for-granted assumptions of traditional quantitative research. I had established my credibility as a quantitative researcher wearing a white laboratory coat in the early 1970s, doing obligatory rats and maze work, even counting their pellets (a measure of stress), and a large-scale quantitative investigation into the interplay of personality, neurophysiology and environmental variables. I used state of the art electronic and computer equipment to count (EEGs, ECGs, electro-galvanic skin response rate measures and so on and so forth). I aimed for neutral objectivity. but I wanted 'the truth'. I did not find either. I did, however, learn how to do quantitative research to Doctoral standard and was awarded distinctions twice by my viva examiners who included two members of the Royal Society of Medicine.

But I have moved on. And so has the field of research itself. Not that the old forms are discarded, but the new forms are gaining their own unique place. And my interest is now in what possible relationship we can establish between knowledge and practice. between reading and thinking, between doubting and believing, between standardisation and invention, between safety and risk, between self and other, individual and profession, consumer and provider and of course – always – between body and soul. And if we fail again, nevertheless the search itself will bear the hallmarks of honest endeavour and soulful encounter and the possibility of hope.

We can speak of roughly two kinds of education. To evolve a differentiation between the role, place and usefulness of these contrasted polarities, Table 12.1 is offered.

The research questions of phenomenological research methods '*reflect the interest, involvement and personal commitment of the researcher . . . viewing experience and behaviour as an integrated and inseparable relationship of subject and object and of parts and whole*' (Moustakas, 1994: 21). My interest in what appeared to be the most conclusive common factor across

Table 12.1 Two kinds of education

Old paradigm of education	New paradigm of education
Expectation of pathology	Expectation of potential
Authority based	Resource based
Motivated by threats/fear	Motivated by curiosity/élan vital
Local	Global
Cumulative	Systemic
Content	Context
Rule bound	Situational
Body of 'knowledge'	Body of 'method'
Consensus driven	Exception-al
Reward for ideological (theoretical) adherence	Reward for rigour and variety of inquiry
Consolidate practice standards when circumstances change	Change practice standards when circumstances change
Sectarian boundaries and disputes	Awe
Scholarship	and authorship
Neutrality and objectivity	Engagement and subjectivity
Absorption of other's knowledge	Learning from other's learning
Compliance	Questioning
Mass-produced	Individual
Incremental progressions	Second-order shifts in knowledge
Imposed teachers, supervisors, therapists	Teachers, supervisors, therapists employed as consultants by autonomously directed individuals to assist their learning process
Introjected collective ethics	Questioned and researched personal ethics
Closed systems	Open systems
Modernist	Postmodernist
Newtonian and Cartesian	Quantum and chaos/complexity inclusive

psychotherapeutic disciplines and approaches formed the substance of a twenty-year qualitative research project which Hinshelwood (1990: 119), the editor of the *British Journal of Psychotherapy*, described as

> a careful analysis of the various levels of the psychotherapeutic relationship in an *attempt to find a perspective from which an overview might become possible*. She [Clarkson] offers a way of circumventing the inherent contradictions and incompatibilities that exist *between* different psychotherapies; instead of incompatibilities we have different priorities and emphasis.

This work has recently culminated in a book (Clarkson, 1995a) and an accompanying paper (Clarkson, 1996b), 'Researching the "Therapeutic Relationship" in Psychoanalysis, Counselling Psychology and Psychotherapy – A Qualitative Inquiry' both of which have been well received nationally and internationally as exemplars of postdoctoral level qualitative research in action.

In the light of an absence of documented research on the training and education of psychotherapists, psychologists and supervisors, I now wanted to explore for myself the capacities and limitations of qualitative research on learning about psychotherapy, psychology and supervision which was grounded in the life, liveliness and livelihood of the consulting process.

In terms of effectiveness, there is not much to distinguish between different approaches to psychotherapy (Norcross, 1986; Beutler, 1989; Lambert, 1989; Mahoney, Norcross, Prochaska and Missar, 1989; Norcross and Newman, 1992; Lambert, 1992; Glass, Victor, and Arnkoff, 1993; Arnkoff, Victor, and Glass, 1993). The recent *Consumer Reports* study in the USA also bears this out (Seligman, 1995). Of course it is also always possible to contest or question research results – and the justifications are infinite. They range from methodological criticisms to a treasuring of the essentially ineffable mystery of the therapeutic encounter which intrinsically cannot be measured. Perhaps this objection comes from the archetypal nightmare of the scientists dissecting ET in a way which destroys not only awe but also life.

So, outcome studies do not particularly favour any one theory more than another or even give much evidence to the idea that theory has much to do with practice at all. However, in the old days it used to be argued that one needed to have a theory to match one's practice (we are back to Farrell's (1979) WOT). One needed a firm theoretical/ideological base upon which to stand before considering or – heaven forfend – *integrating* other ways of thinking, feeling and doing. Indeed, even if theory were irrelevant, the fact that the individual practitioner believed it would be likely to make it more effective. Yes. And what else would the practitioner have to believe on such grounds? In order to 'pass' their exams some Gestalt therapists now have to use a diagnostic categorisation of their clients such as a gender-biased DSM-IV which is intrinsically opposed to the very core of classical Gestalt therapy, Gestalt psychology *and* phenomenology. In order to become a training psychoanalyst it may still be important to believe, as Sociarides did, in the developmental immaturity of people with homosexual love choices. In order to be accredited as a 'person-centred' counsellor by some organisations, one has to make 'no-suicide contracts'. Someone from psychosynthesis may *have* to 'use' transference in order to belong to a particular professional society. I am not objecting to the existence or creation of *options* and *possibilities*; I am questioning the imperatives which *mandate* accreditation and 'respectability'. (Examples from all sides could be proliferated *ad infinitum*.)

Indeed what seems to be missing most of all is a privileging of the activity of questioning, of experimenting, of discovery, of invention, of searching and *re*-searching, of interrogating the subject (*not* object) in dialogic relationship with the existentially experienced world we seek to understand and in which we live, move and have our being. Of course *all relationship is also experiment* – open to the notion that the novel and exciting can unfold in an unexpected and unpredictable way – unless it is a rehash of some 'treatment plan' introjected or swallowed whole from someone else's received superior wisdom.

According to the primarily theoretical framework adopted in order to comprehend the atttempt to transform unruly inimicality into docile obedience [Foucault, 1979], the secretly vicious disciplinary order is a *cultural-historical process* into which we are born. Psychology's methods of dealing with persons are structurally no different from those in the areas of medicine, criminal justice, education and industry . . . and yet I do argue that we as individual persons and as psychologists are responsible for our participation in this order and are free to abandon the project of domination and control, to practice a psychology that recognizes, embraces, liberates and empowers the Other through a practice of open dialogue. This entails not an eradication but a respectful acknowledgement of the presence of inimicality in others and in ourselves (Wertz, 1995: 451).

So what could be the very best kind of therapy or supervision training for psychologists and others of such ilk which would centralise and value this questioning, questing, relational mode of investigation? This became my question. Research on training for consultants, psychotherapists, counsellors and psychologists is apparently very hard to find or non-existent. (There may be good reasons for this.) How might we educate professionals in this field and enable their most efficient highly effective functioning *whilst* still meeting externally measured criteria of academic rigour and practical professionalism?

The answer to an apparently obscure and intractable problem may sometimes appear quite obvious once found. The hypothesis of this whole project emerged with the notion that the ideas, ideals and methods of qualitative psychological research are in themselves the closest approximation to good intervention – whether with individuals, groups or organisations. Psychotherapy, supervision and organisational process consultancy are all seen as areas of applied psychology which is a discipline that revolves around research. Once this is accepted, the need for psychological research in these fields becomes apparent and indeed imperative.

Qualitative research, although around for some decades, has comparatively recently experienced an enormous influx of attention, energy, imagination, a spate of excellent textbooks and even professional academic recognition. Very briefly it proposes methodological answers to my questions above by focusing on: (a) a preference for qualitative data – the use of words rather than numbers; (b) a preference for naturally occurring data – such as are created and available in the consulting room; (c) a preference for subjective meanings instead of quantities of units of behaviour; (d) a rejection of Newtonian natural science as a model; and (e) preference for, but not exclusively, inductive, hypothesis-generating research (adapted from Hammersley, 1992: 160–72).

There is a great deal more to say about this – one may refer to the most excellent handbook by Denzin and Lincoln (1994a). For our purposes here, let it suffice to say that I anticipate that this focus on the *how of experience*, on the *quality of learning*, on the process of *learning about learning*, the *questioning of all assumptions,* the *vitality of engaged commitment* and of *discovery about discovery itself,* promises to be, if not the best, certainly an excellent form within which and through which to explore the tensions, disagreements, creativities, responsibilities, competencies and applicabilities of psychology and its role in all our disciplines.

This new project (Dierotao) would draw, of the necessity of the time and my own situatedness, from *a postmodern qualitative research methodology, context and content which was grounded in a moral universe* where issues of values, ethics and the cultural/ecological situatedness of everyone constantly and inevitably accompanies the investigation, instead of maintaining a pretence of objectivity, illusion of neutrality or, even, authority. Everything changes.

> The early postmodern years are bringing, instead of a collapse of morality, a renaissance of searching for principles of life that we variously call morals, ethics, values. And this is not merely a single shift of values but a continual dynamic process of moral discourse and discovery. Morals are not being handed down from the mountaintop on graven tablets; they are being created by people out of the challenges of the times. The morals of today are not the morals of yesterday, and they will not be the morals of tomorrow (Anderson, 1990: 259).

CONCEPTUAL FRAMEWORK

The conceptual framework for this investigation draws broadly from the fields of psychoanalysis/psychotherapy, psychology, organisational consultancy, supervision and counselling. These can be visualised as overlapping circles at the heart of which, and in the place of maximum overlap, is the relationship.

This whole project is inevitably located in its place and time. 'Postmodern' is one of the words which has been used to try to encapsulate the current *Zeitgeist* (or spirit of our time.) Postmodernism is a story about all the different stories of our time coexisting in our world. 'We are seeing in our lifetimes the collapse of the objectivist worldview that dominated the modern era, the worldview that gave people faith in the absolute and permanent rightness of certain beliefs and values' (Anderson, 1990: 268).

In 'Toward reflexive methodologies' Gergen and Gergen (1991: 86) have suggested that: 'By taking a reflexively dialogic approach to research, a new form of scientific work can be developed'. Clinicians have often in the past defended their hostility, avoidance and rejection of scientific research on the grounds that the mystery of human relationship cannot be subjected to the analyses of the white coats. I have in the past myself likened it to trying to catch butterflies with tractors. Traditional scientific method has often seemed inappropriate, if not damaging, to the mystery and elusiveness of the healing human relationship.

However, the new form of scientific work may already have, or develop, the capacity to honour both the mystery and its greater appreciation by understanding. Perhaps this dialogic approach to research could become acceptable – even desirable to clinicians/facilitators of all kinds and to their co-researchers into the human psyche – their clients. 'The intentional nature of human practices is well captured by *qualitative methods*. There is an acceptance of diverse ways of producing knowledge . . . also encompassing qualitative methods involving inter-active and contextual approaches and including case studies' (Kvale, 1992: 51).

I specifically begin with 'but a provisional stance towards a subject', and progressively elaborate the "the nature of the problem" as it is refracted through the intelligibilities of others' (Gergen and Gergen, 1991: 79) intending to use the metaphor (and reality) of writing as learning, while engaging with learning and unlearning as well as engaging with the writings of others about the nature and range of their understandings, lack of understandings and questionings in these fields.

Or as the phenomenologist Merleau-Ponty (1962: 354) phrases it:

> In the experience of dialogue, there is constituted between the other person and myself a common ground; my thought and his are interwoven into a single fabric, my words and those of my interlocutor are called forth by the stage of the discussion, and they are inserted into a shared operation of which neither of us is the creator. We have here a dual being, where the other is for me no longer a mere bit of behaviour in my transcendental field, nor I in his; we are collaborators for each other in consummate reciprocity.

THE QUALITATIVE METHODOLOGY

The study would be based on the use of my own personal and professional experience as client, teacher and supervisor of psychotherapists (and allied professions) as locus of the exploration. Instead of an 'objective experimenter' on an object, I am engaging from the subjective realities of my ongoing existen-tial situation. This would correspond to Shelef's (1994: 2) *'heuristic incubation'*. The period of my personal and professional engagement with this question spans some twenty-five years, several psychotherapists/analysts, over one hundred pro-fessional chapters/papers, twelve books, and several continents. My background is considered uncommonly wide and thorough in my profession. It is during this period of immersion that I followed a strategy similar to that which is reported by Bamberger and Schön (1991: 187): 'searched for such boundaries without trying to be explicit about the criteria'.

In addition the proposed exploration is engaging the partipants of the project in their relationship with me, with each other, with the relevant disciplines and approaches and a variety of external recognising/accrediting or awarding bodies. Clandinin and Connelly (1994: 425) also view research itself as about relation-ship. conducted in relationship and through relationship:

> Personal experience methods inevitably are relationship methods. As researchers, we cannot work with participants without sensing the funda-mental human connection among us; nor can we create research texts without

imagining a relationship to you, our audience. Voice and signature make it possible for there to be conversations through the texts among participants, researchers, and audiences. It is in the research relationships among participants and researchers, and among researchers and audiences, through research texts that we see the possibility for individual and social change. We see personal experience methods as a way to permit researchers to enter into and participate with the social world in ways that allow the possibility of transformations and growth.

Indeed one can consider the possibility that relationship is at the very heart of the recognition and growth of qualitative methodology because the qualitative research paradigm is based on the *interrelatedness of subjects*, not the apparently disembodied study of *objects* by some non-involved value-neutral analytic experimenter. It is centrally concerned with the researcher–researched unit where one can never authentically be peeled off from the other except in abstract compartments. In this sense it is consistent and congruent with the observer–field interdependence which is the particular contribution of quantum physics and the emerging sciences of chaos and complexity which I have discussed elsewhere (Clarkson, 1993a, 1993b, 1993c).

Any inquiry into relationship is by the same token research. And if psychotherapy is about relationship, then it must also *be* research in a sense. The fact that the work of the clinic is too frequently left unreflected and unreported in a rigorously reflected qualitative way does not mean that it cannot be done. In the future, responsible clinical practice may require that it does not remain undone. Both supervisors and clinicians need to write in order not only to reflect on their experience, but also to offer it to the community of professionals for their edification, challenge and support. As the 'unexamined life may not be worth living', the unexamined therapy may not be worth doing. As Richardson (1994) has suggested, writing itself is of course a method of inquiry in its own right. And any writing done consistently over a large number of years inevitably has the mark of the researcher upon it.

> All qualitative researchers are philosophers in that 'universal sense in which all human beings . . . are guided by highly abstract principles' [Bateson, 1972: 320]. These principles combine beliefs about ontology (What kind of being is the human being? What is the nature of reality?), epistemology (What is the relationship between the inquirer and the known?), and methodology (How do we know the world, or gain knowledge of it?) [Lincoln and Guba, 1985; Guba, 1990; Guba and Lincoln, 1994]. These beliefs shape how the qualitative researcher sees the world and acts in it (Denzin and Lincoln, 1994b: 12–13).

> And writing is a primary way of both seeing and acting in the world. . . . [Not] trying to write a single text in which everything is said to everyone. . . . *Writing is validated as a method of knowing* (Richardson, 1994: 518, emphasis added).

Bor and Watts (1993) wrote that researchers in counselling psychology should conduct their research using a methodology which is congruent with their theoretical framework and approach to counselling and psychotherapy. It is possible to argue that the serious and dedicated writing up of subjective experience, the theories of others and the invention of one's own, the questioning of received wisdom and popular assumptions, the encounter with the other in the consulting room and their words and images, the prose as well as the poetry of healing form a congruent representation of the work of the clinician supervisor in this field. It is thus my opinion and recommendation that research should be inseparable from supervision or clinical work. This theme is developed in this book and elsewhere (Clarkson, 1995b).

The purpose of this study described here is to experiment with new ways of learning and educating practitioners and supervisors in psychotherapy and organisations. A literature search revealed no other attempt of this kind in this country or abroad. In this study the generation of data would be inextricably intertwined in a feedback loop fashion with the interpretation or analysis phase in the sense that the information sought and the data collected were constantly subject to analysis and evaluation in terms of posibility of 'fit' within the framework being tested.

SAMPLING

The naturalist is likely to eschew random or representative sampling in favour of purposive or theoretical sampling because he or she thereby increases the scope of range of data exposed (random or representative sampling is likely to suppress more deviant cases) as well as the likelihood that the full arrray of multiple realities will be uncovered (Lincoln and Guba, 1985: 4).

On the advice of Denzin and Lincoln (1994a: 200), it was my hope to 'seek out groups, settings and individuals where (and for whom) the processes being studied are most likely to occur'. The participants of the proposed series of workshops would ideally be a group of self-directing intellectually and professionally able individuals of varying levels of experience, different theoretical approaches, a diversity of professional directions and a wide spread of previous experience. To my delight and surprise so many suitable individuals applied for the series that I had to make two groups even allowing for people who decided to postpone their starting date to the following year or whom we thought would not be suitable for or benefit from this particular format. Two more groups have since completed.

The sample for this study eventually comprised a self-selected sample of novice and experienced practitioners, qualified and unqualified, supervisees or supervisors who felt drawn to the following announcement:

The Psychology of Advanced Psychotherapy, Supervision and Organisations (A professional and academic educational concept)

Uses, Applications and Accreditation

- Towards obtaining Chartered Status as a Counselling Psychologist.
- Towards UKCP registration as a Psychotherapist.
- Towards a Masters or Doctorate in Psychology or Psychotherapy or Organisational Consultancy or Training via independent study and/or research.
- As a framework for writing applications/ BAC/UKCP/BPsS/IMC/Organisational Diploma case studies/dissertations in any of these disciplines.

For

Psychologists as well as trainee and experienced Psychotherapists, Psychologists and Consultants and supervisors to supplement or complete their training. People from any orientation are welcome and may be able to progress their qualifications within this format, provided they are interested in developing beyond a 'narrow schoolism'. It is particularly designed for free thinking, meta-bureaucratic, independently minded, creative individuals who like to take responsibility for their own learning process, who enjoy thinking as well as feeling; and being bodies as well as souls, engaging with research as well as art and poetry. *Supervision and research are conceptualised as inseparable from ongoing professional work and all work is perceived within the context of organisations and social structures.*

Objectives

This course will provide the structure and opportunity for participants to: (a) review and clarify the disciplines of individual and group psychotherapy, consulting and counselling psychology; (b) re-evaluate and critique the major theoretical traditions in this field and their contributions to clinical practice; (c) do live work and bring cases, audio- or video-tapes for supervision; (d) do personal exploration and experiential work; (e) get supervised supervision for novice and experienced supervisors/trainers (towards recognition with BAC, BPsS, GPTI and other bodies) and (f) do one or more ongoing supervised writing/research projects, (either a case study, Master's or Doctoral dissertation or paper to be prepared for publication) with group support; (h) library supervision and ongoing writing consultation. The emphasis will be on the person rather than the course, the therapy of the soul rather than the diagnosis, the honoring of the work rather than an examination *per se*. There will be also be consultation on preparing applications and research proposals. All work will be externally assessed. The series itself is a qualitative research project teaching by modelling of qualitative research in action.

The training structure

Ten 2-day weekend modules over the academic year. A day may comprise: (a) Group Process – the integration of individual and group therapy within organisational contexts; (b) Theory Review with Practical Application; (c) Personal work; (d) Supervised Supervision, and (e) On the first evening of every event there will be library supervision, Internet access and allocated time for forming and sustaining a learning contract pair and collegial writing support group.

The educational spine of the series

The series will be based on previously unavailable parts of Clarkson's recent books, *Change in Organisations* [1995c] as well as *The Therapeutic Relationship* [1995a]. The series follows the framework of the five therapeutic relationships which encompass most, if not all, of the different approaches to, and critiques of psychotherapy and consultancy and provides a framework for supervision. This makes it compatible with (and extends the) 'training' in any particular school, whether Psychoanalytic, Cognitive/Behavioural, Existential, Archetypal, Jungian, Pluralistic, Humanistic, Gestalt, TA, Person Centred or Integrative Psychotherapy and independent forms. Every two-day event will additionally be structured to comprise all *seven levels of experience, universes of discourse or knowing (epistemology)*. For further information see 'Systemic Integrative Psychotherapy Training' P. Clarkson (1992), published in *Integrative and Eclectic Therapy: A Handbook*, pp. 269–295, Milton Keynes: Open University Press. The philosophy is described in this document entitled 'Dierotao – Learning by Inquiry' and the counselling psychology framework in the paper called 'Counselling Psychology – The Next Decade' [Clarkson, 1995b].

The course was officially recognised by the British Psychological Society as a recommended course for Continuing Professional Education.

It soon becames clear that 'training' is a misnomer for this kind of educational concept. Of course processes similar to, and end products resembling the outcome of, other trainings occur and can be achieved. However, it would probably be preferable if everyone referred to this particular series of ten learning events as participation in *a qualitative research project*. It is of course also in itself and intentionally training and supervision in qualitative research. It is thus concerned not so much with a specific syllabus or content, but with process. Not necessarily only with process as feelings or emotions or 'unconscious' processes, although these are of course part of the field. It is intended as a wholehearted engagement with process in the sense of how one thinks, reads, writes, argues, disagrees, explores, gets confused, investigates, consults or does therapy, supervises or learns, admires and applauds. It is indeed meant to be what the ancient Greeks referred to as *dierutau* – learning by inquiry.

At the selection interview and/or afterwards it was made clear that the project would itself be a qualitative research study within which everyone could pursue their own academic learning, professional recognition objectives or alternative goals.

SELECTION CRITERIA

In addition everyone participating would meet the following selection criteria (or have plans to meet them in the time):

(a) be mature, independent self-directing individuals with a track record of autonomous questioning and learning;

(b) possess willingness to take responsiblity for their own learning, study and exploration within the universe of discourse of psychology and allied disciplines;

(c) have academic fluency – proven ability to read, think and write autonomously about the psychology of their subject;

(d) possess a disinclination to 'sit down and be lectured at' or incorporate pre-digested material whether ethical positions, technicalities of practice or theoretical conclusions;

(e) carry an insistence on seeking and finding their own academic or professional external accrediting systems whether they be universities, professional bodies such as the BAC or BPS and/or sections of the UKCP or informed decisions to reject these or develop alternatives;

(f) be willing to take responsibility for finding and using support, advice and input from multiple sources in order to set their self-chosen personal and professional goals;

(g) have a liking for experimentation, dialogue, response-able relationship, innovation, discovery and invention;

(h) as opposed to a need for following pre-set structures and adapting to pre-set syllabuses or expectations;

(i) be familiar with the outcome of my previous major qualitative research study – The Therapeutic Relationship' (1995a) or its organisational companion – Change in Organisations (1995c) and show a willingness to consider applying this device in a thematic analysis of the field of research itself;

(j) show a willingness to experiment with using the seven-level model of epistemological discourse analysis, i.e. to differentiate in discussion between the realms of (1) the body and the sensations, (2) feelings and emotions, (3) the labels or nominations of language and linguistics, (4) values, ethics and ideals, (5) facts, logic and probabilities, (6) theories, myth, narrative and stories and (7) a transpersonal realm (which may be on the one hand the imponderables of quantum physics and chaos theory or, on the other hand, the inexplicables of spiritual or other awe-inspiring experiences);

(k) bring a desire for education or trainings based on value-systems which do not in what they do (as opposed to in what they claim) militate against creativity, diversity, exception-ality, individuality, uniqueness, unusualness, response-ability, non-conformity, beauty, poetry, artistry, craft, intuition, sensuality, etc.;

(l) have an interest in participating in learning environments where the leader is a respected facilitator, a senior researcher, an experienced enabler and/or a valuable professional resource and not, for example, a 'holding' mother, a 'task-master' father, a transferential object, an organisational embodiment or 'the fount of all wisdom';

(m) show an interest in flexibility, spontaneity and creativity in the service of learning, productivity and the 'elegance' of well-made experiments and inquiries;

(n) possess substantial personal experience of psychotherapy, counselling psychology or similar self-development activities;

(o) welcome the opportunity to pursue relevant applied work with suitable supervision so as to form a fulcrum for developing the course work;

(p) possess a clearly defined individual professional goal or objective, e.g. pursuing the BPS independent route to become a chartered counselling or occupational psychologist, preparing a Masters or PhD proposal, finishing a Masters or Doctoral thesis, completing and submitting a case study/dissertation for accreditation with organisational bodies such as BPsS., BAC, GPTI, ITA, AHPP, London Convivium, University bodies, etc.

(q) be committed to attend all ten two-day workshops of the series from 9.45 (for coffee and settling in) to 5 pm on the planned days (with the proviso that some changes may be necessary in the light of changing circumstances);

(r) be willing to co-operate with one or two other participants in a mutual co-learning structure which would entail at least a weekly telephone contact for feedback, challenge, succour and support focused on the progression and achievement of the primary learning objective;

(s) share responsibility to preserve and enhance the learning environment by taking responsible care of books, journals and other resources, cleaning of used spaces and generally improving or facilitating the physical and educational environment as far as is possible and appropriate;

(t) be willing to maintain, preserve and cherish (or at least explicitly monitor) the confidentiality of the learning 'vas' or alchemical vessel for the duration of the academic year, thereby increasing the likelihood of achieving intensity of experience and quality of learning relatively uncontaminated with the fantasies, projections, transferences and opinions of those who are not part of the project;

(u) be willing to take responsibility for each honouring their own learning styles (visual, auditory or kinaesthetic for example), moving when they need to, drawing on sketchpads or using multi-coloured pens for brainmaps etc. as suits them best whilst still allowing for compatibility with the needs of the others in the group;

(v) be willing to inform themselves of the relevant arguments and to choose responsibly if they want to engage with the leading researcher of this project in any other professional situation such as group or supervision situations;

(w) be willing to keep a journal, log, or ongoing record of some kind (from dreams to graphs to patchwork quilts illustrating their process over the year); any sharing of such material will be optional;

(x) be accepting of the notion that my role would be that of an educator – one who leads forth the drive to experiment, to know, to create, to heal from within – not that of an assessor or evaluator;

(y) accept responsibility for taking up, refusing, conforming, disagreeing, complying, negotiating, fighting or agreeing with external assessors and evaluators from professional or external academic bodies of their own choice on their own behalf;

(z) and last, but not least, like or at least tolerate dogs. (Dogs always attended in the healing chambers of Aesclepius and his companions since time immemorial.)

DISCOURSE ANALYSIS

All sessions of the series were recorded on audiotape. If at any point a participant wished the tape to be switched off, this would be agreed. If anyone wanted to lay specific individual claim to authorship of any particular idea, they could be sure to make that claim on tape. Transcripts were made by a highly experienced confidential and ethically sound research/editorial assistant and could be available to participants at cost.

This leads to the possibility of discourse analysis especially at two primary levels: (a) our own discourse during the time together; (b) the analysis of the discourses of our fields – the writings, tapes, observations of other professionals, ancient and contemporary, experienced and inexperienced, in good or bad standing, with whom we agree and with whom we disagree, those who are in the thick of 'where the disagreements are' and most of all – those who lead us to question.

> Learning about such things, continually re-examining beliefs about beliefs, becomes the most important learning task of all the others needed for survival in our time. . . . We don't really know how to do such learning or such teaching, and it is likely that wherever people try to do such teaching they will be opposed – as the educators of 'moral reasoning' have been (Anderson, 1990: 268).

This project will be an attempt to discover how to do such learning and such teaching. All discourses will be considered in accordance with the phenomenological principle of horizontalisation – the attempt to avoid making kneejerk 'habitual hierarchically based judgements' (Spinelli, 1989: 19) by treating each one's articulated world as of potentially equal interest. All narratives, all stories – even myths and poetry – are assumed to have their value.

As I have explored elsewhere (Clarkson, 1995a and Clarkson, 1997), I do not believe a developmental model is *necessarily* the most appropriate (definitely not the only) paradigm for the training, nurture, sustenance and blossoming of psychologists, psychotherapists or others in the helping professions. Samuels (1981: 217) was one of the first to say it openly: 'In general, there are three places to start a training – at the beginning, where you're told, or you can look for where the explosion is and start there'. As he pointed out this goes against the

> apparently more sensible and customary view that you should start with what is known and agreed, and when that has been mastered or at least understood, engage in *grown-up disagreements*. [emphasis added] The discourses under investigation will not assume that starting at the beginning is a guarantee of comprehension [or] . . . that students are not equipped to make choices and handle problem areas . . . (Samuels, 1980: 216).

VERIFICATION PROCESSES

> We will have to come to terms, as we stagger into the postmodern era, with the hard-to-avoid evidence that there are many different realities, and different ways of experiencing them, and that people seem to want to keep exploring them, and that there is only a limited amount any society can do to insure that its official reality is installed in the minds of most of its citizens most of the time (Anderson, 1990: 152).

The design and construction of a training course for psychotherapists based on this model would test the theoretical framework as a formula for learning the practice of psychotherapy by externally assessed standards. Although obviously not tightly controlled in the more traditional quantitative mode, the students would be indeed engaged as co-researchers testing and using the framework to support their learning and their practice. This is research tested *by application.*

This is partly for Kvale's (1992: 39) suggestion: 'by discarding a modern legitimation mania, justification of knowledge is replaced by application, with a pragmatic concept of validity'. This criterion of validity is particularly applicable in this case where usefulness of the framework is its *raison d'être* – not its 'truth' *per se.* As Jim Hartle said: 'anyone over the age of twelve knows there is no such thing as certainty, right?' (Hawking, 1992, p.177).

At the same time, the work of Dierotao would be, in addition to my own regular weekly professional supervision, supervised at *termly intervals by two external* supervisors specifically to monitor and improve the academic, supervisory and qualitative research aspects of the study.

In addition this work would be supported by my own personal and professional application of the device or framework in learning, supervising and consulting about psychotherapy, supervision and organisational consultancy at least over the period of duration of the study. All people in therapy, supervision and training interact dialogically with me living the material day by day *in* relationship. From them I learn what makes sense, what works, what does not. They are my first co-researchers and my best teachers. I have always wanted 'the advantages of allowing a multiplicity of voices to speak to the research issues of concern' (Gergen and Gergen, 1991: 79).

This is the interweaving of researcher and researched, folding in on the self and out into the practice. 'It is through this spiral movement, through experiencing lived space with others, that the researcher would learn, illuminate, and generate data' (Shelef, 1994, p. 3). Also, of course, it is necessary to test the data. In this sense it reflects a contemporary postmodernist attempt to give validity to all the 'different stories about stories' (Anderson, 1990: 267) which currently constitute the body of knowledge and practice we call psychotherapy. It also allows for future development.

According to Rudestam and Newton (1992: 38), 'Because the researcher is regarded as a person who comes to the scene with his or her own operative reality, rather than as a totally detached scientific observer, it becomes vital to understand, acknowledge and share one's own underlying values, assumptions and expectations'. A further exploration of the ethical and moral situatedness of the researcher/clinician/supervisor in psychotherapy is thus indicated. This may involve taking the postmodern works concerning ethics, politics and moral action of for example Anderson (1990), Bauman (1993) and Hutcheon (1989) as well as a qualitative investigation into the cultural, social and psychological aspects of bystanding behaviour into the discursive domain of avowed and enacted values (Clarkson, 1996a).

This is in keeping with Denzin and Lincoln's (1994a: 115, 199) description:

> Qualitative researchers . . . understand the social, political, cultural, economic, ethnic and gender history and structure that serve as the surround for their inquiries . . . self-consciously draw upon their own experiences as a recourse in their inquiries. They always think reflectively, historically and biographically. They seek strategies of empirical inquiry that will allow them to make connections among lived experience, larger social and cultural structures, and the here and now.

I can imagine sifting the literature and our experiences in the nature of a thematic analysis to explore the clarity or ambiguity with which researchers in theory and practice deal with quantitative methods and data distortion and expectancy effects (1) as learning or educational acts for the researcher and researched; (2) as engagement and dialogue of the kind which qualitative research valorises; or (3) as allowing space for the ultimately mysterious – even itself as a kind of research exploring the human quest for knowledge or the end of it where individuality or a separate voice no longer exists.

> The competition between different stories, whether based on religion or ideology, is far less critical to the prospects for peace in the world, and to the emergence of a global civilization, than the competition between different stories about stories – between absolutist/objectivist and relativist/constructivist ideas about the nature of human truth. A pluralistic civilization can only

be built with a great amount of tolerance, and the kind of tolerance that comes from people who believe in the cosmic certainty of their truth (and theirs alone) is both limited and patronizing. You can only become truly tolerant of other people's realities by having found some new way to inhabit your own (Anderson, 1990: 267).

The practice of the clinic or the consulting room should not be separated from rigorous and constant research (Clarkson, 1995b), for it is by this that the therapeutic relationship can be returned to itself. A qualitative research project should not be just a one-off study – I believe it needs to be conducted with every client, every session, for as long as a clinician/supervisor works professionally.

Inter-rater reliability in assessing between clinician, client and supervisor whether an intervention was effective or not is just one example of such reflexive practice and the analysis of transcripts or disciplined inquiry by means of writing can augment this. The supervisor or trainer is then not someone to whom one is in a hierarchical relationship, but becomes someone who acts as a co-worker researching the clinical as well as the supervisory work at every step. The engagement of the client in this process is also to be explored.

To do this, it would be necessary for all clinicians to become familiar and at ease with research, particularly the paradigms and disciplines of qualitative inquiry. Qualitative research may be the method favoured by clinicians, supervisors and organisational consultants because it overcomes the sterility and alienation of much quantitative research in its close relationship with the ambiguities, imponderables and unmeasurables of the facilitative encounter.

Supervisors and change agents of any kind would need to be skilled in acting as co-researchers in every case or situation brought to disciplined reflection as well as subjecting their own clinical and supervisory work to constant investigation. Conjoining the work of *doing and reflection* in this way might even signal the end of the difference between research and clinical supervision in training. (If we would still use a term so closely aligned with behaviourism instead of the awakening of the inquiring drive for excellence (*physis*) in every person – no matter what their objectively assessed ability.) Learning with the client in such a way introduces a praxis of the recovery of knowledge which is surely at the very heart of the therapeutic endeavour itself.

EXAMPLE OF HEURISTIC ANALYSIS OF THE EXPERIENCE OF LEARNING BY INQUIRY

The investigation into the meaning, experience and uses of learning by inquiry for psychologists and others of cognate disciplines is proceeding by many routes: the individual experience of every participant *vis à vis* their individual learning and professional goals; the discourse analysis of the tape-recordings of all the sessions – some 200 hours of tape-recorded material; the analysis of the module evaluation forms completed at the end of every tenth of the educational structure and also by means of asking the respondents to write about it as well as interviewing them about their experience. Different parts of this investigation are being conducted by different inquirers.

This section conveys the flavour of another slice of the investigation through a different aspect of the prism – the composite textural description made by Clarkson on the basis of transcripts of answers to the same question in interviews conducted by Haslam with four co-researchers. The method is explained by Moustakas (1994) as well by Clarkson and Angelo in Chapter 2 in this present book.

The question Haslam asked the respondents was: What do you see as the defining characteristics of this form of learning (learning by inquiry) which differentiate it from other kinds of learning experiences that you have had? The composite textural description of the experience of learning by inquiry reads thus:

> Learning by inquiry is a learning environment, not a provider of courses. It feels not like an actively mentoring relationship. It means a very fluid kind of learning allowing for maximum diversity in terms of content, issues, people, attention to your own awareness. It's high on experience of interaction and depends on a relationship with the material rather than learning the material or even being presented with it. I'm there to practise relating – relating to it, how it relates to me. I am given the space to struggle with the material and share it in the process. It feels comfortable, easygoing, without pressure. An environment where you can get what you need as an individual personally to keep on learning in the times in between and doing and relating to yourself in the world as learner and teacher even as someone who can pass something else on as well as discover things and so it enables you to see yourself in the world in a different way. It is more a holding experience than a 'bonding' experience. I can choose what to do with it – it's a resource like food which I can swallow, create or use in my own recipes. I can create my own individual awareness of the issues in which I am interested. It allows my own interests to plug into some of the joint energy, recharge my batteries. It has a culture of 'you put your two-pence worth in'.

> If members of the group were purely all on the same learning route, for example, or on the organisational route or all on the counselling psychology route, that would not be conducive to what I need from it because what I'm actually trying to do is integrate my counselling psychology experience and knowledge and just trying to kind of apply that and how it might work in organisations on a dynamic sort of level. Learning by inquiry does not mean 'things being put down or shoved down your throat', it's not an actively mentoring relationship.

EXAMPLES OF PARTICIPANTS' DEFINITION OF 'LEARNING BY INQUIRY'

What does learning by inquiry mean to you in your experience over this last year?

- Learning by inquiry has meant that I take responsibility for listening, connecting and opening up to new possibilities. I have become co-creator of an extraordinary integration of personal, political, emotional and theoretical ideas. The creative process moves beyond the limitations of language. It is like the mist from the bottle; the bottle is the container, the water the content. The mist is transient yet tangible – it is in the mist that we have become pioneers of the soul.
- I have woven silken threads across the membrane of my soul and connected with others. The generosity has at times moved me deeply.
- I am asking questions of myself and others and not predetermining the answers. Unexpected jewels have been found, new ways of understanding. The story is still being told.
- I am expanding and growing, travelling lighter, making connections, reading, integrating theory yet also remaining in touch with Level 1 and respecting my intuition.
- I am learning that poetic expression can be underpinned by theoretical understanding, yet also remain beautiful and transcendent. Poetry gives expression to the transpersonal, the restriction of language creates a distillation of emotion.
- We are seekers of knowledge exploring a vast continent – I have set sail from the shore.
- Between wrongness and rightness there is a field. I will meet you there. Rumi.
- Learning by inquiry moves beyond shame-based rigidity and retains an integrity that respects the individual's journey to knowledge, through knowledge, through experience. Learning by inquiry means rejecting neat solutions and seeking to understand the complexities of living in the world and beyond.
- For me it means saying, 'I don't like this . . . but I'm going to have fun finding out and when I've found out I'll understand that I may still not know, and it will be OK'. Inquiry avoids seeking absolute truths and needing absolute ideas. What a relief!
- Expanding. Growing. Deepening yet remaining aware and in touch with Level 1.
- Creativity. Sharing/generosity of spirit. Pioneers of the soul.
- Seekers of knowledge exploring a vast continent. Openly asking without predetermining the answer.

* * *

- It means quintessentially experiencing myself as a fractal of an infinitely moving, spiral universe/voyage where I find myself riding the crest of a wave and believing that this is *The Big One* – California.

- Style: I'm surfing, only to discover that I'm moving down a tunnel to infinitely greater worlds, in-out now I'm a dot on the edge of a vast universe; now centre, dead in the middle, balanced, poised at the still centre of the turning world, the dance to the music of the spheres, in one the macro-microcosm, the pearl in the oyster, a leaf on the tree of life, the tree, the egg, a blot on the landscape, the void, exploding into infinity; sharing with others in a wonderful game of hunt the thimble, where anyone can play and everyone's thimble is *The Thimble* for a moment. A feeling of intoxicating expansiveness. Chaos, stop the world I want to get off. Am I doing it right? Am I doing this exercise right? The way you want it? Does it express what I want to say? Not having the right words. Confronting the limits of my consciousness, understanding, ability to express. My hand is aching. I feel fired up. Process as being more – no, as important as content. Being part of a Bos–Einstein condensate. Understanding the meaning of space/time; feeling myself shift in space/time. Learning to shift paradigms; using language, imagery, metaphorically feeling caught on a train ride to infinity. Infinity in a grain of sand. Joy, humility, fear.
- Trance-ference, turning the Trance, through fire, into something solid – a crystal, which in its essence expresses the crackedness of everything. I am mad and it's wonderful. Wierd, wyrd, to know, wirsen, wicke, witch.
- Ring out the bells that still can ring. Forget your perfect offering.
- There is a crack in everything. That's how the light gets in.
- What makes it essentially different from other forms of learning is that it frees me to think, do, move in ways that have been blocked for me up until now. I can go in or out, up or down, home in one fractal of the whole, focusing on the five kinds of therapeutic relationship, analysing the discourse in terms of the seven levels. Standing by Your Man, By-standing as injustice is perpetrated. By-standing on myself.
- Fractals. Dead in the middle. Breakthrough. Dogs/birds.
- Being out, beyond the edge. Juggling. Having fun.
- Alternative systems and their interconnection. Finding connections.
- Going through the flash-point where I can no longer hold everything together (if I ever could).
- Deepening knowledge. Aha! Fear of failure. Fear of success.
- Sharing each other's insights/dreams. Irritation with self and others. Valuing of self and others. Love and friendship. Stories/different stories.
- The transpersonal. Being creative. Naming the discourse.
- Aladdin's cave – music – of the spheres. Having curiosity whetted/sharpened.
- Inspiration. Gut laughter.
- Re-experiencing shame/humiliation and moving beyond them (at moments).

* * *

- Re-creating the experience of building pyramids for other purposes.
- Including and weaving different realities.
- A structure that becomes clearer with time.
- Every participant in the group is a learner and teacher and resourcer.
- Centring quest for understanding as focus for research/developing *understanding*.
- Visions of playing hula hoops on a slope with a group of similar learners.
- Rambling up and down slopes . . .
- Discovering/uncovering, clarifying other perspectives.
- Collective stories in difference voices.
- Working outside 'normative' ideologies and inclusivity – not exclusions.
- Asking questions to get more questions to clarify scope of the field in view.
- Learning *how* to ask questions and what to ask.
- Choruses of realities in cosmic harmonies.
- Ancient, future and contemporary.
- Exploring ideas at different levels simultaneously.
- Getting to know a particular group of travellers on uncharted sands.

* * *

Learning by inquiry

With disciplined infidelity as my
  learning tool, I face the rush
  of models and models
  and more models,
  overwhelming me like the
  uncertainty of a new love.
Ideas smashing the crust which
  separates conscious
  from unconscious . . .
  Zap, Insight.
Weekends as a welcomed return
  to the experiential truths
  I always forget amidst
  the struggle of becoming;
  Weekends as flowers
  and scents and associations,
  as therapeutic friendship.
Inquiry as becoming a counsellor,
  as becoming a person,
  as becoming,
  as Being.

© *Bill Wahl, 1996*

* * *

I have brought my story and shared with others who also have their stories.
In relationship and at different levels I have explored . . . beliefs,
  experiences.
Transmission of old and new knowledge can occur at various levels . . .
  relationship.
Everything is interrelated, connected – professional/personal, artistic/poetic.
No one truth exists, which is exciting and gives scope for . . . exploration.
Boundaries and no boundaries.
When questions evolve questions.
Evolution of questions . . .
Unending . . .

* * *

- Learning by inquiry is a 'looking into', a questioning, a starting out from a conscious state of not knowing, and doing this in both a personal and inter-penetrating group process.
- I learned in the library, more than in school. The teacher couldn't or wouldn't answer my questions, but the books always did.
- At PHYSIS I LISTENED, and in listening I discovered so much that I knew. Either because it struck a chord – I RECOGNISE THAT, SHAKE MY HEAD, YES, YES, YES. Or because I had a thought that I thought was silly, but when I shared it with somebody outside the main group (in a one-to-one) it was valued and therefore seemed valuable.
- Not everybody understood psychological research – I do. Even if I feel that everybody knew so much more than I do.
- I began to understand transference (only began). I now know what congruence is. False emotions explained, not just GRIEF, JOY, ANGER, FEARS, but that which can be resolved.

  1 I want to be a family.
  2 I want to be a child therapist.
  3 I can conceive an idea and make it grow.
  4 I can run groups.

- The last two I could not have had the courage to do without PHYSIS. The first two were insights verbalised by two other members of the group.

* * *

My strangeness is no longer a strangeness.
My interests are not weird.
Or as was once said of me, 'Oh her, . . . you don't want to meet her, she hasn't
got all her marbles'.

* * *

- A structure that allows the creation of my own structure for change and learning, and allows the dissolution of structure and rearrangement. Constant flow and interest highlighting the interconnectedness of timelessness of knowledge. The possibility to endless discovery, and to discover that I cannot know very much, ever, no matter what I find out.

- To be able to support others in the discovery of learning, from seeking out and creating/partaking of the process. To not hold false gods, and to allow all gods.
- To learn (relearn) how I learn – to watch and to listen and to seek and to make connections with places and people, here and not-here, with voice and touch and through books. To be open to ideas that don't fit. Affirmation for the use of story and metaphor, left and right brain.
- To allow the highest standard I can find, and to discover the joy of the brilliance of others and to learn from this.
- Richness and diversity, the valuing of all paths and the integration of theories and perspectives.
- To call upon 'proper' study and use what is of value in traditional methods with how and where to find the names and the dates. To do this more effectively and efficiently than I've ever learned in the whole of the rest of my education, despite its emphasis on this to the exclusion of all else.
- Support for the difficulty and discipline of writing and a sight of the possibility that I can enjoy the discipline and find it less difficult.

* * *

- Never having to say you're sorry! Play. Growth.
- A gift to myself – dust-free and vital. A journey. Food for thought.
- What is the question? Provoking. Relevance. Growth. Discovery.
- Development. Many paths. Non-linear. Group dynamics.
- Integration. Wonder. Thought. Feeling. Experiential learning. Using my brain.
- Not-knowing. Holographic knowledge. Making my own path.
- Complexity. Affirmation. Support for practising my abilities.
- Process about using process. The business/stuff of my life. Network.
- Finding. Chaos. Taking into the world. Teaching (facilitating).
- Explore. Companions/journeying. Resourcing. Re-sourcing.
- Ways of approaching/organising/viewing.

* * *

- Learning to open my heart and begin to show my 'true colours'. To face the anxiety of part learning and take the risk to voice what is here and now, using my experience and trusting my intuition.
- To test the boundaries of myself and others. To bring laughter and tears into the process.
- To start to listen – really listen for the first time. This comes from being heard myself – it's like being a baby again and offered food to grow into the sunflower.
- To experience intimacy at different levels or in different aspects.

- To juggle with several balls at once.
- To be able to allow the balls to drop and be picked up later.
- Music – disruptions and harmonic moments.
- Fighting for a place, then taking a deep breath and knowing there is a place – no need to battle – that I can relax.
- Each of us is so different. Yet the commonality of need is also there – as evidenced in the five aspects – just different ways of expressing.
- The will began to surface, and the passion being released – and still not knowing, but a richness of choice emerging.
- Releasing the inhibitions – find one's unique melody.
- Bringing heart and mind together. Finding one's TRUE COLOURS.
- Being fully receptive to ideas and being able to express and continue the process of enlarging and changing the way we think and the way we put that into practice.
- Not bystanding on the self. STANDING BY ANOTHER.
- MENTORING ANOTHER.
- NOT KEEPING SECRETS ABOUT OURSELVES OR OUR ABILITIES/ SKILLS.
- Listening. Confusion. Excitement. Anxiety.
- Laughter. Seeds. Willing. Voicing.
- Colours. Food. Intimacy. Boundaries.
- Nourishment. Challenge.

* * *

- Learning by inquiry involves learning to ask questions rather than answering them. It is a process-driven activity, as opposed to an objective-driven one. It involves 'discovery as you go along' – a kind of collapsing of time, or, as the physicists call it, 'collapsing the wave function'. It is what happens when creativity emerges – a feeling of Eureka!
- Describing learning by inquiry through the techniques employed by objectivist reductionists is almost impossible, partly because it involves describing a qualitatively different picture. It involves a holistic perspective of human action – like Wordsworth's description of the scientist and the buttercup the act involves 'dissect and destroy'.
- Learning by inquiry is a method of research. It emphasises holism, synthesis and inclusion. It is a way of relating to the world – an activity whereby we learn how we discover meaning – an epistemology.
- Learning by inquiry acknowledges that we live in a changing, evolving world, where nothing stays the same.

* * *

- Trips you up at times. Instability. Uncertainty. Change. Asking.
- Thinking. Fear of power. A feeling of competence. Listening.
- Talking. Seeking. Doing. Finding. Being.

- Researching. Feeling. Food for thought. Feeling barriers.
- Space. Resistance. Freedom. Going into the world.
- Something that never stops. Being an agent in my world. Competence.
- Confidence. Achievement. A breath of fresh air. Sharing.
- Like tasting cheese for the first time, and olives, aubergines, new things and experiences. Synergy. Synthesis. Physis. Holism.
- Eureka! Relating. Discovery.

* * *

- This is a very different way of teaching and learning from conventional, hierarchical ways. Probably, you imagine that teaching means there is a teacher who teaches and students who are taught. They have clear roles and boundaries. Sometimes it is even difficult to ask questions in the circumstances, because the social norm might say that questioning the teacher is degrading the teacher. Also, if the teacher can't answer properly, it becomes shame. However, in the style of learning by inquiry, both the teacher and students learn from the questions. Questioning means not giving pressure, but extracting insight and heightening awareness.
- I teach Japanese to an American man. He always asks questions. I learn Japanese culture from the process.
- Facilitator and receiver can learn together. Facilitator is allowed not knowing.
- Multi-ways (not one way). Not hierarchical. Empowerment.

RANDOM EXCERPTS FROM TAPE-RECORDED TRAINING WORKSHOPS

What do you see as the defining characteristics of this form of learning which differentiate it from other kinds of learning experiences that you have had?

A It's very fluid. So in a sense that kind of allows all diversity. Nothing's kind of put down or shoved down your throat, as it were.

The lack of content, in a way, you know, the lack of specific structure and content allows for a diverse range of issues to be raised.

It actually allows my own interests to plug into some of that energy, so I can do with what comes. It's as if it's like a resource, food, food for thought which is actually . . . I'm able to swallow in a way. And, and kind of put my own recipe on and create.

There's just kind of a basic structure there that I can plug into and put my own content into. So it's much more of a holding experience as opposed to, um, and a bonding experience within which I can create my own individual awareness of the issues that I'm interested in.

It allows you to extend your own awareness your way.

I would say fluidity, um, kind of very loose structure, um, not high on content, high on experience and process and just the experience of interaction, relating to the material as opposed to learning the material or even being presented with it. Kind of about relating to it, how it relates to me. You know, being given the space to relate to the material and struggle with it and share it, so very much a process.

It is a learning environment. It's not a provider of courses, it's not a provider of qualifications. It's a comfortable, quite easy-going sort of experience, no pressure. It kind of feels more like a mentoring type of, not an actively mentoring one, just an environment where you can get what you need as an individual personally to keep on learning in the times between doing and relating to yourself in the world as a learner and a teacher, even, as someone who can pass something else on as well and discover things, and so it enables you to see yourself in the world in a different way.

I'm there to practise relating.

I was just seeing it as a place where I kind of recharge my batteries.

If the members of the group were purely all on the same learning route, for example, all on the organisational route, or all on the counselling route – that would not be conducive to what I need from it, because what I'm trying to do is actually integrate my counselling experience and knowledge, and just trying to kind of apply that and how it might work in organisations on a dynamic sort of level. But I mean the main thing I get from it anyway is, as I say, a kind of recharging of my batteries.

* * *

B We have a culture here that says you put the twopence-worth in, you know, and, if you're a good person, you'll work with the other person's twopence-worth. . . . It has an available pattern to it and an available range of subject matter, so that is similar. It doesn't feel to me to be so prescriptive in how that area is explored and there is more, sort of, following the discourse, if you like, more discursive attention to what comes up and finding the relevance of what is coming up in the group and the exploration. So there's much more allowance of exploration and broadness. Um, I usually find that education is aimed at narrowing focuses in order to get qualifications, in this country, in my experience, and it is broadening and allowing inquiry, and supporting inquiry that for me is the difference, so I don't feel, I do not feel stifled. I can feel stifled by what I perceive to be the conventional education. I've done all right in it but frankly it's only done me good, because our culture needs me to have done it. You know, it's like a little passport, but emotionally or spiritually in terms of a bigger development, I think it has not particularly functioned for me in that way and this is more likely to.... And an allowance for the place of the whole person. I'm not just a brain. I am also a brain.... It's quite frustrating at times ... it's something to do with being such a diverse group of people.... It doesn't have the linearity and I have been brought up with linearity so I experience frustration at the same time as I want to have non-linearity, circularity, complexity.... And a richness. there's a richness which I find rather unusual.... This is a supportive group ... trying to express ideas that I'm struggling with and find difficult. In fact, you know, bits about chaos or complexity or postmodernism, these are all things I've read about. I'm interested by them and I see their connections with me and my world and my work, and they are not easy, and being able to bring them to a forum like this just helps to shine a bit more light and get some more views, and it just opens things up, so that's very useful to me because it gives me more clarity on things and a greater understanding through talking.

We are a learning and change group.... That was very helpful to me, this writing stuff we did, because although I've been paid to be a writer, I don't always find it easy. I just find it very difficult. I mean certain styles of writing I find difficult. And having just done an academic thing, I've laboured intensively trying to produce the right sort of work. So, to have more sort of free-flowing input. say, right, do, write about this, explore about that, do it now, do it to get over those blocks, is good.

* * *

C And people were very out, very much outside, um, the white concepts, values. um, and subject areas that academic institutions usually cover.... I, I feel very, um, familiar with the kind of things that Petrŭska is doing.... And that's because when I was working as a youth worker and we were trying to develop resources for working with young black people around things like sexuality, drugs, relationships and so on, there were no resources that were immediately relevant to young black people ... so we started off by asking one of the advisers from County Hall to come down and to facilitate our growth through running a group a bit like Petrŭska has done, in which we were given the information as such, but we had to come with some prepared work about how you were going to progress with these resources, and, um, through the kind of discussions that we had, we were given access to further information as to where to look for what, who to speak to. Often it was going and talking to other people. So. in that sense, you know, as a kind of, I suppose there's a kind of action learning thing that was, that was open to lots of different perspectives. Because although we were all black women, we had very, some of us, there was a very wide spectrum of perspectives on how ... the work should progress. What kind of terms we should use that came from different political approaches.... So in, in a sense, in terms of what Petrŭska is doing, which is giving us access to information saying, well here it is and here's the thinking. What will you do with it? It's similar in that sense for me. But it is very unlike any other experience I've had in a white-led organisation. . . . Where the knowledge base is something that is up for grabs, where you access and you interpret, but you don't take on wholesale and try and reproduce. You try and make something of, you know, the sources available that relate to the environment that you are working in.

I was wondering, given what you've just said here, um, whether in fact this form of learning, if you like, learning by inquiry, is one that is familiar in a, in a, in an African context – um, and I see you nodding. What you learn is often rarely ever learned between yourself interacting with a thing or one other; it's often within a group. . . . And the learning that you do in a group is always challenged by other people . . . because you can't but express your interpretation or your interaction with what you're hearing, so that you're, if you like, a person's thinking is sharpened and moulded by the people around them. You can still not hear a lot of things that people are saying, but you certainly will be aware of the arguments . . . whilst you, whilst you're learning. . . . So I think there are lots of similarities. I think also Petrūska does use symbols in the work that she does and they're very, very powerful because they contain so many messages, and people can relate to them and interpret simultaneously – if they're ten people, ten different things . . . which makes it so much more exciting than reading texts. . . . That's one person's idea . . . So, um, I suppose, yes, in terms of the form Petrūska is using I can see similarities with what I would call earth-based cultures . . . cultures that are, that still use a lot of their traditional approaches. . . . Still very much in touch with their spirituality, the environment, the earth around them. They have a pace of life that respects all living things and they live in harmony with them.

REFERENCES

Anderson. W. T. (1990) *Reality Isn't What it Used to Be*, San Francisco: Harper & Row.

Arnkoff, D. B., Victor, B. J. and Glass, C. G. (1993) Empirical research on factors in psychotherapeutic change. in G. Stricker and J. R. Gold (eds) *Comprehensive Handbook of Psychotherapy Integration*, pp. 27–42, New York: Plenum.

Bamberger, J. and Schön. D. A. (1991) in F. Steier (ed.) *Research and Reflexivity*, Newbury Park, CA: Sage.

Bateson. G. (1972) *Steps to an Ecology of Mind*, New York: Ballantine.

Bauman. Z. (1993) *Postmodern Ethics*, Oxford: Blackwell.

Beutler. L. E. (1989) 'The misplaced role of theory in psychotherapy integration,' *Journal of Integrative and Eclectic Psychotherapy*, 8: 17–22.

Bor. R.. and Watts, M. (1993) 'Training counselling psychologists to conduct research', *Counselling Psychology Review* 8 (4): 20–21.

Clandinin. D. J. and Connelly. F. M. (1994) 'Personal experience methods', in N. K. Denzin and Y. S. Lincoln (eds) *Handbook of Qualitative Research*, pp. 413–427, Thousand Oaks, CA: Sage.

Clarkson. P. (1993a) 'A small kitbag for the future', in *Order, Chaos and Change in the Public Sector* Conference. pp. 17–27, London: Association of Management Education and Development.

Clarkson, P. (1993b) New perspectives in counselling and psychotherapy (or adrift in a sea of change), in P. Clarkson, *On Psychotherapy*, pp. 209–232, London: Whurr.

Clarkson, P. (1993c) Two thousand five hundred years of Gestalt – from Heraclitus to the Big Bang, *British Gestalt Journal* 2, 1: 4–9.

Clarkson, P. (1995a) *The Therapeutic Relationship in Psychoanalysis, Counselling Psychology and Psychotherapy*, London: Whurr.

Clarkson, P. (1995b) Counselling psychology – the next decade, *Counselling Psychology Quarterly* 8 (3): 197–204.

Clarkson, P. (1995c) *Change in Organisations*, London: Whurr.

Clarkson, P. (1996a) *The Bystander (An End to Innocence in Human Relationships?)*, London: Whurr.

Clarkson, P. (1996b) Researching the 'Therapeutic Relationship: A Qualitative Inquiry in Psychoanalysis, Counselling Psychology and Psychotherapy, *Counselling Psychology Quarterly*, 9, 2: 143–62.

Clarkson, P. (1997) Integrative psychotherapy, integrating psychotherapies, or psychotherapy after schoolism, in C. Feltham (ed.) *Which Psychotherapy?*, pp. 33–50, London: Sage.

Corsini, R. (1984) *Current Psychotherapies*, Itasca, IL: F. E. Peacock.

Denzin, N. K. and Lincoln, Y. S. (eds) (1994a) *Handbook of Qualitative Research*, London: Sage.

Denzin, N. K. and Lincoln, Y. S. (1994b) 'Introduction: Entering the field of qualitative research', in N. K. Denzin and Y. S. Lincoln (eds) *Handbook of Qualitative Research*, pp. 1–17, Thousand Oaks, CA: Sage.

Farrell, B. A. (1979) 'Work in small groups: Some philosophical considerations', in B. Babington Smith and B. A. Farrell (eds), *Training In Small Groups: A Study of Five Groups*, pp. 103–115, Oxford: Pergamon.

Gergen, K. J. and Gergen, M. M. (1991) 'Toward reflexive methodologies' in Steier, F. (ed.) *Research and Reflexivity*, pp. 76–95, Newbury Park, CA: Sage.

Glass, C. G., Victor, B. J. and Arnkoff, D. B. (1993) 'Empirical research on integrative and eclectic psychotherapies', in G. Stricker and J. R. Gold (eds) *Comprehensive Handbook of Psychotherapy Integration* (pp. 9–26), New York: Plenum.

Guba, E. G. (ed.) (1990) *The Paradigm Dialog*, Newbury Park, CA: Sage.

Guba, E. G. and Lincoln, Y. S. (1994) 'Competing paradigms in qualitative research', in N. K. Denzin and Y. S. Lincoln (eds) *Handbook of Qualitative Research*, pp. 105–117, Thousand Oaks, CA: Sage.

Hammersley, M. (1992) 'On feminist methodology', *Sociology* 26 (2): 187–206.

Hawking, S. (ed.) (1992) *Stephen Hawking's A Brief History of Time: A Reader's Companion* (prepared by G. Stone), London: Bantam.

Hinshelwood, R. D. (1990) Editorial, *The British Journal of Psychotherapy* 7 (2): 119–120.

Hutcheon, L. (1989) *The Politics of Postmodernism*, New York: Routledge.

Kvale, S. (1992) 'Postmodern psychology: a contradiction in terms?', in S. Kvale (ed.), *Psychology and Postmodernism*, pp. 31–57, London: Sage.

Lambert, M. J. (1989) 'Contributors to treatment outcome', paper presented at the annual meeting of the Society for the Exploration of Psychotherapy Integration, Berkeley, CA.

Lambert, M. J. (1992) 'Psychotherapy outcome research: implications for integrative and eclectic therapists', in J. C. Norcross and M. R. Goldfried (eds) *Handbook of Psychotherapy Integration*, pp. 94–129. New York: Basic Books.

Lincoln, Y. S. and Guba, E. G. (1985) *Naturalistic Inquiry*, Beverly Hills, CA: Sage.

Mahoney, M. J., Norcross, J. C., Prochaska, J. O. and Missar, C. D. (1989) 'Psychological development and optimal psychotherapy: converging perspectives among clinical psychologists', *Journal of Integrative and Eclectic Psychotherapy* 8: 251–263.

Mandelbrot, B. B. (1974) *The Fractal Geometry of Nature*, New York: Doubleday Anchor.

Merleau-Ponty, M. (1962) *Phenomenology of Perception* (trans. Colin Smith), London: Routledge & Kegan Paul.

Moustakas, C. (1994) *Phenomenological Research Methods*, London: Sage.

Mowbray, R. (1995) *The Case Against Psychotherapy Registration*, London: Transmarginal Press.

Norcross, J. C. (ed.) (1986) *Handbook of Eclectic Psychotherapy*, New York: Brunner/Mazel.

Norcross, J. C. and M. R. Goldfried, M. R. (eds) (1992), *Handbook of Psychotherapy Integration*, New York: Basic Books.

Norcross, J. C. and Newman, C. F. (1992) 'Psychotherapy integration: setting the context', in J. C. Norcross and M. R. Goldfried (eds) *Handbook of Psychotherapy Integration*, pp. 3–45, New York: Basic Books.

Polkinghorne, D. E. (1992) 'Postmodern epistemology of practice', in S. Kvale (ed.) *Psychology and Postmodernism*, pp. 146–165, London: Sage.

Prioleau, L., Murdock, M. and Brody, N. (1983) 'An analysis of psychotherapy versus placebo studies', *The Behavioral and Brain Sciences* 6: 275–310.

Richardson, L. (1994) 'Writing: a method of inquiry', in N. K. Denzin and Y. S. Lincoln (eds) *Handbook of Qualitative Research*, pp. 516–529, Thousand Oaks, CA: Sage.

Rilke, R. M. (1993) *Letters to a Young Poet* (trans. M. D. Herter Norton) (revised edn), New York: W. W. Norton.

Rudestam, K. E. and Newton, R. R. (1992) *Surviving your Dissertation: A Comprehensive Guide to Content and Process*, Newbury Park, CA: Sage.

Samuels, A. (1981) *Fragmentary Vision: A Central Training Aim*, Spring, pp. 215–225.

Samuels, A. (1993) 'What is a good training?', *British Journal of Psychotherapy* 9 (3): 317–323.

Seligman, M. E. P. (1995) 'The effectiveness of psychotherapy', *American Psychologist* 50 (12): 965–974.

Shelef, L. O. (1994) A simple qualitative paradigm: the asking and the telling, *The Qualitative Report* 2, 1: 1–6.

Spinelli, E. (1989) *The Interpeted World – An Introduction to Phenomenological Psychology*, London: Sage.

Von Glaserfeld, E. (1991) 'Knowing without metaphysics: aspects of the radical constructivist position', in F. Steier (ed.) *Research and Reflexivity*, pp. 12–29, Newbury Park, CA: Sage.

Wertz, F. J. (1995) 'Yerkes' Rabbit and Career: From Trivial to More Significant Matters', *Theory and Psychology* 5 (3): 451–454.

Chapter 13

Phenomenological research on supervision

Supervisors reflect on 'Being a supervisor'[1]

Petrūska Clarkson and Orit Aviram

A study using a phenomenological research method was performed to reveal the meanings of the concept 'supervision' from the supervisor's perspective. Eleven supervisors of counselling and psychotherapy from a humanistic/existential framework answered the open question: 'What does being a supervisor mean?' Content analysis and frequency measuring were performed, revealing six groups of statements; six facets describing the experience of supervision: 'structuring', 'teaching', 'nurturing', the 'supervisor as person', 'supervisor as colleague', and the 'triangle, client–therapist–supervisor'. Structuring was the largest category, and the first three categories together represented more than 75 per cent of the statements. The results showed that 'teaching' and 'nurturing' were very similar in their importance, as represented by the number of statements in each. Further research should address the possible relation between supervisors' perception and experience of their role and the theoretical framework of counselling and psychotherapy in which they are based. The phenomenological research method in this study has shown the possibility of doing research on processes without 'betraying' the subjective perspective.

INTRODUCTION

There is relatively little research in counselling, psychotherapy and supervision (Hicks and Wheeler, 1994; Wheeler and McLeod, 1994).

> It appears that authors and researchers have embraced the idea that cross-theoretical approaches to supervision are fruitful and informative. This development shifts the field of scientific inquiry into a new period; one that is separated from the past by its recognition of supervision as a process unique from counseling and related to knowledge gained from the foundational disciplines of psychology and sociology (Holloway, 1992: 205).

Some research has been done on the perception of the supervisor's role (Ellis *et*

1 This chapter was first published 1995 in *Counselling Psychology Quarterly* 8 (1): 63–80. We gratefully acknowledge permission to reproduce the material here.

al.. 1986); but the relation between those perceptions and the theoretical framework has not been extensively discussed. As far as we know, there have been no studies of the phenomenological concept of the supervisor in a clinical psychotherapeutic context.

Carroll (1988: 387) raises crucial questions about counselling and psychotherapy supervision: 'Supervision is still little understood. There are few agreed definitions and certainly no agreed tasks, roles, or even goals of supervision'.

> Although each supervisor and supervisee will have particular idiosyncratic expectations of roles and functions, there needs to be a more explicit and empirical set of competencies that are expected of the supervisor and of the counsellor-in-training as both a supervisee and a counsellor. As in any working relationship, the clarity of these expectations from the beginning will probably enhance the development of the relationship and the establishment of specific learning goals (Holloway, 1992: 194).

Supervision is, of course, also carried out in related professions such as social work. and youth work (Hawkins and Shohet, 1989; Marken and Payne, 1987; Mattinson, 1992). This paper is a small contribution on each of the following fronts: (1) supervision, (2) research and (3) phenomenological investigation.

TOWARDS A PHENOMENOLOGICAL DEFINITION OF SUPERVISION

Referring to the definition of supervision, Carroll (1988: 390) claims: 'There is no such thing as "supervision" if we use that term, and that concept, in a uniform way. It means different things in different situations'. He also points out (p. 388) that 'One of the major dilemmas in the area of counselling supervision is precisely how judgemental the supervisor should be. Supervision, like psychotherapy, runs the risk of being treated with the "uniformity myth" [Kiesler, 1966]'.

> It seems that whatever approach or method is used, in the end it is the quality of the relationship between supervisor and trainee therapist (or counsellor) that determines whether supervision is effective or not. . . . There needs to be a degree of warmth. trust and genuineness and respect between them in order to create a safe enough environment for supervision to take place (Hunt, 1986: 20).

There is little research on supervision and models of the supervisor role (Holloway, 1992; Ellis *et al.*, 1986; Ellis *et al.*, 1988). Ellis and his associates focused on the perceptions of the role of supervisor in supervisors and supervisees. They analysed the dimensionality of the supervisor role and found it to be represented in three dimensions (Ellis *et al.*, 1986; Ellis *et al.*, 1988): namely, they contrast the supervisory functions of process versus conceptualisation as indexed by behavioural versus non-behavioural nature of the functions; contrast the supervisor roles of consultant with the combined roles of teacher and counsellor (issues of who structures the interaction and who has power in it are important to decisions about this dimension); and, lastly, they contrast the function of personalisation with the role of teacher. This dimension is best understood by its indicators, cognitive versus emotional; non-supportive versus supportive (Ellis *et al.*, 1988).

Yet, as has been argued by Carroll (1988: 389), existing research is confined largely to the United States and few attempts have been made to apply findings to Britain: 'Some recent research has indicated a difference between the counselling climate in America and Britain [Munt, 1987]. We need to be careful that we do not transport theories that work well in other climates to Britain without serious investigation that they will adapt well to the changing environment. Counselling supervision may not be a good traveller'.

But even if great care is taken with regard to American perceptions of supervision, few questions are raised by Ellis *et al.*'s (1988) results. The perceptions they yielded were bound to the stimuli with which they presented their participants: 'Future researchers could use different stimuli (e.g., supervisor behaviors) derived from other models of supervisions than Bernard's [1979] and Littrell *et al.*'s [1979]' (Ellis *et al.*, 1988: 323).

It seems most important, at this stage, to further research and knowledge about counselling and psychotherapy in Britain. The aim of the present study was to explore the way 'supervision' is perceived. As mentioned above, 'supervision' (as well as any other construct) is perceived through the prism of one's theoretical framework, beliefs and attitudes. In order to expand upon the questions raised by Ellis *et al.* (1986), it is important to enable a wide range of meaning and dimensions of the perceptions of supervision. One way of achieving this was making the question unstructured and non-reactive; in other words, asking participants themselves to present the stimuli, instead of giving the participants the stimuli to which to respond. In order to control the theoretical background of the participants, we specifically aimed in this research to explore how supervisors define from their own (humanistic and existential) approach what supervision means.

Elsewhere I have identified three major distinct emphases in the tradition and development of psychotherapy in this century (Clarkson, 1994); namely, the conceptual/ideological traditions emanating from Freud (psychoanalytic), Pavlov (behavioural to cognitive traditions) and humanistic/existential originating from Moreno and the European existentialists. The main focus has been on the process rather than the product in most approaches to psychotherapy; particularly in the psychodynamic and humanistic/existential approaches.

Independent of the research findings regarding what supervisors must do or what they have learnt in their training, this research is focusing on how they experience themselves and their individual construing of the role of supervisor by means of answer to the question: 'What does being a supervisor mean?' The emphasis is therefore on being rather than doing, on existence rather than essence; a key word in why this is existential rather than empirical or objective.

PHENOMENOLOGICAL APPROACH TO RESEARCH

Today's new trend in psychology is to focus on consciousness (e.g. Kessel *et al.*, 1992). An interest is spreading quickly in capturing processes via the eye of the beholder, in order to describe processes through *subjective experience* (Greenberg, 1986). Existential and humanistic psychology are close to one another, but represent two different approaches. Yet they share a lot in common; and one of the themes that absolutely unites them is phenomenology. 'The goal of the phenomenological method is not to expose and explore what is truly real – since that remains an impossibility – but, rather to clarify both the variables and invariants of phenomenal reality' (Spinelli, 1989: 80).

The relationship between the humanistic and phenomenological elements of the 'third force' (Maslow, 1968: iii) in psychology is that of outlook and method. By adopting the phenomenological method of comprehending the world, it is argued, we are driven to an essentially humanistic position on human psychology (Robinson, 1979). Phenomenological research would be the methodology to approach and 'scientifically' describe human processes and experiences 'as given'. Phenomenological research is based on describing subjective experience in an authentic manner (Keen, 1975). Phenomenological or qualitative research is now being acknowledged (e.g. Keen, 1975; Kuiken *et al.*, 1989; Sanders, 1982). Discerning an essence, according to Husserl, is neither more nor less than discerning the complex of properties that defines a phenomenon when instances of that phenomenon are already known (Kuiken *et al.*, 1989). The procedure by which this goal is pursued defines the phenomenological approach to psychological research.

One of the most important criteria as to which research methodology one chooses when carrying out research on counselling and psychotherapy is the congruence between the psychotherapist/counsellor theoretical framework and the research method. Researchers should conduct their research using a methodology which is congruent with their theoretical framework and approach to counselling and psychotherapy (Bor and Watts, 1993). So it became clear that phenomenological research would be the appropriate approach to supervision in order to be faithful to a humanistic and existential framework. Yet it is important to note that phenomenology should not be bound to a specific theoretical approach – phenomenology offers a useful and rewarding starting point for any research (Spinelli, 1989).

In order to understand the subject's intentional world of lived experience, one must first arrive at it by a suspension, or bracketing off, of all presumptive constructs about it (Aanstoos, 1983). In this research, the phenomenological approach to research into perceptions of supervision enabled an open-ended inquiry into what constitutes supervision. At the same time, this approach is congruent with the theoretical framework of the participating supervisors (as well as the researchers themselves). This has specific importance as the 'subject' or participant in the research is not simply a subject but also a co-researcher (Keen, 1975).

The aim of this research project was to surface the concept of 'supervisor' as represented phenomenologically in the construct system of professionals providing clinical supervision. As a phenomenological view of psychological research suggests an approach rather than a strict method (Keen, 1975), the inquiry in this research was dictated by our specific interest in exploring how 'supervision' is experienced and perceived by clinical supervisors.

METHOD

Subjects

Eleven clinical supervisors participated in the study (three men and eight women). They came from different humanistic and/or existentially based schools of psychotherapy and counselling: client-centred therapy, Gestalt psychotherapy, transactional analysis and integrative psychotherapy.

Questionnaire and procedure

The questionnaire was aimed at eliciting descriptions of the concept 'Being a supervisor'. The subjects got the following written instructions:

> We would like you to think about the concept 'Supervisor' or, more precisely, 'Being a supervisor'. By that question we aim to surface the different layers of meaning you relate to this concept, as well as to the meanings other people relate to it. On the attached paper please write down all ideas, associations and experiences that come to mind.

The subjects met to hear about phenomenological research and were then asked to answer the questionnaire as a demonstration of 'What is phenomenological research?'

RESULTS

Listening and analysing the data

The attributes given by the subjects yielded a wide range of expressions. The first stage of analysing the written reports was to list units of meaning; either sentences or one meaningful word, e.g. 'Explaining theoretical issues relevant to work supervisee is doing', or 'Teaching'. We will refer to each meaning unit as a statement. Altogether there were 270 statements related to 'Being a supervisor'; the mean number of statements was twenty-four per subject. Table 13.1 represents a report as given by one of the participants.

The second stage was to list the given statements. All responses were recorded verbatim, without changing anything in the original, authentic way the subjects phrased their statements.

Table 13.1 Demonstration of a report protocol

BEING A SUPERVISOR

Being a supervisor means

Being an outsider – outside the relationship of counsellor and client – with extra rather than 'super' vision
Providing a listening and supportive place for the counsellor to explore feelings and ideas about her client
Sometimes offering information, teaching
Providing a relationship
Watching for ethical issues and addressing them when necessary
Being available as far as possible for emergencies or discussion
Challenging, exciting
Responsibility
Relationship
Supporting
Monitoring quality and development
Teaching
Assessment
Administration of contract
Power – 'Am I good enough?'

The third stage consisted of two judges arranging the statements in the list by grouping together identical or very similar statements. This arrangement created thirty-seven 'groups' of statements which represent thirty-seven meaning units or. as they are called by Kuiken *et al.* (1989), 'constituents'. These thirty-seven constituents actually represent the first stage of grouping the statements.

For example:

- support;
- being supporting;
- giving support;
- supportive of supervisee's development;
- patiently supporting;
- holding hands.

Inter-reliability between the judges was computed using the conservative method of evaluating percentage agreement (i.e. percentage of attributes that the two judges grouped in the same category). The inter-judge agreement was higher than 95 per cent. Several statements that could not be grouped and did not make logical sense, idiosyncratic by their nature, were omitted. The thirty-seven paraphrases or 'groups' of statements can be seen in Table 13.2.

At the fourth stage the two judges created broader categories of content. Each category included the groups of statements from the previous stage creating a content category factor. The inter-judge agreement on this stage was 82 per cent. The thirty-seven constituents given by the participants created a structure of six

Table 13.2 Thirty-seven groups of statements describing 'Being a supervisor'

1	Responsibility	19
2	Teaching and education	19
3	Triangle: supervisor, supervisee, client	14
4	Guidance, growth promoter	13
5	Procedure, ethics and practice	12
6	Support	11
7	Benefits	10
8	Sharing	10
9	Process, transference, counter-transference	9
10	Monitoring	9
11	Contracting (including administration)	9
12	Modelling	9
13	Doubts and uncertainty	8
14	Professionalism – qualification	8
15	Challenging	7
16	Power issues	7
17	Relationship	7
18	Boundaries	6
19	Personal growth and self-support	6
20	Overseen – extra vision	5
21	Availability	5
22	Confrontation	5
23	Mourning	4
24	Checking	4
25	Professionalism – competence	4
26	Creativity	4
27	Praising	4
28	Enabling	4
29	Listening	3
30	Celebrating	3
31	Caring	3
32	Assessment	3
33	Management	3
34	Understanding	2
35	Holding	2
36	Collegial relationship	2
37	Boundaries between supervision and therapy	1

factors. or six dimensions of the concept 'Being a supervisor'. Table 13.3 represents these six factors. The full list of the statements on which they are based can be seen in Appendix 1 (pp. 285–92).

'Structuring' is the largest content category and involves properties that connect to procedure, process, ethics, professionalism, monitoring transference and countertransference, responsibility and boundaries. More than 43 per cent of the statements given in the report included this factor. The second category makes up 17.7 per cent of the statements and represents the supervisor as educator, teacher and a source of information about both theory and practice. The third category includes 14.6 per cent of the statements and represents the

Table 13.3 Six dimensions of 'Being a supervisor'

A Structuring (110 statements: 43.3%)		C Nurturing (37 statements: 14.6%)	
1	Responsibility	6	Support
5	Procedure, ethics and practice	21	Availability
9	Process, transference and	27	Praising
	countertransference	28	Enabling
10	Monitoring	29	Listening
11	Contracting (including	31	Caring
	administration)	34	Understanding
14	Professionalism – qualification	35	Holding
15	Challenging		
16	Power issues		
18	Boundaries	D	*Supervisor as person*
22	Confrontation		*(24 statements: 9.4%)*
23	Mourning	7	Benefits
24	Checking	13	Doubts and uncertainty
25	Professionalism – competence	19	Personal growth and
33	Management		self-development/support
32	Assessment		
		E	*Triangle (19 statements: 7.5%)*
B	*Education and teaching*	3	Responsibility for the client
	(45 statements: 17.7%)		Triangle: Supervisor/supervisee/
			client
2	Teaching and education	20	Overseeing – extra vision
4	Guidance		
12	Modelling	F	*Supervisor as colleague*
26	Creativity		*(19 statements: 7.5%)*
		8	Sharing
		17	Relationship
		36	Collegial relationship

'nurturing' facet of supervision where the supervisor is a source of support. The fourth category includes 9.4 per cent of the statements and focuses on the supervisor as a person with their own benefits, doubts and personal growth. The fifth category includes 7.5 per cent of the statements and describes the special 'triangle' of supervisor, therapist and client, and focuses on the specific role the supervisor plays in this triangle. The sixth category includes 7.5 per cent of the statements and describes the supervisor as a colleague.

Figure 13.1 shows the relative proportions of the six categories.

As can be seen, the 'structuring' category is the most dominant, representing nearly half of the statements. This is not unexpected as the contents of this category can be seen to be the very 'essence' of supervision. By adding to it the two other largest categories which are 'education' and 'nurturing' we get very close to the description of the concept 'supervisor' as was given in this study. It is interesting to note that the 'teaching' and 'nurturing' categories have similar proportions.

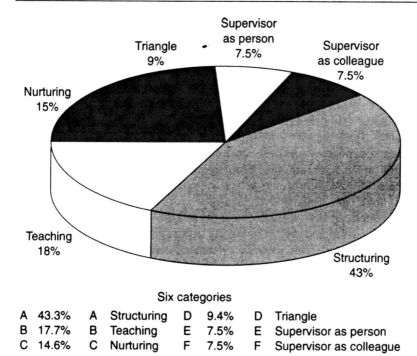

Six categories

A	43.3%	A	Structuring	D	9.4%	D	Triangle
B	17.7%	B	Teaching	E	7.5%	E	Supervisor as person
C	14.6%	C	Nurturing	F	7.5%	F	Supervisor as colleague

Figure 13.1 Phenomenological research on supervision

Whereas 'structuring', 'teaching' and 'nurturing' describe what the supervisor provides professionally, the category 'supervisor as person' shifts the focus of attention to the person and what s/he gets from the supervision given. The last two categories, 'triangle of supervisor, supervisee and client' and 'supervisor as colleague', refer to the unique situation of supervision or the unique status of supervisee.

DISCUSSION

The aim of this study was to approach supervision of counselling and psychotherapy with phenomenological methods of research and in so doing to describe the 'supervisor's experience' from their own perspective. Eleven supervisors, humanistic/existential in their theoretical frame of work, were asked to describe in their own words what 'Being a supervisor' meant.

Content and frequency analysis performed on the protocols revealed six content categories which can be seen as six facets of 'Being a supervisor' as it exists in this study's participants. The largest category was 43 per cent (structuring), built of statements referring to process, monitoring, transference and countertransference, confrontation, etc. The next two categories, 'educating/ teaching' and 'nurturing' were very similar in their importance as revealed by their relative proportions (17 per cent and 14 per cent respectively). These three categories are similar to Proctor and Inskip's (1988) three main processes, which they identify as 'normative', 'formative' and 'restorative'.

The first three categories resemble the perceptions of the supervisor's role in the studies of Ellis *et al.* (1986 and 1988). The themes of process versus conceptualisation, as well as the roles of teacher versus counsellor were found in the perceptions of supervisees (Ellis *et al.*, 1986) as well as supervisors (Ellis *et al.*, 1988). However, the supervisees distinguished between roles of teacher and counsellor, whereas supervisors did not. The importance of support within the supervisory relationship has been demonstrated to be related to trainees'/supervisees' perceptions of the effectiveness of supervision (Heppner and Roehlke, 1984; Hutt *et al.*, 1983).

Our research yielded the clear distinction made by supervisors between the roles of teacher and that of nurturing and supporting. It seems to show that, according to the perceptions of these supervisors, 'support' is a salient part of supervision. It seems that the importance given to 'nurturing' here may be a characteristic of the values which formed the basis of the training of these subjects. It is tempting to speculate what the statements would be if the subjects were from other schools of psychotherapy. Further research is needed to study similarities and differences between schools. This is perhaps due to the humanistic/existential frame of work of the supervisors in our study. The similar proportion of 'teacher' and 'support' corroborates with Blocher (1983), who indicated the importance of balancing challenge and support in supervision. In our study they did indeed show very similar, balanced proportions.

Whereas 'structuring', 'teaching' and 'nurturing' describe what the supervisor provides, the category 'supervisor as person' shifts the focus of attention to the person and what the supervisee gets from the supervision given. The last two categories, 'triangle of supervisor–supervisee–client' and 'supervisor as colleague' refer to the unique situation of supervision or the unique status of supervisee. Among the supervision models mentioned by Hess (1980), each with its own goals, is the 'collegial–peer' relationship. In supervision the relations are not simply defined between two parties, such as the relationships between teacher and student, client and therapist. There are two therapists, one more senior than the other, and there is the silent but nonetheless strong presence of the client. This unique combination specifically characterises the supervision situation.

The last three categories deal with contents not described by previous studies (e.g. Ellis *et al.*, 1986; Ellis *et al.*, 1988). These and other studies dealing with the supervisor's role and its dimensions share a limited focus on 'doing' and, to some extent, 'being'. The uniqueness of this research is its emphasis on 'being', which was dictated by the phenomenological point of view, and enabled and facilitated by the phenomenological research method. The aim of phenomenological research is to describe rather than explain conscious phenomena. We could see that the open question to describe the meanings of 'Being a supervisor' facilitated descriptions relating to the supervisor as a person; his/her feelings, benefits and own development/process, and to the special frame of relationship in the supervision setting.

In his article, *Counselling supervision: the British context,* Carroll (1988: 395) states that supervision may be regarded as being at the adolescent stage of development. 'So far it has been nurtured and cared for by counselling and psychotherapy. It has talked the same language, entailed similar behaviours and thoughts and been researched along similar lines. . . . It has begun looking for independence'. As an adolescent, one of the main tasks supervision has to face is that of 'self-identity' and 'self-definition'. The present study has researched, using a phenomenological approach, how supervisors describe, from their own perspective, what supervision means. By exploring these perceptions this research has contributed to the development of this 'young creature', and further studies are anticipated.

Phenomenological studies are infrequent. This partly stems from their relative newness as a research methodology. From this point the present study has also contributed to a new way of conducting research, in the hope that it will appeal to those potential researchers who would otherwise be reluctant to join the conservative, objective, quantitative approach to research. In our research, we have referred to the meaningful, subjective, valuable experience of 'Being a supervisor' (e.g. Mearns, 1991). In an attempt to draw on the benefits of both qualitative and quantitative research, the data hopefully capture phenomenological experience without losing the personal perspective, yet do not generalise. Rather, they help to create and research a new field of cumulative information.

The categories that emerged from the protocols of our study participants did not reveal anything new; in a way, they repeat the themes considered to be a part of the supervision role and relationship. What is unique, however, is to see the way in which these themes are expressed by the supervisors themselves. Looking through several protocols and counting the frequency of this content we can measure some of its importance. Phenomenological research does not aim to uncover the new, but to reveal further the known (Keen. 1975).

Although in this chapter the phenomenological method has been applied to a group of supervisors who would consider themselves humanistic or existential, the method *per se* would be equally suitable to supervisors from another tradition. Future research will investigate such hypotheses. This research focused on the perspective of the supervisor. No less important is the perspective of the other party, i.e. the supervisee (e.g. Greenberg, 1980). Further research should complete this picture.

This study represents the application of a research method which is particularly suited to investigating the subtle processes of human experience. It so happens that the phenomenological method is by its philosophy and methodology associated with the humanistic and existential approaches, but can be validly used as an integrative research methodology across and between traditions.

APPENDIX 1: FULL LIST OF STATEMENTS

Groups of statements   *Frequency of statements*

A Structuring

8 Confrontation (5 statements)

Being prepared to confront harmful interest	1
Being prepared to confront unprofessional behaviour	1
Being prepared to confront inappropriate referrals	1
Being prepared to confront unethical behaviour	1
Being prepared to confront caseload	1

9 Process, transference and countertransference (9 statements)

Watching for transference and countertransference	1
Watching on a context and process level the work of the supervisee	1
Watching on a context and process level the work of the clients	1
Acknowledgement and working with transference between supervisor and supervisee	1
Share own issues that get in way of work with client countertransference issues	1
Helping to sort out process problems	1
Importance of parallel process – how the difficulties get passed on up the line from client to counsellor to supervisor	1
Process	1
Process management	1

10 Procedure, ethics and practice (12 statements)

Ethics, ethical issues	5
Watching for ethical issues	1
Addressing ethical issues when necessary	1
Being prepared to confront unethical behaviour	1
Working within the law	1
Being moral	1
Ensuring that the job is being done adequately	1
Liaising with trainers where appropriate	1

11 Challenging (7 statements)

Challenging/challenge	4
Challenging bad practice to get better	1

Groups of statements	*Frequency of statements*
Initiating	1
Exciting	1

15 Mourning (2 statements)

Mourning	1
Mourning the work	1

19 Monitoring (9 statements)

Monitoring	3
Monitoring development	2
Monitoring quality	2
Monitoring – looking over	1
Guarding quality	1

20 Checking (4 statements)

Checking	2
Checking quality	1
Checking that something is being done right	1

21 Assessment (3 statements)

Assessment	2
Judgement	1

22 Professionalism – qualification (8 statements)

Being a counsellor/psychotherapist	1
Being professional/professionalism	3
Skills appropriate	1
Being qualified to do the job appropriately	1
Being able to work with a wide variety of client groups and nationalities	1
Working with people to enable them to do their counselling/psychotherapy better	1

23 Professionalism/competence (4 statements)

Being competent/competence	3
Ability to understand and work at different levels of abilities	1

Groups of statements	*Frequency of statements*

24 Responsibility (19 statements)

Responsibility/being responsible	5
Responsibility to supervisee	2
Responsibility to client	2
Responsibility – supervisee-client-organisation – balance of responsibility to ourselves	1
The supervisor needs to be clear who is responsible for the client, the counsellor and the referral	1
Ethical responsibility for the client	1
Responsibility to theory, knowledge	2
Responsibility to self, to ourselves	2
Responsibility to law	1
Shared responsibility	1
Being accountable	1

25 Contracting (including administration) (9 statements)

Contract	3
Having a contract re. the work of the supervisee	1
Contracting – business, pleasure, domestic	1
Contract: what supervisee wants – what supervisor wants	1
Working to an agreed contract as to what they want from a supervision hour or session	1
Clarifying at end what supervisee has gained/is taking away	1
Expectations/what expectation they have from supervision	1

26 Management (3 statements)

Good time management	1
Process management	1
Content management	1

29 Boundaries (6 statements)

Boundaries	2
Understanding or knowing limits	1
Statutory laws	1
Hands off	2

32 Boundaries between supervision and therapy (1 statement)

Knowing the fine line between therapy and supervision	1

Groups of statements	*Frequency of statements*

33 Power issues (7 statements)

Power	1
Power balance	1
Power relationship	1
Power imbalance	3
Balancing issues – supervisor's need and counsellor's need	1

B Education – teaching

1 Teaching and educating (20 statements)

Elder sharing of knowledge and wisdom	1
Teaching	5
Teaching when asked – or necessary?	1
Supervisor as a teacher sometimes	2
Being an educator	2
Sometimes giving information	1
Information giver	2
Offering, sometimes, information explaining theoretical issues relevant to type of work supervisee is doing	1
Offering different theories at different times according to stage of supervisee	1
Making theory alive and real	1
Theory and practice	1
Possibly with a training element also	1
Ongoing training	1

2 Modelling (9 statements)

Modelling	4
Modelling Rogers' concepts	1
Demonstrating Rogers' concepts	1
Norming	1
Working in same mode as mode of therapy/counselling being learned	1
Congruent	1

3 Guidance – growth and development promoter (13 statements)

Parental at times	1
In theory, not such a parental checking-up role	1
Someone who the therapist wants to approach for help	1
Someone who the therapist wants to approach to unburden	1

Groups of statements	*Frequency of statements*
Development of the supervisee, their workload and the appropriate referral of clients to them	1
Development of the trainee	1
Help supervisee to grow their inner supervisor	1
Growth promoting	1
Guidance	1
Direction	1
Recommending	1
Providing options	1
Involves consultation	1

28 Creativity (4 statements)

Being creative	2
Being imaginative	1
Flexibility	1

C Nurturing

4 Availability (5 statements)

Being as available as possible for emergencies	1
Supervisor as someone who acts as an SOS post in emergencies	1
Ready access to	1
Being available as far as possible for discussion	1
Being available – telephone	1

5 Listening (3 statements)

Providing a listening and supportive place for the counsellor to explore her feelings and ideas about her client	1
Listening on context and process level to the work of the supervisee	1
Listening on context and process level to the work of their clients	1

6 Understanding (2 statements)

Understanding	2

7 Enabling (4 statements)

Enabling environment where supervisee feels free enough to share:

• their difficulties	1

Groups of statements	*Frequency of statements*
• their mistakes	1
• their successes	1
Being tolerant	1

12 Support (11 statements)

Supporting/supportive/giving support	6
Supporting in the context of counselling	1
Supportive of supervisee's development	1
Patiently supporting – holding hands	1
Holding	1
Unburdening element (to move to enabling?)	1

13 Praising (4 statements)

Praising	4

14 Celebrating (3 statements)

Celebrating	3

17 Caring (3 statements)

Caring	3

18 Holding (2 statements)

Holding	1
Holding hands	1

D Supervisor as person

34 Doubts and uncertainty (8 statements)

Power – 'Am I good enough?'	1
'Who am I to say?'	2
Humility/humbling	1
Uncertainty	1
Fear of facing the expectations of the supervisee	1
Being able to know when to ask for help	1
Do they need feedback?	1

Groups of statements	*Frequency of statements*

35 Benefits (10 statements)

The 'valid consideration' – both have to get something out of it	1
Satisfaction	1
Exchange of services	1
Providing challenges to my own	1
Received ideas of how to do things	1
Refreshing my interests in TA/counselling/psychotherapy	1
Improving my own supervision skills	1
Money	2
Fun	1

36 Personal growth and self-development/support of supervisor (6 statements)

Being in therapy myself	1
Being in supervision myself	1
Having a peer group of like-minded people	1
Ongoing training	1
New inputs to psychotherapy literature	1
Healthy	1

E Supervisor as colleague

16 Sharing (10 statements)

Sharing	3
Share own issues that get in way of work with a client – countertransference issues	1
Shared responsibility?	1
Sharing of experience	1
Sharing of knowledge	1
Sharing of knowledge but as much if not more the facilitation of someone's expansion of thinking and skills	1
Share and group	1
Working together to address these issues	1

27 Relationship (7 statements)

Relationship	3
Providing a relationship	1
Meeting with individual or group, depend on issues or what wanted in supervision	1

Groups of statements	Frequency of statements
Relationship – intruding advocate	1
Commitment	1

31 Collegial relationship (2 statements)

Able to talk as colleagues at times	1
Being a colleague professional friend – fellow explorer	1

F Triangle

30 Responsibility for the client/Triangle: supervisor, supervisee, client (14 statements)

Advocacy/being the unseen advocate of the client	2
Intruding advocate	1
Being invisible in the dance	1
Intruding in dyad of counsellor–client	1
With aim of providing better service for client	1
Is there a conflict of interest that may be damaging for the client?	1
Responsibility to the client/s	2
Responsibility – supervisee–client–organisation	1
The supervisor needs to be clear who is responsible for the client, the counsellor and the referral	1
Protecting the client	2
Being an outsider – outside the relationship of counsellor and client – with extra rather than 'super' vision	1

37 Overseeing – extra vision (5 statements)

Being an outsider – outside the relationship of counsellor and client – with extra rather than 'super' vision	1
Super vision	1
Overseeing a colleague in the workplace	1
The 'loaded' view of each individual supervisor	1
Goodwill overseen	1

APPENDIX 2: THE THERAPIST AS SCIENTIST-PRACTITIONER

A method of self-supervision for helping professionals*

In an earlier paper (Clarkson, 1995) I suggested that perhaps the end of the divide between clinical supervision and academic research can begin to be made as the work of doing and reflection becomes integrated. What would be required is a reconceptualisation of the primary task of supervision from that of an expert to that of a consultant or co-researcher in every case or situation brought for disciplined reflection.

The purpose of this appendix then is to record a simple method of self-supervision and describe an attitude of scientific interest and ethical experimentation in the everyday practice of counselling psychology which many students, practitioners and supervisors have found helpful. It is not intended to be science, but to explore the use of a kind of scientific metaphor to serve as guide through the vagaries and vicissitudes of everyday clinical practice.

It is probably a truism that people who feel intelligent, resourceful and encouraged learn more efficiently and enjoyably than people who feel stupid, limited and constantly criticised. Practitioners in the helping professions tend to be conscientious, well-motivated and often hypercritical of themselves. Concerns about 'doing damage' saying or doing 'the wrong thing' and appearing in an unfavourable light to colleagues, trainers, supervisors or peers seem to be on the increase. Frequently on training courses, and in the privacy of the bedroom, the worst criticism does not come from trainers and supervisors, but from the inner supervisor, critic, professional superego or internal parent figure.

Naturally, early in training the prohibitions against what *not* to do outweigh the fund of knowledge or skills about what actually to do that may be helpful. (It is only later in a professional training that it becomes clear why and how one should not treat friends and family for example.) It is not unusual in the learning cycle that this concern about the normative aspects of our work sometimes can interfere with the open, curious, non-judgemental attitude which is most conducive to learning once the warnings, cautions and dangers have been taken on board. When learning energy becomes, so to speak, tied up in avoiding mistakes, learning is impeded and creativity and innovation halted.

Elements of a model or metaphor for self-supervision

An attitude modelled on the ideal of a scientist-practitioner has advantages which can overcome this problem and enhance reflective learning as well as creative assessment of one's functioning. The elements seem to be the following:

---

* By Petrŭska Clarkson.

1 *An idea or goal, purpose, contract, direction or outcome measure*

There has to be something that someone wants in order to have some idea of whether they got all or half or none of what they wanted or not. This will obviously depend on the values, the epistemology and conceptualisations of whichever theory is being learnt, practised, integrated or expanded.

For theory read introject. Theory is always someone else's idea or your idea with which someone else agrees. Every such outcome measure carries implicitly or explicitly values, epistemologies, ideology as Foucault and others have shown. In one model the goal may be *insight* into childhood roots of a disturbance (Symington, 1986), in another *symptom relief* (Beck, Emery, Greenberg, 1985), in another *congruent self-statements* (Rogers, 1951), in another *authentic expression of feeling in a fully felt cathartic release* (bioenergetics), and so on and so forth. We can proliferate examples indefinitely. But you or the client have some idea that if the person does x, something has happened. This is perhaps physiological at a fundamental level – the answer to the client's question, am I getting something which I want?

This of course needs to be differentiated from the therapist 'having their own agenda' in a proactive countertransferential way, such as when we want our clients to get better so that we can protect ourselves against feelings of inadequacy, to impress our supervisors or to avoid getting into trouble with the agency, for example. There has to be a goal, and ideally an explicit goal on both sides. Ethical issues about clarity of contract, consensual agreement, exploitation are all relevant here.

2 *A scientific paradigm*

There has to be some way in which we judge what's going on. There has to be some epistemological paradigm: at the simplest level, how do we know, what shall we call knowledge? Experiments are often conducted using the notion of a null hypothesis – that is the postulate that the intervention, experiment, manipulation of variables, etc. will not make any difference greater than chance. A 5 per cent or 1 per cent probability region is identified where the difference potentially attributable to the experimenter intervention is likely to be due to such intervention rather than random chance fluctuations. This is a statistical measure of likelihood. One way of saying this is that the chances are that 95 per cent of what we do has little or no influence on what would have happened anyway.

If we translate this as a *metaphor* for clinical practice we could say that the null hypothesis states that nothing the therapist does or does not do will make more than a chance difference to the situation of the client. The experimenter attitude then requires careful observation of the client in order to judge whether an intervention actually does make a difference or not. (An intervention may of course be *active* such as an interpretation or empathic comment or *apparently passive* such as looking away or not answering a question while a silence grows in the room.)

The use of the null hypothesis here is obviously meant as paradigm and metaphor to help the practitioner to be more objective about their own work, less judgemental, but more discriminating. It is not meant as exact or exemplary science. The intention is firstly to serve the client and to resource the clinician which may or may not eventually be translated into single-case design or other more conventional blending of applied and scientific practice. Hopefully the importation of an open expectant but largely unbiased interested attitude can foster the abilities as well as the desire to grade such a practice to conventional scientific standards.

There is in fact not that much scientifically acceptable evidence that 'undoing retroflections' or 'empathic reflection' or 'making interpretations' makes that much difference to the problem that people bring. This goes well against the grain particularly of 'acceptable attitudes' in psychotherapy trainings which are based on theoretical compliance instead of scientific inquiry and constant methodological inquiry. I think we have a ethical obligation to pay very precise attention to what we do and what happens, moment by moment, in the consulting room and session by session in disciplined reflection – with or without the aid of another researcher. An experimenter attitude is: Did x make a difference or did it not make a difference? How can I find out if it did? Was it indeed as a result of something I did? Was it in the desired direction? This is the legitimate experiment. not: Am I following the rules I learnt on my last training day.

Obviously we are not talking about laboratory work in the exact, exemplary or classical sense. Yet there is a sense in which the consulting room is always a laboratory. It matters what we explore, test or discover in this laboratory. The intention of using this null hypothesis metaphor is here offered to help the clinician to be less judgemental, but more discriminating, more questioning, more accountable.

3 Units of analysis or attention

These can be stimulus response pairs, transactions, interpretation and the next dream image, the five relationships, identification and so on. There has to be something that we're looking at. The methodology has developed rapidly and excellently recently in psychology. It may or may not be translated into a single-case design. There are not very fine examples of how one case is conducted as an experiment. Working with one case within a paradigm of inquiry is already possible and may well be adaptable to one's work. In order to do this, one needs units of observation – even if these are phenomenological self-reports.

This is contrasted with some recent examples where trainees build their competencies on demonstrated adherence to theory – i.e. meeting the requirements of the organisation. The training organisation naturally exists to further its own theoretical, ideological and financial purposes and the case study often becomes a way of getting the approval of the people who designed the curriculum. It does not meet the criterion of measurable difference in the direction that people are wanting attributable to what the practitioner has done or not done. I am not suggesting that this is easy or can comfortably be imported into traditional models. I am pleading for an importation of these very serious questions and aspirations to pre- or transtheoretical rigour and discipline in every piece of work we do.

In other words, just because you're not a PhD laboratory-trained scientist, it doesn't mean that you should not be thinking, adapting and improving on the scientific method in ways to suit your clinical work. In this way the locus of evaluation is shifted from outside to inside. Instead of worrying about 'Am I doing Gestalt?' or 'proper Kleinian analysis?', the locus becomes 'I did this with that person and this is the evidence I am adducing to indicate that what I did was within this region of probability related to the outcome this person desired'. (Of course the language you use is up to you.) So when you go for examination or accreditation it is not a case of 'Do I meet your subjective compliance criteria?', but more 'This is the way I conceptualised and thought about and judged my work and I would like to share it with you'.

Competence is here defined as having the internal competence to meet external criteria in a consistent way as well as knowing the limits of competence and the areas of development.

Is therapy and therapy training perhaps primarily a social influence process? There has been for the last hundred years a proliferation of theory in therapy and there are many very intelligent and excellent professionals throughout the world who are questioning the very theory of theory. Too often theory is the vehicle for achieving submission, compliance, decisions about who shall have certification, recognition, status – essentially a vehicle for the establishment and maintenance of power relations.

There are probably no easy solutions for this. These are the problems. We have seen how 'objective' experimenters influence outcomes. We know observers affect physics experiments in the best, most controlled laboratories in the world. I don't think it is as simple as 'having a control group' or 'following theory'. Of course it does not mean that theory is without value. It is a responsibility to be curious about what is going on. The fact that we probably can't find out fundamentally for sure and for always should not absolve us from the effort of trying. I would like us to work consciously knowing that we are active in a problematised area.

4 An attitude of interest, curiosity about one's own skills and process

A willingness is needed to engage in a genuine self-feedback exercise untrammelled with transferential distortions self-reflexive in the best way. I perceive that professionals in training are not curious enough about what happens in their consulting rooms. A man of 50 is worried about saying something to his patient because of what his supervisor may say.

The Oxford philosopher of psychology, B. A. Farrell, after intensive research on five training groups concluded that a group therapist or leader helps to produce material that fits in with his WOT – or 'way of talking'. Farrell suggests that (perhaps always) the person, the organisation, the training group is therefore declared 'cured', 'mature', 'competent' to the extent that they have adopted the WOT of the trainer or leader. 'Therefore, the insight and understanding etc. that the operator helps his groups to acquire are not only dependent on his own perspective; they are also dependent on the very method [and thus theory] he uses' (Farrell, 1979: 108).

You'll notice if you are curious about something that you are not trapped in 'This is good WOT' or 'This is bad WOT', 'Am I doing it right?' or 'Will my supervisor "like" it?' Rather, curiosity is 'What will happen if . . . ?' and I submit that that is the appropriate attitude for the practitioner scientist – to question the WOTs. In this way we may develop the ability as well as the desire to upgrade our practices to exemplars of inquiry and competence.

It is probably important to realise that every piece of research will always be contestable now or later. There are always faults to be found in any method or piece of human inquiry. There is no place to hide even behind the scientific paradigm. There are many different languages for many different purposes.

5 A desire to make a contribution to the common stock of clinical knowledge

This is achieved by sharing observations and experience, questioning and writing, contributing to conferences and the development of the discipline overall. (I suppose this is the old desire to 'save the world' in one of its multitude of guises.) At the very least it is: 'I will write this down so that other people – for example, the client – may benefit from it'.

REFERENCES

Aanstoos, C. M. (1983). The think aloud method in descriptive research. *Journal of Phenomenological Psychology*, 14 (2): 243–366.

Beck, A. T., Emery, G., and Greenberg, R. L. (1985). *Anxiety Disorders and Phobias: A Cognitive Perspective*. New York: Basic Books.

Bernard, J. M. (1979). Supervisory training: a discrimination model. *Counselor Education and Supervision*, 19, 60–68.

Blocher, D. H. (1983). Toward a cognitive developmental approach to counseling supervision. *Counseling Psychologist*, 11 (1), 27–34.

Bor, R. and Watts, M. (1993). Training counselling psychologists to conduct research. *Counselling Psychology Review*, 8 (4), 20–21.

Carroll, M. (1988). Counselling supervision: the British context. *Counselling Psychology Quarterly*, 1 (4), 387–396.

Clarkson, P. (1994). The nature and range of psychotherapy. In P. Clarkson and M. R. Pokorny (eds), *Handbook of Psychotherapy* (pp. 3–27). London: Routledge.

Clarkson, P. (1995) Counselling psychology in Britain – the next decade. *Counselling Psychology Quarterly*, 8 (3): 197–204.

Ellis, M. V., Dell, D. M. and Good, G. E. (1986). Dimensionality of supervisor roles:

supervisors' perceptions of supervision. *Journal of Counseling Psychology*, 33 (3), 282–291.

Ellis. M. V., Dell, D. M. and Good, G. E. (1988). Counselor trainees' perceptions of supervisor roles: two studies testing the dimensionality of supervision. *Journal of Counseling Psychology*, 35 (3), 315–324.

Farrell. B. A. (1979) Work in small groups: some philosophical considerations, in B. Babington Smith and B. A. Farrell (eds), *Training In Small Groups: A Study of Five Groups* (pp. 103–115), Oxford: Pergamon.

Greenberg, L. S. (1980). Supervision from the perspective of the supervisee. In A. K. Hess (ed.). *Psychotherapy Supervision: Theory, Research and Practice*. New York: Wiley.

Greenberg, L. S. (1986). Research strategies. In L. S. Greenberg and W. M. Pinsoff (eds), *The Psychotherapeutic Process: A Research Handbook* (pp. 707–734). New York: Guilford.

Hawkins, P. and Shohet, R. (1989). *Supervision in the Helping Professions*. Milton Keynes: Open University Press.

Heppner, P. P. and Roehlke, H. J. (1984). Differences among supervisees at different levels of training: implications for a developmental model of supervision. *Journal of Counseling Psychology*, 31, 76: 90.

Hess. A. (1980). Training models and the nature of psychotherapy supervision. In A. K. Hess (ed.), *Psychology Supervision: Theory, Research and Practice*. New York: Wiley.

Hicks. C. and Wheeler, S. (1994). Research: an essential foundation for counselling, training and practice. *Counselling*, 5 (1), 29–31.

Holloway, E. L. (1992). Supervision: a way of teaching and learning. In S. D. Brown and R. W. Lent (eds), *Handbook of Counseling Psychology* (2nd edn), (pp. 176–214). Chichester and New York: Wiley.

Hunt. P. (1986). Supervision. *Marriage Guidance*, Spring, 15–22.

Hutt. C. H., Scott, J. and King, M. (1983). A phenomenological study of supervisees' positive and negative experience in supervision. *Psychotherapy: Theory, Research and Practice*, 20, 118–128.

Keen. E. (1975). *A Primer in Phenomenological Psychology*. Washington, DC: University Press of America.

Kessel. F. S., Cole, P. M. and Johnson, D. L. (eds) (1992) *Self and Consciousness*, London: Lawrence Erlbaum Associates.

Kiesler. D. J. (1966). Some myths of psychotherapy research and the search for a paradigm. *Psychological Bulletin*, 65, 110–136.

Kuiken. D., Schopflocher, D. and Cameron, W. (1989). Numerically aided methods in phenomenology: a demonstration. *Journal of Mind and Behavior*, 10 (4), 373–392.

Littrell. J. M., Lee-Borden, N. and Lorenz, J. (1979). A developmental framework for counseling supervision. *Counselor Education and Supervision*, 19, 129–136.

Marken. M. and Payne, M. (eds) (1987). *Enabling and Ensuring: Supervision in Practice*. Leicester: National Youth Bureau.

Maslow, A. H. (1968). *Toward a Psychology of Being* (2nd edn). New York: Van Nostrand.

Mattinson. J. (1992). *The Reflection Process in Casework Supervision* (2nd edn). London: Tavistock.

Mearns. D. (1991) On being a supervisor. In W. Dryden and B. Thorne (eds), *Training and Supervision for Counselling in Action* (pp. 116–128). London: Sage.

Munt. S. (1987). Personality characteristics of counselling students with particular regard to indicators of psychopathology. MSc Dissertation. London: Roehampton Institute.

Robinson. D. N. (1979). *Systems of Modern Psychology*. New York: Columbia University Press.

Rogers. C. R. (1951) *Client-Centered Therapy*, Boston MA: Houghton Mifflin.

Sanders. P. (1982). Phenomenology: a new way of viewing organizational research. *Academy of Management Review*, 7 (3), 353–360.

Spinelli. E. (1989). *The Interpreted World: An Introduction to Phenomenological Psychology*. London: Sage.

Symington, N. (1986) *The Analytic Experience: Lectures from the Tavistock*, London: Free Association Books.

Wheeler. S. and McLeod, J. (1994). Editorial: Special edition of counselling on the relevance of research for practice. *Counselling*, 5 (1), 28.

Further reading

Breese. J. (1987). The supervision of counsellors. *British Psychological Society Section Review*, 2 (2), 17–21.

Greenberg, L. S. (1991). Research on the process of change. *Psychotherapy Research*, 1 (1). 3–16.

Stenack. R. J. and Dye, H. A. (1982). Behavioural description of counseling supervision roles. *Counselor Education and Supervision*, 21, 295–304.

Chapter 14

Writing as research in counselling psychology and related disciplines

Petrūska Clarkson

ENTROIT

'But why does opening the box and looking reduce the system back to one probability, either live cat or dead cat? Why don't *we* get included in the system when we lift the lid of the box?'

There was a pause. 'How?' Rover barked, distrustfully.

'Well. we would involve ourselves in the system, you see, the super-imposition of two waves. There's no reason why it should only exist *inside* an open box, is there? So when we came to look there we would be, you and I, both looking at a live cat and both looking at a dead cat, see?'

A dark cloud lowered over Rover's eyes and brow. He barked twice in a subdued, harsh voice, and walked away. With his back turned to me he said in a firm. sad tone, 'You must not complicate the issue. It is complicated enough' (LeGuin. 1982: 47).

INTRODUCTION

Psychology as a discipline grew out of the early European laboratories, where white-coated researchers emulated the physical scientists of their time, to the profession today where millions more people throughout the world are in effect of the reverberations of our work. The professions of counselling, psychotherapy and psychoanalysis have also more recently seen the development of an interest in research joining the psychologists in their quest for understanding, study and investigation of the psychological dimensions of being human and the impact of our interventions in this field.

Attitudes of individual practitioners may be hostile or dismissive of the attempt to subject the delicate and mysterious project of the healing encounter to the harsh and unsympathetic instrumentation of statistical probability and factor analysis – not to mention the presence of the recording measures. Others are ambivalent, sometimes torn between the desire to know on the one hand and the lack of resources, ability or technology on the other. For many in these professions, market forces and political as well as ethical considerations are further shaping the necessity for engagement with the research project so that the day of the scientist–practitioner seems to be drawing closer. Fortunately the models and permissible parameters of acceptable paradigms of research are also proliferating – perhaps even in response to the late twentieth-century changes in our cultural field.

RESEARCH AS RELATIONSHIP

Clandinin and Connelly (1994: 425) comment on the way in which research itself is about relationship, conducted in relationship and through relationship:

> Personal experience methods inevitably are relationship methods. As researchers, we cannot work with participants without sensing the fundamental human connection among us; nor can we create research texts without imagining a relationship to you, our audience.

NEW PARADIGMS AND OLD PARADIGMS

The research component of most academic psychology programmes is the one that is often least attractive to students and most burdensome to the teachers. The attempt to blend the excitement and stimulation of the consulting room with the dry and sometimes tedious methodology of parametric statistics and other similar forms of processing wet and living data fail too frequently. New ways are being forged from these necessities (Reason, 1988; Reason and Rowan, 1981; Kvale, 1992). In particular, counselling psychology as a newly emerging discipline in Britain has a unique opportunity to develop, encourage and sustain a model of blending practice and research in an ongoing, interesting and satisfying way. Process as well as outcome will be investigated – perhaps even considered equally important (Elton Wilson and Barkham, 1994). New research questions and new kinds of research questions can perhaps follow the interests of clinicians rather than the funding priorities of the laboratory. The divide between the academy and the consulting room could potentially become a meeting place as their inhabitants learn to speak and work and supervise in the same language.

NEW QUESTIONS, NEW METHODS

Our conceptual and cultural world has changed irrevocably over the last few decades. Much of what we were certain about, believed in, fought for, lies in tatters. Science has exploded into the indeterminate paradigms and multiple realities of the quantum physical world, the implications of chaos and complexity models or impossibilities are gradually filtering through to the humanities, while cultural critique has left us incapable of moral or academic innocence. Now, according to Lyotard (1989: 34), the 'meta-narrative' has collapsed. There is no more one story or even the hope of one *grand* story. The ideal used to be that we could build our knowledge piece by piece based on previous research. As Gergen (1990: 27) points out, 'we do not improve our knowledge of the world through systematic study . . . so much as shift our way of seeing the world'.

For example, the almost automatic assumptions of a causal relationship between childhood trauma and adult pathology, the comforting notion of an individual self as autonomous agent, the separability of subject and object, the idea that the magnitude of the effect may have little relevance to the magnitude or timing of our interventions, the possibility of representative samples and the generalisability of our so-called scientific findings are all being questioned (Clarkson, 1993a, 1993b, 1993c). Some perspectives indicate, for example, that

> conceptions of the child may depend on a host of factors uncorrelated to the actual nature of the child. Beliefs about the child vary markedly as a result of history, culture and personal disposition; yet the genetic make-up of the actual child seems to remain relatively constant. Perhaps the most radical view within this domain is that of Kessen [1979]. As Kessen proposed, 'the child is essentially and eternally a cultural invention and . . . the variety in the child's definition is not the removable error of an incomplete science' (1979: 815). From this perspective the concept of the child is essentially a social construction, and no amount of observation will provide the basis for an unconstructed or interpretation-free account of the child's nature. Yet is this process of inquiry, learning and re-evaluation of perception in itself not also research? (Gergen *et al.*, 1990, p. 108)

WRITING AS RESEARCH

Richardson (1994) suggests that writing itself is a method of inquiry. It is a primary way of both seeing and acting in the world. Richardson (1994: 517) warns against the importation of the ideals of objectivity and non-involvement even as we write:

> Specifically, poststructuralism suggests two important things to qualitative writers: first, it directs us to understand ourselves reflexively as persons writing from particular positions at specific times; and second, it frees us from trying to write a single text in which everything is said to everyone. Nurturing our own voices releases the censorious hold of 'science writing' on our consciousness, as well as the arrogance it fosters in our psyche. Writing is validated as a method of knowing.

Certainly it has been my experience from my earliest experimental training counting faecal pellets in rat laboratories as a measure of their stress (distress?) that the work of writing itself is another process of discovery, both about myself, my discipline and the work of thinking and writing itself. The poet in me went into hiding and it is only with my increasing grasp of the postmodernist, poststructuralist *Zeitgeist* that I begin to see the possibilities – not necessarily of a wholesome final product called 'integration', but a continuing endeavour of validating all the forms of my search and my knowing even as I subject these very processes to both intuition, dialogue and objective inquiry.

An interest is spreading in our field to capture processes via the eye of the beholder, in order to describe, document or write up processes through *subjective experience* (Greenberg, 1986). For Spinelli (1989: 80) as well: 'The goal of the phenomenological method is not to expose and explore what is truly real – since that remains an impossibility – but, rather to clarify both the variables and invariants of phenomenal reality'. Discerning an essence, according to Husserl, is neither more nor less than discerning the complex of properties that define a phenomenon when instances of that phenomenon are already known (Kuiken *et al.*, 1989). The procedure by which this goal is pursued defines the phenomenological approach to psychological research. Bor and Watts (1993) wrote that researchers in counselling psychology should conduct their research using a methodology which is congruent with their theoretical framework and approach to counselling and psychotherapy. It is possible to argue that the serious and dedicated writing up of subjective experience, the theories of others and the invention of one's own, the questioning of received wisdom and popular assumptions, the encounter with the other in the consulting room and their words and images, the prose as well as the poetry of healing, form a congruent representation of the work of the clinician or supervisor in this field.

THE OBJECTIVITY OF THE CLINICIAN-RESEARCHER

Much as Pavlov lived the ideals of the neutral researcher in his laboratories, Freud tried to do it in his. The ideal of neutrality is still taught, however impossible to practise or to sustain logically, in many training schools for analysts and psychotherapists. The origin of this attitude is beautifully illustrated in the scientific use Freud made of the 'untoward event' (Jones, 1953) when Anna O fell in love with his colleague – Breuer.

> Breuer then decided straight away that his method was unethical for a medical practitioner, and he left the field for Freud to struggle on alone. Freud was more circumspect. He looked around the edges of the ethical problem and, *being a well-brought-up natural scientist, he adopted the characteristic neutrality to ethical questions*. Thus, transference was looked at anew – from being an untoward and unethical happening it could become a phenomenon for study, and then for use in practice (Hinshelwood, 1989: 447, emphasis added).

Elsewhere (Clarkson, 1994, 1996), there have been explorations of the ethical and moral consequences of this 'scientific' attitude in the clinician – as well as its impossibility. It has been argued that a value-free practice is as impossible as a value-free science and that all of us are involved in the structuring and construction of our world, complicit with its ideological assumptions and never free from the moral and epistemological consequences of our actions or non-actions. In the words of Robert Hariman (1989: 211): 'Why do those who are pursuing knowledge not encounter tragic knowledge, or otherwise confront the penalties of knowledge, and why do they declare themselves free of sentiment and patriotism and religious conviction, and who are they writing for anyway?'

PROFESSIONALISM

Gergen (1992) for our profession is one of the first and most eloquent psychologists to address the issues of postmodern consciousness *per se*. He claims that psychologists and society are being brought closer together by 'demystifying the grand narrative of modernism' (p. 28). The grand narrative can be understood as the expectation that there is an ultimate story behind all human experience which, when found, would precipitate Utopia or, at the very least, enlightenment. Such a grand narrative was the hope of the enlightenment project of the Renaissance. It was encapsulated in the conviction that, somehow, human beings could find an ultimate answer or solution to the dilemmas of human existence, whether in religion, communism, or the final findings of a positivistic science. The world has, however, become more complex than even da Vinci imagined. New technology and discoveries have meant that we have more realities to contend with. New, more complex, technological language has proliferated, with which we seek to explain it all, but fail repeatedly.

> We live in a world in which the authority of previous guides has apparently crumbled. They have become fragments, bits of a particular archive (of Western Europe, of the white male voice), part of a local history that once involved the presumption (and power) to speak in the name of the 'world' (Boradori, 1986: 82).

We have seen ideological dream after ideological dream flower, and fail to solve the monumental problems facing our world – the impending destruction of the planet, the millions of people dying of hunger and disease, the rise of fundamentalism to an extreme degree. There is a profound sense in which we have become disillusioned, and yet many lack the energetic, courageous despair of Existentialists such as Kierkegaard. While they largely conform to the externals, the young seem to listen to authorities now with a built-in scepticism. At the same time there is a 74 per cent increase in suicides among young men alone in the UK in the last ten years (Pepinster, 1993).

Thus the criticism of our culture can be read in such statistics as well as in the postmodern movement. Whereas modernism tended to be both upper class and Eurocentric, the ideas of postmodernism are characterised by the presence of *the other* – many different cultures find a voice, and the place of women and minority groups become of significant interest.

Postmodern consciousness ... by demystifying the grand narrative of modernism, attempts to bring psychologists and society closer together. Not only is technology placed in the service of values to which one is committed; more importantly, the psychologist is encouraged to join in forms of valuation advocacy and to develop new intelligibilities that present new options to the culture. There is no promise of utopias here, but the possibility of active and engaged participation in cultural process is significantly enhanced (Gergen, 1990: 33).

THE EPISTEMOLOGICAL VALUES OF THE THERAPIST

In comparing the values of behavioral scientists with non-behavioral scientists in psychology, Krasner and Houts [1984] found the former to endorse quantitative, empirical, and objectivist approaches to the study of human behavior, whereas the latter endorsed humanistic and subjectivist approaches. As Norcross [1981: 1544] has pointed out, 'clinical investigators have repeatedly encountered numerous and predictable differences in both the activities and beliefs of therapists of differing theoretical orientations' [e.g. see McGovern, Newman, and Kopta, 1986; Plutchik, Conte and Karasu, 1988] (Messer, 1992: 150).

FINALLY – AESTHETIC REASONS FOR QUALITATIVE RESEARCH LIKE THIS

Before going ahead, I ought to say that I am not trying to settle these matters once and for all. I am on a poetic plane where the yes and no of things are equally true. Were you to ask me, 'Is a moonlit night of one hundred years ago identical to a moonlit night of ten years ago?' I could demonstrate (as could any other poet who is master of his craft) that it was. But with the same ring of indisputable truth, I could also prove that it was not. I am trying to avoid the sort of ugly erudite data that tire out audiences; it is emotional data I shall try to emphasize. You are surely more interested in knowing whether a melody can give birth to a finely sifted, soporific breeze, or whether a song can place a simple landscape before the child's newly jelled eyes, than in knowing whether the melody is of the seventeenth century or whether it is written in ¼ time, information the poet ought to know but not to repeat and which is, after all, within reach of anyone who dedicates himself to these matters (Garcia Lorca, 1980: 8).

REFERENCES

Bor, R. and Watts, M. (1993) Training counselling psychologists to conduct research, *Counselling Psychology Review* 8 (4): 20–21.

Boradori, G. (1986) Weak thought and the aesthetics of quotationism: the Italian shift from deconstruction, Working Paper, No. 6, Center for Twentieth Century Studies.

Clandinin, D. J. and Connelly, F. M. (1994) Personal experience methods, in N. K. Denzin and Y. S. Lincoln (eds) *Handbook of Qualitative Research* (pp. 413–427), Thousand Oaks, CA: Sage.

Clarkson, P. (1993a) A small kitbag for the future, in *Order, Chaos and Change in the Public Sector: Papers from the Third Public Sector Conference* (pp. 17–27), London: Association of Management Education and Development.

Clarkson, P. (1993b) New perspectives in counselling and psychotherapy (or adrift in a sea of change), in P. Clarkson, *On Psychotherapy* (pp. 209–232), London: Whurr.

Clarkson, P. (1993c) Two thousand five hundred years of Gestalt – from Heraclitus to the big bang, *British Gestalt Journal* 2 (1): 4–9.

Clarkson, P. (1994) Values in psychotherapy, paper presented at 'What is Human' Conference, Keele University, August 1994.

Clarkson, P. (1996) *The Bystander (An End to Innocence in Human Relationships?)*, London: Whurr.

Elton Wilson, J. and Barkham, M. (1994) A practitioner-scientist approach to psychotherapy research and evidence, in P. Clarkson and M. R. Pokorny (eds), *Handbook of Psychotherapy* (pp. 49–72), London: Routledge.

Garcia Lorca, F. (1980) *Deep Song and Other Prose* (ed. and trans. C. Maurer), London: Marion Boyars.

Gergen, K. J. (1990) Toward a postmodern psychology, *The Humanistic Psychologist* 18: 23–34.

Gergen, K. J. (1992). Toward a postmodern psychology, in S. Kvale (ed.) *Psychology and Postmodernism* (pp. 17–30), London: Sage.

Gergen, K. J. , Gloger-Tippelt, G. and Berkowitz, P. (1990) The cultural construction of the developing child, in G. S. Semin and K. J. Gergen (eds) *Everyday Understanding: Social and Scientific Implications* (pp. 108–129), London: Sage.

Greenberg, L. S. (1986) Research strategies, in L. S. Greenberg and W. M. Pinsoff (eds) *The Psychotherapeutic Process: A Research Handbook* (pp. 707–734), New York: Guilford.

Hariman, R. (1989) The rhetoric of inquiry and the professional scholar, in H. W. Simons (ed.) *Rhetoric in the Human Sciences* (pp. 211–232), London: Sage.

Hinshelwood, R. D. (ed.) (1989) *A Dictionary of Kleinian Thought*, London: Free Association Books.

Jones, E. (1953) *Sigmund Freud: Life and Work*, Vol. I, London: Hogarth Press.

Kessen, W. (1979) The American child and other cultural inventions, *American Psychologist* 34: 815–20.

Krasner, L. and Houts, A. C. (1984) 'A study of the value systems of behavioural scientists', *American Psychologist* 39: 840–50.

Kuiken, D., Schopflocher, D. and Cameron, W. (1989) Numerically aided methods in phenomenology: a demonstration, *Journal of Mind and Behavior* 10 (4): 373–392.

Kvale, S. (1992) Postmodern psychology: a contradiction in terms?, in S. Kvale (ed.) *Psychology and Postmodernism* (pp. 31–57), London: Sage.

LeGuin, U. (1982) 'Schrödinger's Cat', in *The Compass Rose*, New York: Harper and Row.

Lyotard, J.-F. (1989) *The Postmodern Condition: A Report on Knowledge*, Manchester: Manchester University Press.

McGovern, M. P., Newman, F. L. and Kopta, S. M. (1986) Metatheoretical assumptions and psychotherapy orientation: clinician attributions of patients' problem causality and responsibility for treatment outcome, *Journal of Consulting and Clinical Psychology* 54: 476–481.

Messer, S. B. (1992) A critical examination of belief structures in integrative and eclectic psychotherapy, in J. C. Norcross and M. R. Goldfried (eds) *Handbook of Psychotherapy Integration* (pp. 130–165) New York: Basic Books.

Norcross, J. C. (1981) 'All in the family? On therapeutic commonalities', *American Psychologist*, 36: 1544–5.

Pepinster, C. (1993) Presence of mind, *Time Out* (20 May), London: Time Out Publications.

Plutchik, R., Conte, H. R. and Karasu, T. B. (1988) Psychodynamic and behavioral therapy: a survey and discussion of integrative models, *Integrative Psychiatry* 6: 22–26.

Reason, P. R. (1988) *Human Inquiry in Action: Developments in New Paradigm Research*, London: Sage.

Reason, P. R. and Rowan, J. (eds) (1981) *Human Inquiry, A Sourcebook of New Paradigm Research*, Chichester: Wiley.

Richardson, L. (1994) Writing: a method of inquiry, in N. K. Denzin and Y. S. Lincoln (eds) *Handbook of Qualitative Research* (pp. 516–529), Thousand Oaks, CA: Sage.

Spinelli, E. (1989) *The Interpreted World: An Introduction to Phenomenological Psychology*, London: Sage.

Chapter 15

The psychology of 'fame'
Implications for practice

Petrūska Clarkson

This qualitative research study was undertaken to begin a phenomenological exploration of the subjective experience of what is meant by the notion of 'fame'. It is here defined as being discussed or 'known' by strangers through report, reputation, media appearance, position or writing as a result of some achievement or accomplishment. The respondents were members of the therapy profession in one country considered as being 'renowned' or 'famous' in their disciplinary world. From the sixteen possibilities who were identified, eleven agreed to be interviewed. It was the assumption that as therapists, psychologists or psycho-analysts they could not only report, but also reflect psychologically on their own human experience of this phenomenon, as well as consider the effects of this factor on their therapeutic practices.

> Our Deepest Fear is not that we are inadequate. Our deepest fear is that we are powerful beyond measure. It is our light, not our darkness, that most frightens us. We ask ourselves: 'Who am I to be brilliant, gorgeous, talented, fabulous?' Actually, who are you not to be? You are a child of God. Your playing small doesn't serve the world. There's nothing enlightened about shrinking so that other people around you won't feel insecure. We are all meant to shine, as children do. We are born to manifest the glory of God that is within us. It is not just in some of us: it is in everyone. And as we let our light shine, we unconsciously give other people permission to do the same. As we are liberated from our own fear, our presence automatically liberates others (from Nelson Mandela's Inaugural Speech, 1994).

INTRODUCTION

The *Oxford English Dictionary* defines the notion of fame as 'renown; the state of being famous; much spoken of' (Onions, 1973: 510). The psychological liter-ature does not reveal much research on this theme, yet the daily newspapers, for example, devote many column inches to describing or discussing the lives and activities of people who could be regarded as famous or infamous in some way. There is anecdotal or biographical material discussing the effects of fame on rock artists, child filmstars and other people of achievement or notoriety, but as far as can be established not a great deal of serious psychological study in terms of the subjective experience of this collective phenomenon. My own professional world was also not immune to aspects of this phenomenon.

> I began to write when I realized all I had to do was speculate, question, argue, create a model, take a position, define a problem, make an observation, propose a solution, illuminate a possibility to participate in a (continuous) written conversation with my peers ... not to deliver the Truth (Murray, 1986: 147).

AIMS AND OBJECTIVES OF THE STUDY

The aim of this study is to describe qualitatively the human experience of being known outside of one's immediate relationships as a result of achievement of some kind. This is different from fame or renown which comes about sociologically as in celebrities 'famous for being famous' or arbitrarily such as by birth or accident. The careful and diligent search here is for the particular themes or experiences which constitute this collective phenomenon. The method is phenomenological and descriptive.

CONCEPTUAL REALMS

The conceptual framework will include the notion that the phenomenon essentially concerns a relationship – usually between an individual and other people. (One cannot be famous in isolation from the report of others.) It was therefore considered that the experience of therapists (whose work and expertise by definition concern relationship) would offer a valuable entry-point. Choosing psychologists, psychotherapists and psychoanalysts potentially had an additional advantage in that they are trained to be self-reflective – trained in taking into account their own feelings, thoughts and behaviours as well as the experiences of their patients or clients. The third aspect concerned a possible contribution in exploring, to the benefit of therapists who have become or may become 'renowned', the effect of this kind of phenomenon on their ordinary clinical practice. These considerations led to a method which also acknowledges research as dialogic relationship – the interview.

It is probably universally acknowledged that apparently benign events (such as promotion at work, buying a new house, having a longed-for baby) have negative as well as positive consequences for the people involved, even when these events were much desired. We can thus also anticipate that there will be negative as well as positively experienced effects for our respondents attendant on recognised achievement.

It is understood that the 'fame' referred to in this study is 'renown within a small circle of people in a specific field for professional accomplishment of some kind' – a very specific and confined aspect of fame isolated for this study. Whether or how it corresponds psychologically or collectively to the more generalised notion of 'fame' as in the wider type of fame which may involve millions of people from all walks of life may need to be followed up in a future study.

This investigation was commenced with comparatively little literature search in accordance with the suggestion (Denzin and Lincoln, 1994) that the researcher engages with the issue before doing extensive literature search. Furthermore in spite of more than two decades of scholarship and study in these fields, I actually knew of little or nothing about fame in counselling, psychology, psychoanalysis or psychotherapy, with the exception of the 1992 Lingdale Paper by Michael Jacobs. This excellent and considered theoretical paper discussed historiometry, the work of Schiffer on charismatic leadership and the almost symbiotic relationship between the famous and their followers, concluding with an application to therapy of the need for the client to be 'famous for an hour each week' (Jacobs, 1992: 2). A subsequent literature search on this topic turned up an Ellis (1989) paper on 40 plus years of negative experiences with the media, but showed nothing of direct relevance on this topic.

METHOD

Qualitative research

It was judged that a qualitative research method was more suitable to the exploration of this phenomenon because it concerned according to Polkinghorne (1991: 112) the 'generation of categories for understanding human phenomena and the investigation of the interpretation and meaning that people give to events they experience'. It is more preoccupied with relationship, subjectivity, description and discovery than with testing or verifying hypotheses. For a comprehensive review of the issues and methods in the field of qualitative research see Denzin and Lincoln (1994) or Banister, Burman, Parker and Taylor (1994). I will not review their arguments here. Suffice it to say that I drew extensively from these sources in informing, guiding and structuring my investigation.

Selection of respondents

In the country of research there are at least twelve and at most twenty therapists – psychotherapists, psychologists or psychoanalysts – who would be recognisable by name within and perhaps outside the disciplines. However, this recognition or repute would exist even then only for some respondents in certain circles. Given such a small pond from which to obtain data, the criteria for confidentiality would be paramount. It would not be difficult for anyone to guess who had been asked to participate, but who agreed to contribute is essentially the researcher's information alone.

A letter was sent to the possible participants explaining the study and inviting them to interview. After some exchange of telephone calls, arrangements were made to meet and record. Confidentiality and method were explained. Each participant signed a consent to record and publish given that they would see the final manuscript before publication. This would also serve as a kind of 'member check' (Lincoln and Guba, 1985).

Instrumentation

The research would be done to describe the phenomenological experience of the notion of fame and its subjectively judged positive or negative effects on the professional and personal life of the participant. Textual analysis or discourse analysis would not be suitable because of the requirement to protect not only the identity, but also the identifying achievements and the particularly unique and recognisable 'voices' of the participants.

The themes identified would be drawn from the reported experiences of each of these people. The focus would not be on their particular theoretical frameworks, but on common human issues understood in everyday language. In order to elicit these themes, an interview within a dialogic relationship would be used. A dialogic relationship is here defined as one where both subject and researcher are present as human beings engaged in a common quest of exploring the human condition. It acknowledges that 'objectivity' in research has severe limitations, is also fundamentally value laden, and that it is probably impossible when we accept that the observer is always part of the field.

Only seven questions would definitely be asked of all respondents. This is in line with the recommendation of Huberman and Miles (1994: 441) to err in 'the direction of minimally predesigned instrumentation' (p. 441). So the concerns mentioned above were encapsulated in the following seven questions.

The research questions

- What do you understand by the concept of fame?
- What are some of the positive effects which you have experienced as a result of this kind of phenomenon?
- What are some of the negative effects, if any?
- How do you feel it has impacted on your practice as a psychotherapist?
- How do you feel it has impacted on you as a professional *vis-à-vis* your colleagues?
- How has it affected you as a person?
- Is there anything else you would like to add?

Although, in two interviews, I wished I had phrased them slightly differently, I ensured that all participants had an opportunity to answer questions in this form.

Amplification and elaboration of the questions

It was anticipated that as the interview progressed, different questions may become necessary or interesting and that the interviewer and interviewee would prefer to follow the flow of a collegial discussion rather than a strictly structured format. Since our interest was in the phenomenology of this experience, the spontaneous developments of the dialogue would be of equal, if not more, value to the project.

Given as well that the discussion was likely to elicit a train of thought and reflection which would continue for at least the next couple of days, the interview was always followed with a letter thanking the respondent and asking them for further thoughts on their subjective experiences of 'fame'.

Interview protocol

Since the interviewer was known by name, reputation or friendship to all the respondents who participated, the establishment of rapport was easy and comfortable on all occasions although the degree of formality varied with the duration of the previous collegial relationships.

In order to obtain a reasonably uncontaminated description of the experiences the interviewer would (a) prompt with the specific open-ended questions, (b) then follow where they led and (c) only in some instances, to facilitate the conversation. or where it would have been unnatural not to say something, showed empathy by reporting a similar personal experience. As far as possible I would engage in the epoch process of the phenomenological method (Spinelli, 1989), bracketing my own theories and assumptions as I listened to and facilitated their descriptions of their experiences.

It is my conviction that the independence and uniqueness of these individuals and their relationship with me would be sufficiently self-regulating so as to prevent their adapting to or uncritically incorporating any of my personal experiences shared dialogically during the course of the interview. Nonetheless I took care not to lead, but only to reflect a similar experience on occasion to support the flow of the interview or to ask a question about something specific which piqued my curiosity. Several individuals later commented on the fact that they had enjoyed talking about and reflecting on the topic with me in this way.

Data collection

The interview was recorded on audio tape – in some cases with simultaneous secretarial notetaking. The raw data were first expunged of names, identifying details and characteristic speech patterns of the participants. Because these people are precisely those whose characteristic styles of expression, 'voice', history and particular concerns could identify them, discourse analysis was not suitable as a method without potentially disturbing the freedom of the interviewee. The identification of *themes* was the extent of the earliest analysis.

An audit trail was however constructed consisting of raw data (after identity protection checks), data reduction and analysis products, data reconstruction and synthesis products, process notes, materials relating to intentions and dispositions. and instrument development information (Halpern, 1983 in Lincoln and Guba. 1985: 319–320). This was checked at several intervals in consultation with external qualitative research supervisors.

Organising, analysing and synthesising data

According to Polkinghorne (1983: 280), the qualitative researcher of the post-positivist era:

> needs to develop a strategy that will indicate which systems to use and how to use them in a particular investigation. Research results are not obtained merely by using a method correctly. A project must be designed, and design problems are compounded in a science of multiple logics and methodological tools.

An adaptation of Aronson's (1994) pragmatic approach to thematic analysis was devised for this exploration taking into account (a) the enhanced demand for confidentiality because of the very phenomenon under view – enhanced visibility or known-ness; (b) the intention of identifying themes of subjective experience, not number of instances of occurrence: and (c) the fact of a relatively small sample of sixteen – even though it probably represents two-thirds to a half of people in these professions which would impressionistically be described by professionals familiar with all three disciplines concerned (psychologists, psychotherapist and psychoanalysts) as 'well-known'. The value of the study was not intended to get a definitive result, but to get more understanding of the nature and aspects of the experience.

The following series of steps were followed:

1 transcribing of audiotapes with simultaneous editing out for purposes of confidentiality;
2 keeping a research log over the period of transcription which included identifying themes as they emerged;
3 reading through all transcriptions;
4 listing clearly identifiable patterns of experience or theme sets and adding new ones as they became clear;
5 checking through the transcripts for representation of the experiences – perhaps using indication of how many respondents identified issues to do with each identified theme or a simple ranking display;
6 submitting all edited materials to an external research supervisor for inter-rater reliability check on theme identification;
7 submitting edited transcripts and draft of this paper to respondents for them to add further thoughts or feelings;

8 getting an additional interview to make eleven usable protocols or further exploration of 'deviant case' – a respondent whose differences from the others showed up at interview as much more profound than expected on invitation (a discussion of this issue would be too identifying as the problem is too individual);

9 incorporating suggestions of external supervisor;

10 incorporating additions and suggestions of respondents;

11 substituting new protocol or deletion of 'deviant case' and

12 preparing for publication.

It should be noted that the fact that some respondents may not have mentioned a theme does not have to mean that it is not an important theme of their subjective experience for them. It may be (a) that their train of thought (or the interviewer's questions) did not lead in that way on the particular day of interview; (b) there may have been other themes which took up more of the foreground, time and interest of interviewee and interviewer on a particular day; and (c) all respondents had a chance to add their identification or articulation of a theme at the pre-publication check stage. Several respondents mentioned informally that they may have stressed slightly different issues at other times although the general themes appear steady over time.

The result of a first graze of the data was sent to the external qualitative research supervisor and to all respondents with a request to (a) check their own transcript for appropriate deletions or changes to identifying material; (b) read the draft and add further comments to their own response in the light of this if they wish; and (c) make any suggestions for improvement which I could incorporate before finalising the data presentation and preparation for publication.

All demographic and geographical data were deleted. I judged that they nevertheless represented a reasonably good (if not random) spread of gender, seniority, age, orientation and discipline – psychology, psychotherapy and psychoanalysis. The reported effects also cut across scale of achievement and duration of phenomenon affecting the life. Originally I had intended to delete or paraphrase all technical terms which may indicate the kind of approach and so identify the respondent. But the results made this surprisingly unnecessary.

One of the clearest findings of this survey was that respondents from all approaches use a vocabulary which is more shared between approaches than a classical or orthodox vocabulary that is used in similar ways by people of nominally the same orientation. It was simply not the case that because someone used, for example, self-actualising language and someone else transferential signifiers that they were respectively talking from within their professional home base and were thus identifiable by theoretical or professional orientation. So I abandoned this attempt, leaving technical terms present and intact on the whole, if not exploring their individual meanings with the respondent, since no valid inferences whatsoever can be drawn from them as to the identity or approach of the respondent.

I have discussed elsewhere (Clarkson, 1995) this apparent postmodern phenomenon of theoretical, technical and linguistic 'contagion', 'integration' or 'pluralistic co-existence' within *and* between so-called different 'schools' or 'approaches' to psychotherapy, but was somewhat surprised to find it so clearly in this experiment where such a result was both unlooked for and indeed quite unexpected. (Further exploration of this aspect of linguistic discourse analysis could be done in future.) All respondents could identify that there is such a phenomenon as 'being known' to people who know you through your work (in any number of ways) or through the report of others which does happen to psychotherapists, psychologists and psychoanalysts. It could be called fame or renown or reputation.

I had explained that my interest was in a fractal or microscopic experiencing of this phenomenon and that I had chosen psychotherapists/psychoanalysts/psychologists for the first investigation because they were trained to be more self-reflective (natural qualitative researchers?). Even so, most respondents thought that the notion of 'fame' did not quite apply to them since they were not famous on a large scale as certain filmstars, royalty or political leaders may be.

This is an interesting echo of a paper on the sociology of science by Woolgar (1985) which was in the main concerned with 'artificial intelligence'. He found that participants were reluctant to treat their own activities as instances of a particular idealised phenomenon. He reported that when he tried to get access to laboratories to study scientists at work, each laboratory team would without exception say that if he was interested in real science, this really was not the best place to study it. For whatever reason, what they were doing did not actually fit what scientific work really should be. These scientists all said that work being done at some other laboratory by some other scientists would be more suited for exploration.

There seems to be a qualitative difference between different kinds of 'fame', 'renown' or 'eminence'. The media give frequent coverage to people who are famous for being famous. Then there is the kind of 'fame' or position which is the result of accident of birth or marriage or situation (for example a peerage) versus the kind of fame or recognition which comes from 'going about one's business', 'just doing one's work' or learning more (for example a doctorate). These categories of personal and professional may of course overlap and are not mutually exclusive. In the context of this investigation, the researcher was exclusively interested in a population where the recognition followed from some kind of achievement, contribution or recognised public service.

Keeping these qualifications in mind, the findings can be presented under six major headings: the concept of fame; effects on professional life; effects on personal life; effects on clinical practice; effects on work with clients; and coping strategies.

The concept of fame

1 The experienced qualities of 'fame' were identified by *most* respondents as: 'being known' by people who may speak or write to you without a prior direct personal or professional relationship.

2 People who don't have such a direct relationship speak or talk about you – 'They stop speaking to you and start talking about you'.

3 All ordinary communications become endowed with exaggerated positive/ idealised or negative/denigrated properties and associations. In a way there is a distortion of the 'volume and importance' of one's communications.

4 This is usually associated with a sense of loss of control, becoming the object of others' fantasies, others' expectations about which you may not know very much or be able to do very much.

5 All respondents recognised *positive and negative effects* as a result of 'becoming better known'. Ironically, this is experienced in its opposite – subjectively becoming less well known.'The name blinds one to any objective judgement'; 'The name becomes too big [and] they can't see beyond it. . . . They don't see anything but the name'.

6 Most reported an awareness that personal and professional effects were experienced somewhat differently.

Effects on professional life

1 Several respondents mentioned enduring pleasure in the ability to create opportunities for others with ambivalent results: for example, exaggerated envy experienced by the recipients in the face of such enhanced perceived abundance, feelings of obligation and resentment in the recipients, unwillingness to take offered autonomy and responsibility simultaneously with a need to spoil, destroy or critically attack to achieve separation 'so that even that which was good in the past is attacked'.

2 All reported specifically that they had experienced *negative reactions from colleagues* which they felt were envy. It was sometimes equated with jealousy or rivalry or competitiveness, with the home base professional group's reactions usually being the most extremely negative. Examples of what respondents have experienced as envious attacks from colleagues have ranged from malicious pathologising gossip, outright lies, versions of being 'sent to Coventry' (colleagues not speaking to you), anonymous letters attempting to prejudice appointment or honours boards, disparaging one's abilities (e.g. *if* so-and-so is successful or successful in one activity, *then* they can't be a good analyst, a good supervisor, etc.), the apparently malicious causation of misunderstandings with editors and publishers on joint projects.

3 Although it may be seen as another manifestation of what has been described as envy or rivalry in general, a specific aspect mentioned by a few respondents concerned *envy or jealousy among trainees, people one supervises or clients*

whose attacks on the creativity of the therapist/analyst/psychologist could take the form of spoiling the therapy and denigrating the analyst or 'biting the hand that's fed you' rather than 'manifesting their own creativity'.

4 Another aspect mentioned by several respondents who often understood it as a manifestation of envy in colleagues (particularly those close associations to whom one would most naturally look for recognition), was one's achievements being ignored or not mentioned. Archetypal patterns reported in the Bible were quoted: 'A prophet is not without honour except in their own land'. A more prosaic version of this one person reported after a particularly successful achievement was: 'it is as if I had farted and it was better not to draw attention to it'.

Effects on personal life

1 Everyone had experienced some form of depersonalisation, loss of humanity, identity, absence of empathy from others, lack of fit between private and public self, being seen as being invulnerable and without feelings, and everyone had been hurt. 'In a way, you've lost your membership card of the human race'; 'There is a film called *The Invasion of the Body Snatchers.* . . . Yes, it's a film in which some alien thing takes over the body so it kind of looks like you, talks like you, but it isn't you'. Or in another's words, 'You sense that the other person has got a complete travesty of the person you really are'.

2 While the perception of invulnerability grows externally, there is often an increase in anxiety of vulnerability to insidious comments, ethics charges, the sowing of suspicion, inexplicable complications with editors, trainees, colleagues, etc. 'I don't think I am being paranoid, but there is a sense in which I am being watched with people almost hoping that I will "put a foot wrong".' '[I was] at a party when someone *warned* me about me. They didn't know who I was but they were telling me to be careful of this person who was me and of course I encouraged them to talk and then someone identified me and then there was an interesting moment [. . . .] I did not recognise the person [they were talking about].'

3 There seems to be a curve which translates as encouragement in the beginning and then a diminishing return as if only a certain level of achievement can be tolerated before the person must be brought down off the pedestal upon which they had been hoisted. An excessive interest and importance is attached to everything about you so 'you need to be cautious/careful about what you say'. 'Getting caught in thinking "If I say this, then they will think this" and "I must make sure that I don't say something which is going to make them feel inferior".'

4 A different measurement is being used than for 'ordinary people who may have not achieved so much in these particular ways – there is a certain lack of compassion and a definite lack of care to understand or empathise'. They have 'unreal expectations regarding your output, workrate, performance and goals'.

'You are made to feel different and separated from others and subject to different rules.'

5 Several respondents reported loneliness, isolation from colleagues and professional communities and difficulties in achieving peer relationships with past employees or past clients even in spite of the best of intentions and attempts. 'You lose people's empathy – you are seen as invulnerable, not needing love and support.'

Effects on clinical practice

1 Although a small number talked about the positive effects on adjacent aspects of their professional activity (invitations to lecture, fees, etc.) in terms of actual practice there was not a single positive effect.
2 Not all, but most people reported that it affected their practice in some ways. Responses ranged from the response being too large or intrusive to cope with to nothing to worry about.
3 Enhancement of life space, travel, friendship, connections, invitations. More calls for supervision, more clients – 'but people often assume that I am full'. Somewhat enhanced lifestyle and improved income – not as much as the fantasies of others, but distinctive in improvement, freedom and, yes – joy.
4 Increased self-respect and self-esteem, healthy narcissistic gratification. A sense of contribution and value to the community, an historical awareness, a legacy of some kind found in the next generations of the profession and/or literature.
5 Several themes related to the negative aspects of being somehow different or separated from others – aloneness/loneliness/isolation. These related sometimes to the professional and sometimes to the personal domain: 'You are made to feel different/separated from others/subject to different rules, dehumanised.'

Effects on work with clients

1 Vicarious status. Some clients want to come into therapy with you for reasons of status – clients may talk with others about what you do in therapy sessions and you cannot respond – powerlessness. One participant described therapeutic sessions in such circumstances as feeling 'crowded' – some clients may be deprived of privacy if others learn they are seeing a famous therapist. One respondent highlighted that a possible side-effect may be that some clients may find it difficult to believe they are important to you and that your interest in them is genuine.
2 Unrealistic expectations. Clients who are or become familiar with your writing, create expectations about how you will operate in therapeutic sessions. 'On principle, I don't take patients who come to me on the basis of [hearing about my work]. I'm not interested in either the idealisation that leads them into

wanting to come to meet [me] or the disillusion when they find that I'm not like that. They might say for example "On page 94, you said that and now you do this . . . ". It can interfere with the freedom "to be" for both.'

3 Client envy. Clients who want to undermine or destroy you (note the theme of envy resurfacing here but this time client envy) or who just wait for you to slip up. '[One reason why a client might seek therapy] is that she sometimes thinks her own creativity is blocked, so I think she/he is hugely motivated by envy and one way of using the contact here is that instead of actually receiving something from me which might unblock her creativity, she does her best to destroy mine'. This may or may not be linked to the notion of envy or sabotage but – 'I get increasing numbers of difficult clients'.

4 Mixed third-party hearsay effects. Others tell clients things about you which not only compromise therapeutic anonymity, but definitely slant expectations in particular ways positively or negatively. 'One can get hooked into other people's positive evaluation . . . have to be/play the role of a successful therapist.' Most respondents cope with this by proceeding symbolically, as if it's a story, without confirming or denying it. Several confirmed that the need for therapeutic anonymity is a myth.

5 Meetings or encounters with the analyst's work, public appearance, books or organisational position outside of the consulting room can be anticipated or talked through. The patient can, for example, take avoiding action by not watching TV on a particular date/channel. This is not dissimilar in principle to meeting one's analyst in the supermarket or in the office of one's PhD supervisor (Clarkson, 1995).

Coping strategies

1 Everyone had devised ways of coping ranging from 'I just repress it' to considering action for libel, retiring, going shopping.

2 The most common coping strategy was the need to make meaning, to understand their experience in some way by the construction of a narrative or an explanation. Theories ranged from the human need to 'incorporate' the productive/achieving person, the idea that much of what is termed *transference* in British culture may actually equally well be called *admiration* in another culture which does not use shame collectively to punish enthusiasm or achievement. (The investigation of this belongs elsewhere as it is beyond the remit of this present chapter.)

3 Along with this almost everyone mentioned the importance and need for support and friendship which was not predicated on or veiled by one's achievements. There was a need to talk things over with friends (who are not part of the professional world).

4 Several reported the need to 'get away' and/or that they wish they could retire, stop, be released from the pressure or responsibility in some way. 'Having a place you can withdraw to in order to get things into perspective/spend time

alone', thinking about retiring and stepping 'off the bandwagon altogether (but people would want to know why you are not doing it any more and what has gone wrong)' were some of the experiences reported.

5 Other ways of coping with this included: bringing the private self into your public products; realising it's not personal; talking to someone who really knows who you are and can affirm who you are; carrying on being an active member of the home group but do not refer to own ideas; keeping out of the political side of things; toughening yourself; recognising your responsibility; being cautious about the invitations you accept and the proposals you make; and finally, acknowledging a sense of powerlessness – that there's simply not a lot you can do about it.

SUMMARY

Eleven semi-structured interviews were conducted with psychologists, psychoanalysts and psychotherapists who would be considered to be 'well known' or comparatively famous on a microscopic sociological scale, as a result of their achievement or contribution in the field, in order to explore their subjective experience of 'fame' or recognition of their personal and professional lives and their practice.

THE RELATIONSHIP OF STUDY FINDINGS TO FINDINGS OF LITERATURE REVIEW

Given the scarcity of material in the literature review, this may be the first qualitative inquiry or phenomenological investigation into the subjective experience of 'fame', 'renown' or public 'recognition' as it affects the personal and professional lives and practice of psychoanalysts, psychotherapists and psychologists.

The issue under review was not charismatic leadership as in the Jacobs (1992) paper, but some phenomena similar or identical to the symbiotic relationship between the famous and their followers which he described may indeed exist between the 'famous' achievers and the collective in society, professions and therapy.

POSSIBLE FUTURE RESEARCH

This study is merely a small beginning which may or may not hold the seeds for broader generalisations to other populations or to other aspects of the phenomenon of renown. It may be a fractal – a term taken from chaos and complexity theory (Gleick, 1989) which indicates self-similarity across scale. It may contain within its structural characteristics much if not all of the elements or have at least a similar shape to other experiences on a larger or smaller scale. The uniformity of results suggests universality. However a much larger sample will be required to make extensive generalisations.

Some of the future research studies which may follow are:

- A phenomenological exploration of a group discussion where respondents meet each other to share and contrast their individual subjective experiences and coping mechanisms.
- A replication study of the original group of respondents in five or ten years time.
- A replication study in another country.
- A replication study over several countries.
- A replication study of different professional groups, e.g. high achievers in sports, literature, the media, politics or business.
- Construct theory explorations.
- A similar study with respondents who would have experience of this phenomenon on a much larger scale, i.e. being known to millions of strangers through film or TV.
- A similar study with respondents who have experienced this phenomenon for longer periods (say twenty or thirty years) compared with respondents new to this experience.
- The study of fluctuations in this experience over time. This could be based on the one above.
- A phenomenological investigation of a group of people specifically brought together because of their interest in some 'famous' person such as an Elvis Presley fan club.
- A phenomenological exploration of infamy – repute based on notoriety or crime – for example the attraction of certain kinds of murderers for certain people.
- An exploration of gender differences in the subjective and objective experience and management of the positive and negative effects of fame.
- A theoretical exploration of the group dynamics of the exceptionally achieving individual and the collective response particularly in relation to the dynamics of envy and gratitude.
- An archetypal exploration of the group dynamics of the exceptionally achieving individual and the collective response.
- A theoretical exploration of the phenomenological self-concept structures or experiences of the vicissitudes of vicarious self-esteem or self-denigration.
- A theoretical exploration of the original concept which I have termed 'third-party transference' to discover more about its nature and management.
- The development of individual textural and structural descriptions; composite textural and composite structural descriptions and a synthesis of textural and structural meanings.
- A comparison between individuals' intrapsychic ambivalence about their own creative achievements and society's ambivalence towards creatively achieving individuals in their midst.

PERSONAL OUTCOMES

Personally I have learned a great deal from these focused conversations with professional people all of whom I respect and admire. This is in the face of the fact that I have overheard positive appreciation as well as negative disparaging attacks on their integrity or their reputations on several occasions. I am personally and professionally concerned with the attempt to transform such negative gossip about achievers in society into a spur for everyone to fulfil their own dreams rather than spoil those of others.

I have developed a range of ways of coping with these kinds of events which I plan to publish in a forthcoming paper and which are also outlined in an unpublished paper on the management of gossip in organisations (Clarkson and Sunderland, 1992). My understanding emotionally and intellectually is greatly enhanced and my compassion for the human dilemma even more sensitised.

THE RELATIONSHIP OF THE STUDY TO PROFESSIONAL OUTCOMES

I undertook this study partly to review and relearn qualitative research methodology under the guidance of competent qualitative research supervisors. I have thoughtfully read quite a large number of works in this field, only some of which are referenced in this chapter. Also, having had the opportunity to think and work through a live issue for me as a person and a professional in the field, this study has been lively, interesting and challenging at every step. I hope that in addition to my previous experiences of quantitative (my Master's and Doctorate) as well as qualitative research (see Chapters 5 and 13 in this book and Clarkson and Aviram, 1995), it will help me to be a better and more helpful supervisor of others engaged in research – but particularly those grappling with the peculiar idiosyncrasies, satisfactions and demands of qualitative inquiry and methodology.

RELATIONSHIP OF STUDY TO SOCIAL MEANINGS AND RELEVANCE

I am concerned with the care and nurturance of the creative capacity in every individual and the care and nurturance of individuals who constellate this capacity in groups and organisations and our world as a whole. I think that understanding leads to greater empathy with others with different experiences from our own and to greater tolerance. I would like to hope that this can reduce the confusion, pain, cruelty, scapegoating and distress in our world (whether we call it evil, Thanatos, envy or some kind of 'ism'). It is also my current belief that the more every person can connect with the creative, unique and life-enhancing drive in themselves (however it may be defined by temperament, culture or history) the more these capacities can grow in individuals as well as in the collective we call organisations or 'society'. Heraclitus called this drive *Physis* (Guerrière, 1980).

FUTURE DIRECTION AND GOALS

I imagine that I will be engaged in some aspect of this study for the rest of my life. At this stage I envisage at least an annual paper, updating and expanding as well as taking into account feedback, criticisms and contributions of colleagues and research respondents, world events and the meanderings of my own experiences. I intend it as an ongoing conversation. I would very much like others – students or colleagues – to work with me on aspects of this theme if it interests them, because the job is clearly too big for one – or even a few – people. The world needs all of us.

REFERENCES

Aronson. J. A. (1994) Pragmatic view of thematic analysis, in *The Qualitative Report* 2 (1): 1–2.

Banister, P., Burman, E., Parker, I., Taylor, M. and Tindall, C. (1994) *Qualitative Methods in Psychology: A Research Guide*, Buckingham: Open University Press.

Clarkson. P. (1995) *The Therapeutic Relationship*, London: Whurr.

Clarkson. P. and Sunderland. M. (1992) *The Management of Gossip in Organisations*. Unpublished paper.

Denzin, N. K. and Lincoln. Y. S. (eds) (1994) *Handbook of Qualitative Research*, London: Sage.

Ellis. A. (1989) Four decades of experience with the media, *Journal for Psychotherapy in Private Practice* 7 (1): 47–55.

Gleick. J. (1989) *Chaos: Making a New Science*, London: Heinemann.

Guerrière, D. (1980) Physis, Sophia, Psyche, in J. Sallis and K. Maly (eds) *Heraclitean Fragments: A Companion Volume to the Heidegger/Fink Seminar on Heraclitus* (pp. 87–134), Tuscaloosa, AL: University of Alabama Press.

Huberman, A. M. and Miles. M. B. (1994) Data management and analysis methods. In N. K. Denzin and Y. S. Lincoln (eds) *Handbook of Qualitative Research* (pp. 428–444), London: Sage.

Jacobs. M. (1992) *The Significance of Fame for the Famous and for Those who Make Them So* (Frank Lake Memorial Lecture), Lingdale Paper 20, Oxford: Clinical Theology Association/Bocardo Press.

Lincoln. Y. S. and Guba, E. G. (1985) *Naturalistic Inquiry*, Beverly Hills, CA: Sage.

Murray. D. (1986) One writer's secrets, *College Composition and Communication* 37: 146–153.

Onions. C. T. (ed.) (1973) *The Shorter Oxford English Dictionary: On Historical Principles*, Vol. 2, Oxford: Clarendon Press.

Polkinghorne, D. (1983) *Methodology for the Human Sciences, Systems of Inquiry*, Albany, NY: State University of New York Press.

Polkinghorne, D. E. (1991) Two conflicting calls for methodological reform, *The Counseling Psychologist* 19: 103–114.

Spinelli. E. (1989) *The Interpreted World, An Introduction to Phenomenological Psychology*, London: Sage.

Woolgar. S. (1985) Why not a sociology of machines? The case of sociology and artificial intelligence, *Sociology* 19 (4): 557–572.

Name Index

Aanstoos, C.M. 276, 297
Acharyya, S. 101, 117
Acker, J. 61, 72
Adams, T. 95, 101, 117
Addington-Hall, J. 132
Aitken, G. 169, 173
Alexander, L. 239, 241
Amudson, J. 129, 133
Anderson, H. 238, 240
Anderson, W.T. 90, 91, 92, 248, 256–9
  passim, 270
Angelo, M. xi, 20, 21, 26, 33, 35, 95, 260
Ani, M. 115, 117
Arborelius, E. 126, 131
Argyris, C. 165, 173
Arnkoff, D.B. 233, 240, 246, 270, 271
Aronson, E. 39–42 passim, 45, 51, 54
Aronson, J.A. 313, 323
Aronson, J.T. 81, 92
Arrenondo, P. 118
Asen, K. 132
Astington, J.W. 184, 187
Atkinson, J.M. 212–18 passim
Atkinson, P. 60, 72
Avens, R. 21, 35
Aviram, O. xi, 322, 323

Bakhtin, M. xvi, 213, 217
Balint, M. 125, 131
Ballachey, W.L. 114, 117
Bamberger, J. 77, 92, 249, 270
Bandler, R. 14
Banister, P. 81, 83, 92, 115, 117, 310,
  323
Barker, C. xvi, xvii, 104, 117
Barkham, M. 13, 14, 301, 306
Barry, K. 61, 72
Barthes, R. 213, 219

Bartlett, F.C. 27, 36
Bateson, G. 79, 93, 250, 270
Bauman, Z. 90, 93, 258, 270
Bayes, M. 238, 240
Beck, A.T. 294, 297
Bellinger, N. 123, 132
Berelson, B. 199, 203
Berg, D.N. 158, 173
Bergin, A.E. 239, 240
Berkowitz, P. 306
Berman, S. 128, 131
Bernard, J.M. 275, 297
Beutler, L.E. 189, 192, 246, 270
Billig, M. 214, 217, 219
Blacker, C.V.R. 119, 131
Blackmon, B. 118
Blakey, R. 124, 131
Bloch, S. 145, 146, 148, 155
Blocher, D.H. 282, 297
Bolton, N. 226, 230
Bond, F.W. xi, 37, 45, 54
Boot, D. 119, 122, 123, 131
Bor, R. xi–xii, 80, 93, 125–31 passim,
  251, 270, 276, 297, 303, 305
Boradori, G. 304
Borders, L.D. 189, 192
Borkovec, T.D. 46, 54
Boscolo, L. 132
Boulton, M. 195, 198
Brady, K. 14
Brannen, J. 71, 72
Bray, D. xii, 180, 199–203
Breakwell, G.M. 58, 59, 72, 124, 131
Breese, J. 299
Bremberg, S. 126, 131
Brenner, M. 59, 72
Brennman, D. 132
Breuer, J. 303

Brewer. J. 199, 203
Brody. N. 235, 241, 272
Brown. A.C. 119, 132
Brown. L.M. 57, 72
Brown. S.D. 30, 36
Bryman. A. 56, 65, 72, 182, 187
Burman. E. 92, 115, 117, 169, 173, 310, 323
Burnard. P. 70, 72
Burns. J. 169, 173
Butler. S.F. 193
Buyers. C. 38, 55

Cameron. W. 298, 306
Campbell. T.L. 127, 131
Canter. R. 54
Carlsmith. J.M. 39–42 passim, 45, 51, 54
Carroll. M. 1, 2–3, 14, 274, 275, 283, 297
Carter. J.A. 15
Casas. J.M. 238, 241
Cecchin. G. 132
Charmaz. C. 185, 187, 206, 210
Chatterjee. S.G. 95
Cheng. E. 170
Christensen. L.B. 185, 187
Christoph-Lemke. C. 85, 93
Clandinin. D.J. 79, 93, 249, 270, 300, 305
Clare. A.W. 119, 131
Clark. D.M. 49, 55
Clark. T. 54
Clarkson. P. xi, 5,6, 11, 14, 20, 26, 27, 30, 32, 36, 76, 79, 80, 90, 93, 97, 100, 112, 117, 231, 237–40 passim, 245, 250–3 passim, 256, 258–60 passim, 270–1, 275, 293, 297, 302, 303, 306, 315, 319, 322, 323
Cohen. M. 239, 241
Cole. P.M. 298
Connelly. F.M. 79, 93, 249, 270, 300, 305
Considine. M. 14
Conte. H.R. 305, 307
Coolican. H. 194, 198
Cooper. B. 119, 132
Cooper. J. 39–42 passim, 45, 47, 51, 54
Corbin. J. 204, 207, 209–11 passim, 214, 219
Corney. R. 119, 122, 130, 131
Cornford. F.M. 230
Corsini. R. 14, 74, 93, 242, 271
Costall. A. 226, 230
Cowie. H. xii, 30, 180, 194, 198

Coyle, A. xii, 56, 60, 72
Cremona, R. 95
Cristol, A.H. 235, 241
Crits-Cristoph, P. 239, 241
Crossley, D. 122, 123, 131
Crouch, E. 145–8 passim, 155
Crutchfield, R.S. 114, 117
Cummings, A.L. 189, 192
Cunningham, I. 163, 173

Dabbs, J.M. 175
Dammers, J. 119, 132
Dann, S. 194, 198
D'Ardenne, P. 99–101 passim, 117
Dell, D.M. 298, 306
Denzin, N.K. 75, 93, 98, 117, 182, 187, 210, 244, 247, 250, 251, 258, 271, 310, 323
Derrida, J. 213
De Saussure, F. 213
Dickerson, P. xii, 181, 212–18, 219
Didsbury, P. 232, 233, 240
Doherty, W. 127, 128, 131, 132
Donaldson, M. 185, 187
Drew, P. 212, 215, 219
Dryden, W. xii, xv, xvii, 14, 37, 45, 49, 54, 96, 118, 231, 236, 240, 241, 297
Duffy, M. 14
Dukes, S. 132
Dye, H.A. 299
Dym, B. 128, 131

Earll, L. 122, 131
East, P. 120, 122, 125, 127, 130, 131
Eckhartsberg, R.V. 20, 36
Egan, G. 70, 72
Eisner, E.W. 87, 93
Elden, M. 165–7, 173
Eleftheriadou, Z. 95, 97, 101, 117, 238, 240
Elliott, R. xvi, xvii, 104, 117
Ellis, A. 310, 323
Ellis, M.V. 273–5, 282, 298, 306
Elton Wilson, J. 13, 14, 301, 306
Emery, G. 294, 297
Enright, J. 165, 173
Esseveld, J. 60–1, 72

Fahey, T. 131
Fairclough, N. 212, 218, 219
Farrell, B.A. 93, 97, 117, 243, 246, 271, 296–7, 298
Faulkner, R.R. 175

Feldman, M.S. 32, 36
Fenelon, J. 131
Ferguson, J. 49, 54
Fernando, S. 102, 117
Fiedler, F.E. 10, 14
Finch, J. 57, 72, 169, 173
Fletcher, J. 121, 131
Fong, M.L. 189, 192
Forward, J. 43, 48, 54
Foucault, M. 213, 219, 247, 294
Foulkes, S.H. 137, 143
Fowler, R. 212, 213, 218, 219
Fox, W. 172, 173
Frank, J.D. 239, 240
Fransella, F. 165, 173
Freedman, A.M. 4, 14
Freedman, J.L. 39, 40, 45, 51, 54
Freeling, P. 132
Freeman, E.M. 118
French, J.R.P. 36
Freud, A. 194, 198
Freud, S. 10, 167, 238, 275, 303
Friedman, W.H. 145, 155

Gale, J. 205, 210
Garcia Lorca, F. 305, 306
Gask, L. 126, 132
Gaskins, S. 232, 240
Gawinski, G. 132
Geller, D.M. 41–5 passim, 48–51 passim, 54
Gelso, C.J. 15
Gergen, K.J. 26, 36, 56, 72, 77, 81, 86, 89, 93, 205, 210, 213, 218, 219, 238, 241, 248, 249, 258, 271, 302–6 passim
Gergen, M.M. 77, 81, 86, 93, 238, 240, 248, 249, 258, 271
Gill, C. 126, 132
Gillett, G. 184, 187
Gillies, P. 131
Gilligan, C. 57, 72
Glachan, M. xii, 179, 181, 182–8, 220
Glaser, B.G. 57, 72, 185, 187, 204–10 passim
Glass, C.G. 233, 240, 246, 270, 271
Gleick, J. 320, 323
Gloger-Tippelt, G. 306
Gold, J.R. 272
Goldberg, C. 189, 192
Goldberg, D. 132
Goldfried, M.R. 9–10, 15, 74, 93, 239, 241, 242, 272
Goldman, E. 125, 129, 131

Gomes, M. 160, 173
Good, A.M.C. 61, 72
Good, G.E. 298
Goolishan, H. 238, 240
Graham, H. 121, 125, 129, 132
Gray, D.P. 120, 132
Gray, P. 131
Green, A. 186, 187
Greenberg, L.S. 276, 283, 298, 299, 303, 306
Greenberg, R.L. 294, 297
Greenwood, J.D. 40, 45, 51, 54
Griffiths, T. 122, 133
Grinder, J. 14
Grof, C. 162, 174
Grof, S. 162, 174
Guba, E.G. 79–80, 87, 93, 158, 174, 183, 186, 188, 210, 211, 227, 250, 251, 271, 311, 313, 323
Guernina, Z. 1
Guerrière, D. 322, 323
Guy, J.D. 189, 193

Hall, B. 165, 174
Hallberg, E.T. 192
Halpern, E.S. 313
Hammersley, M. 60, 72, 247, 271
Hampden-Turner, C. 165, 174
Handy, C. 21, 36
Hants, A.C. 304, 306
Hare-Mustin, R.T. 238, 240
Hariman, R. 304, 306
Harmon, G. 95
Harp, J. 132
Harre, R. 184, 187, 226, 230
Harris, P.L. 187
Harrison, R. 170, 174
Hartle, J. 257
Harvey, J.H. 58, 72
Haslam, D. 260
Hatch, M.J. 32, 36
Hawking, S. 257, 271
Hawkins, P. 34, 36, 168–74 passim, 274, 298
Heibett, R. 192
Heidegger, M. 228, 230
Helman, C.G. 97, 117
Helms, J.E. 115, 117
Henwood, K.L. 57, 72, 73, 186, 187, 204–6 passim, 210, 211
Heppner, P.P. 282, 298
Hepworth, J. 128, 132
Heritage, J. 212–19 passim

Heron. J. 160–2 *passim*, 167, 170, 174
Herth. K. 59, 72
Hess. A. 282, 298
Hicks. C. 273, 298
Higgs. R. 119, 132
Hill. C.E. 239, 241
Hillman. J. 28, 31, 34, 36
Hinshelwood, R.D. 76, 93, 245, 271, 303, 306
Hirschkop. K. xvi, xvii
Hobson. R. 194, 198
Holloway. E. 112, 117, 273, 274, 298
Holmes. J. 5, 15
Holsti. O. 199, 203
Hoshmand, L. 78, 93
Howe. A. 126, 132
Howell. D.C. 200, 203
Howell. E. 238, 240
Huberman, A.M. 76, 80, 93, 272, 311, 323
Hughes. T. 27, 36
Hunt. P. 274, 298
Hunter. A. 199, 203
Hurd. J. 127, 132
Husserl. E. 276, 303
Hutcheon. L. 90, 93, 258, 271
Hutt. C.H. 282, 298
Hylton. B. 49, 54
Hynan. M.T. 239, 240

Inskip. F. 282, 299
Irving. J. 125, 127, 132

Jacobs. M. 310, 320, 323
Jaffe. D.T. 170–1, 174
Jameson. F. 298
Jenkins. R. 119, 122, 130, 131
Joba. C. 171, 174
Johnson. D.L. 298
Johnson. M. 95
Johnston. M. 132
Jones. E. 303, 306
Jung. C.G. 238

Kalton. G.W. 119, 132
Kamuf. P. 213, 219
Kanner. A.A. 160, 173
Kaplan. H.I. 4, 14
Karasu. T.B. 9, 15, 305, 307
Kareem. J. 101, 117
Kaye. J. 26, 36, 218, 219
Kazdin. A.E. 185, 188
Keen. E. 276, 277, 283, 298

Kelly, G. 15
Kelman, H.C. 43, 54
Kendall, J. 95
Kenney, G.E. 96–7, 117
Kessel, F.S. 276, 298
Kessen, W. 301–2, 306
Keter, V. 95
Kierkegaard, S. 304
Kiesler, D.J. 274, 298
Kilmann, R.H. 173, 174
Kincey, J. 122, 131
King, E. 61, 72
King, M. 298
Kirk, J. 81, 93
Kirsch, N. 54
Kivlighan, D.M. 189, 192
Klineberg, O. 100, 117
Kofler, L. 95
Kohut, H. 10, 15
Koluchova, J. 194, 198
Kopta, S.M. 305, 306
Krasner, L. 305, 306
Krech, D. 114, 117
Krippendorf, K. 199, 203
Krueger, R.A. 64, 72
Kuhn, T.S. 9, 15, 157, 174
Kuiken, D. 276, 278, 298, 303, 306
Kvale, S. 75, 77, 85, 89, 93, 249, 257, 271, 301, 306

Lago, C. 116–17, 118
Lambert, M.J. 233, 239, 240, 246, 271
Langenhove, L.V. 230
Langer, S. 228, 230
Laplanche, J. 15
Laver, R. 195, 198
Lazarus, M. 132
Lazarus, R.S. 49, 55
Lee, R.M. 57, 58, 71, 72
Lee-Borden, N. 298
Le Guin, U. 300
Lent, R.W. 30, 36
Light, P. 185, 188
Lincoln, Y.S. 75, 79–80, 87, 93, 98, 117, 158, 174, 182, 183, 186, 187, 188, 210, 211, 227, 244, 247, 250, 251, 258, 271, 310–13 *passim*, 323
Lindley, R. 5, 15
Littlewood, R. 97, 101, 117, 118
Littrell, J.M. 275, 298
Logan, S.L. 118
Lorenz, J. 298
Loughly, J. 15

Lowenstein, L.F. 101, 118
Luborsky, L. 239, 241
Lyotard, J.-F. 301, 306

Macaskill, A. 189, 193
Macaskill, N. 189, 193
McCaul, E.J. 114, 118
McClelland, S. 160, 174
McDaniel, S. 128, 132
McDavis, R.J. 118
MacDevitt, J.W. 189, 193
McGovern, M.P. 305, 306
McGrath, G. 132
Machado, P.P.P. 192
McLeod, J. 96, 118, 127, 132, 273, 299
McNamee, S. 57, 72, 238, 241
McRoy, R.G. 112, 118
McTeague, S. 49, 54
McWilliam, J. 131
Magritte, R. 213
Mahoney, M.J. 233, 241, 246, 271
Mahtani, A. 99–101 passim, 117
Mair, M. 29, 36
Mandela, N. 308
Mandelbrot, B.B. 242, 272
Maquet, J. 115–16, 118
Marcel, G. 92, 93
Marcus, G.E. 84–5, 93
Margolis, M. 239, 241
Marken, M. 274, 298
Markoff, J. 199, 203
Markus, A.C. 128, 132
Marrett, V. 241
Martin, J. 32, 36, 192
Maruyama, M. 167, 174
Maslow, A.H. 276, 298
Massarik, F. 59, 72
Mattinson, J. 274, 298
May, R. 160, 174
Mayer, R. 132
Maynard, A. 125, 132
Maynard, H.B. 171, 174
Mead, G. 19, 36
Meade, M. 169, 174
Mearns, D. 283, 298
Mendelson, M. 194, 198
Merleau-Ponty, M. 91, 93, 249, 272
Messer, S.B. 305, 306
Mies, M. 169, 174
Miles, M.B. 76, 80, 93, 272, 311, 323
Milgram, S. 44–5, 54
Millar, T. 132
Miller, A.G. 34, 40–7 passim, 51, 53, 55

Miller, M.C. 81, 93
Miller, R. 125–31 passim
Miranda, J. 38, 55
Missar, C.D. 193, 233, 241, 246, 271
Mitroff, I.I. 173, 174
Mixon, D. 40, 41, 44–5, 49, 51, 55
Moorhouse, S. 101, 117, 118
Moran, J. xii–xiii, 24, 36, 181, 222–9
Moreno, J.L. 275
Morris, P. 213, 219
Morson, G.S. 213, 219
Moustakas, C. 75, 93, 98, 118, 244, 260, 272
Mowbray, R. 243, 272
Munt, S. 275, 298
Murdock, M. 235, 241, 272
Murray, D. 309, 323
Myers, M.P. 122, 123, 131

Nadirshaw, Z. 95–7 passim, 102–3, 108, 118, 238, 241
Nelson-Jones, R. 58, 64, 73
Neufeldt, S.A. 192
Newman, C.F. 233, 241, 246, 272
Newman, F.L. 305, 306
Newnes, C. 98, 118, 237, 241
Newton, R.R. 90, 94, 258, 272
Nicolson, P. 61, 73
Niemeyer, G.J. 192
Nippoda, Y. xiii, 100, 118
Norcross, J.C. 5, 9–10, 15, 74, 93, 189, 193, 233, 239, 241, 242, 246, 271, 272, 305, 306

Oakley, A. 59, 60, 67, 73, 169, 174
O'Callaghan, J. xiii, 180, 204–10
Oerter, R. 111, 118
Olson, D.R. 187
O'Malley, S.S. 239, 241
Onions, C.T. 1, 15, 308, 323
Orbuch, T.L. 58, 72
Orford, J. 307
Orne, M.T. 40, 42, 48

Palazzoli, M.S. 129, 132
Papadopoulos, L. xiii
Paris, G. 24–5, 36
Parker, I. 92, 115, 117, 310, 323
Parkes, M.C. 132
Pauli, R. xiii, 180, 199–203
Pavlov, I.P. 275, 303
Paykel, E. 119, 132
Payne, M. 274, 298

Penrose. R. 224, 230
Pepinster. C. 304, 307
Persons. J.B. 38, 55
Phillips. J.R. 211
Phoenix. A. 169–70, 174
Pickard. E. 2, 14
Pidgeon. N.F. 57, 72, 73, 186, 187,
    204–6 passim, 210, 211
Pistrang. N. xvi, xvii, 104, 117
Pitts. J. 119, 133
Plutchik. R. 305, 307
Pokorny. M. 6
Polkinghorne, D.E. 12, 15, 20, 32, 36, 74,
    75, 78, 93, 98, 118, 226, 230, 238, 241,
    243, 272, 310, 313, 323
Polyani. M. 224, 230
Pontalis. J.B. 15
Pontoretto. J. 238, 241
Potter. J. 56, 73, 213, 219
Prata. G. 132
Prioleau. L. 235, 241, 272
Prochaska. J.O. 233, 241, 246, 271
Proctor. B. 15, 282, 299
Prosch. H. 230

Quartaro. G.K. 211

Ralph. N. 189–91, 193, 200, 201
Raven. B.M. 36
Ray. M. 171, 174
Reason. P. 34, 36, 157–60 passim,
    167–74 passim, 301, 307
Rennie. D.L. 205–7 passim, 211
Renzetti. C.M. 57, 72
Reubin. R. 131
Ribeiro. J.P. xiii, 155, 156
Richardson. L. 79, 80, 94, 250, 272, 302,
    307
Ricour. P. 227, 230
Rilke. R.M. 242, 272
Roberts. H. 59, 73
Robinson. D.N. 276, 299
Robson. C. 195, 198
Roehlke. H.J. 282, 298
Rogers. C. 15, 58, 73, 238, 288, 294, 299
Romanyshyn, R.D. 223, 230
Romney. A.K. 202, 203
Ronnestad, M.H. 191, 193
Rosenthal, R. 43, 55, 185, 188
Rosnow. R.L. 43, 55
Rosser. C.L. 193
Rowan. J. xiii, 157, 160, 162, 165, 174,
    301, 307

Rowland, N. 125–7 passim, 132
Rudduck, J. 194, 198
Rudestam, K.E. 90, 94, 258, 272
Russell, R. 235, 241

Salm, A. xiv, 30, 179–81 passim, 194–8,
    204, 206–7, 220–1
Salmon, P. 123, 132
Sampson, E.E. 212, 213, 218, 219
Samuels, A. 243, 256–7, 272
Sanders, P. 276, 299
Sanford, N. 165, 174
Sartre, J.P. 162
Scheuffgen, K. 95
Schiffer, I. 310
Schön, D.A. 77, 92, 249, 270
Schopflocher, D. 298, 306
Schwankovsky, L.P. 119, 133
Scott, C.D. 170–1, 174
Scott, J. 298
Seaburn, D. 125, 128, 132
Seligman, M.E.P. 235, 241, 246, 272
Senior, R. 128, 132
Settle, S.E. 238, 241
Shadock, B.J. 4, 14
Shapiro, G. 199, 203
Sharma, N. 123, 132
Shelef, L.O. 75, 77, 86, 94, 249, 258,
    272
Shepherd, D. xvi, xvii
Shepherd, M. 119, 132
Sheppard, J. 127, 132
Shields, C. 132
Shohet, R. 274, 298
Shotter, J. 77, 83, 89, 94, 213, 217, 219
Sibbald, B. 124, 132
Silverman, D. 212, 217–19 passim
Sinclair, J. 124, 131
Sitkin, S.B. 32, 36
Skinner, B.F. 39, 55, 238
Skovholt, T.M. 191, 193
Slemon, A. 192
Slipp, S. 156
Sloane, R.B. 235, 241
Smith, C.A. 49, 55
Smith, E.M.J. 101, 118
Smith, J.A. 226, 230
Smith, K.K. 158, 173
Smith, P.B. 156
Smith, P.K. 195, 198
Sociarides, G. 246
Spinelli, E. 256, 272, 276, 299, 303, 307,
    312, 323

Stanley. L. 60, 73
Staples. R.F. 235, 241
Steier. F. 94, 272
Stenack, R.J. 299
Stewart. K. 129, 133
Still. A. 226, 230
Stopa. L. 49, 55
Strauss. A.L. 57, 72, 78, 85, 94, 185, 187, 204–11 passim, 214, 219
Strausser-Kirtland. D.J. 193
Stricker, G. 272
Strupp. H.H. 189, 193, 239, 241
Sue. D.W. 118
Suh. C.S. 239, 241
Sunderland, M. 322, 323
Sutter, J.A. 114, 118
Symington, N. 294, 299

Taijfel. H. 114, 118
Tarcher, J. 174
Tart, C.T. 160, 174
Taylor. M. 92, 115, 117, 310. 323
Taylor. R. 124, 131
Taylor. S.E. 120, 133
Thomas. L. 99, 101, 118
Thompson, S.C. 119, 133
Thorne. B. 297
Thurnberg, L. 230
Tichenor. V. 239, 241
Tindall. C. 92, 115, 117, 323
Tomson. P. 132
Traylen. H. 170, 174
Trepka. C. 122, 133
Truax. C.B. 146

Valentine, L. 129, 133
Valori. R. 123, 132
Van Dijk. T.A. 238, 241
Van Maanen, J. 157, 175
Victor. B.J. 233, 240, 246, 270, 271

Von Glaserfeld, E. 244, 272

Wahl, B. 263–4
Walker, R. 157, 175
Waseem, A. 119, 133
Watkins, J.G. 4, 15
Watts, M. 80, 93, 251, 270, 276, 297, 303, 305
Waxman, D. 132
Waydenfield, D. 121, 133
Waydenfield, S.W. 121, 133
Weber, A.L. 58, 72
Weitman, S. 199, 203
Weller, S. 202, 203
Wellman, H.M. 184, 188
Wells, K. 194, 198
Wertz, F.J. 247, 272
Wetherell, M. 56, 73, 213, 219
Wheeler, S. 189, 193, 273, 298, 299
Whipple, K. 235, 241
Whiteman, J.H.M. 160, 175
Widiger, T.A. 238, 241
Wilber, K. 158, 175
Wilkins, M. 131
Wilkinson, G. 122, 123, 131
Wilkinson, S. 169, 175
Wilson, K. 120, 133
Wilson, S. 120, 133
Wise, S. 60, 73, 182, 188
Wolman, B.B. 4, 15
Wood, D. 125, 133
Wooffitt, R. 212, 217, 219
Woolfe, R. 96, 118, 231, 232, 241
Woolgar, S. 315, 323
Worthington, E.L. Jnr 299
Wright, C.M. 61, 73

Yalom, I.D. 146, 156
Yin, R. 195, 197, 198
Yorkston, N.J. 235, 241

Subject Index

acceptance 139–48, 152–3
access to training 8–9, 216
Accreditation of Prior Experiential
  Learning (APEL) 8
active roles 41–5, 48–50
agreement 161
ahistoricity 11–12
alienation 162–8
alignment 170
altered states 160–2, 167
analysis: changing process 151–5; content
  137–8, 180, 199–203; correspondence
  202; data 64, 105, 180, 199–203;
  discourse 81–4, 181, 212–18, 256–7;
  heuristic 259–60; learning by inquiry
  259–60; procedures 207–10;
  self-supervision 295–6; session
  contents 137–8; stories 22–4;
  strategies 207–10; thematic 81–4,
  313–15
anxiety 46, 139–50, 151–2: finding
  course placements 216
applied psychologists 1–4
attunement 170
Axial Coding 209

balance 170; qualitative and quantitative
  182–7
behaviour 2; physicians influencing 126;
  predictions 40–1
beliefs: affecting internal events 38–46;
  manipulating 38–41; rational and
  irrational 45–6
bias 61, 66–7; see also prejudice
British Association for Counselling
  (BAC) 4
British Psychological Society (BPS):
  Counselling Psychological Diploma

Examination 231–2; Counselling
  Psychology Division xv, 2–3, 231

case studies 194–8
categories 199–201; core 209
catharsis 138–50, 153
causal relationships 37–54
changing: conditions 146; process 151–5
characteristics: clients 5; counselling
  psychologists 3
chartered psychology qualifications 2,
  7–8, 231–40
clichés 24
client characteristics 5
clinical psychologists 2
co-creation 171
code of ethics 9
coding 204, 207–9
Cohen's Kappa 200
collaborative research 159, 160, 165–8
commonality 110–11
comparisons 208–9
competence 189; issues 113;
  self-supervision 296
consciousness: altered states 160–2, 167;
  four levels 158–60; planetary 172
conservatism 9
constructionism 212–18
constructivism 222
consultancy: stories in 23, 28–30
content analysis 137–8; qualitative data
  180, 199–203
contextuality, cultural 11–12
conventional norms 173
coping strategies 319–20
core categories 209
corrective emotional experience 139–48,
  153

correspondence analysis 202
counselling 3; definition 4; interviews
57–71; *see also* counselling psychology
Counselling in Primary Care Trust 125
counselling psychologists 2–4; selection
7–9
counselling psychology xv–xvii;
comparison with counselling 3, 5–6;
comparison with psychotherapy 5–6;
cross-cultural issues 95–117;
definitions 1–6; future 6–13;
interviews in research 56–71;
organisational 19–35; practice 11–12;
primary health care 119–31;
professionalism 6–9; qualitative
research 56–71, 182–7; quantitative
research 182–7; research 12–13;
theory 9–11; therapeutic relationship
74–92; *see also* counselling,
psychology
counsellors 3,4; liaison with other
professionals 120–2
counter norms 173
cover stories 43, 47; pro-social 47
creativity 11, 172
Critical Realism 222–3
cultures 11–12, 29–30; concepts 100–3;
in groups 138, 143, 145, 154; issues in
practice 95–117; literature 100–3;
research 103–17; training omissions
238–9
cure factors 145–6
Cure Helping Agents 145
Cure Psychodynamic Mechanisms 145
cycle: research 162–8

data analysis 64, 105, 180, 199–203;
coding 207–9; quantitative methods
103
debriefing 59
deconstruction 9–10
definitions: learning by inquiry 261–7
dependency 126
dialogue 91, 225, 249
Dierotao programme 242–70
differences, individual 110–11
discourse analysis 81–4, 181, 212–18,
256–7
distressed interviewees 57–9, 71

education *see* training
emotional involvement 42–3, 46
emotional level 33

emotions 38; positive 111
empathy 65–6
empowerment 170–1
enactment *see* role enactment
energy streaming 161
enrichment 111
epistemological values of therapists
305
Eros 181, 222–9
errors 112
ethics xvi; code 9; interviews 70–1
ethnic minorities *see* cultures
European *utamawazo* 116
evaluation: by general practitioners 124;
of findings 209–10; primary care
treatment 122–5
exclusion criteria 47–8
experimental realism 42
experimenter intent 43
experiments: internal events 37–54;
involved participation 41–4, 52–3;
problems 40–1; realism 42–3, 46; role
enactment 37–54; using 38–9; validity
41–51
explanation 146–7, 152–3
external validity 41–9; maximising 45–8

fame: clients 318–19; clinical practice
318; concept 316; coping strategies
319–20; definitions 308, 309–10; future
research 320–1; personal life 317–18;
professional life 316–17; psychology
of 308–23
Family Health Service Authorities
(FHSAs) 130
family therapy 127–9
feelings: inferiority 114; reflecting 58;
structures 96; use of own 190
feminism 169–70; interviewing 59–60
field perspectives 10–11
five relationship framework 83–7
four levels of consciousness 158–60
functionality of inferences (FI) 45–6, 52
future: counselling psychology 6–13;
recommendations 13–14, 91–2;
research 89–91, 116–17, 320–1

GBR 26, 27, 237
gender 29–30
General Health Questionnaire 123
general practitioners *see* GPs
genuineness in interviews 66–7

Gestalt therapy 154; code of ethics 9;
    training 246
GPs 119–31
graduate basis for registration *see* GBR
grand narrative 20, 27–8, 301–2, 303–4
Greek thought categories 222–9
grounded theory 57, 180, 204–10
group psychotherapy 134–56
guidance 152

healing 111
health care: psychological counselling
    119–31
Hermes 21–35, 181, 222–9
heterogeneity 161
heuristic analysis 259–60

identification 139–50, 151–2
imagined scenarios 46, 48–9
independence 162
individuals 12; differences 110–11; in
    groups 136–7, 153; perspectives
    10–11; uniqueness 100
inferences 38, 205; functionality (FI)
    45–6, 52
inferiority feelings 114
inquiry: learning through 242–70;
    relationships 249–50; writing 250–51;
    see also research
integration 9–10
intelligence tests 39–40
intelligibility 227
inter-rater reliability 186–7, 259, 278
internal events: beliefs 38–9; causal
    relationships 37–54; hypothesis testing
    38; interaction 38, 50–1; manipulation
    37–40
interpsychic factors 152–5
interviews: data analysis 200–3; discourse
    analysis 212–18; empathy 65–6;
    ethical issues 70–1; feminist 59–60;
    genuineness 66–7; paraphrasing 58,
    62–3; practical issues 70–1; reflecting
    63; research 56–71; summarising
    63–5; therapeutic value 68–9;
    unconditional positive regard 67–8;
    with known respondents 312
intrapsychic factors 139–52
intuition 171
involved participation 41–5, 52–3
irrational beliefs 45–6

knowledge 171

language 56, 184–5; constructionism
    212–18; medical 120–1, 128; within
    communities 81
learning 110; experience of trainees
    179–229; through inquiry 242–70;
    vicarious 153; *see also* training
liaison between professionals 120–2
logic 172

manipulation: beliefs 38–40; checks 47–8
meaning 208, 224–5, 227–9
medical language 128
memos 209
messy texts 84–5
meta-integrative approach 21–2, 27
metaphors 24, 32, 65–6; self-supervision
    293–7
Metaphysical Realism 222–3
minorities *see* cultures
mirror reaction 151
mistakes *see* errors
motivation 147, 152–3; to train 191–2
multicultural organisations 95–117
myths 19–35, 160

Nafsiyat Intercultural Therapy Centre
    101, 103
Naive Realism 222
narratives *see* stories
National Health Service *see* NHS
National Vocational Qualification *see*
    NVQ
negative statements 105–8, 112–14
neutral statements 105–6, 109
new paradigm: and feminism 169–70;
    education 245; Greek categories of
    thought 222–9; research 12–13,
    157–60, 165–7, 181, 183–4, 301
NHS 7; *see also* primary health care
nominative level 33
non-active roles 41–5, 48–50
normative level 33
norms 173
nurturing: supervision 279–81, 289–90
NVQ 11; *see also* training

objectivity: researchers 303
old paradigm: education 245; research
    12–13, 301
open coding 207–9
organisations: as clients 19–20;
    counselling psychology 19–35; stories
    22, 28–9

paraphrasing 58, 62–3
participation, involved 41
patients 122–5
personal qualities *see* characteristics
perspectives 10–11
phenomenological research 98, 103, 244;
 on supervision 273–97
physiological level 33
PHYSIS 242–70
planetary consciousness 172
positive emotion 111
positive regard: unconditional 67–8
positive statements 105–8, 110–12
positivism 12
postculturalism 80
postmodernism 12, 301–5: therapeutic
 relationship 89
power 27–8
practice 11–12; implications of fame
 308–23
predicting behaviour 40–1
prejudice 97–9, 113, 114: overcoming
 112: *see also* bias
premature certainty 129
presences 161
primary health care: evaluation of
 psychological treatment 122–5: family
 therapy 127–9; GPs counselling
 125–7: guidelines 130–1: liaison
 120–2
pro-social cover stories 47
professionalism 6–9, 304
projects 162–3
psychoanalysis: therapeutic relationship
 74–92
psychologists: definitions 1–4
psychology: academic 21, 236–7;
 archetypal 21: cultural 21: definition
 1–4: nomination 236–8: of fame
 308–23: practitioners 1–4: *see also*
 counselling psychology
psychotherapeutic factor 138–9
psychotherapists 4–6, 138–9, 146, 148,
 152–4
psychotherapy: cultural implications
 115–16: definitions 4–6; groups
 134–55: psychological level 33:
 therapeutic relationship 74–92: training
 organisations 5; *see also* counselling
 psychology

qualification statements 105–6, 109
qualifications *see* training

qualitative research 56–71, 98, 103,
 157–8, 182–7, 247, 258, 313; aesthetic
 reasons 305; content analysis 180,
 199–203; Greek thought categories
 222–9; learning through inquiry
 249–51; methodology 77–80, 249–51;
 multicultural organisations 95–117;
 relationships 249–50; stories 24–35;
 therapeutic relationships 74–92
quantitative evidence 74–5, 103, 182–7
questionnaires 104; final therapeutic 138;
 General Health 123; supervision
 277–81; therapeutic self-evaluation 137

race *see* culture
racism *see* prejudice
rational beliefs 45–6
rational level 33
realism: experimental 42–3, 46;
 metaphysical 222–3; naive 222
recognition 27–8
recommendations for the future 13–14
referrals 129
reflecting feelings 58, 63
reflective processes 20
regression 147–9, 151–2
relationships: causal 37–54; family
 127–9; framework of five 83–7;
 importance 239–40; in qualitative
 research 249–50; internal events
 37–54; patient–counsellor 120;
 practitioner and client 3, 5; practitioner
 and other professionals 120–2; research
 300; therapeutic 74–92; training
 omissions 239–40
reparation 111
repertoire 26–7
research xv–xvii, 12–13; action 165–6;
 balancing qualitative and quantitative
 182–7; case studies 194–8;
 collaborative 159, 160, 165–8; cycle
 162–8; endogenous 165–7; experiential
 165–7; future 89–91, 320–1;
 intervention 165–6; interviews 56–71;
 learning 179–230, 242–70;
 multicultural organisations 95–117;
 new paradigm 12–13, 157–60, 165–7,
 169–70, 301; old paradigm 12–13, 301;
 participatory 165–7; personal construct
 165–6; phenomenological 98, 103,
 273–97; positivic 12; postmodernist
 12; procedures 30–1, 81, 82;
 qualitative 56–71, 75–6, 98, 103,

157–8, 182–7, 247, 249–51, 305;
quantitative 74–5, 103, 182–7;
questionnaire 104; relationships
249–50, 300; selecting participants
47–8, 103–4; stories 20–35, 168–70;
supervision 273–97; therapeutic
relationship 74–92; transformational
157–73; writing 79–80, 250–1, 300–5
researcher influence 185–6, 206–7, 303
resistance 139–41
responsiveness 27
revolution 9
rhetorical techniques 65–6
ritual 161
Rogerian approach 190
role enactment: active 41–5, 48–50;
criteria 43–4, 50; defining experiment
39–40; Geller's four types 41–2;
internal events 38–9, 50–1; non-active
41–5, 48–50; problems 40–1; types
41–2; using 38–9, 51–3; validity
40–51
Royal College of General Practitioners
132

sampling 80–1, 209, 251–4
selecting participants 47–8, 103–4,
254–6, 310–11
Selective Coding 209
self-descriptions 106, 107, 283
self-disclosure 139–48, 152–3
self-evaluation questionnaires 137
self-supervision 293–7
semiosis 218
sensitive issues 57–9
sensitivity: theoretical 208
seven-level model of epistemological
discourse 32–4
silence 139, 140, 143
skills: feeling lack of 113; see also
training
spatial reference 162
spontaneity 162
standards see training
statements: classification 105–14
stimuli 40
stories: analysis 22–4; changes 31–5;
competition between 258–9;
consultancy work 23; cover 43, 47;
dangers 23; fragments 24; grand 27–8,
301–2, 303–4; location 25–8;
organisations 19–35; power 27–8;
quality 30–1; retelling 24–35; seven

levels 32–4; tellers 20–2, 25, 28–31;
telling 22–4, 160, 168–70; unexamined
23; uniqueness 32
structures of feeling 96
structuring: supervision 279–82, 285–8
subject exclusion criteria 47–8
subjective experience 276–7, 303
summarising 63–5
supervision: definition 274–5; perceptions
277–84; phenomenological research
273–97; self 293–7
supervisors: as colleagues 291–2; as
people 290–1
support to patients 123–4
synchronicity 162
Synergistic Realism 222–3
systems 12

thematic analysis 81–4, 313–15
theme summary 64–5
theoretical level 33
theoretical sampling 209
theoretical sensitivity 208
theory 9–11; grounded 57, 180, 204–10
therapeutic factors in group therapy:
definitions 134–5; questionnaires 137,
138; study methodology 136–8; study
results 138–55
therapeutic relationships: GPs 123–31;
research 74–92
therapists: as scientist-practitioners
293–7; epistemological values 304–5;
see also counsellors, psychotherapists
training 3; access 8–9; altered states
160–2; anxiety finding placement 216;
British Psychological Society 231–2;
course elements 201–2; Dierotao
programme 242–70; diversity 7–8;
excitement 216; GPs 130; independent
route 231–40; inquiry 242–70;
learning experiences of counsellors
179–229; longitudinal study 189–92;
motivation 191–2, 196–7, 216–8; new
paradigm 245; old paradigm 245;
omissions 238–40; PHYSIS 242–70;
postgraduate courses 125, 189–92;
primary care 124–5, 130;
psychotherapy 5; quality 7;
supervision 273–97; uniformity 7–8
transferability 186–7
transference 101, 113, 141–9
transformational research: four levels of
consciousness 158–62; research cycle

162–8: storytelling 168–70: themes 170–2
transpersonal ecology 172
transpersonal level 33–4
treatments 2; effectiveness of forms 233–5
Tree of Life 33
triangles: supervision 280–1. 292
truth 227–8

unclear statements 105–6. 108–9
unconditional positive regard 67–8
understanding 110, 226–7
uniformity 7–8
uniqueness: individuals 100: stories 32

United Kingdom Conference for Psychotherapy (UKCP) 4, 5, 243
units of meaning 199, 208

validity: external 41–9; five relationship framework 85–7; individual reports 207; role enactment experiments 40–51; study methods 186; training framework 257–9
verification processes 85–6, 257–9
vicarious learning 153
visions 161

way of talking (WOT) 97, 243, 246, 297
writing as research 79–80, 250–1, 300–5

Printed in the United Kingdom by
Lightning Source UK Ltd., Milton Keynes
138689UK00003B/6/P